20/10/1994

Lou Reed

Lou Reed

The Biography

VICTOR BOCKRIS

HUTCHINSON
London

1 3 5 7 9 8 6 4 2

This edition first published in 1994 by
Hutchinson

Random House (UK) Group Ltd
20 Vauxhall Bridge Road, London SW1V 2SA

Random House Australia (Pty) Ltd
20 Alfred Street, Milsons Point, Sydney, NSW 2061, Australia

Random House New Zealand Ltd
18 Poland Road, Glenfield, Auckland 10, New Zealand

Random House South Africa (Pty) Ltd
PO Box 337, Bergvlei, 2012, South Africa

A CIP catalogue entry for this book is available from the British Library

ISBN 0 09 178031 4

Set in Garamond by Deltatype Ltd, Ellesmere Port, Cheshire
Printed and bound in Great Britain by
Clays Ltd, St Ives plc

When I think of Lou I remember what a romantic he was. And fun. And then when he had you hooked with that sweetness he had to destroy you in order to survive. He couldn't help himself, like any predator. He always warned his prey, partly as a challenge and partly to cover his ass for any later moral responsibility. What made the process interesting was the fact that it was an ongoing intellectual and artistic work - a performance piece.

An acquaintance

This book is dedicated to Stellan Holm and to the writers Lester Bangs, Richard Meltzer, Mary Harron, Nick Kent, Miles, Robert Christgau, Charles Shaar Murray, Albert Goldman, Richard Witts, Legs McNeil, John Holmstrom, Clinton Heylin, Nick Tosches, Kurt Loder, Julie Burchill, David Dalton and John Wilcock.

Contents

Acknowledgements

Thanks for input and enlightenment to Andy Warhol, Lisa Krug, Andrew Wylie, Albert Goldman, Robert Dowling, Gerard Malanga, Syracuse University Rare Book Room, the staff of Creedmore Mental Hospital, Paul Sidey, Ingrid von Essen, Dawn Fozard, Stellan Holm, Marianne Erdos, Barbara Wilkinson, Jessica Berens, Chantal Rosset, Elvira Peake, Anita Pallenberg, Marianne Faithfull, Allen Ginsberg, David Dalton, Miles, Jeff Goldberg, Ira Cohen, Rosemary Bailey, Phillip Booth, Allen Hyman, Andy Hyman, Richard Mishkin, Bob Quine, Raymond Foye, Diego Cortez, Clinton Heylin, Jan van Willegen, John Holmstrom, Legs McNeil, Bobbie Bristol, Ann Patty, Carol Wood, John Shebar, Charles Shaar Murray, Mick Farren, Michael Watts, Ernie Thormahlen, Gisella Freisinger, William Burroughs, John Giorno, Stewart Meyer, Terrence Sellers, Chris Stein, Bob Gruen, David Bourdon, Jonathan Cott, Ed & Laura DeGrazia, Bobby Grossman, Art and Kym Garfunkel, Patti Giordano, Stephen Gaines, Lee Hill, Marcia Resnick, Michelle Loud, Terry Noel, Glenn O'Brien, Robert Palmer, Rosebud, Geraldine Smith, Walter Stedding, David Schmidlapp, Lynn Tillman, Hope Ruff, James Carpenter, Tei Carpenter, Toshiko Mori, Gus van Sant and Mary Woronov.

chapter one

Kill Your Son

1959–60

[In which Lou Reed has
twenty-four shock treatments
followed by intense
psychotherapy and falls into
a deep depression.]

I don't have a personality.

LOU REED

Any biography of Lou Reed must necessarily begin in the summer
of his seventeenth year, 1959, with the most traumatic event of his
life – the series of twenty-four electroshock treatments administered to him at Creedmore State Hospital in Queens Village,
Long Island, on the East Coast of the United States.

That optimistic summer introduced the bikini and the Barbie
doll to a generation of American boys in button-down-collar
shirts and Bermuda shorts, and girls in straight-legged white duck
pants and their boyfriends' letter sweaters, sock-hopping to Dion
and the Belmonts' 'Teenager in Love'. Under the banner of a new
species – the teenager – American youth culture had suddenly and
joyously erupted. However, reeling from the recent deaths of
Buddy Holly, Ritchie Valens and the Big Bopper, plus the arrests
of Chuck Berry and the number-one rock-and-roll DJ, Alan
Freed, a small segment of that teen population would spend a
darker season tuning into the premiere of the *Twilight Zone*
television series, and listening to Frank Sinatra's latest hit, 'A Hole
in the Head'.

It was a bad year, and Lou, who had been studying his bad-boy role ever since he'd worn a black armband to school when Johnny Ace shot himself back in 1954, grabbed the chance to drive everyone in his family nuts. Slithering around the house like a snake on speed, he alternately slashed screeching chords on his electric guitar, practised an effeminate way of walking that caused acute embarrassment to anyone who saw it, drew his sister aside in conspiratorial conferences that excluded his parents, and threatened to throw the mother of all moodies if everyone didn't pay complete attention to him immediately. Like many of his peers and their hero James Dean who had rebelled against the confines of 1950s mainstream America by attacking their parents, Lou was labelled a 'problem case'. Allen Ginsberg captured the teenager's rebellious attitudes in his poem *Howl*. Just like Ginsberg's characters, some of the best minds of Lou's generation would be judged mad by the authorities and dissolve into mental confusion. Many were committed to institutions where electro-shock treatments were routinely performed, and the unlucky few could still receive lobotomies.

That spring, Lou's conservative parents, Sidney and Toby Reed, sent their difficult son to a psychiatrist, requesting that he cure Lou of his homosexual feelings and alarming mood swings. The doctor prescribed a then popular course of treatment recently undergone by, among many others, Mrs Jacqueline Kennedy and the American poet Delmore Schwartz. He explained to the Reeds that their hostile son would benefit from a series of visits to the Creedmore Psychiatric Hospital. Located in a hideous stretch of Long Island wasteland, the large state-run facility was equipped to handle some six thousand patients. There, young Lewis would be given an electroshock three times a week for eight weeks. After that, he would need intensive post-shock therapy. According to the *History of Psychiatry* by Franz G. Alexander and Sheldon T. Selesnick, 'The use of nonconvulsive electrotherapy as a method for alleviating symptoms through suggestion dates back to Scribonius Largus (*c.* AD 47), who treated the headaches of the Roman emperor with an electric eel'.

In 1959 you did not question your doctor. 'His parents didn't want to make him suffer,' explained a family friend. 'They wanted him to be healthy. They were just trying to be parents, so they wanted him to behave.' Consequently, the Reeds nervously accepted the diagnosis.

Creedmore State Psychiatric Hospital's Building 60, a majestically spooky edifice which stood twenty-four storeys high and spanned some 500 feet, loomed over the landscape like a monstrous pterodactyl. Within Building 60, hundreds of corridors led to padlocked wards, offices and operating theatres, all painted a bland, watery cream. Bars and wire mesh covered the windows inside and out. Among the creepiest of these units was the Electro Shock Treatment Center.

Into this unit one early summer day walked the cocky, troubled Lou, unaware, he later claimed, that his first session at the hospital would consist of volts of electricity pulsing through his brain. Lou had amused himself playing mind games with his psychiatrist and not even objected to the then romantic notion of going into a 'nuthouse', but electroshock treatment was not what he had in mind. 'I didn't know what was going to happen,' he explained. 'I'm very passive that way.' Lou was escorted through a labyrinth of corridors. Each door he passed through would be unlocked by a guard, then locked again behind him. Finally he was locked into the electroshock unit and made to change into a scanty hospital robe. As he sat uncomfortably in the waiting room with a group of what looked like human vegetables, Lou caught his first sight of the operating room. A thick, milky-white metal door studded with rivets swung open, revealing an unconscious victim who looked dead and defiled. The body was wheeled out on a stretcher and hurried into a recovery room by a stone-faced nurse. One patient scheduled for the treatment was so frightened that he dissolved into tears and had to be assisted into the chamber, after which the door slammed shut behind him. Lou suddenly found himself next in line for shock treatment.

When wheeled into the small, bare operating room, furnished with an alien-looking machine from which two large wires dangled, Lou was gripped with ball-biting fear. Strapped down on the table, he stared helplessly at the overhead fluorescent lights as his sedative started to take effect. Then he felt the nurse apply a salve to his temples and stick a clamp into his mouth to make sure that he would not swallow his tongue. 'Relax, please!' she instructed the terrified boy. 'We're only trying to help you. Will someone get another pillow and prop him up? One, two, three, four. Relax.' Seconds later, conductors were attached to his head. At the height of his acid fear, he lapsed into unconsciousness. The last thing that filled his vision was a blinding white ceiling light.

The current searing through Lou's body altered the firing pattern of his central nervous system, producing a minor seizure which, although horrid to watch, in fact caused no pain. In the 1950s, the voltage administered to each patient was not adjusted to their size or mental state. Everybody got the same dose. Thus, the vulnerable seventeen-year-old received the same degree of electricity as was given to a heavyweight axe-murderer. When Lou revived several minutes later, a deathly pallor clung to his mouth, he was spitting and his eyes were tearing and red. Gradually, as his body stopped twitching and grew calm, the clamp was removed, and he regained full consciousness.

Like a character in a story by one of his favourite writers, Edgar Allan Poe, the alarmed patient now found himself prostrate in a dim waiting room under the gaze of a blank-faced nurse. Over the next half-hour, as he struggled to return to normalcy, he was panicked to discover his memory had gone. According to experts, memory loss was an unfortunate side effect of shock therapy. 'There is almost always some loss surrounding the time of treatment,' they said. 'Amnesia could last for several weeks or months following the treatment. Eventually gaps in memory may extend a few weeks or months before the therapy, and to a lesser degree, afterward. In time, some memory will return, but some will not. Whatever brain changes occurred were considered reversible, and persisting brain damage was very rare.' As Reed left the hospital to return home, he thought, he recalled later, that he had 'become a vegetable'.

'You can't read a book because you get to page seventeen and you have to go right back to page one again. Or if you put the book down for an hour and went back to pick up where you started, you didn't remember the pages you read. You had to start all over. If you walked around the block, you forgot where you were. It was a problem. It was like a very prolonged bad acid trip with none of the benefits.' For a man with plans to become, among other things, a writer, this was a blow. At the end of the eight-week treatment, Lou was put on tranquillizing medication. 'I HATE PSYCHIATRISTS. I HATE PSYCHIATRISTS. I HATE PSYCHIATRISTS,' he later screamed in one of his best poems, 'People Must Have to Die for the Music'.

Lewis Alan Reed was born on 2 March 1942 at Beth El Hospital in Brooklyn, New York. His father, Sidney George Reed, a diminutive, black-haired man who had changed his name from Rabinowitz, was a tax accountant. His mother Toby Futterman Reed, seven years younger than her husband, a former beauty queen, was a housewife. Both parents were native New Yorkers, recent arrivals in the middle-class community of Freeport, Long Island, Sidney from Manhattan, Toby from Brooklyn.

Lewis developed into a small, thin child with kinky black hair and a sensitive, nervous disposition. By that time, his mother had shaped her beauty-queen personality into an extremely nice, polite, formal persona that Lou later characterized as 'Standing on Ceremony' ('A song I wrote for my mother'). She wanted her son to have the best opportunities in life, and dreamed that one day he would become a doctor or a lawyer, not just an accountant like his father. When Lewis was five the Reeds had a second child, Elizabeth, affectionately known as Bunny. While Lou doted on his little sister, there is no doubt that her arrival was also cause for alarm.

The emotional milieu that dominated Lewis's life throughout childhood was a kind of suffocating love. 'Gentiles don't understand about Jewish love,' explained Albert Goldman in his biography of one of Lou's role models, Lenny Bruce.

They can't grasp a positive, affectionate emotion that is so crossed with negative impulses, so qualified with antagonistic feelings that it teeters at every second on a fulcrum of ambivalence. Jewish love is love, all right, but it's mingled with such a big slug of pity, cut with so much condescension, embittered with so much tacit disapproval, disapprobation, even disgust, that when you are the object of this love, you might as well be an object of hate. Jewish love made Kafka feel like a cockroach . . . Like a sign in the flesh, like a genetic code, this fusion of self-love and self-hate is transmitted from one generation to another.

In Lou's case, his mother's love became a trap from which he has not escaped. It was built around emotional blackmail. First, since the mother's happiness depends upon a son's happiness, it becomes a responsibility for the son to be happy. Second, since the mother's love is all-powerful, it is impossible for the son to return an equal amount of love, therefore he is perennially guilty. Third, with the arrival of a sibling, the mother's love can no longer be total. All three elements combine to make the son feel impotent, confused and angry. The trap is sealed by an inability to talk about such matters so that all the bitter hostility boiling below the surface is contained until the son marries a woman who replaces his mother. Then it explodes in her face.

Goldman could have been describing Reed as much as Bruce when he concluded, 'the sons develop into twisted personalities, loving where they should hate and hating where they should love. They attach themselves to women who hurt them, and treat with contempt the women who offer them simple love. They often display great talents in their work, but as men they have curiously ineffective characters.'

One friend recalled that Toby Reed smothered her son with too much attention and concern. 'I think his mother was fairly overbearing. Just in the way he talked about her. She was like a protective Jewish mother. She wanted him to get better grades and be a doctor . . .' Such attentions, of course, were fairly typical of full-time mothers in the family-oriented fifties. Lou's best friend in high school, the genial Allen Hyman, never found her particularly unusual. 'I always thought Lewis's mother was a very nice person,' he said.

> I mean, she was very nice to me. I never viewed her as overbearing, but maybe he did. My experience of his parents was that they were very nice people. He might have perceived them as being different than they were. They were very involved parents. His mother was never anything but really nice. Whenever we went there she was anxious to make sure we had food. But Lewis was always on the rebellious side and I guess that the middle-class aspect of his life was something that he found disturbing. My experience of his relationship with his parents when we were growing up was that he was really close to them.
>
> His mother and father put up with a lot from him over the years and they were always totally supportive. His father was very quiet, his mother had a lot more energy and a lot more personality. She always wore her hair short, she had a lovely figure and dressed immaculately. She was a very attractive woman. I got the impression that Mr Reed was a shy man. He was certainly not Mr Personality. You know how when you went out with certain parents it was fun and they were the life of the dinner and they bought you a nice meal. But when you went out with Sidney Reed, you paid. When you're a kid, that's unusual. The check would come and he'd say, 'Now your share is . . .' Which was weird. But that was his thing, he was an accountant.

Another friend who knew what made Lou tick would later comment:

> Lou's mother had the Jewish-mother syndrome with her first child. They overwatch their first child. The kid says watch me, watch me, watch me. You can't watch them enough, and they're never happy, because they've spent so much time being watched that's what they expect. His mother was not off to work every morning, the mothers of this era were full-time mothers. Full-time watchers. They set up a scenario that could never be equalled in later life.

'He'd always found the idea of copulation distasteful, especially when applied to his own origins,' Lou began in the first short story he ever published. The untitled one-page piece, signed Luis Reed, was featured in a magazine, the *Lonely Woman Quarterly*, that

Lou edited at Syracuse University in 1962. It hit on all the dysfunctional family themes that would run through his life and work.

His quixotic/demonic relationship to sex was intense. The psychology of gender was everything. Lou either sat at the feet of his lovers or devised ingenious ways to crush their souls. No one understood Lou's ability to make those close to him feel terrible better than the special targets of his inner rage, his parents. In the story, Lou had his mother say, 'Daddy hurt Mommy last night,' and climaxed with a scene in which she seduced 'Mommy's little man'. From all accounts, it appears that neither scenario ever took place in the Reed household. However, these Oedipal fantasies revealed a turbulent interior life and profound reaction to the love/hate workings of the family. Lewis would later write, in 'How Do You Speak to an Angel', of the curse of a 'harridan mother, a weak simpering father, filial love and incest'. He both resented and was jealous of the overbearing affection. And at the same time, he realized that it was a powerful weapon to be wielded.

Lewis enjoyed the comforts of his middle-class upbringing, but acted as if he was estranged from the dominant values of suburban American life. Some of his most famous songs, written in reaction to his parents' values, have a stark, despairing tone that spoke for millions of children who grew up in the stunned and silent fifties of America's postwar affluence. Lou would rewrite his childhood repeatedly in an attempt to define himself. Virtually everything he wrote examined the forces that formed his personality. In fact, Lou Reed became one of the most self-conscious writers who ever lived. Virtually his only subject was and is himself. According to Lou, he never felt good about his parents. 'I went to great lengths to escape the whole thing,' he said when he was forty years old. 'I couldn't relate to it then and I can't now. Even today it kills my father that I didn't fail. My parents would both have been much happier if I had come home a failure with my tail between my legs.' As he saw himself in one of his favourite poems by Delmore Schwartz, '. . . he sat there / Upon the windowseat in his tenth year / Sad separate and desperate all afternoon / Alone, with loaded eyes . . .'

One friend really put her finger on the pulse of the problem when she pointed out that Lou had an extreme case of *shpilkes* – a Yiddish term.

> A person with *shpilkes* has to scratch not only his own itch, he can't leave any situation alone or any scab unpicked. If the teenage Lewis had come into your home, you would have said, 'My God, he's got *shpilkes*! Because he's cute and he's warm and he's lovable, but get him out of here because he's knocking the shit out of everything and I don't dare turn my back on him. He's causing trouble, he's aggravating me, he's a pain in the ass!

'In the time frame that we grew up in, in the fifties and early sixties, for the most part we were pretty unconscious,' recalled Allen Hyman. 'We were living in the fifties, it was like *Happy Days*. And most people were just into having a good time. There was not a tremendous amount of consciousness about what was happening on the planet or anything like that. Lou was always interested in questioning authority, being a little outrageous and he was certainly a person who would be characterized as mildly eccentric.'

Lou's eccentric rebellious side found a lot to gripe about within the conservative, white confines of his neighbourhood. Hyman remembered that, though outwardly polite, Lou harboured a hatred of Allen's right-wing father. 'The reason he disliked my father so much was because he always viewed him as the consummate Republican lawyer. He was very aware early on of political differences in people. We lived in an area that was Republican and conservative and he always rebelled against that. I couldn't understand why that upset him so much. But he was always very respectful to my parents.'

Mr Reed and Mr Hyman discouraged musical careers for their sons. 'He thought there were bad people involved, which there were,' recalled Lou. According to Richard Aquila in *That Old Time Rock and Roll*:

Adult fear of rock and roll probably says more about the paranoia and insecurity of American society in the 1950s and early 1960s than it does about rock and roll. The same adults who feared foreigners because of the expanding Cold War, and who saw the Rosenbergs and Alger Hiss as evidence of internal subversion, often viewed rock and roll as a foreign music with its own sinister potential for corrupting American society.

In his late thirties, Lou wrote a series of songs about his family. In one he said that he originally wanted to grow up like his 'old man', but got sick of his bullying and claimed that when his father beat his mother it made him so angry he almost choked. The song climaxed with a scene in which his father told him to act like a man. He did not, he concluded in another song, want to grow up like his 'old man'. Lou dramatized his father's benevolent dominance into Machiavellian tyranny, and viewed his mother as a victim when this was not the case at all. Friends and family were shocked by Lou's stories and songs about interfamily violence and incest, claiming that nothing could have been further from the truth. The fact is that Sid and Toby Reed adored and enjoyed each other. After twenty years of marriage, they were still crazy about each other. As for violence, the only thing that could have possibly angered Sidney Reed was his son's meanness to his wife.

Another charge Lou would lob at his unprotected parents was that they were filthy rich. Again, this was purely a figment of his imagination. During Lou's childhood his father made a modest salary by American standards. The kitchen-table family possessed a single car and lived in a simply furnished house with no vestiges of luxury or loosely spent funds. Indeed, what with the shock treatments, Lou's college tuition and their daughter Elizabeth's coming into her teens, the Reeds were stretched about as far as they could reach by the beginning of the 1960s. Sidney Reed never took vacations, never stayed out late or partied with his male friends. He essentially sacrificed his life for his family, poured all his energy and everything he earned into providing a home and education. He was the consummate family man, post–World War II East Coast suburban division. Mr and Mrs Reed have worn the crown of thorns squashed onto their heads by their errant son with dignity and silence, never attempting to set the record straight.

Since puberty Lou had honed a sharp edge, wounding his parents with both public and private insults and what they saw as destructive, hostile behaviour. According to his own testimony, what made Lewis different from the all-American boys in Freeport was the fact, discovered at the age of thirteen, that he was homosexual. As he explained in a 1979 interview, the recognition of his attraction to his own sex came early, and so did the immediate attempts at subterfuge: 'I resent it. It was a very big drag. From age thirteen on I could have been having a ball and not even thought about this shit. What a waste of time. If the forbidden thing is love, then you spend most of your time playing with hate. Who needs that? I feel I was gypped.'

In his teens, Lou led Mr and Mrs Reed to believe he would become both a rock-and-roll musician *and* a homosexual – the stuff of nightmares for most suburban parents of the 1950s. Actively dating girls at the time, and giving his friends every impression of being heterosexual, Lou enjoyed the shock and worry that gripped his parents at the thought of having a homosexual son.

'There was no indication of homosexuality except in his writing,' said Hyman.

Towards our senior year some of his stories and poems were starting to focus on the gay world. Sort of a fascination with the gay world, there was a lot of that imagery in his poems. And I just thought of it as his bizarre side. I would say to him, 'What is this about, why are you writing about this?' He would say, 'It's interesting. I find it interesting.' We used to play basketball at a place called Northwest Park in Freeport, we used to go there all the time and there was always this kid hanging out there, a couple years older than we were – I can't remember his name – and I believe a lot of the kids from that time had early gay experiences with this kid, on a very innocent basis. And I believe that Lou may have had some very early, very innocent experiences with this kid. Little masturbatory experiences. A number of my friends would participate in these games. But it was not something that was ever communicated, we never talked about it much.

'I always thought that the one way kids had of getting back at their parents was to do this gender business,' said Lou. 'It was only kids trying to be outrageous. That's a lot of what rock and roll is about to some people: listening to something your parents don't like, dressing the way your parents won't like.' In fact, throughout his adolescence, Lou had neither an active male partner nor a long-term girlfriend. He was far more interested in his real passion, rock and roll.

Lou had fallen for the new R&B sounds in 1954, when he was twelve. Almost instantly, he had started composing songs of his own. Like his fellow teenager Paul Simon, who grew up in nearby Queens, Lou formed a band and put out a single at the age of fifteen, appropriately called 'So Blue'. To Lou's parents, these early signposts of a musical career were ominous. Their dreams of having their only son become a doctor or, like his father, an accountant, were vanishing in the haze of pounding music and tempestuous moods. 'His mother was very upset,' recalled a friend. 'She couldn't understand why he hated them so much, where that anger came from. At first, they had no malice, they tried to understand. But they got fed up with him.'

Lou suffered through the eight weeks of shock treatments that dreadful summer of 1959 haunted by the fear that in an attempt to obliterate the abnormal from his personality, his parents had nearly destroyed him. In his heart he believed that if his parents really loved him they would never have allowed the shock treatments to happen. He felt betrayed.

The death of the great jazz vocalist Billie Holiday in July, and the haunting refrain of Paul Anka's number-one teen-angst ballad 'Lonely Boy', heightened Lou's sense of distance and loss.

According to Reed, the shock treatments eradicated any feeling of compassion he might have had and gave him an even more fragmented view of people. 'I think everybody has a number of personalities,' he told a friend, to whom he showed a small notebook in which he had written 'From Lou #3 to Lou #8 – Hi!' 'You wake up in the morning and say, "Wonder which of them is around today?" You find out which one and send him out. Fifteen minutes later, someone else shows up. That's why if there's no one left to talk to, I can always listen to a couple of them talking in my head. I can talk to myself.' But the aftereffects of shock therapy put Lou, as Ken Kesey described it in *One Flew Over the Cuckoo's Nest*, 'in that foggy, jumbled blur which is a whole lot like the ragged edge of sleep, the grey zone between light and dark, or between sleeping and waking or living and dying'. Lou's nightmares had become dominated by the sad, off-white colour of hospitals. Now he was afraid to go to sleep. Insomnia would become a life-long habit. As he put it in a poem, 'How does one fall asleep / When movies of the night await / And me eternally done in.'

The year 1959 through the summer of 1960 was a lost time for Lou. From then on, the central thrust of his life became a struggle to express himself and get what he wanted. The first step was to remove himself from the control of his family, which he now saw as an agent of punishment and psychological confinement. 'I came from this small town out on Long Island,' he stated. 'Nowhere. I mean nowhere. The most boring place on earth. The only good thing about it was you knew you were going to get out of there.' In August he registered and published a song called 'You'll Never, Never Love Me'. A gut resentment of his parents was blatantly expressed in another song, 'Kill Your Sons'. 'I keep a distance from my family for my own emotional safety, and so I can do the things I want to get done,' he said years later. The music gave him back his heartbeat so he could dream again.

In order to continue their friendship, Lewis and Allen had conspired to attend the same university. 'In my senior year in high school Lou and I and his father drove up to Syracuse for an interview,' Allen recalled. It is a large, prestigious, private university in northwest New York State, hundreds of miles from Freeport.

> We didn't speak to his father much, he was quiet. Quiet in the sense of being formal – Mr Reed. We stayed at the Hotel Syracuse, which was then a real old hotel. There were also a bunch of other kids who were up for that with their parents – would-be applicants to Syracuse. Lou's father took one room and Lou and I took another. We met a bunch of kids in the hall that were going to Syracuse and we had this all-night party with these girls we met. We thought this was going to be a gas, this is terrific. The following day we both knew people who were going to Syracuse at the time who were in fraternities. And the campus was so nice, I think it was the summer, it was warm at the time, it looked so nice. We made an agreement that both of us would go to Syracuse if we got in.
>
> We both got in. And the minute I got my acceptance I let them know I was going to go and I called Lou very excited and said, 'I got my acceptance to Syracuse, did you?' And he said, 'Yes.' So I said, 'Are you going?' and he said, 'No.' And I said, 'What do you mean, no? I thought we were going, we had an agreement.' He said, 'I got accepted to NYU and that's where I'm going.' I said, 'Why would you want to do that, we had such a good time up there, we liked the place, I told them I was going, I thought you were going . . .' He said, 'No, I got accepted to NYU uptown and I'm going.'

In the autumn of 1959, Lou headed off to college. Located in New York City, New York University seemed like a smart choice for a man who loved nothing more than listening to jazz in the Greenwich Village clubs. But the Village was not the NYU campus Lou chose. Almost incomprehensibly, he signed up for the school's branch located way uptown in the Bronx. NYU uptown provided him with neither the opportunities nor the support that he needed. Instead, he was left floundering in a strange and hostile environment. One of his few pleasures came from visiting the Mecca of modern jazz, the Five Spot, but he didn't always have the money to get in, and often stood outside the place listening to Thelonius Monk, John Coltrane and Ornette Coleman as the music drifted out to the street.

However, Lou's main concern was not college. The Bronx campus was conveniently close to the Payne Whitney psychiatric clinic on the Upper East Side of Manhattan, where he was undergoing an intensive course of post-shock treatments. According to Hyman, who talked to him on the phone at least once a week throughout the semester, Lou was having a very, very bad time:

He was in therapy three or four times a week. He hated NYU. He really hated it. I always viewed him as an overly sensitive person, a person who would be affected by his environment. He would see something and be blown away by it when I would just look at it and say, Why does that disturb you? He would ponder it and think about it and go ape shit and finally little stuff like that just got to him. He was going through a very difficult time and he was taking medication. He was having a lot of difficulty dealing with college and day-to-day business. He was a mess. He was going through a lot of very, very bad emotional stuff at the time and he probably had something very close to a minor breakdown.

Part of Lou's problem stemmed from his aloneness. Lou always wanted to be in his own centre but he wanted somebody to share it with. He needed another person in whom he could see those sides of himself he wanted to develop reflected. So far he had not found any one person but combined the disparate shards of personalities who had made an impression on him.

After completing his Payne Whitney sessions, in the spring of 1960 he left NYU and returned to Freeport on prescription tranquillizers. The only thing that seemed to break through the fog he felt enveloped in was the, to him, awesomely beautiful rock and roll music he was listening to on the radio and collecting like an art dealer. According to Lou it not only gave him back his heartbeat but saved his life. Like many artists who explore their darker sides, Lou began to find his way to be himself in his darkest hours.

It cannot have been an easy time for the Reeds. Their eighteen-year-old son alternately sat around like a helpless zombie and immersed himself in the fractured music of Ornette Coleman or

James Brown. It better mirrored his temperament than anything in the neat, ceremonial Reed home.

chapter two   *Pushing the Edge*

1960–1962

[In which Lou recovers from his
shock treatments, enrols at
Syracuse University, challenges
the status quo and meets
his first love, Shelley Albin.]

Lou liked to play with people, tease them and push them to an
edge. But if you crossed a certain line with Lou, he'd cut you
right out of his life.

ALLEN HYMAN

One of the few people who encouraged Lou during his year-long
depression was his stalwart childhood friend Allen Hyman, who
now urged him to get away from his parents and join him at
Syracuse. In the autumn of 1960, shaking off the shadows of
Creedmore and the medication of Payne Whitney, Reed took
Hyman's advice and enrolled at Syracuse.

The Syracuse campus looked like the set for a horror movie
about college life in the early 1960s. Its buildings resembled
Gothic mansions from a screenwriter's imagination. Indeed, the
scriptwriter of the *Addams Family* TV show of the 1960s, who
attended the university at the same time as Lou, used the
classically Gothic Hall of Languages as the basis for the Addams
Family mansion. The surrounding four-block-square area of
wooden Victorian houses, Depression-era restaurants, stores and
bars completed the college landscape. It provided a perfect
backdrop for the beatnik lifestyle. A pervasive ochre-grey paint
lent a sombre air to the seedy wooden houses tucked away in side

streets covered, most of the time, with snow, wet leaves or rain. The atmosphere was likely to elicit either poetic contemplation or depressive madness.

The surrounding city of Syracuse presented no less dour a landscape. The manufacturing town got dumped with snow seven months of the year, and heavy bouts of rain the rest of the time. Only during the summer, when most of the students had scattered to their homes on Long Island or in New Jersey, did the city receive warmth and sunshine. Syracuse seemed at first an unlikely place for Lou. A thriving industrial metropolis popularly known as the Salt City, also specializing in metals and electrical machinery, it was 200 miles northwest of Freeport, 40 miles south of Lake Ontario on the Canadian border and five miles southwest of Oneida Lake. Syracuse was aggressively conservative and religious, but at the time of Reed's arrival it was fast turning into the academic hub of the Empire State. However, despite high academic standards, Syracuse was still primarily seen as a football school. The city supported its university, whose popular football team, the Orangemen, was undefeated during Lou's four years, and its residents proudly turned out in great numbers for athletic events. 'Where the vale of Onondaga / Meets the eastern sky / Proudly stands our Alma Mater / On her hilltop high' ran the opening verse of the school song, a ditty Lewis, as many of his friends called him, would not forget.

The coeducational university, attended by some 19,000 sciences and humanities students, had been established in 1871. It was located on a 640-acre campus atop a hill, in the middle of the city. Tuition was $800 per term, relatively high for a private university. Most of the students lived in sororities and fraternities and were enjoying one last four-year party before putting aside childish notions for the responsibilities of economic adulthood. Among the student population was a large and wealthy Jewish contingent, generally straight-arrow fraternity men and sorority women bound for careers in medicine and law. There was a small margin of artists, writers and musicians with whom Lou would throw in his lot, enjoying, for the first time in his life, a niche in which he could find a degree of comfort. Among many other talented and successful people, the artist Jim Dine, the fashion designer Betsey Johnson and the film producer Peter Gruber all graduated in Reed's class of 1964. As a freshman, Lou was assigned to the far southwestern corner of the North Campus in Sadler Hall, a plain, boxlike dormitory resembling a prison. However, much of his time was spent in the splendid, large, grey stone Hall of Languages, which overlooked University Avenue and University Place at the north end of campus and housed the English, History and Philosophy departments.

To his advantage, Reed already had the perfect agent to introduce him to the university, his great childhood friend, the smooth operator and prince of good times, Allen Hyman, now entering his sophomore year. Another pampered suburban kid, who drove both a Cadillac and a Jaguar, Allen was generous, full of good humour and sharp-witted. Furthermore, he genuinely appreciated Lou and was willing to put up with a lot of flak to remain his friend. Allen was well connected with the straight fraternity set to which he aspired and was eager to introduce Lewis to his world.

'Rushing was a really horrendous experience and most people were very intimidated by it,' Hyman explained later. Inductees were forced to drink themselves into oblivion and were often humiliated physically, sexually and mentally by the fraternity brothers. When Allen told Lou stories about what he went through to join a fraternity, Lou shot him a blank look, snapping, 'What are you into – masochism?' (A good question, considering Reed's later reputation as a champion of S & M.)

'He had said that he didn't want anything to do with it and that it was fascistic and disgusting,' Hyman recalled, 'and he couldn't believe anybody would be willing to go through hazing without killing the person who was hazing them.' However, typically perversely, Reed agreed to attend a rush session at Allen's fraternity Sigma Alpha Mu (also known as the Sammies).

From the outset it was clear that he intended to make a strong impression. Reed came to the initiation in a suit three sizes too small and covered in dirt. It was a radical departure from the blue blazer, smart tie and neatly combed hair of the other recruits. Allen immediately realized how much Lou was getting off on being outrageous. When one of the brothers criticized Lou's appearance, Reed riposted, 'Fuck you!' and his fraternity career came to an abrupt end. Hyman was asked to escort his friend out immediately. Walking Lou back to his dorm, Allen hung his head regretfully, but Lou, far from being despondent, appeared exhilarated by the event. 'I guess this isn't for you,' Allen said.

'Yeah, that's right,' Lou replied. 'I told you I wouldn't get along with those assholes. How can you live there?'

Another trial that Lou failed was with the Reserve Officers' Training Corps. As part of his freshman course requirements, he had to choose between physical education and ROTC. (In those days it was common to join ROTC in order to be able to go into the army as an officer and a gentleman.) Claiming that he would surely break his neck in phys ed or else kill somebody in ROTC, Lou attempted to evade both requirements, but in the end grudgingly signed up for the latter. ROTC activities consisted of two classes a week in how to be a soldier and possibly a leader. However, Lou's military experience was almost as short-lived as his fraternity stint. Just weeks into the semester, when he flatly refused a direct order from his officer, he was booted out.

But Reed made an impact with his very own radio show. Employing a considerable boyish charm to overcome the severe doubts of the programme director Katharine Griffin, during his first semester Lou hustled his way onto the Syracuse University radio station WAER FM with a jazz programme called *Excursions on a Wobbly Rail* (a wicked Cecil Taylor piece used as his introductory theme). The classical, conservative station, Radio House, was situated in a World War II Quonset hut tucked away behind Carnegie Library. Freezing his balls off through many icy Syracuse evenings, hunched over his ancient machinery like some underground resistance fighter for two hours, three nights a week, Lou blasted a melange of his favourite sounds by the avant-garde leaders of the free-jazz movement, Ornette Coleman leaders of the free-jazz movement, Ornette Coleman and Don Cherry, the doo-wopping Dion and the sexually charged Hank Ballard, James Brown and the Marvelettes. The mixture presented the essence of Lou Reed. 'I was a very big fan of Ornette Coleman, Cecil Taylor, Archie Shepp,' he recalled. 'Then James Brown, the doo-wop groups, and rockabilly. Put it all together and you end up with me.'

Unfortunately, the Reedian canon was not appreciated by the station's staff and numerous faculty members, including the Dean of Men (administrator), who lodged complaints about the – to them – hideous, unintelligible cacophony that emanated from Reed's programme. And the authorities' reaction was not Lou's only problem. Disguising his voice, Allen Hyman would often call Lou at the station and harass him with ridiculous requests. On one occasion, Allen recalled:

> I asked him to play something he hated and I knew he would never play. He said, 'No, I'm not going to play that, forget it.' So I said, 'Listen, if you don't play this I'm gonna fucking have you killed. I'll wait for you myself and I'm gonna kill you!' And, thinking it was some lunatic, Lou got scared. Then I called him back and told him it was me and he screamed at me, saying that if I ever did that again he'd never speak to me.

As it turned out, Allen's pranks didn't continue long enough to lose him Lou's friendship because before long Griffin, ever vigilant in her duties as WAER's programme director, was forced to conclude that 'Excursions on a Wobbly Rail was a really weird jazz show that sounded like some new kind of noise. It was just too weird and cutting edge.' Before the end of the semester, she dumped it from the air, causing Lou considerable anguish.

In retrospect, Griffin and her contemporaries realized that Reed was simply ahead of his time. 'Most of us who were in power on campus were children of the fifties,' she explained. 'Kids in those days wore chinos and madras shirts, a clean-cut Kingston Trio kind of thing. Lou looked more like what a rock person from later in the sixties would look like. Lou was presaging the sixties and seventies and we just weren't ready for it. He was right on the cusp of two generations. A little too far ahead to be admired in the fifties.'

During his first year at Syracuse, the scholarly Griffin concluded, 'it was just Lou versus everybody else'.

Lou quickly defined himself as an oddball loner. Eschewing all organizations, he was on the track of creating an image that would in time become widely acknowledged as the essence of the hip New York underground man. Lou was a year older than most freshmen and fully grown, measuring five foot eight inches (although he claimed to be five foot ten). He was a little chubby and some way yet from the Lou Reed of 'Heroin'. He wore loafers, jeans and T-shirts, tending, if anything, to be a little sloppier than the majority of men at school who wore the fraternity uniform of jacket and tie. His hair was a trifle longer than theirs. Otherwise, he would not have been noticed in a crowd. His looks tended toward the cute, boyish, curly-haired, shy, gum-chewing. He had a small scar under his right eye. His most unusual feature was his fingers. Short and strong, they broadened into stubby, almost blocklike fingertips, making them perfect tools for the guitar.

Syracuse University had excellent faculty and academic courses. Though Lou may have sleepwalked through much of the curriculum, he threw himself into the music, philosophy and literature studies in which he excelled. In music appreciation, theory and composition classes, Lou soaked up everything. First, he tried his hand at journalism, but he dropped that after a week when the teacher told him his opinions were irrelevant. Lou then immersed himself in philosophy. He devoured the existentialists, obsessed over the torturous *Dialectics* of Hegel and embraced the *Fear and Trembling* of Kierkegaard. 'I was very into Hegel, Sartre, Kierkegaard,' Reed recalled. 'After you finish reading Kierkegaard, you feel like something horrible has happened to you – Fear and Nothing. That's where I was coming from.' He also loved Krafft-Ebing's nineteenth-century study of sexual behaviour and the writing of the beat generation, particularly Kerouac,

Burroughs and Ginsberg. To complete his freshman image, he took imagistic inspiration from the brash, tortured figures of James Dean, Marlon Brando and, most of all, Lenny Bruce.

Lou had already formed his ambition to be a rock-and-roll writer. The university's rich music scene consisted of an eclectic mix of talents like Garland Jeffreys, a future singer-songwriter and Reed acolyte two years younger than Lou; Nelson Slater, for whom Lou would later produce an album; Felix Cavaliere, the future leader of the Young Rascals; Mike Esposito, who would form the Blues Magoos and the Blues Project; and Peter Stampfel, an early member of the Holy Modal Rounders, who would become a pioneer of folk rock. The best bands at Syracuse were Felix Cavaliere's the Escorts and Mike Esposito's the Daiquiris. While colleges in New York and Boston produced folk singers in the style of Bob Dylan, Syracuse created a bunch of punk rockers, and, like Reed, some of them produced early records. In 1963, Cavaliere and Esposito put out a single called 'Saved' / 'The Syracuse'.

Most importantly for Lou musically, it was at Syracuse he met his fellow guitarist Sterling Morrison, a resident of Bayport, Long Island, who had a similar background. Just after Lou got kicked out of ROTC, Sterling, who was never actually enrolled at Syracuse but spent a lot of time there hanging out and sitting in on some classes, was visiting Jim Tucker, who occupied the room below Lou's. Gazing out of Tucker's window at the cadets marching up and down the quad one afternoon, Sterling suddenly heard 'ear-splitting bagpipe music' wail from someone's hi-fi system. After that, the same person 'cranked up his guitar and gave a few shrieking blasts on that'. Excited, Sterling realized, 'Oh, there's a guitar player upstairs,' and prevailed on Jim Tucker for an introduction.

When they met at three o'clock the following morning, Lou and Sterling discovered they had a common love for black music, rock and roll and that nasty, stultifying Long Island attitude exemplified in the 1990s by the gun-toting Lolita Amy Fisher. They also loved Ike and Tina Turner. 'Nobody even knew who they were then,' Morrison later recalled. 'Syracuse was very, very straight. There was a 1 per cent lunatic fringe.'

Luckily, the drama, poetry, art and literary scenes were just as alive as the music scene for that 1 per cent fringe. Soon Lou was spending the majority of his time playing guitar, reading and writing or engaging in long rap sessions with like-minded students. Many of Lou's long conversations about philosophy and literature took place in the bars and coffee shops he and his friends began to call their own. Each restaurant had its social affiliations. Lou's crowd set up camp at the Savoy coffee shop run by a lovable old character, Gus Josephs, who could have walked right out of a *Happy Days* TV episode. At night, they drank at the Orange Bar, frequented predominantly by the more intellectual students. According to Lou, he took two steps out of school and there was the bar. 'It was the world of Kant and Kierkegaard and meta-physical polemics that lasted well into the night,' he remembered. 'I often went to drink alone to that week's lost everything.' He had become accustomed to taking prescription drugs and smoking pot, but he was not yet a heavy user of mood-altering substances. At the most he might have a Scotch and a beer.

The rules that governed a freshman's life at Syracuse were greatly to the advantage of the male students as opposed to the females. Whereas the girls in the dorm atop Mount Olympus were locked in at 9 p.m., and any girl who dared break curfew was subject to instant expulsion, the boys, who had no curfew, were able to use the night to live a whole other life, exploring the town, drinking in the Orange or in frat houses and getting up to all sorts of mischief. Naturally Lou, who had developed the habit of staying up most of the night reading, writing and playing music, lost no time exploring his new home. He quickly checked out Syracuse, discovering the neighbouring black ghetto where he could hear funky jazz and R&B as well as finding a whole culture, centered around drugs, music and danger, which strongly appealed to the explorer of the dark side in Reed.

Lou's first college girlfriend, Judy Abdullah, was an Arab and it may be that she was of more interest to him as an exotic object than as a person – he called her 'the Arab'. Judy revealed an interesting quirk in Lou's sexuality: he was turned on by big women. Judy Abdullah was twice his size. She was a sensual woman and they apparently had a good time in bed, but at least one acquaintance added a shade to Reed's personality profile when she pointed out that his attraction to big women offered both a challenge and an escape route. Lou could take the attitude that he had no responsibility to be serious about her or even try to satisfy her.

The relationship petered out before the end of the year. Lou, who persisted in not wasting time with dates and always coming on obnoxiously, was mean to Judy, and when they broke up she was pissed off with him for good reason. Still, they remained acquaintances and Lou saw her occasionally throughout his college years.

At Syracuse Lou presented himself as a tortured, introspective, romantic poet. Following the dictate that the first step to becoming a poet is to look and act like one, Lou liked, for example, to give the impression that he was unwashed, but that wasn't true. According to one friend, 'he wasn't about to go out unless he took a shower first'. As far as his costume was concerned, he was still stuck somewhere between the suburban teenager in loafers and button-down shirts and the rumpled blue jeans and work shirts of the Kerouac rebel. In his demeanour, Lou was just beginning to swing with the whole James Dean–inspired 'I've suffered so much everything looks upside down' routine. According to one student who occasionally jammed with him, 'Part of his aura was that he was a psychologically troubled person who in his youth had had electroshock treatments which had clearly had an effect on him. He used that as part of his persona. Where the reality and the fantasy of what he was crossed, who knew.'

For a sarcastic kid who had grown up with buck teeth, braces and a nerd's wardrobe, Lou wasn't doing badly turning himself into the image of a totally perverse psycho. However, whatever he did with his turtleneck sweaters and his attitude to make himself hip, there was one detail about his looks that seemed always to overwhelm him – his hair. His frizzy helmet had plagued him since he'd started looking into the mirror with intense interest in his twelfth year. What stared back at him throughout his adolescence was a Jewish version of Alfred E. Neumann, the obnoxiously nerdy kid on the cover of *Mad* magazine.

Since America had been an anti-Semitic nation, the Jewish 'afro' was seen as geekishly ethnic. In the early sixties, Bob Dylan single-handedly changed the image of what a hip young boy could look like. Although the film industry and media characters like Allen Ginsberg had begun to turn the whole Jewish male persona into something ultra-chic, nobody came close to having the pervasive influence of Bob Dylan. As Ginsberg explained to his biographer Barry Miles, when Dylan appeared, particularly in his 1965 *Bringing It All Back Home* incarnation, he made the hooked nose and frizzy hair the very emblem of the intellectual avant-garde. By the time Lou got to college, however, and started to sculpt himself into the Lou Reed who would emerge in 1966 as the closest competition to Dylan for the most articulate rock star in the world, he was ready to do something about it. At Syracuse he discovered a hair-treatment place in the black neighbourhood, and on several occasions had his hair straightened. Naturally, the effect did not last long enough to solve the problem permanently so Lou finally finessed it by wearing his hair either exceedingly short, to avoid the biblical curls, or long enough to be considered a weirdo.

Just like his British counterparts Keith Richards of the Rolling Stones or John Lennon of the Beatles, Lou rejected the lifestyle that came before the bomb, and was remaking himself out of a combination of his favourite stars. Such self-creation was not difficult for Lou, who often claimed he had as many as eight personalities. He now clothed these personalities in the costumes and attitudes of a cast of media characters who were as important to his image as the first creative friends he would hook up with at Syracuse.

First among them was Lenny Bruce. Though soon to be damned by his legal problems to a horrible fate, Bruce was at the apogee of his career. In the eyes of the public he was the hippest, fastest-talking American poet and philosopher around. Bruce spiked his act – a kind of Will Rogers on fast forward – by injections of pure liquid methamphetamine hydrochloride, which would in time become Lou's own drug of choice. Many of Reed's mannerisms, his hand gestures, the way he answered the phone, part of the rhythm of his speech came directly from Bruce.

As for the rest of Lou's media idols, you only have to look at a panel of head shots of the stars of the era to see what Lou would take in time from Frank Sinatra, Jerry Lewis in *The Bellboy*, Montgomery Clift and William Burroughs, to name but a few of the more obvious ones. In fact, one of Lou's most attractive characteristics was the way he was able to appreciate and celebrate his heroes. He was always trying to get Hyman, for example, a straight law student whose path would lead in a direction diametrically opposite to Lou's, to read Kerouac and then rap with him about it. Lou loved turning people on to the new sounds, the new scenes and the new people.

A lot of the artistic kids who went to Syracuse look back upon it with disdain as being a football school dominated by the Orangemen. In fact, in that watershed period between the end of McCarthyism and the death of Kennedy, a new permissiveness had swept through colleges across the country. Syracuse con-tained and nurtured a lot of different environments. Certainly the fraternity culture still dominated the American campus and the majority of male and female students aligned themselves with a fraternity or sorority in sheeplike fashion. There was, however, a vital cultural split between the Jewish and the non-Jewish fraternities. The Jewish fraternities were for the most part more receptive to the new culture and open to alternative ways of living. Despite completely rejecting Sigma Alpha Mu and attaching himself primarily to the arty intellectual crowd, some of whom even had apartments off campus, Lou maintained a loyal friendship with Hyman and was even adopted by the Sammies as their residential oddball. They weren't about to miss out completely on a character who had already, in the first half of his freshman year, carved out an image for himself as tempestuous and evil. In fact, Jewish fraternities in colleges across America would provide some of the most receptive of Lou Reed's audiences throughout his career.

By the end of his first year at Syracuse, according to one of the Sammies:

> Lou's uniqueness and stubbornness made him different from anyone I had ever known. He marched to his own drum. He was for doing things for people, but his way. He would never dress or act in a way so that people would accept him. Lou had an unbelievably wry, caustic sense of humour and loved funny things. He played off people. He would often act in a confrontational manner. He wanted to be different. Lou was a funny guy in an extremely dry, witty sense. Certainly not the type of comedian that would make you laugh at him. He wasn't making fun of things but seeing the humour in things – the banal and the normal. There was an undercurrent of saneness in everything he did. He was screwed up, but that was schizophrenia too.

What Lou Reed needed most was to find a co-conspirator, an equal off whom he could bounce his ideas and behaviour and receive inspiration in return. Almost miraculously, he found such a person in what would become the second golden period of his life (the first being his discovery of rock and roll). Lou's first great soulmate, mirror and collaborator, whom he now roomed with in his sophomore year, was the brilliant, eccentric, talented but tortured and doomed Lincoln Swados. Swados came from an upwardly mobile middle-class and, by all accounts, outstandingly empathetic Jewish family from upstate New York. Like Reed, he had a little sister called Elizabeth, upon whom he doted (and to some extent, like Lou, identified with). The two students fell into each other's arms like lost inmates of some Siberian prison of the soul who finally discover after years of isolated exile a comrade and fellow voyager. To make matters perfect from Lou's point of view, Lincoln was an aspiring writer (working on an endless Dostoevskian novel); his favourite singer was Frank Sinatra; Lincoln's side of the room was covered in more crap than Lou's and – this was the clincher – Swados was agoraphobic. He spent most of his time holed up in their basement room either hunkered over a battered desk or playing Frank Sinatra records and rapping with Lou. Whenever Lou needed a receiver for one of his new songs, poems or stories, Lincoln was *always* there. Their relationship was the first of many good collaborations in Lou's life.

One of Lou's strongest personalities was the controlling figure who always needed to be the centre of attention and the most outstanding person in the room. Here again Lincoln was his perfect match, for if Lou ever worried that he might not yet possess the hippest look in the world, Lincoln presented no threat. He was usually togged out in a pair of trousers that ended somewhere above his ankles and were belted in the middle of his chest. His customary short-sleeved shirt invariably clashed with the trousers. A pair of bugged-out eyes stared out of a cadaverous face capped by a head of dirty, dishevelled, blondish hair. Lincoln's body was as much of a mess as was his mind. He rarely bathed or brushed his teeth, and at times emanated an odour that obviated any close physical relationships. He generally wore a Cheshire Cat smile that clearly indicated, at least to somebody of Lou's perceptiveness, just how far out in space Lincoln really was most of the time.

Their basement room was furnished like some barren writer's cell out of the imagination of the great Franz Kafka. The two black iron bedsteads, identical desks and battered chairs set out upon a green concrete floor and lit by a harsh bare lightbulb could not have better symbolized both the despair and the ambition at the heart of their twin souls. They both despised the world of their parents from which they had at least temporarily escaped. Both were intent upon destroying it and all its values with some of the most vitriolic, driven pages since Burroughs spat *Naked Lunch* out of his battered typewriter in Tangier. The room became their arsenal, their headquarters, their cave of knowledge and learning, and the engine of their voyage into the unknown. In time, Lou would rip off Lincoln's entire repertoire of attitudes, gestures and habits. He later confessed, 'I'm always studying people that I know, and then when I think I've got them worked out, I go away and write a song about them. When I sing the song, I become them. It's for that reason that I'm kind of empty when I'm not doing anything. I don't have a personality of my own, I just pick up other people's.'

Having met his male counterpart, Lou now needed, in order to pull out the male and female sides warring within him, a female companion. Within a week of settling in with Swados, Lou saw her riding down the university's main drag, Marshall Street, in the front seat of a car driven by a blond football player who belonged to the other Jewish fraternity on campus and recognized Reed as their local holy fool. Thinking to amuse his date, a scintillatingly beautiful freshman from the Midwest named Shelley Albin, he pulled over, laughing, 'Here's Lou! He's very shocking and evil!' making, as it turned out for him, the dreadful mistake of offering 'the lunatic' a ride.

Although in no way as twisted and bent as Lincoln Swados, Shelley was as perfect a match for Lou as his roommate was. Shelley was at Syracuse because it was the only university her parents in Wisconsin would let her attend. In preparation for the big move away from home, Shelley, along with a childhood girlfriend, had come to Syracuse fully intending to mend her ways and acquiesce to the college and culture's co-ed requirements. Discarding the jeans and work shirts she wore at home, where she had lived the frustrated life of a beatnik tomboy, she donned instead the below-the-knee skirt, tasteful blouse and string of pearls seen on girls in every yearbook photo of the period. When Lou hopped into the back seat eager to make her acquaintance, Shelley was squirming with the discomfort of the demure uniform as well as her dorky date's running commentary.

She vividly recalled Lou's skinny hips, baby face and give-away eyes, and 'knew we were going to go out as soon as he got into the car'. She also knew she was making a momentous decision and that Lou was going to be trouble, but that it certainly wasn't going to be boring. 'It was such a relief to see Lou, who was to me a normal person. And I was intrigued by the evil shit.'

The feeling was clearly mutual. As soon as the couple let Lou off in front of his dorm, he sprinted in and breathlessly told Swados about the most beautiful girl in the world he had just met, and his plans to call her immediately.

Lincoln had a strangely paternal side which would often appear at inappropriate moments. Seeing his role as steering Lou through his emotional mood swings, Swados put the kibosh on Lou's notion of seducing Shelley by informing him that this would be out of the question since he, Lincoln, had already spotted the pretty co-ed and, despite not yet having met her, was claiming her as his own.

Lou, for his part, saw his role in the relationship as primarily to calm the highly strung, hyperactive Swados down. Reasoning that the nerdy Lincoln, who had been unable to get a single date during his freshman year, would only be wounded by the rejection he was certain to get from Shelley, Lou wasted no time in cutting his friend off at the pass by calling Shelley at her dorm within the hour and arranging an immediate date. That way, Lou told himself, he would soon be able to give Swados the pleasure of her company.

Shelley Albin would not only become Lou Reed's girlfriend through his sophomore and junior years – 'my mountaintop, my peak' as he would later describe her – but would remain for many years thereafter his muse. 'Lou and I connected when we were too young to really put it into words,' Shelley said.

> There was some innate connection there that was very strong. I knew him before everything was covered up. My strongest image of Lou is always as a Byronesque character, a very sweet young man. He was interesting, he wasn't one of these bland, robotic people, he had a wonderful poetic nature. Basically, Lou was a puffball, he was a sweetie.

For all of Lou's eccentricities, Shelley found him

> very straight. He was very coordinated, a good dancer and he could play a good game of tennis. His criteria for life were equally straight. He was a fifties guy, the husband of the house, the God. He wanted a woman who was the end-all Barbie and would make bacon when he

wanted bacon. I was very submissive and naive and that's what appealed to him.

But Lou also had his 'crazy' side, which he played to the hilt. Like many bright kids who have just discovered Kierkegaard and Camus, he was the classic arty bad boy. Alternating between straight and scary, Lou revelled in both. 'There was a part of Lou that was for ever fifteen, and a part of him that was a hundred,' Shelley fondly recalled. Fortunately for Lou, she embraced both parts equally. And going out with Lou gave Shelley the jolt she needed to throw off her skirt and pearls for jeans and eventually letting her perm return to her natural long straight hair. Seeing her metamorphosis, the boy Shelley had left so brazenly for Lou was soon chiding her, 'You went to the dogs and became a beatnik. Lou ruined you!' In fact, Shelley, an art student, had simply reverted to being herself. But she enjoyed the taunt, knowing how much Lou liked it when people accused him of corrupting her, and enjoyed the notoriety it won him. Shelley was also astonishingly beautiful; to this day, Lou's Syracuse teachers and friends remember above all else that Lou Reed had an 'outrageously gorgeous girlfriend who was also very, very nice'.

Shelley Albin had a unique face. Looked at straight on, what struck you first were her eyes. An inner light glimmered through them. Her nose was straight and perfect. The planes of her face each side of it were smooth and angled so as to give the impression of being neither sharp nor dull. Her jawline and chin were so finely sculpted they became the subject of many an art student at Syracuse. It was an open and closed face. Her mouth was a 'yes' mouth; 'yes,' it said, 'yes'. Yet her face had a Modigliani Madonna quality that bade you keep your distance. Her light-brown hair reflected in her pale cream skin gave it an, at times, reddish tint. At five foot seven inches and weighing 115 pounds, she was close enough in size to Lou to wear his clothes. Close enough, in fact, to feel confident that she could beat him up.

'We were literally and physically inseparable from the moment we met,' Shelley recalled. 'We were always literally wrapped up in each other like a pretzel.' Soon Shelley and Lou could be seen at the Savoy, making out in public for hours at a time. 'He was a great kisser and well coordinated. I always thought of him as a master of the slow dance. When we met it was like long-lost friends.' For both of them it was their first real love affair. They quickly discovered that they could relate across the board. They had a great sexual relationship. They played basketball and tennis together. When Lou wrote a poem or a story, Shelley found herself doing a drawing or a painting that perfectly illustrated it. Shelley had been sent to a psychiatrist in her teens for refusing to speak to her father for three years. And just as he had rushed the fraternity, she, much to his delight, rushed a sorority and then told them to go fuck themselves an hour after she got accepted. Lou wrote 'I'll Be Your Mirror' two years later about Shelley.

His appeal was as a little boy [she said]. He was, however, a little too strong, a dangerous little boy you can't trust who will turn on you and is much stronger than you think. He had the strength of a man. You really couldn't win. You had to catch him by surprise if you wanted to deck him.

The electroshock treatments were very fresh in his mind when we met. He immediately established that he was erratic, undependable and dangerous, and that he was going to control any situation by making everyone around him nervous. It was the ultimate game of chicken. But I could play Lou's game too, that's why we got along so well.

What appealed to me about Lou was that he always pushed the edge. That's what really attracted me to him. I was submissive to Lou as part of my gift to him, but he wasn't controlling me and I could have beaten him up any time. If you look back at who's got the power in the relationship it will turn out that it wasn't him.

Whereas the entrance of a stunning female often disrupts the male bonding between collaborators, in the tradition of the beats established by Kerouac and his friend Neal Cassady, Lou correctly presumed that Shelley would enhance, rather than break up, his collaboration with Lincoln. In fact, it became such a close relationship that Lou would occasionally suggest, only half jokingly, that Shelley should spend some time in bed with Lincoln. Their relationship mirrored that of the famous trio at the core of their generation's favourite film, *Rebel Without a Cause*, with Lou as James Dean, Shelley as Natalie Wood and Lincoln as the doomed Sal Mineo.

Lou presented Lincoln to Shelley as an important but fragile figure who needed to be nurtured. Lincoln was very homely, but Shelley's vision of him in motion was 'like Fred Astaire. Lincoln was debonair and he would spin a wonderful tale and I think Lou could see this fascination. Lou felt very responsible and protective toward Lincoln because nobody would see Lincoln and we liked Lincoln.' The first thing Lou said to Shelley was, 'Lincoln wants you, and if I were a really good guy I should give you to Lincoln because I can get anybody and Lincoln can't. Lincoln loves you, but I'm not going to give you to him because I want you.' Lincoln, Shelley realized,

> was a wonderful gold mine for Lou. Many of Lou's ways of being charming and his gestures were taken straight from Lincoln. A lot of what I really loved about Lou was Lincoln, who was absolutely Lou's best friend and in many ways like Jiminy Cricket standing on Lou's shoulder whispering words into his ear. In many ways both of them saw me as their Elizabeths. They were going to take care of me and straighten me out and educate me.

The most important thing about Lincoln and Shelley was their understanding and embracing of Lou's talent and personality. If Lincoln was a flat mirror for Lou, Shelley was multidimensional, reflecting Lou's many sides. Perceptive and intuitive, she understood that Lou appreciated events on many different levels and often saw things others didn't. For the first time in his life Lou found two people to whom he could actually open up without fear of being ridiculed or taken for a ride. To a person who depended so much on others to complete him, they were irreplaceable allies.

At first, Lou's first love affair was idyllic. Lou rarely arose before noon, since he stayed up all night. He and Shelley would sometimes meet at 6 a.m. at the bottom of the steps leading to the women's dorm in the snow. Or else in the early afternoon she would take the twenty-minute hike from the women's dorm to Lou and Lincoln's quarters. Like all co-eds on campus, she was forbidden to enter a men's dorm on threat of expulsion, so she would merely tap on their basement window and wait for Lou to appear. When he did, he would gaze up at one of his favourite views of his lover's face smiling down at him with her long hair and a scarf hanging down. 'I liked looking in on their pit,' she recalled. 'It was truly netherworld. I liked being outside. I liked my freedom. And Lou liked that I had to go back to the dorm every night.' From there, the threesome would repair to a booth at the Savoy where they would be joined by the art student Karl Stoecker, a close friend of Shelley's, and the English major Peter Locke, a friend of Lou's to this day. With Jim Tucker, Sterling Morrison and a host of others, they would commence an all-day session consisting of writing, talking, making out, guitar playing and drawing. Lou was concentrating on playing his acoustic guitar and writing folk songs. The rest of the time was spent napping, with an occasional sortie to a class. When the threesome got restless at the Savoy, they might repair to the quaint Corner Bookstore, just half a block away, or the Orange Bar. But they always came back to home base at the Savoy, and to the avuncular owner, Gus Joseph, who saw kids come and go for fifty years, but still recalls Lou as one of his special favourites.

Lou was so enamoured of Shelley that in the autumn of 1961 he decided to bring her home to Freeport for the Christmas/ Hanukkah holidays. Considering the extent to which Lou based his rebellious posture on the theme of his difficult childhood, Shelley was fully aware of how hard it would be for Lou to take her to his parents' home. She remembered him thinking that he would score points with his parents: 'It was sort of subtle. He was going to show his father that he was OK. He knew that they would like me. And I suspect in some ways he still wanted to please his parents and he wanted to bring home somebody that he could bring home.'

Much to her surprise, Lou's parents welcomed her to their Freeport home with open arms, making her feel comfortable and accepted. Lou had given her the definite impression that his mother did not love him, but to Shelley, Toby Reed was a warm and wonderful woman, anything but selfish. And Sidney Reed, described by Lou as a stern disciplinarian, seemed equally loving. They appeared to be exact opposite of the way Lou had portrayed them. In her impression, Mr Reed 'would have walked over the coals for Lou'.

At the same time Shelley realized that Lou was just like them. He not only looked like them, but possessed all their best qualities. However, when she made the mistake of communicating her positive reaction, commenting on the twinkle in Mr Reed's eyes and noting how similar his dry sense of humour was to Lou's, her boyfriend snapped, 'Don't you know they're killers?'

After spending a happy, if at times tense, week in the Reed household, Shelley put together the puzzle. In a war of wits that had been going on for years, Lou went on the offensive as soon as he stepped through the portals of his home. Attempting by any means necessary to horrify and paralyse his loving parents, Lou had learned to control them by threatening to explode at any moment with some vicious remark or irrational act that would shatter their carefully developed harmony. For example, one night Mr Reed gave Lou the keys to the family car, a Ford Fairlane, and some money to take Shelley out to dinner in New York. However, such an exchange between father and son could not pass without conflict straight out of a cartoon. As Lou was heading for the door with Shelley, Sid had to make the observation that if he was going into the city he might, under the circumstances, put on a clean shirt. Instantly spinning into a vortex of anger that made him feel like a cockroach, Lou threw an acerbic verbal dart at his mother before slamming out the door. On the way into New York he almost killed himself and Shelley by driving carelessly and with little awareness of his surroundings. 'I remember him taking this little flower from the Midwest to the big city,' Shelley said. 'Chinatown. We drove in a hair-raising ride I'll never forget in my whole life. Lou showed me how to hang out on the heating grate of the Village Gate so you could hear the music and stay warm.'

His parents, she realized, 'had no sense of what was really in his mind and they were very upset and frightened by what awful things he was thinking. He must have been really miserable, how scary.' As a result, in order to obviate any disturbance, Lou's tense and nervous family attended to his every need just as if he were the perennial prodigal son. The only person in the house who received any degree of affection from Lou was his little sister, Elizabeth, who had always doted on Lou and thought he was the best.

Given their kind, gracious, outgoing manner, the Reeds were sitting ducks for Lou's brand of torture. He would usually begin by embracing the rogue cousin in the Reed family called Judy. As soon as he got home, Lou would enthusiastically enquire after her activities and prattle on about how he wanted to emulate her more than anyone else in the family, often reducing his mother to tears. Next, Lou would make a bid to monopolize the attentions of the twelve-year-old Elizabeth. Confiding to her his innermost thoughts, he could make a big point of excluding his parents from the pow-wow. 'She was cute,' thought Shelley, 'she looked just like Lou. So did his mother and father. They all looked exactly like him. It was hysterical. Lou was very protective of her. And she was so sweet. She didn't have that much of a personality, but she was not unanimated.' Every action was aimed to cut his parents out of his life, while keeping them prisoners in it. Meanwhile, like every college kid home on vacation, Lou managed to extract from them all the money he could, and the freedom to come and go as if the house were a hotel. As soon as everybody at 35 Oakfield Avenue was in position ready to do exactly as he wanted, Lou began to enjoy himself.

In fact, so extreme was the situation that on this first visit Toby Reed, looking upon Shelley as the perfect daughter in law, took her into her confidence. 'They were very nervous about what was he bringing home,' she remembered. 'So they really took it as a sign that, "Oh, God, maybe he was OK." We recognized with each other, she and I, that we both really liked him and we both loved him.' Mrs Reed filled her in on Lou's troublesome side and tried to find out what Lou was saying about them. Shelley got the impression that the Reeds bore no malice towards Lou, but just wanted the best for him. Mrs Reed seemed completely puzzled by how Lou had got on the track of hating and blaming them. Pondering the strange state of affairs unfolding behind the façade of the Reeds' attractive home, Shelley drew two conclusions. On the one hand, since his family seemed quite normal and had no apparent problems, Lou was moved to create psychodrama in order to fuel his writing. On the other hand, Lou really did crave his parents' approval. He was immensely troubled by their refusal to recognize his talent and needed to break away from their restricted life. One point of Lou's frustration was the feeling that his father was a wimp who gave over control of his life to his wife. This both horrified and fascinated Lou, who was a dyed-in-the-wool male supremacist. Lou was secretly proud of his father and wanted more than anything else that the old man should stand up for himself. But he simply could not stand the thought of sharing the former beauty queen's attention with his father.

However, at least for the time being, Lou's introduction of Shelley into their lives caused his parents unexpected joy. Ecstatic that his son had brought home a clean and beautiful Jewish girl, Mr Reed increased Lou's allowance.

If he had had any idea of the life Lou and Shelley were leading at Syracuse, he would probably have acted in the reverse. As the year wore on, sex, drugs, rock and roll and their influences began to play a bigger role in both their lives, although Shelley did not take drugs. Already a regular pot-smoker, Lou dropped acid for the first time and started experimenting with peyote. Taking drugs was not the norm on college campuses in 1961. Though pot was showing up more regularly in fraternities, and a few adventurous students were taking LSD, most students were clean-cut products of the 1950s, preparing for jobs as accountants, lawyers, doctors and teachers. To them, Lou's habits and demeanour were extreme. And now, not only was Lou taking drugs, he began selling them to the fraternity boys. Lou kept a stash of pot in a grocery bag in the dorm room of a female friend. Whenever he had a customer, he'd send Shelley to go get it.

Lou was by now on his way to becoming an omnivorous drug user. Apart from taking acid and peyote, Lou would at times buy a codeine-laced cough syrup called turpenhydrate. Lou was stoned a lot of the time. 'He liked me to be there when he was high,' Shelley remembered. 'He used to say, "If I don't feel good, you'll take care of me." Mostly he took drugs to numb himself or get relief, to take a break from his brain.'

Meanwhile, having presented himself as a born-again hetero-sexual, Lou now wasted no time in making another shocking move by shoring up his homosexual credentials. In the second semester of his sophomore year, he had what he later described as his first, albeit unconsummated, gay love affair. 'It was just the most amazing experience,' Lou explained. 'I felt very bad about it because I had a girlfriend and I was always going out on the side, and subterfuge is not my hard-on.' He particularly remembered the pain of 'trying to make yourself feel something towards women when you can't. I couldn't figure out what was wrong. I wanted to fix it up and make it OK. I figured if I sat around and thought about it I could straighten it out.'

Lou and Shelley's relationship rapidly escalated to a high level of game playing. Lou had more than one gay affair at Syracuse and would often try and shock her by casually mentioning that he was attracted to some guy. Shelley, however, could always turn the tables on him because she wasn't threatened by Lou's gay affairs and often turned them into competitions for the subject's attentions, competitions she usually won. If Shelley was a match for Lou, Lou was always ready to up the stakes. They soon got out of their depth playing these and other equally dangerous mind games which led them into more complexities than they could handle.

Friends had conflicting memories of Lou's gay life at Syracuse. Allen Hyman viewed him as being extraordinarily heterosexual right through college. There was no indication that he was either bisexual or gay in those years. He started doing a lot of writing at Syracuse. In a lot of his early poetry he seemed fascinated by the gay world. The writing suggests that he had his first homosexual experience at Syracuse. It was then I started talking to him about the, from my perspective, very bizarre work he was doing.

'He tried the gay scene at Syracuse, which was really repellent,' recalled Sterling Morrison, who thought Lou was mostly a voyeur. 'He had a little fling with some really flabby effete fairy. I said, "Oh, man, Lou, if you want to do it, I hate to say it but let's find somebody attractive at least."'

Homosexuality was generally presented as an unspeakable vice in the early 1960s. Nothing could have been considered more repellent in 1962 America than the image of two men kissing. The average American would not allow a homosexual in his house for fear he might leave some kind of terrible disease on the toilet seat, or, for that matter, the armchair. There were instances reported at universities in America during this time when healthy young men fainted, like Victorian ladies, at the physical approach of a homosexual. In fact, as Andy Warhol would soon prove, at the beginning of the 1960s the homosexual was considered the single most threatening, subversive character in the culture. According to Frank O'Hara's biographer Brad Gooch:

A campaign to control gay bars in New York had already begun in January, 1964, when the Fawn in Greenwich Village was closed by the police. Reacting to this closing by police department undercover agents, known as 'actors,' the *New York Times* ran a front-page story headlined 'Growth of Overt Homosexuality in City Provokes Wide Concern.'

Besides the refuge large cities such as San Francisco and New York provided for homosexuals, many cultural institutions, especially the private universities, became home to a large segment of the homosexual community. Syracuse University, where there was a hotbed of homosexual activity, led in part by one of Lou's drama teachers, who had a strong influence on the budding Lou, was no exception.

'As an actor, I couldn't cut the mustard, as they say,' Reed recalled. 'But I was good as a director.' For one project, Lou chose to direct *The Car Cemetery* (or *The Automobile Graveyard*) by Fernando Arrabal. Reed could scarcely have found a more appropriate form (the Theatre of the Absurd) or subject (it was loosely based on the Christ mythology) as a reflection of his own life. The story line followed an inspired musician to his ultimate betrayal to the secret police by his accompanist. Everything Lou wrote was about himself, and had the props been available, perhaps he would have considered a climactic electroshock torture scene. In giving the musician a messianic role against a backdrop of cruel sex and prostitution, the play appealed to the would-be writer and musician. 'I'm sure Lou had a homosexual experience with his teacher,' attested another friend. 'This drama teacher used to have guys go up to his room and put on girls' underwear and take pictures of them and then he'd give you an A. One Dean of Men either committed suicide or left because he was associated with this group of faculty fags who were later indicted for doing all kinds of strange stuff with the students.'

The 'first' gay flirtation cannot be simply overlooked and put aside as Morrison and Albin would want it to be. First of all, it had happened before. Back in Freeport during Lou's childhood, he had participated in circle jerks, and the gay experience left him with traits which he would develop to his advantage commercially in the near future. Foremost among them was an effeminate walk with small, carefully taken steps, by which friends could identify him from a block away.

Despite his apparent desire originally to concentrate on a career as a writer, just as his guitar was never far from his hand, music was never far from Lou's thoughts. In fact, his first band at Syracuse was a loosely formed folk group comprising himself; John Gaines, a good-looking, tall black guy with a powerful baritone; Joe Annus, a remarkably good-looking, tall white guy with an equally good voice; and a great banjo player with a big Afro hairdo who looked like Art Garfunkel.

The group often played on a square of grass in the centre of campus at the corner of Marshall Street and South Crouse. They also occasionally got jobs at a small bar called the Clam Shack. Lou didn't like to sing in public because he felt uncomfortable with his voice, but he would sing his own folk songs privately to Shelley. He also played some traditional Scottish ballads based on poems by Robert Burns or Sir Walter Scott. Shelley, who would inspire Lou to write a number of great songs, was deeply moved by the beauty of his music. For her, his chord progressions and the way he slid from chord to chord were just as hypnotic and seductive as his voice.

In addition to how to direct a play, Lou was also taught how to dramatize himself at every opportunity. The showmanship would come in handy when Lou hit the stage with his rock music. Though he was devoting himself to poetry and folk songs, Lou had not dropped his initial ambition to be a rock-and-roll star. In fact, Reed's development of folk music was put in the shade in his sophomore year when he finally formed his first bona fide rock-and-roll band, LA and the Eldorados. LA stood for Lewis and Allen, since Reed and Hyman were the founding members. Lou played rhythm and took the vocals; Allen was on drums; another Sammie, Richard Mishkin, was on piano and bass; and Mishkin brought in Bobby Newman on saxophone. A friend of Lou's, Stephen Windheim, rounded out the band on lead guitar. They all got along well except for Newman, a loud, obnoxious character from the Bronx, who, according to Mishkin, 'didn't give a shit about anyone'. Lou hated Bobby and was greatly relieved when he was kicked out of school that semester and replaced by another sax player, Bernie Kroll, whom Lou fondly referred to as 'Kroll the troll'.

There was money to be made in the burgeoning Syracuse music scene, and the Eldorados were soon being handled by two students, Donald Schupak, who managed them, and Joe Divoli, who got them local bookings. 'I had met Lou when we were freshmen,' Schupak explained. 'Maybe because we were friends as freshmen nothing developed into a problem because he could say, "Hey, Schupak, that's a fucking stupid idea." And I'd say, "You're right."' Soon, under Schupak's guidance and Reed's leadership, LA and the Eldorados were working most weekends, playing frat parties, dances, bars and clubs, making $125 a night, two or three nights a week.

Lou was strongly drawn to the musician's lifestyle and haunts. Just off campus was the black section of Syracuse, the fifteenth ward. There he frequented a dive called the 800 Club, where black musicians and singers performed and jammed together. Lou and his band were accepted there and would occasionally work with some of the singers from a group called the Three Screaming Niggers. 'The Three Screaming Niggers were a group of black guys that floated around the upstate campuses,' said Mishkin. 'And we would pretend we were them when we got these three black guys to sing. So we would go down there once in a while and play. The people down there always had the attitude, the white man can't play the blues, and we'd be down playing the blues. Then they'd be nice to us.' The Eldorados also sometimes played with a number of black female backing vocalists.

At first, what made LA and the Eldorados stick out more than anything else was their car. Mishkin had a 1959 Chrysler New Yorker with gigantic fins. He and his roommate, an industrial-design student who was also friends with Lou, painted red guitars with flames shooting out of them on the side of the car and 'LA and the Eldorados' on the trunk. Simultaneously they all bought vests with gold-lamé piping, jeans, boots and matching shirts. Togged out in lounge-lizard punk and with Mishkin's gilded chariot to transport them to their shows, the band was a sight when it hit the road. They had the kind of adventures that bond musicians. Mishkin remembered:

One time we played Colgate and we were driving back in Allen's Cadillac in the middle of a snowstorm which eventually stopped us dead. So we're sitting in the car smoking pot around 1 a.m., and we realized that we can't do that all night because we'd die. The snow was deep, so we got out of the car and schlepped to this tiny town maybe half a mile away. We needed a place to stay so we went to the local hotel, which was, of course, full. But they had a bar there. Schupak was in the bar telling these stories about how he was in the army in the war, and Lewis and I are hysterical, we are dying, it was so funny. Then the bartender said, 'You can't stay here, I have to close the bar.' We ended up going to the court house and sleeping in jail.

The Eldorados further distinguished themselves by mixing some of Lou's original material into their set of standard Chuck Berry covers. One of Lou's songs they played a lot was a love song he wrote for Shelley, an early draft of 'Coney Island Baby'. 'We would do some of his material, but we were doing fraternity parties,' Mishkin recalled. 'We did a fifteen-minute version of "Comin' Home Baby" – that thing that Herbie Mann did – it would just go on and on. We did the Chuck Berry kind of thing and then we'd do some of Lou's stuff. We did a thing called "Fuck Around Blues". It was an insult song. It sometimes went over well and it sometimes got us thrown out of fraternity parties.'

LA and the Eldorados played a big part in Lou's life at Syracuse, providing him with many basic rock experiences, but he kept the band separate from the rest of his life at Syracuse. At first Lou wanted to make a point of being a writer more than a rock-and-roller. In those days, before the Beatles arrived, the term 'rock-and-roller' was something of a put-down, associated more with Paul Anka and Pat Boone than the Rolling Stones. Lou preferred to be associated with writers like Jack Kerouac. This dichotomy was spelled out in his limited wardrobe. Like the classic beatnik, Lou usually wore black jeans and T-shirts or turtlenecks, but he also kept a tweed jacket with elbow patches in his closet in case he wanted to come on like John Updike. However, in either role – as rocker or writer – Lou appeared somewhat uncomfortable. Therefore, in each role he used confrontation as a means both to achieve an effect and dramatize an inner turmoil that was quite real. For Hyman and the others, this sometimes made working with Lou exceedingly difficult. According to Allen:

One of the biggest problems we had was that if Lou woke up on the day of the job and he decided he didn't want to be there, he wouldn't come. I remember one fraternity party, it was an afternoon job, we were all set up and ready to go and he just wasn't there. I ran down to his room and walked through about 400 pounds of his favourite pistachio nuts – and then I found him in bed under about 600 pounds of pistachio nuts – in the middle of the afternoon. I looked at him and said, 'What are you doing? We have a job!' And he said, 'Fuck you, get out of here. I don't want to work to today.' I said, 'You can't do this, we're getting paid!' Mishkin and I physically dragged him up to the show. Ultimately he did play, but he was very pissed off.

Reed seemed at once to want the spotlight and to hate it. 'Lou's uniqueness and stubbornness made him really different than anyone I had ever known,' added Mishkin.

He was a terrible guy to work with. He was impossible. He was always late, he would always find fault with everything that the people who had hired us expected of us. And we were always dragging him here and dragging him there. Sometimes we were called Pasha and the Prophets, because Lou was such a son of a bitch at so many gigs he'd upset everyone so much we couldn't get a gig in those places again. He was as ornery as you can get. People wouldn't let us back because he was so absolutely rude to people and just so mean and unappreciative of the fact that these people were paying us to get up and play music for them. He couldn't have cared less. So we used the name Pasha and the Prophets in order to play there again. And then the people who hired us were so drunk they wouldn't remember. He would never dress or act in a way so that people would accept him. He would often act in a confrontational manner. He wanted to be different.

Lou was ambitious. He wanted to be – and said this to me in no uncertain terms – a rock-and-roll star and a writer. He didn't have a great way to put it together yet, and he was so ornery and difficult to work with that he made it hard. He probably would have been more successful if he had been nicer.

In May 1962, sick of the stodgy university literary publication and keen to make their mark, Lewis and Lincoln, together with Jim

Tucker and some other students, put out two issues of a literary magazine called the *Lonely Woman Quarterly*. The title was based on Lou's favourite Ornette Coleman composition, 'Lonely Woman', and the editors operated out of the Savoy coffee shop with the encouragement of Gus Joseph. The first issue contained an untitled story, mentioned in the previous chapter, signed Luis Reed. It described Sidney Reed as a wife beater and Toby as a child molester. Shelley, who was involved in the publication, was convinced that, just as Lou's homosexual affair was mostly an attempt to associate with the offbeat gay world, the story was a conspicuous attempt to build his image as an evil, mysterious person. He was smart enough, she thought, to see that this was going to make readers uncomfortable. 'And that's what Lou always wanted to do,' she said, 'make people uncomfortable.'

The premier issue of *LWQ* brought 'Luis' his first press mention. In reviewing the magazine, the university's newspaper, the *Daily Orange*, had interviewed Lincoln, who boasted that the magazine's 100 copies had sold out in three days. Indeed, the first issue was well received, but when everyone else on its staff apparently got lazy, Lou put out issue number two, which featured his second explosive piece, printed on page one. Called 'Profile: Michael Kogan – Syracuse's Miss Blanding', it was the most attention-grabbing project Lou ever pulled off at Syracuse: a deftly executed, harsh attack upon the student who was head of the Young Democrats Party at the university. Allen Hyman recalled, 'It said something like he (Kogan) should parade around campus with an American flag up his ass, which at the time was a fairly outrageous statement.' Unfortunately, Kogan's father turned out to be a powerful corporation lawyer. 'He decided that the piece was libellous,' Sterling remembered, 'and he'd bust Lou's ass. So they hauled him before the dean. But this guy and his father were so offensive, the dean started shifting to Lou's side. Afterwards, the dean told Lou to finish up his work and get his ass out of there, and nothing would happen to him.' By May 1962 Reed's literary career was off to a running start.

Despite this, Lou's relationship with Shelley – who was not in his classes – dominated his sophomore year. They had spent as many of their waking hours together as was possible, camping out over the weekends in friends' apartments, using fraternity rooms, cars and sometimes even bushes to make love, but in the second semester problems overwhelmed them. Shelley was sick with bronchitis a good deal of the time, spending as much as one third of the semester in the infirmary. From March through May 1962, neither of them went to school at all. 'We were very close, we were absolutely terrific together,' Shelley recalled, 'but we were having a terribly difficult time living. The kind of things we were dealing with completely detached us from school. It was like, "Oh, God, we're supposed to go to class, we're supposed to have a test. Oh, yeah, well, screw it." We had other stuff to do.'

Lou received a D in Introduction to Math and an F in English History. Then he got into trouble with the authorities again when another student, who occasionally played with LA and the Eldorados, was busted for smoking pot and ratted on a number of people, including Lewis and Ritchie Mishkin.

'We smoked all the time,' Mishkin admitted.

> But we didn't smoke and work. We may have played and then smoked after and then jammed. Anyway, the Dean of Men called Lou, me and some other people into his office and said, 'We know you were smoking pot, so give us the whole story.' We were terrified, at least I was. But nothing happened. Lou was angry – with the authorities and the student. But they were pretty soft on us. We were lucky, but then all they had to go on was the 'he said, she said' kind of evidence, so there was a limit to what they could do. But they had us in the office and they did the old, 'We know because so and so said . . .'

As a result of these numerous transgressions, and with his apparent academic torpor at the end of his sophomore year, Reed was put on academic probation.

The summer of 1962 was somewhat difficult for Lou. This was the first time he had been apart from Shelley for more than a day, and he took it hard. First, in an attempt to exert his control over her across the thousand miles that separated them, he embarked on a zealous letter-writing campaign, sending her long, storylike letters every day. They would begin with an account of his daily routine – he would go to the local gay bar, the Hayloft, every night, and tweaked Shelley with suggestive comments. Then, suddenly, in the middle of a paragraph the epistle would abruptly shift from reality to fiction and Lou would take off on one of his short stories, usually mirroring his passion and longing for Shelley. An exemplary story sent across the country that summer was 'The Gift', which appeared on the Velvet Underground's second album, *White Light/White Heat*, and summed up Lou's image of himself as a lonely Long Island nerd pining for his promiscuous girlfriend. 'The Gift' climaxed with the lovelorn author desperately mailing himself to his lover in a cardboard box. The final image, in the classic style of Yiddish humour that informed so much of Reed's work, had the boyfriend being accidentally killed by his girlfriend during her attempt to open the box with a large sheet-metal cutter.

Shelley, a classic passive-aggressive character, rarely responded in kind, but she did talk to Lou on the phone several times that summer and he did not like what he heard at all. Lou had expected Shelley to remain locked in her room for the duration of the summer, thinking of nothing but him. But Shelley wasn't that kind of girl. Despite having commenced the vacation with a visit to the hospital to have her tonsils out, by July she was regularly dating more than one guy and at least one was madly in love with her. The emotions Lou addressed in 'The Gift' were his. He paced up and down his room in frustration. He couldn't stand not having Shelley under his thumb. It was driving him insane.

Then he hit on a plan. Why not go out and visit her? After all, he was her boyfriend, he was writing to her every day or so and had called her several times. It sounded like the right thing to do. His parents, who had kept a wary eye on their wayward son that summer, still frowning on his naughty visits to the Hayloft and daily excursions on the guitars, were only too happy to support the venture that they felt was taking him in the right direction. At the beginning of August he flew out to Chicago.

Shelley had been adamantly against the planned visit, warning Lou on the phone that her parents wouldn't like him, that it was a big mistake and wouldn't work out at all. But Lou, who wanted, she recalled, 'to be in front of my face', insisted.

By now Lou had developed a pattern of reaction to any new environment he entered. His plan was to split up any group, polarizing them around himself. In a family situation as soon as he walked into anybody's house he took the position that the father was a tyrannical ogre from whom the mother had to be saved. On his first night in the Albins' home, he cleverly drew Mr Albin into a political discussion and then, marking him for the bullheaded liberal Democrat that he was, expertly lanced him with a detailed defence of the notorious conservative columnist William Buckley. While Shelley sat back and watched, half horrified, half mesmerized, Mr Albin became increasingly apoplectic. Lou was obviously not the right man for his daughter. In fact, he didn't even want him in the house.

The Albins had rented a room for Lou in nearby Evanston, at Northwestern University. Lou pulled a double whammy on Mr Albin, driving their car into a ditch later the same night when bringing Shelley back from the movies at 1 a.m., forcing her father to get up, get dressed, come out and help haul out the mauled automobile.

Things went downhill from there. Lou made a valiant attempt to win over Mrs Albin. Having dinner with her and Shelley one night when the man of the house was absent, Lou launched into his classic rap saying, 'Gee, you're clearly very nice. If it wasn't for that ogre living in the house . . .' But Mrs Albin was having none of his boyish charm. She had surreptitiously read Lou's letters to Shelley that summer and formed a very definite opinion about Lou Reed: she hated him with a passion – and still does, more than thirty years later. In her opinion, Lou was ruining her daughter's life.

As an upshot of Lou's visit, Shelley's parents informed her that if she continued to see Lou in any way at all, she would never be allowed to return to Syracuse. Swearing that she would never set eyes upon the rebel again, Shelley now embarked upon a secret relationship with Lou that trapped her exactly where he wanted. Since Shelley had no one outside Lou's circle in whom she could confide about her relationship with him, she was essentially under his control. From here on Lou would always attempt to program his women. His first move would always be to amputate them from their former lives so that they accepted the fact that the rules were Lou's.

chapter three

Shelley, If You Just Come Back

1962–1964

[In which Lou finds his first
mentor in Delmore Schwartz,
breaks up with Shelley and
composes 'Heroin' and
'I'm Waiting for the Man'.]

*The image of the artist who follows a brilliant leap to success
with a fall into misery and squalor, is deeply credited, even
cherished in our culture.*

IRVING HOWE, foreword to *In Dreams Begin Responsibilities
and Other Stories* by Delmore Schwartz

When Lou returned to Syracuse for his junior year, he rented a
room in a large apartment inhabited by a number of like-minded
musicians and English majors on Adams Street. The room was so
small that it could barely contain the bed, but that was OK as far as
Lou was concerned because he lived in the bed. He had his
typewriter, his guitar and Shelley, who was now living in one of
the cottage-style dorms opposite Crouse College that were far less
supervised than the big women's dorm. She was consequently able
to live with Lou pretty much full time.

The semester began magically with Shelley's arrival. Lou
whipped out his guitar and a new instrument he had mastered over
the summer, a harmonica which he wore in a rack around his neck,
and launched into a series of songs he had written for Shelley over
the vacation, including the beautiful 'I Found a Reason'. Shelley,

who was completely seduced by Lou's music, was brought to tears by the beauty and sensitivity of his playing, the music and the lyrics.

In his new pad, he could play his music as loud as he wanted ('The music played all day and all night,' Shelley recalled. 'I could sleep with the music on') and take drugs with impunity. It also became another stage on which to develop 'Lou Reed'. He rehearsed with the band there, and maintained a creative working environment essential to his writing. He was really beginning to feel his power. His band was under his control. He had already written 'The Gift', 'Coney Island Baby', 'Fuck Around Blues', and later classics like 'I'll Be Your Mirror' were in the works.

By the mid-1960s, the American college campus was going through a remarkable transformation from a bastion of conservatism to one of the brighter beacons of politics and art. One of the marks of a particularly hip school was its creative-writing department. Few American writers were able to make a living out of writing books. Some time in the 1950s someone put together the bogus notion that you could haul in a bigwig writer like Ernest Hemingway or Samuel Beckett and get him to teach a bunch of ten to fifteen young men (no chicks in the band!) how to write. However, it had succeeded in dragging a series of glamorous superstars like T. S. Eliot (a rival with Einstein and Churchill as the top draw in the 1950s) to Harvard for six weeks to give a series of lectures about how he wrote, leading hundreds of young men to write poor imitations of *The Waste Land*. The concept of the creative-writing programme looked good on paper, but it was, in reality, a giant shuck, and the (mostly) poets who were on the lucrative gravy train in the early sixties were, for the most part, a bunch of wasted dudes who had helped popularize the craft during its glorious years 1920–50, when poets like W. H. Auden had the cachet rock stars would acquire in the second half of the century.

Delmore Schwartz was one of the most charismatic, stunning-looking poets on the circuit. He had been foisted onto the Syracuse University creative-writing programme by two heavy-weights in the field who had known him in his prime as America's answer to T. S. Eliot: the great poet Robert Lowell and the novelist Saul Bellow, who would go on to win the Nobel Prize. Unfortunately for both himself and his students, Schwartz had by then, like so many of his calling, expelled his muse with near-lethal daily doses of amphetamine pills washed down by copious amounts of hard alcohol. Despite having as recently as 1959 won the prestigious Bollingen Prize for his selected poems, *Summer Knowledge*, when he arrived on campus in September 1962, Schwartz was suffering through the saddest and most painful period of his life.

He was then fifty-two, and his skin had a greenish-yellow tinge, which gave the impression he was suffering from a permanent case of jaundice or trying out for a stock role as Frankenstein, with his pair of mad eyes that boiled out of his big bloated face with unrestrained paranoia. On a good day this brilliant man could still hold a class spellbound with the intelligence, sensitivity and conviction of his hypnotic voice once it had seized upon his religion – literature. Schwartz once received a ten-minute standing ovation at Syracuse after giving his class a moving reading of *The Waste Land*. Unfortunately, by 1962 his stock was so low that none of the performances he gave at Syracuse – in the street, in the classroom, in bars, in his apartment, at faculty meetings, anywhere his voice could find receivers – was recorded.

Until the arrival of Delmore Schwartz, Lou Reed had not been overly impressed by his instructors at Syracuse, with the exception of his drama teacher. However, Lou only had to encounter Delmore once to realize that he had finally found a man impressively more disturbed than himself, from whom he might be able to get some perspective on all the demons that were boiling in his brain.

If Lou had been looking for a father figure ever since rejecting his old man as a silent, suffering milquetoast, he had now found a perfect one in Delmore Schwartz. In both Bellow's novel about Schwartz, *Humboldt's Gift*, and James Atlas's outstanding biography, *Delmore Schwartz, The Life of an American Poet*, many descriptions of Schwartz's salient characteristics could just as well apply to what Lou Reed was fast becoming.

As Lou already did, Delmore entangled his friends in relationships with unnatural ardour until they finally made him unbearable to everyone. Like Lou, Delmore ultimately always caused those around him more suffering than pleasure. Like Lou, Delmore possessed a stunning arrogance along with a nature that was as solicitous as it was dictatorial. Both presented astonishing displays of self-hatred mixed with self-love, and finally concluded, in concurrence with many of their friends, that they were evil beings. Both were wonderful, hectic, nonstop inspirational improvisators and monologists as well as expert flatterers. Grand, erratic, handsome men, they both gained much of their insights during long nights of insomnia.

But there the comparison ended. For Delmore Schwartz was already singing himself in and out of madness, and when his heart danced it never danced for joy, whereas Lou possessed a marvellous capacity for unadulterated joy and a carefully locked hold on reality. He had no doubt that he was going to succeed and most of his friends – some of them becoming disciples – equally believed in his talent. Lou may have shared with Delmore moments of sublime inspiration alternated with moments of indescribable despair, but unlike Schwartz, Reed had not read himself out of American culture.

In his junior year, Reed took a number of courses with Schwartz apart from creative writing. They read Dostoevsky, Shakespeare and Joyce together and when studying *Ulysses*, Lou was seeing himself as Daedalus to Schwartz's Bloom. They developed a friendship that would go on until Lou graduated.

At first Schwartz would actually manoeuvre himself to the various classrooms in which it was his duty to entertain students. Soon, however, rather than attempting to teach them how to write, he would fall into wandering, often despondent rants about the great men he had known, the sex life of the Queen of England, and other irrelevant subjects, conveying his information in tones so authoritative and confiding that he convinced his astonished audiences that he really knew what he was talking about. When he grew tired of these exercises in nostalgia for a lost life, he would often fill in the time reading aloud or, on bad days, mumbling incoherently. He also set up an office at the far-back left-hand corner table of the Orange Bar, where, usually sitting directly opposite Lou, who was one of the few students able to respond to him, and surrounded by several rows of chairs, Schwartz would do what he had now become best at. Saul Bellow called him 'the Mozart of conversation'.

Shelley, who was always at the table with them, recalled that Lou and Delmore

adored each other. Delmore was always drinking, popping Valiums and talking. I can picture Delmore sitting in the Orange just as clear as day. He was kind of edgy, big. His hands would move, picking things up, putting them down; he was always lurching over and I got the feeling he was slobbering because he was always eating and talking and spitting things out. Then he'd be popping his pills. He really adored Lou. He could see Lou as he was, that he was really sweet. But he kept berating Lou for not treating me nicely. At the same time Delmore told me not to leave Lou no matter how obnoxious he was and to make sure he became a writer. He was very direct to me. He said, 'I love Lou. You have to take care of Lou because he has to be a writer. He is a writer. And it is your job to give up your life to make sure that Lou becomes a writer. Don't let him treat you like shit. But tolerate everything he does to stay with him because he needs you.'

His attitude was like, 'Lou, pay attention because in ten years sitting here talking to these kids will be your job.' He was riveted on Lou.

Both Delmore and another strong influence on Lou, the poet and lecturer Phillip Booth, saw Reed as one of them, a writer. If Lou learned how to act from Lincoln, he learned how to spin a tale from Delmore. In the bar Schwartz was an old drunk guy with a drug habit who had to be escorted home every night. But when he read Joyce aloud the beautiful young poet would briefly emerge.

Both Lou and Shelley were wildly excited by the new connection. They made the final pages of Molly's monologue in *Ulysses* their credo. Whenever Shelley heard Lou's chord changes she always wanted to answer, 'Yes, yes, yes.'

Later in his life, perhaps to some extent to demolish the notion that he was just a dumb rock-and-roll guitar player, Lou liked nothing better than to reminisce about his relationship with Delmore.

Delmore was my teacher, my friend, and the man who changed my life. He was the smartest, funniest, saddest person I had ever met. I studied with him in the bar. Actually, it was him talking and me listening. People who knew me would say, 'I can't imagine that.' But that's what it was. I just thought Delmore was the greatest. We drank together starting at eight in the morning. He was an awesome person. He'd order five drinks at once. He was incredibly smart. He could recite the encyclopedia to you starting with the letter A. He was also one of the funniest people I ever met in my life. He was an amazingly articulate, funny raconteur of the ages. At this time Delmore would be reading *Finnegans Wake* out loud, which seemed like the only way I could get through it. Delmore thought you could do worse with your life than devote it to reading James Joyce. He was very intellectual but very funny. And he hated pop music. He would start screaming at people in the bar to turn the jukebox off.

At the time, no matter how strange the stories or the requests or the plan, I was there. I was ready to go for him. He was incredible, even in his decline. I'd never met anybody like him. I wanted to write a novel; I took creative writing. At the same time, I was in rock-and-roll bands. It doesn't take a great leap to say, 'Gee, why don't I put the two together?'

Schwartz's most famous story, 'In Dreams Begin Responsibilities', was a real eye-opener for Lou. The story centres on a hallucination by a son who finds himself in a cinema watching a documentary about his parents and flips out, screaming a warning to them not to have a son. '"In Dreams Begin Responsibilities" really was amazing to me,' Lou recalled. 'To think you could do that with the simplest words available in such a short span of pages and create something so incredibly powerful. You could write something like that and not have the greatest vocabulary in the world. I wanted to write that way, simple words to cause an emotion, and put them with my three chords.'

Delmore, for his part, clearly believed in Lou as a writer. The climax of Lou's relationship with Delmore came when the older poet put his arm around Lou in the Orange Bar one night and told him, 'I'm gonna be leaving for a world far better than this soon but I want you to know that if you ever sell out and go work for Madison Avenue or write junk I will haunt you.'

'I hadn't thought about doing anything, let alone selling out,' Reed recalled. 'I took that seriously. He saw even then that I was capable of writing decently. I never showed him anything I wrote – I was really afraid. But he thought that much of me. That was a tremendous compliment to me, and I always retained that.'

Shelley remembered the moment vividly:

Delmore was larger than life. He put his hand on Lou and said, 'Lou, this is your job, you have this responsibility.' Like 'Redeem me. If you're not a writer, I haven't lived for anything.' That was very much the impression that we all had: if Lou didn't become a writer, Delmore was wrong. Delmore said, 'You are good enough to become a writer.' Lou took it to heart but nothing was very heavy because nothing lasted very long. Delmore moved at a very high speed. He did it all very quickly and lightly, yet he knew that it was very important. We didn't doubt this for a minute.

Delmore also gave Lou signed copies of his books and taught him that his character would be determined by how he handled his fate and the pressures of life. 'I think he wanted to pass his legacy on. But the moment you put responsibility on Lou, he's going to resent you,' Shelley observed. 'In time I think he felt a great guilt about that, but that was a real attachment.'

Close though they were, they had two serious differences of opinion. As a man of the forties, Delmore was an educated hater of homosexuals. The uncomprehending attitudes common among straight American males towards gays in the early sixties put homosexuals on the level of communists or drug addicts. Therefore, Lou was unable to show Delmore many of his best short stories, since they were based on gay themes.

Then there was rock and roll. Delmore despised it, and in

particular the lyrics, which he saw as a cancer in the language. Delmore knew Lou was in a band but wrote it off as a childish activity he would outgrow as soon as he commenced his graduate studies in literature.

Delmore Schwartz was thus barred from two of the most powerful strands of Lou's work.

Lou's relationship with Shelley reached its apotheosis in his junior year when, she felt, he really gained in confidence and began to transform himself. Ensconced in the Adams Street apartment muddle of guitars and amps, books, clothing and cigarettes, Lou now lived in a world of music accompanied by the spirit of Shelley. She knew every nook and cranny of him better than anybody, and before he put his armour on. She had become his best friend, the one who could look into his eyes, the one he wrote for and played to.

Lou needed to be grounded because, although Lincoln could be cooler than whipped cream and smarter than amphetamine, he was a lunatic. Lou always needed a court jester nearby to keep him amused, but he also required the presence of a straight, 1950s woman, who could cool him down when the visions got too heavy. Shelley Albin became everything to Lou Reed: she was mother, sister, muse, lover, fixer-upper, therapist, drug mule, mad girl. She did everything with Lou twenty-four hours a day.

Lou was drinking at the Orange as Delmore told stories of perverts and weirdos, and fulminated over the real or imaginary plots that were afoot in Washington. Lou was flying on a magic carpet of drugs. Pages of manuscripts and other debris piled up in his room, which she felt was a purposeful pigsty. Lou was having an intensely exciting relationship with Lincoln, who was going bonkers, lost in a long hysterical novel mostly dictated by a series of voices giving him conflicting orders in his head. Lou was also displaying that special nerve that is given to only very few men, getting up in front of audiences three or four times a week, blowing off a pretty good set of rock and roll, playing some wild inventive guitar, becoming a lyrical harmonica player, turning his voice into a human jukebox.

Everything was changing. Rock was 'Telstar' by the Tornados, 'Walk Like a Man' by the Four Seasons, 'He's So Fine' by the Chiffons – all great records in Lou's mind – but what was really happening on campuses across the USA was folk music. Dylan was about to make his big entrance, beating Lou to the title of poet laureate of his generation.

At this point, Lou appeared to have several options. He could have gone to Harvard under the wing of Delmore Schwartz, and perhaps been an important poet. He could have married Shelley and become a folk singer. He could have collaborated with any number of musicians at Syracuse to form a rock-and-roll band. Instead, he began to separate himself from each of his allies and collaborators one by one.

The trouble started with Lou's acquisition of a dog, Seymour, a female cross between a German shepherd and a beagle-cum-dachshund, three and a half feet long, standing four inches off the ground. If you believe that dogs always mirror their people, then Seymour was, in Shelley's words, 'a Lou dog'. Lou appeared to be able to open up more easily and communicate more sympathetic-ally with Seymour than with anybody else in the vicinity. As far as Shelley could tell, the only times Lou seemed to really feel at peace with himself was when he was rolling on the floor with Seymour, or sitting with the mutt on the couch staring into space. Soon, however, Lou's love for the dog became obsessive and he started remonstrating with Shelley about treating Seymour better and paying more attention to her.

Meanwhile, Lou's behaviour increasingly hinted at the complex nature Shelley would have to deal with if she stayed with him. 'I mean, he got crazy about being nice to that dog,' she commented later. 'He was a total shit about it, so that was a clue.' But then he couldn't be bothered to take the dog out for a walk in the freezing cold. It soon became evident that it fell to Shelley to feed and walk the dog. Even so, the mercurial Lewis decided to get rid of the dog. Shelley had to persuade him not to. Then he hit on another diabolical plan. He would take the dog home to Freeport and dump it on his family, without warning. And he knew exactly how to do it.

That Thanksgiving, Lou and Shelley returned to Freeport with the surprise gift. Displaying its Lou-like behaviour, the dog rushed out of the cargo area, where it had been forced to travel, and immediately proceeded to piss all over the floor, leading Lou's mother to start screaming, 'A dog! Oh, my God, a dog in my house! We don't need a dog!' Riposting with the artful aplomb that would lead so many of Reed's later collaborators to despair, Lou presented an offer that could not be refused, announcing that the dog was, in fact, a gift for Bunny.

Dismayed at first by this invasion of their domain, the Reeds were, in time – much to Lou's chagrin – unexpectedly delighted by the new arrival. As it turned out, the dog possessed some of Lou's charm without any of his less attractive attributes. Soon Seymour was scurrying around the Reeds' living room or snuggling up to Toby as if she were her long-lost mother. In short, Seymour became the light of Toby's life in a way Lewis never could be. According to Shelley:

> It was the only kid she had that wouldn't talk back. She fell in love with the dog. Seymour was a comfort to her. She said many times, 'This dog kept me together over the years when I became so upset about Lou. That dog would just curl up in my lap, that dog became my other child.' She was maternal and the fact that Lou had brought the dog home touched her very much. So that also reminded her that Lou was who he was. Lou could be sweet, and Lou gave this dog to Bunny, but I think in a way Lou gave the dog to his mother also. He felt she was in there alone.

Sixteen years later he would complain in a song, 'Families', that at first nobody wanted Seymour, but then she became more important than him.

Naturally, as soon as Lou saw how much his family liked the dog, he quickly reversed his decision to bestow her on Bunny and insisted on taking her back to Syracuse, where she would live with him until he graduated, after which Seymour would spend the remainder of her life as the most popular member of the Reed household.

During their visit Lou took Shelley into Harlem on a risky expedition. 'He said, "Come on, we've got to pick something up," ' she recalled.

I remember going up to 125th Street. Really vile, nasty hallways. It was a guy who was a musician, I remember him sitting at this grand piano in his apartment in Harlem. I think there was a connection between the guys in the bar in Syracuse and the guy there. I knew we were going to pick up drugs, my memory was that it was heroin, but I couldn't swear to it. I was more worried about his driving. And I knew I wasn't supposed to be in Harlem. For white kids to do that at the time was stupid. It was dangerous. I could have gotten raped or killed. He loved that.

It was neither the drugs nor the dog that finally caused his relationship with Shelley to break down. Although there was no doubt that Lou was in love with Shelley and their relationship was romantic and enlightening for both of them, Lou engaged in sexual experimentation. Though, as one friend recalled, 'he would do whatever Shelley wanted. He was very much in love with her and she would call the shots,' other friends remembered that Lou seemed obsessed by sex. According to Mishkin, for example, Lou had a thing for big girls, especially 'one big fat ugly bitch who he also really loved to fuck on the side'. He also occasionally had sex with one of the black female singers who sang with the Eldorados. 'I never observed him being particularly nice to Shelley,' Hyman commented, 'but then I never observed him being particularly nice to anyone.'

When Lou wasn't nice to women, he could, it turned out, be particularly cruel, constantly pushing them to an edge, thereby testing the strength of their love. His idea, Shelley said, was:

I'm going to remake you and then I'm not going to like you, and I'm going to push you around and see when you're going to leave me. The worse I treat you the more it proves to me that you love me and you'll stay with me for ever. He clearly got very obnoxious. He had to have somebody to kick around so he felt big, and at that point I was the kickee.

She was not the sort of girl to take this kind of treatment lying down, and retaliated with several thrusts of her own. On one occasion the Eldorados were booked to play a fraternity at Cornell. Shelley had been dating one of the fraternity brothers sporadically on the side and decided to go along for the ride. When Lou walked in with the slightly effeminate walk he had mastered, the brothers were enraged to see Shelley on his arm. She had spent several weekends at the fraternity house and now this little Jewish fag . . . Shelley had not told Lou about the predicament and even he was impressed by the hostility that greeted him. 'Jesus, they're so nasty, they're a bunch of animals,' he told Shelley. Somewhere during the evening she casually explained, 'They're so hostile because I've been here on various weekends with this guy Peter. I'm his girlfriend.' They barely got out of there alive.

Back at Syracuse the relationship between Lou and Shelley came to a climax one night at another fraternity job, when Lou came up to her between sets and said, 'I'm going to go into the back room with that girl. Do you want to watch?' Seeing Ritchie Mishkin smirk at her, Shelley finally snapped, decided that she had taken enough abuse from Lou, and left the fraternity. It was February 1963 and bitterly cold. Lincoln accompanied her on the long walk back to her dorm telling her not to worry, that he was still there and that she was right to leave. That she shouldn't have let Lou treat her so badly for so long.

'Lou and I had had such dire things going on between us for the previous few months,' Shelley explained.

> The groupie thing just finally put me over the edge. I never had any doubt that Lou was going to be a rock star and that if I was going to stay with Lou I was going to be a rock star's wife. I made the decision to leave him and to stay away from him based on the next ten years of my life.

The next day he said, 'I was so stoned I don't remember doing that. Why are you mad at me? Did I do that?'

But Shelley had finally come to understand what made Lou tick, and she didn't like what she discovered. The struggle to conquer and control was much more important to him than the possession, just as being a voyeur was becoming more important to him than natural sex. Basically, Lou was incapable of maintaining any kind of normal, nurturing relationship. Like a shark, he had an urge to poke at bodies until he found a live one and then devour it as ferociously and completely as he could, letting the blood run down his chin.

By the middle of his junior year, Lou had turned himself into a monster with eight different faces. It was in these various guises that he would slither through his life, building up great bands only to tear them down, devouring and destroying everybody he could seduce, because he resented the whole situation of life and didn't want anybody else to have any fun if he wasn't able to.

Ever since Lou had moved into his own apartment, the relationship with Lincoln Swados had been less close. As the junior year ground on, Lincoln showed alarming signs of having a real nervous breakdown. 'I don't think either of us knew that Lincoln was truly schizophrenic,' Shelley remembered. 'Lou was so busy pulling so much of his drama from Lincoln that I don't know how much he realized Lincoln was truly ill, or whether he just thought Lincoln just had a better scam going. He was trying to pick up on Lincoln's traits and abilities. Much of Lou is Lincoln.' Shelley claimed that for both men, the trajectory of a love relationship went something like this: 'I'm going to stroke you and treat you kindly and bless you with my knowledge and presence, and then kill you.' Allen Hyman agreed that Lou had picked up many of his twisted ideas about life from Lincoln. 'You couldn't get much weirder than Lincoln,' he said, 'without being Lou.'

Shortly after Shelley left Lou, Lincoln was carted off to the bug house by his parents who found him in a state of agitation far beyond their wildest fears. According to Swados's sister,

Elizabeth, he had got into 'a helplessly disoriented state. He was unable to go to classes, unable to leave his room. The voices in his head were directing him to do too many different things.'

In short order, Lou had lost his best friends, his two mirrors. Delmore was still there, but he was going in and out of hospital himself and was hardly in a position to give Lou a shoulder to cry on.

However, despite her determination to avoid her former lover, the break-up threw Shelley into a black depression, and she went out and did the one thing that was bound to draw Lou's attention back to her: she dyed her hair orange. 'I remember Lou seeing it and saying, "Wow! Now you're appealing, now you really look like Miss Trash."' Typically, Lou had to race back to Freeport to show his parents what he had done to the nice Jewish girl they had so doted on.

> They saw this nice, wholesome girl turned into trash and they said, 'Oh, my God, Lou has done it again. He has ruined somebody, he has won, he has turned her into trash' [Shelley recalled]. At that point, his mother even said to me, 'I hope he doesn't treat you like he treats us.' We did horrify his mother. We were in the same room and she knocked and we were half undressed – you didn't do this then, and the last time we hadn't been so brazen. She just looked at me like *trash*! He loved it. It was hysterical, his mother just about died. And of course Aunt So-and-so came over to meet me. It was horrible!

As soon as they got back to school, they broke up again. By then she was determined not to go back to him, 'not because I'm stubborn,' she explained, 'but because he'd pushed me so far and I was so tolerant of things that other people weren't. I remember writing a letter to his parents telling them I was sorry I was cutting out. I said I was depressed that I was going to be gone, but I couldn't stand Lou any more because he was such a shit.'

In Lou's senior year, Shelley took up with a boyfriend who 'would keep Lou from me, he was my protection. We were still tied to each other,' she said, 'but studiously avoided each other. If I saw him at two in the morning, my new boyfriend would kick someone else's head in the next day. So Lou and I couldn't even have a conversation.'

November 1963 was a cathartic month for Lou. It started with a Syracuse concert by Bob Dylan. 'Lou idolized Dylan when Dylan came on the scene with his first album,' Mishkin explained.

> We knew every inch of his music inside and out. All of a sudden there was this music and poetry together and it wasn't folk music. Lou was blown away by it. It was an exciting thing. And Lewis immediately got a harmonica and was playing that. I remember sitting in the apartment with [Eldorado] Stevie Windheim and Lewis figuring out the chords to 'Baby, Let Me Follow You Down', and we got them and we were playing it and it wasn't the kind of thing we were going to do for a gig, but we had a good time with it.

According to Shelley, however, Lou had been playing harmonica since the beginning of his junior year. He played the harmonica with an intense, mournful air that perfectly complemented his songs, but after Dylan's performance, he put it away for good – he couldn't stand having people think that he was copying somebody else. It was a pity because Lou was a great, expressive harmonica player.

The assassination of President Kennedy on 23 November 1963 struck a blow to Delmore Schwartz from which he would never recover. Lou watched helplessly as his mentor and drinking buddy fell into a paranoid depression. He gave up any pretence of continuing to teach, and retreated permanently to the Orange Bar. Soon Lou was looking after Delmore, walking him home at night after long sessions at the bar, making sure he had his key, his cigarettes, sometimes picking up groceries or other sundries for him. When Schwartz left the Orange, he was often so transported to other realms he might head off in any direction like some human dowsing wand in search of companionship or, as often as not, trouble. Lou always made sure he got home, got himself to bed, and was not in too much danger of burning down the premises with a carelessly dropped cigarette. After a while, however, this kind of care takes on a spooky quality as the young man begins to recognize his own fate in that of the older man. Suddenly Lou, who had been benefiting from Delmore's enlightened encouragement of his favourite student, and seriously considering his recommendation to go to Harvard, found himself taking care of a man who was increasingly incapable of getting from A to B without assistance. 'Lou always felt that he had to stay around and watch Delmore and take care of him,' said Shelley. 'I think Lou began to find that a little tedious. Lou had to help Delmore, not the other way around. And I don't think Lou was getting all he needed from Delmore.'

Ever since he had been put on medication following the electroshock treatments of 1959, Lou had been an inveterate drug user. If he wasn't popping pills, he was inhaling pot, dropping acid, eating mushrooms, horning coke or dropping placidyls – not to mention bolting down enough booze to keep the Orange Bar in business around the clock. Now, for the first time, he added heroin to his drug menu, whereas previously he had only sold it.

Shelley marked Lou's downslide from the time he started to inject heroin. He had always been petrified by needles and said that he would never shoot any drugs into his veins. Once he began taking heroin he insisted he could control it all the time, and stop whenever he wanted to simply because he had elected to do so (revealing a total lack of understanding of the drug). The experience of getting into heroin on and off was pretty horrifying to him, Shelley thought, 'and he was having some bad LSD trips too.'

Shelley had, however, no sympathy for Lou's cries for help. 'If he was having a very bad trip, he'd send somebody to come over and tell me, "God, Lou is really having a bad trip and would like to see you . . ." And I would tell them to buzz off, he gave me a bad trip. I don't care if he dies. To Lou, that's a betrayal.'

Lou had gone into a decline when he realized that not only was Shelley not coming back to him, she was in fact living with two adult men just three doors down from his apartment. On one occasion, when she was sitting in the Orange Bar with her new lover and his Korean vet friends, an acolyte of Lou's came racing in frantically telling her that Lou was having another really bad time. Although she fully expected that he might not make it through the night, Shelley sent back the reply, 'If you send somebody over here to tell me that you're dying, die!' She knew what a difficult time Lou was having, but she had to save herself from him, and she took the attitude that Lou had axed himself. Now he had nobody to talk to. Now he was confused and alone. And it was all his own fault.

Still, Shelley felt sorry for him. 'Lou can't have a good time, it's not in his genes,' she stated later. 'He feels that he doesn't deserve it. The moment you say Lou's OK, he thinks there's something wrong with you. Because if you say he's OK, then you don't see how evil he is, you don't see all the bad things. He can't have a wonderful time any more than he can accept that people like him. That's what's so sad about Lou.'

Swados, after Schwartz the most perceptive man Reed knew at university, was the first to note (in a conversation with a girlfriend a year later) that beneath Lou's often waiflike desperation, his need to be mothered, existed a much tougher, harder, more realistic man. He possessed an ambition and drive of which very few people who knew him at Syracuse had any idea. The fact, for example, that he would continue to experiment with drugs for the next fifteen years and survive alone, suggests that he was at heart not only a survivor, but a student of narcotics who took care to know what it was he was ingesting. Despite the bad trips he may have had (they may, of course, have been faked to win sympathy – heroin doesn't give you any kind of bad trip like a hallucinogenic. Taken in too strong a dose, it simply makes you feel extremely sick), he appeared for the most part to have put the hard time of his senior year – the isolation, the introduction to heroin – to good use.

The most important development in his senior year was literary. Lou leaped across a great gap when he switched from making the short story his primary form to song lyrics, taking his knowledge of the short-story structure with him. In many ways Bob Dylan was a major influence on Lou in this decision as well as his subsequent decision not to apply to the graduate writing programme at Harvard, but to pursue his love of rock and roll as a career. Dylan not only showed him a way to write lyrics, he legitimized being a singer-songwriter with intellectual credentials. That was the vital point. Lou needed to be recognized intellectually. He was concerned about Delmore's response to his decision because he didn't want to disappoint Delmore, he didn't want to hurt his feelings, he didn't want him to think that he didn't consider his words, his opinion, very valuable. Delmore's collapse may have freed Lou, or forced him, to journey into that region he had always aspired to – the combination of serious writing and rock-and-roll lyrics.

'I thought, Look, all these writers are writing about only a very small part of the human experience,' Reed pointed out.

> Whereas a record could be like a novel, you could write about this. It was so obvious, it's amazing everybody wasn't doing it. Let's take *Crime and Punishment* and turn it into a rock and roll song!
>
> But if you're going to talk about the greats, there is no one greater than Raymond Chandler. I mean, after reading Raymond Chandler and going on to someone else, it's like eating caviar and then turning to some real inferior dish. Take the sensibility of Raymond Chandler or Hubert Selby or Delmore Schwartz or Poe and put it to rock music.

Like any foray into oneself, writing proved to be more than exhilarating. It was, for Lou, a long and painful process. 'I love writing,' Lou would tell an interviewer.

> Raymond Chandler, 'That blonde was as pleasant as a split lip.' Hard to beat that. He's talking about a guy's thumbnail, he thought his thumbnail looked like the edge of an ice cube. Boom, you can see it. And that's what I try to do. I try to give you a very visual image in very few words, so that you can picture it in your mind really quick.

During this time, Lou continued to mine his everyday experiences for song material. He spent a lot of time going into New York, scoring drugs and checking out bands. He was fixated on Ornette Coleman, and used to try to see him whenever he performed in New York City. In his last semester, his writing, taking drugs, loneliness and fascination with underground jazz set off a creative explosion. He wrote at least two songs, 'I'm waiting for the Man' and 'Heroin'. The precision and scope of these songs heralded the Lou Reed who would become known as the Baudelaire of New York.

> At the time I wrote 'Heroin', I felt like a very rather negative, strung-out, violent, aggressive person. I meant those songs to sort of exorcise the darkness, or the self-destructive element in me.

It would take Lou a year to work up 'Heroin' from rough lyrics and bare-bone chords into one of the greatest rock-and-roll songs of all time. Mishkin helped Lou by hammering out its unforgettable bass line. Not until Lou met John Cale the following autumn did he develop the two Syracuse songs into the form in which they were recorded.

Reed's senior year was pitted with conflicts and frustrations that emerged in several dramatic incidents. In October the Eldorados had gone down to Sarah Lawrence College to play a series of weekend dates. Now that Hyman had graduated and had been replaced by another drummer, Lou was ever more impatient with his plodding bandmates. One night when they got to the venue, Lou didn't want to play. 'So he said, "Fuck you, I'm not going to play for these assholes,"' remembered Mishkin. 'And suddenly, right in front of everybody, he smashed his hand through a plate-glass window' (in emulation of Lincoln, who had done the same thing years earlier). 'Of course he couldn't play. We took him to the hospital and there were lots of stitches.'

Lou continued to flaunt his bad attitude. Rather than masking his increasing drug consumption, he became its walking advertisement. At 8 a.m., while other students trotted off to class, he would stand outside the Orange Bar to wait for Delmore, on the unmistakable heroin nod. 'I was sitting in the Orange one early spring day,' Sterling Morrison later remembered. 'Lou and this guy were sitting in the guy's red convertible with the radio on full blast, the top down, and they were both nodding out in the front seat so I went out and put the top up and turned the radio off. I remember another time sitting in the Orange and Lou came in and thought he was leaning on his elbow except that his elbow was about a foot above the table.'

The local campus police, who were determined to crack down on drugs, took note of his behaviour and put Reed under surveillance. In 1963, as drugs spread rapidly through college campuses across the country, the Syracuse Police Department had taken a small group of officers, led by Sergeant Robert Longo from the vice squad, and created a brand-new narcotics squad. The heat was closing in, to employ the opening sentence of Lou's favourite book, William Burroughs's recently published *Naked Lunch*. To counterbalance the police pressure, Shelley and a friend of hers had developed a friendship with two of the members of this new Syracuse narcotics squad. 'The police squad car would pull up outside my apartment and they'd supposedly be working, but they'd be having a beer and hanging out,' she recalled.

> And getting a little bit of nookie without my having to commit myself in any way. They came up and got a few hugs and kisses and thought they were making real progress with the lewd, evil girls of the campus. Lou met the cops and knew them through his senior year. We used to see them in the Varsity a lot. Lou was harassed by the same police. They didn't like Lou because the guy on the force liked me a lot so they wanted to get Lou.

Shelley was more aware of how much the cops really wanted to get Lou ('They thought he was a gay faggot evil shit'), and knew that if they got their hands on him they would beat him up badly. She repeatedly made it a condition of seeing the cop that he promised they would not touch Lou. 'Touch Lou,' she told him, 'and you don't touch me.'

At first, the fact that the heavies from the narcotics squad were on Lou's tail was more of an amusement than a hassle for him. He enjoyed entertaining friends with stories about how, after being tipped off about an impending bust, he had buried his stash at a nearby Boy Scout camp. Lou felt confident that he could outsmart the police just as he had outwitted authorities throughout his life.

There were also signs that a calmer, more confident Lou was emerging, a Lou who had passed through the very centre of some internal tornado and survived stronger, surer and more his own man. Larry Goldstein, a freshman whose band the Downbeats won the battle of the bands at Syracuse in 1963, and who had briefly joined LA and the Eldorados, got a chance to hang out with Lou one night.

'We started playing together, doing mostly college gigs,' Goldstein recounted.

> We played Cornell for one, and we used to play the FI – the Fayetville Inn, which was about 20 miles from Syracuse. Lou was really nothing but very nice to us. We were just kids in comparison, but he wasn't a prima donna or a rock-star type, he was very supportive. There was a restaurant called Ben's in the fifteenth ward near Lou's apartment that served really greasy soul food and Lou used to go there a lot. One night after we played a gig we were sitting around Lou's apartment and I remember him as being very gentle and very nice, like a kind of father figure. And he suggested that we go to Ben's to get something to eat. Lou seemed a lot older than us. And he was much more mature in many ways. He had an alternative type of personality that was unlike anyone else. I never remembered him being arrogant about it. He was just advanced.

In June 1964, Lou Reed graduated with a Bachelor of Arts degree from the Syracuse College of Arts and Sciences. The richness of his character, and yet at the same time its awful limitation, was revealed in his last act of human kindness at Syracuse. According to Lou, 'As soon as exams were over, at the graduation ceremony, I was told by the Tactical Police Squad that if I wasn't gone within the hour they'd beat me up. They couldn't get me, but they'd break every bone, every moveable part of my body. So I split, but I still graduated with honours.'

However, according to Shelley, Lou in fact stayed after graduation strictly to take care of her through a particularly bad illness. The two of them had been living half a block apart. Shelley was installed on McDonald Street with her boyfriend; Lou was living alone on the corner of Adams. Near the end of the semester, Shelley's boyfriend had gone on a trip. Lou visited, and found her unable to attend classes. He scooped her up and moved her into his apartment. Knowing she'd fail her course with Phillip Booth if he didn't do something drastic, Lou took her over to Booth's house. 'I remember being bundled over there and being plunked down on the couch and being told, "Just sit there and look hopeless,"' she recalled. 'Which was no effort. My eyes must have been rolling in my head. He just told Booth, "Pass this person" and he did.' As the other students left campus, Shelley was still too ill to travel, so Lou stayed with her and, she said, 'really put me back together'.

Shelley remembered thinking, 'I really love him, he's really fantastic', but also being exhausted and foggy. 'You know how it is when you get back together with someone. He was just terrific. We were really pigs in shit, like two kids let out of jail. He was adorable. It was a perfect time. We were really amazed at having such a good time.'

She stayed with him for one to two weeks. Unfortunately, it was too long, and Shelley found herself being unpleasantly reminded of Lou's need to be in control and had an intuitive feeling that things would never work out between them. And so, when he put her onto the plane to Chicago, she waved goodbye to Lou without wondering when she would see him again.

Two years after Reed graduated from Syracuse he wrote an essay for an avant-garde magazine stating, 'The colleges should be destroyed, they're dangerous.' Lou blamed the faculty of Syracuse for, among other things, the pressures that led to Lincoln's disoriented state of mind, listing 'metaphysical poetry, theology, *Playboy* jazz polls, tests, papers, psychological tests, doctors trying to cure the freaks while they gulp pills,' among the culprits. 'But meanwhile everything was dead,' Lou concluded.

'Writing was dead, movies were dead. Everyone sat like an unpeeled orange. But the music was so beautiful. It was the music that kept us all intact, that kept us from going crazy.'

chapter four

The Pickwick Period

1964–1965

[In which Lou beats the draft
and gets a job as a songwriter
with Pickwick International.]

*The Pickwick experience was the first plateau of Lou's
maturation as a musician. It gave him a point of departure
that I think was critical to his becoming what he became.*

DONALD SCHUPAK

Instead of going into New York like the majority of the other
bright English Lit graduates coming down from Syracuse University, Lou retreated to the comfort and safety of his parents'
home. In the summer of 1964, he turned his full attention towards
evading the draft. He knew he'd have to put on a good show at the
draft hearing to convince the army officials he was sick, crazy, or
both. He chose both.

Providentially, he was aided in his cause by a real illness that
struck a few days after he got home to Freeport. Feeling feverish
and exhausted, he was diagnosed as having a bad case of hepatitis,
which he later claimed to have acquired in a shooting gallery by
sharing a needle with a mashed-faced negro named Jaw. Upon
receiving this news, Lou immediately placed an expensive long-
distance phone call to Shelley, warning her that she too might have
acquired the disease during their recent rapprochement. Then he
set about lining up medical evidence sufficient to stave off his
recruitment into the army.

According to Lou, he managed to pull off this feat in a record ten minutes by walking into his local draft board chewing on his favourite downer, a 750-milligram Placidyl, a large green pill prescribed for its hypnotic, calming effects and to induce sleep. The effects of the pill come on within fifteen minutes to an hour and may be greatly enhanced when combined with alcohol, barbiturates or other central-nervous-system depressants. Although Placidyl was available over the counter during the 1960s, owing to its potential to cause severe, often suicidal depression, as well as drug dependence, it is now available in the USA by prescription only. The 750-mg variety is the highest dose available in pill form, and its effect on Lou would certainly have shocked his recruiter. 'I said I wanted a gun and would shoot anyone or anything in front of me,' Reed recalled. If this smart-aleck claim didn't do the trick, his desiccated liver and the yellow pall cast over his visage by the incipient hepatitis did. 'I was pronounced mentally unfit and given a classification that meant I'd only be called up if we went to war with China. It was the one thing my shock treatments were good for.'

It was the summer of 1964. His father offered him a job in his tax-accountancy business, which he insisted Lou should take over and inherit upon his retirement. Lou did not fancy sitting behind a desk peering at a calculator. He told Sidney that he should give his business to Elizabeth (aged fifteen) because she had a better head for such things. Instead, Lou put together a band and hacked his way through the summer playing local shows, which included, as often as possible, gay bars. Resenting his family's disapproval of his lifestyle, Lou set about stinging them with rejection. As he would sing in one of his catalogues of contempt, 'Families', people in the suburbs moved each other to tears.

However, the battle was not over. Summer fun was one thing allowed the indolent rich graduates on the island, but come autumn, every one of them was expected to take up a calling. Hyman was already in law school. Lou's parents presumed their son would also buckle down to some kind of acceptable career.

How wrong they were! In a move calculated to upset both his parents and Delmore Schwartz, Lou, as they saw it, threw away his expensive education and his finely tuned brain to take a job as a made-to-order pop songwriter for a cheap recording company called Pickwick International. Pickwick specialized in producing bargain-basement rip-off albums for a naive mass audience. For example, something like *Bobby Darin Sings the Blues* featured Darin crooning on exactly one song, squeezed in amid ten songs by Jack Borgheimer; the album of ten hot- rod songs by the Roughnecks sported a cover of four gallivanting lads who looked, at a distance, suspiciously like the Beatles, but were in fact a bunch of dorky session musicians wearing wigs. (Lou was not on the cover.) In retrospect, observed Phil Milstein, one of Lou's most informed and appreciative critics and the founder in 1978 of the Velvet Underground Appreciation Society, 'in many ways this is the craziest part of the entire crazy story. No work Lou has done is so trivial, so prefabricated, so tossed off as what he did at Pickwick.'

The agent of this first step on Lou's path to becoming a songwriter was none other than Lou's old friend from Syracuse, the manager of LA and the Eldorados, Don Schupak. 'I introduced Lou to a guy who I had developed a partnership with back here in the city, Terry Phillips, who had convinced Pickwick to try to go into the rock business,' Schupak recalled. 'They were taught the notion of rock and roll by Terry Phillips and me. They eventually became Musicland, and the people we had to convince to start this studio at the cost of a few hundred dollars have made millions in the rock-and-roll business since then.'

Phillips, who had worked with Phil Spector, hired Reed on Schupak's recommendation. 'Pickwick started Lou's career,' Donald recalled. 'It taught him the discipline of showing up. It put him into the industry.'

The grand, British-sounding Pickwick International consisted, in fact, of a squat cinderblock warehouse in Long Island City across the river from Manhattan. The whole operation was run out of this warehouse full of cheap, slapdash records, with a small basement recording studio in a converted storeroom containing, as Schupak, who worked there as 'record executive', recalled, 'a shitty old Spinnett piano and a Roberts tape recorder'. Lou, who received $25 a week for his endeavours – and no rights to any of his material – made the twenty-five-minute commute from Freeport to Long Island City every day. Once there, he would find himself locked into the tiny studio with three collaborators: the pasty-faced Phillips, whose pencil moustache, slicked-back hair and polyester suits evinced his weird distance from life, and two other songwriters, Jerry Vance (alias Jerry Pellegrino) and Jimmie Sims (Jim Smith). While Schupak tried to figure out what he was supposed to be doing, Phillips took it upon himself to direct the fledgling rock arm of the Pickwick label.

Lou and his fellow songwriters wrote tunes to order as fast as they could. Although the set-up lacked the glamour of the rock-and-roll lifestyle, it did have redeeming educational value. 'There were four of us literally locked in a room writing songs,' Reed recounted.

We just churned out songs, that's all. They would say, 'Write ten California songs, ten Detroit songs,' then we'd go down into the studio for an hour or two and cut three or four albums really quickly, which came in handy later because I knew my way around a studio, not well enough but I could work really fast.

I really liked doing it, it was really fun but I wasn't doing the stuff I wanted to do. I was just hoping I could somehow get an in.

'Lou was trying to develop an identity,' said Schupak.

He had already developed this poet sing-speak style. Lou never could sing, although he has a very nice voice. It's a beautiful resonant voice and it's gotten better since he's gotten older. Lou's sense of music was always to tell a story. His brain never said, 'I have a broad melodic range.' I actually think his voice has more range than his sense of melody. He always wanted to speak his stories and play his guitar.

And then Terry, all he wanted to do was make things sound commercial. What I tried to do was figure out what a guy's talent was and then make the people love it, whereas Terry wanted the artist to do what he thought people loved. Lou thought Terry was a bit of a jerk musically, because he was pushing Lou into areas that Lou was already past. Lou didn't know what Lou was yet, Lou was willing to do what Terry said because it was a gig and a job and a place to go, and

Lou didn't know what it was like to be a star yet. And everyone as they mature has to do some stuff they don't like or don't understand why they're doing it.

Naturally Lou told friends that he hated working at Pickwick, and expressed endless bitterness over the fact that Phillips failed to see any merit in his own compositions. 'I'd say, "Why don't we record these?"' Reed remembered. 'And they'd say, "No, we can't record stuff like that."' (One can only wonder how *Johnny Don't Shoot No More, Ten Drug Songs* would have gone over in that halcyon era.) But the truth is that the detached observer in Lou was making out like a bandit in this situation. In fact, he should have been paying them for the practical education in how to use a recording studio and work with helpful collaborators – for whom he would in time come to realize a strong need. Never was he more prolific than during his Pickwick days. Over the course of a few months Reed and his three collaborators published at least fifteen songs. The five months he spent at Pickwick from September 1964 to February 1965 provided the best on-the-job training he could possibly have had for a career in rock and roll.

chapter five

The Formation of the Velvet Underground

1965

[In which Lou meets John
Cale and the two of them
form the Velvet Underground
with Sterling Morrison and
Maureen Tucker.]

*The best things come, as a general thing, from the talents that
are members of a group; every man works better when he has
companions working in the same line, and yielding to stimulus
and suggestion, comparison, emulation.*

HENRY JAMES

It was through Pickwick that Lou met the man who would be the
single most important long-lasting collaborator in his life, John
Cale.

One day in January 1965, Lou, who had not let a thing like
hepatitis slow him down, had ingested a copious quantity of
drugs. As he felt the rush of creativity coming on, he leafed
through a local tabloid and came across an item about ostrich
feathers being the latest fashion. Flinging the paper down and
grabbing his guitar with the manic pent-up humour that fuelled so
much of his work, Lou spontaneously created a new would-be
dance craze in a song called 'The Ostrich'. It told the dancer to put
his head on the floor and let his partner step on it. What better

self-image could Lou possibly have come up with than this nutty notion, except that the dancers give each other electroshocks?

Although it appeared unlikely that even rock-mad teenagers, currently disporting themselves in nothing more severe than the twist and the frug, would go for this masochistic idea, Terry Phillips, desperate for a hit to back up his claim that the wave of the future was in rock, insisted that this could be the hit single they had been looking for. With his spacy head full of images of millions of kids across America stomping on each other's heads (he was ten years ahead of his time), he got the executives out in the warehouse to agree to his proposal that they should release 'The Ostrich' as a single by a make-believe band called the Primitives. When the record came out, they received a call from a TV dance show, much to their surprise, requesting a performance of 'The Ostrich' by 'the band'. Eager to promote his project, Phillips persuaded the Pickwick people to let him put together a real band to fill the bill. He saw the pleasingly pubescent-looking Lewis as a natural for lead singer. But he was less than enthusiastic about Terry, Jerry and Jimmy, who did not have the requisite look to con the teen market into spending their spare dollars on 'The Ostrich'. Frantic to get the show on the road, Phillips began to search for a back-up band for Lou Reed.

From the Pickwick studio the story cuts to Terry Phillips at an Upper East Side Manhattan apartment jammed with a bunch of party people all yukking it up and trying to be cool despite having no idea at all about anything. Among them, highly amused but feeling themselves to be above it all, were a big-boned, dark-haired Welshman with a sonorous voice by the name of John Cale and his partner and flatmate, Tony Conrad. Cale was a classical-music scholar, Conrad an underground filmmaker, and they were both members of perhaps the mid-sixties' most avant-garde music group in the world, LaMonte Young's Theater of Eternal Music. On the trail of female companions and good times, they had been brought to the party by the brother of the playwright Jack Gelber, who had recently written a famous play about herion called *The Connection*. Spotting these reasonably attractive and slightly eccentric-looking guys with – for those days – long hair, Terry Phillips asked them if they were musicians. Receiving an affirmative response, he took it for granted that they played guitars (in fact Cale played an electrically amplified viola as well as several Indian instruments) and enquired, 'Where's the drummer?'

The two underground artists, who took their work highly seriously, went along with Phillips as a kind of joke, claiming they did have a drummer so as not to jeopardize the opportunity to make some pocket money. The next day, along with their good friend Walter DeMaria, who would soon emerge as one of the leading avant-garde sculptors and was doing a little drumming on the side, they showed up at Pickwick Studios as instructed.

Cale, Conrad and DeMaria were highly amused by the bogus set-up at Pickwick. To them, the Pickwick executives in cheap suits, who shiftily pressed contracts into their hands, were hilarious caricatures of rock moguls. On close inspection, as Conrad recalled it, the contract stipulated that they would sign away the rights to everything they did for the rest of their lives in exchange for nothing. After brushing aside this attempt to extract some kind of feudal allegiance more closely resembling indentured servitude than business management, Conrad, Cale and DeMaria were introduced to Lou Reed. He assured them that it would take no time at all to learn their parts to 'The Ostrich' since all the guitar strings were tuned to a single note. This information left John Cale and Tony Conrad open-mouthed in astonishment since that was exactly what they had been doing at LaMonte Young's rigorous eight-hours-a-day rehearsals. They realized Lou had some kind of innate musical genius that even the salesmen at the studio had picked up on. Tony got the impression that 'Lou had a close relationship with these people at Pickwick because they recognized that he was a very gifted person. He impressed everybody as having some particularly assertive personal quality.' Reed, it seemed, had something in common with the company men: 'Lou was power-oriented in the same way that any executive is,' one college friend commented. 'He's an executive of rock and roll.'

Cale, Conrad and DeMaria agreed to join 'the Primitives' and play shows to promote the record on the East Coast. It was primarily a camp lark, but it would also give them a glimpse into the world of commercial rock and roll, in which they were not entirely uninterested.

And so it came about that in their first appearance together, Lou Reed and John Cale found themselves, without prior rehearsal, running onto the stage of some high school in Pennsylvania's Lehigh Valley following a bellowed introduction: 'And here they are from New York – the Primitives!' Encouraged by the screaming kids, the band launched into 'The Ostrich'. At the end of the song the MC remarked, rather portentously, 'These guys have really got something. I hope it's not catching!'

Far from catching on, 'The Ostrich' died a quick death. After racing around the countryside in a station wagon for several weekends getting a taste of the reality of the rock life without roadies, the band packed it in. Terry Phillips and the Pickwick executives ruefully left off their dream of seeing 'The Ostrich' sail into the charts and returned to the dependable world of Jack Borgheimer.

The attempted break-out had its repercussions, though, primarily in introducing Lou to John, who held the keys to a whole other musical universe. The fact was that Lou, like many creative people, had a low threshold for boredom and realized that Terry Phillips's vision was too narrow to allow him to grow. Donald Schupak thought:

The issue was say the words that you feel, not the words you think the public necessarily wants to hear. If you say them well enough and the music is relevant, people will pick up on it because you are a musician and a smart guy. If it's irrelevant, you'll learn that. Lou has always been outraged at the social order. That's what drives his music. He said, 'I don't want to do this shit and I do want to pursue this.' It gave him some experience to get some sense of what he didn't want to do. Then he was able to pursue other things – some of which he decided ultimately he didn't want to do and other things he decided he wanted to do. It also gave him the juxtaposition of doing what he wanted to do and finding a way of making it successful.

*

When Lou started to visit John Cale in his bohemian slum dwelling at 56 Ludlow Street in the deepest bowels of Manhattan's Lower East Side, Reed knew nothing of LaMonte Young or his Theater of Eternal Music, and had little sense of the world he was entering. In keeping with the egocentric personalities he had been cultivating since his successes on the Syracuse University poetry, music and bohemian scenes, Lou was out for his own ends and at first showed little interest in whatever it was that John was into. Instead, the rock-and-roller set about seducing the classicist.

Cale, for his part, was taken by Reed's rock-and-roll persona and what little he had witnessed of his spontaneous composition of lyrics, but took a somewhat snooty view of Reed's initial attempts to strike up a collaborative friendship.

> He was trying to get a band together. I didn't want to hear his songs. They seemed sorry for themselves. He'd written 'Heroin' already, and 'I'm Waiting for My Man', but they wouldn't let him record it, they didn't want to do anything with it. I wasn't really interested – most of the music being written then was folk, and he played his songs with an acoustic guitar – so I didn't really pay attention because I couldn't give a shit about folk music. I hated Joan Baez and Dylan. Every song was a fucking question!

Despite having been a musical prodigy and, before the age of twenty-five, having studied with some of the greatest avant-garde composers of the century, by 1965 Cale felt his career was going nowhere. 'I was going off into Never-Never Land with classical notions of music,' he said, desperate for a new angle from which to approach music. The sentiment was shared by his family, putting additional pressure on him to 'get a job'. Just like Lou's mother, Mrs Cale, a schoolteacher in a small Welsh mining village married to a miner, complained that John would never make a living as a musician and should become a doctor or a lawyer. The whole thing had been grinding on his nerves.

Like a bull terrier, Lou kept after John, feeling intuitively that the Welshman might provide a necessary catalyst for his music. Eventually, as with most things he pursued, Lou got his way and

Cale began to take Lou's lyrics seriously. 'He kept pushing them on me,' Cale recalled, 'and finally I saw they weren't the kind of words you'd get Joan Baez singing. They were very different, he was writing about things other people weren't. These lyrics were very literate, very well expressed, they were tough.'

Once John grasped what Lou was doing – method acting in song, as he saw it – he glimpsed the possibility of collaborating to create something vibrant and new. He figured that by combining Young's theories and techniques with Lou's lyrical abilities he could blow himself out of the hole his rigid studies had dug him into. Lou also introduced John to a hallmark of rock-and-roll music – fun – and his youthful enthusiasm was infectious. 'We got together and started playing my songs for fun,' Reed recalled. 'It was like we were made for each other. He was from the other world of music and he fitted me perfectly. He would fit things he played right into my world, it was so natural.'

'What I saw in Lou's musical concept was something akin to my own,' Cale agreed. 'There was something more than just a rock side to him, too. I recognized a tremendous literary quality about his songs which fascinated me – he had a very careful ear, he was very cautious with his words. I had no real knowledge of rock music at that time, so I focused on the literary aspect more.' Cale was so turned on by the connection that he started weaning Reed away from Pickwick.

Cale immediately got to work with Reed on orchestrations for the songs. The two men laboured over the pieces, each feeding off the fresh ideas of his counterpart. 'Lou's an excellent guitar player,' Cale said. 'He's nuts. It has more to do with the spirit of what he's doing than playing. And he had this great facility with words, he could improvise songs, which was great. Lyrics and melodies. Take a chord change and just do it.' Cale was an equally exciting player. Unaware of any rock-and-roll models to emulate, he answered Reed's sonic attacks with illogical, inverted bass lines or his own searing electric viola, which sounded, he said, 'like a jet engine!'

Meanwhile, as he got to know Lou, and Reed began to unwrap

the elements of his legend, John discovered that they had something else in common, 'namely,' Lou would deadpan, 'dope'. Reed joked dismissively about their heroin use, commenting that when he and Cale first met, they started playing together 'because it was safer than dealing dope', which Reed was apparently still dabbling in. While fully admitting his involvement with heroin, Lou always insisted, and friends tended to concur, that he was never an addict. 'I had a toe in that situation. Enough to see the tunnel, the vortex. That's how I handled my problems. That's how I grew up, how I did it, like a couple hundred thousand others. You had to be a gutter rat, seeking it out.'

While rationalizing his drug use, Reed also made it clear that it provided him with a shield necessary for both his life and work. 'I take drugs just because in the twentieth century in a technological age, living in the city, there are certain drugs you can take just to keep yourself normal like a caveman,' he said. 'Not just to bring yourself up and down, but to attain equilibrium you need to take certain drugs. They don't get you high, even, they just get you normal.'

Despite the fact that drug taking was widely accepted, practised, and even celebrated among the artistic residents of Cale's Lower East Side community, heroin, because it was addictive, dangerous and could be extremely destructive, had a stigma attached to it that would lead users to keep it private. Thus Cale and Reed found themselves bonded not only by a musical vision and youthful anarchy, but also by the secret society heroin users tend to form. The cozy, intimate feelings the drug can bring on magnified their friendship.

Besides their excited musical collaboration and shared tastes, Lou and John quickly formed a strong, deep friendship. Lou started spending a lot of his spare time at John's, and before long he was staying there for weeks at a time. He would return to his parents' house in Freeport only when in need of money, food or clean laundry, or to check up on the wellbeing of his dog.

Even his involvement with Pickwick was fading under the spell of the Lower East Side lifestyle. 'Lou was like a rock-and-roll animal and authentically turned everybody on,' Tony Conrad recalled. 'He really had a deep fixation on that and his lifestyle was completely compatible and acclimatized to it.'

Cale's was a match for Reed's mercurial personality. Moody and paranoid, he too was easily bored and looking for action. John responded to Lou's driving energy with equal passion, not only sharing Reed's musical explosions but also providing a creative atmosphere and spiritual home for him. Conrad saw that

> there was a real bonding that occurred between John and Lou in that particular relationship. They started thinking about Lou getting out of Freeport, which was a great idea because he was living at home very uncomfortably. I took off, so there was more room in the pad, and John invited him to come over and stay where I had been staying.

'We had little to say to each other,' Lou said of the deteriorating relationship with his parents. 'I had gone and done the most horrifying thing possible in those days – I joined a rock band. And of course I represented something very alien to them.'

The funky Ludlow Street building did as much as anything else to cement the relationship. It had for a long time been host to creative spirits like the underground filmmakers Jack Smith and Piero Heliczer. When Lou moved in, an erratic but inventive Scotsman named Angus MacLise, who often drummed in LaMonte's group, lived in the apartment next door. Cale's L-shaped flat opened into a kitchen which housed a rarely used bathtub. Beyond it was a small living room and two bedrooms. The whole place was sparsely furnished, with mattresses on the floor and orange crates which served as furniture and firewood. Bare lightbulbs lit the dark rooms, paint and plaster chipped from the woodwork and the walls. There was no heat or hot water, and the landlord collected the $30 rent with a gun. But to Lou it was heaven. When it got cold during the first months he was living there, February to March of 1965, they ran out into the streets, grabbed some wooden crates and threw them into the fireplace, or often sat hunched over their instruments with carpets wrapped around their shoulders. Legend has it that when the toilet stopped up, they picked up the shit and threw it out of the window. For sustenance they cooked big pots of porridge or made humungous vegetable pancakes, eating the same glop day in and day out as if it were simply fuel.

Lou maintained a correspondence with Delmore Schwartz which led his mentor to believe that he was still definitely on the path to distilling his essence in words. 'I've had some strange experiences since returning to NY, sick but strange and fascinating even, sometimes ultimately revealing, healing and helpful,' he wrote in one letter in early 1965, just after moving to New York City.

> NY has so many sad, sick people and I have a knack for meeting them. They try to drag you down with them. If you're weak NY has many outlets. I can't resist peering, probing, sometimes participating, other times going right to the edge before sidestepping. Finding viciousness in yourself and that fantastic killer urge and worse yet having the opportunity presented before you is certainly interesting.

'If you want to write the story of the Velvet Underground, you have to begin far beyond any physical things that actually happened,' wrote the rock historian Lenny Kaye.

> You first have to look at New York City, the mother which spawned them, which gave them their inner fire, creating an umbilical attachment of emotion to a monstrous hulk of urban sprawl. You have to walk its streets, ride its subways, see it bustling and alive in the day, cold and haunted at night. And you have to love it, embrace it and recognize its strange power, for there, if anywhere, you'll find the roots.

Their neighbourhood was the loam, as Allen Ginsberg had said, out of which grew 'the apocalyptic sensibility, the interest in mystic art, the marginal leavings, the garbage of society'. As Lou discovered John's ascetic yet sprawling Lower East Side landscape with its population of what Jack Kerouac described as like-minded Bodhisattvas, he found himself walking in the footsteps of Stephen Crane (who had come there straight from Syracuse University at the end of the previous century to write *Maggie: A Girl of the Streets*, and reported to a friend that 'the sense of a city is war'), John Dos Passos, e e cummings and, most recently, the beats. Indeed, Reed could have walked straight out of the pages of Ginsberg's *Howl* for he too would, like one of the poem's heroes, 'purgatory his torso night after night with dreams, with drugs, with waking nightmares, alcohol and cock and endless balls'. Most importantly, the Ludlow Street inhabitants shared with Lou a communal feeling that society was a prison of the nervous system, and they preferred their own individual experience. The gifted among them had enough respect for their personal explorations to put them in their art, just as John and Lou were doing, and make it new. Friends from college who visited him there couldn't believe Lou was living in these conditions, but among the drug addicts and apocalyptic artists of every kind, Lou found, for the first time in his life, a real mental and spiritual home.

As he began to work with Cale to transform his stark lyrics into dynamic symphonies, he drew John into *his* world. John found Lou an intriguing, if at times dangerous, roommate. What they had in common was a fascination with the language of music and the permanent expression of risk. 'In Lou, I found somebody who not only had artistic sense and could produce it at the drop of a hat, but also had a real street sense,' John Cale recalled of his early days at Ludlow Street.

I was anxious to learn from him, I'd lived a sheltered life. So, from him, I got a short, sharp education. Lou was exorcising a lot of devils back then, and maybe I was using him to exorcise some of mine.

From the start I thought Lou was amazing, someone I could learn a lot from. He had this astonishing talent as a writer. He was someone who'd been around and was definitely bruised. He was also a lot of fun then, though he had a dangerous streak. He enjoyed walking the plank and he could take situations to extremes you couldn't even imagine until you'd been there with him. I thought I was fairly reckless until I met Lou. But I'd stop at goading a drunk into getting worse. And that's where Lou would start.

With John in tow, Lou would befriend a drunk in a bar and then, after drawing him out with friendly conversation, suddenly pop the astonishing question, 'Would you like to fuck your mother?' This kind of behaviour got them into some hairy situations, abhorred by Cale – who was not as verbally adroit as Lou, and was at times agoraphobic and lived in fear of random violence. 'I'm very insecure,' said Cale. 'I use cracks on the sidewalk to walk down the street. I'd always walk on the lines. I never take anything but a calculated risk, and I do it because it gives me a sense of identity. Fear is a man's best friend.'

John was, at times, a little intimidated by Lou, who was prepared to break all the rules showing Cale alternative ways to get what he needed, and seemingly afraid of no one. This was a new world to John, whose explorations out of bounds had been purely musical.

Money was a constant problem. Although Lou often had use of his mother's car and could return to Freeport whenever he desired, after quitting Pickwick in the spring he had no steady income. Instead, he picked up whatever money he could in doing gigs with John, some of them impromptu. Once, they went up to Harlem to play an audition at a blues club. The two young white men showed up with their guitar and viola to play 'Heroin' and 'Venus in Furs'. When the odd-looking couple were turned down by the club management, they went out to play on the pavement and raked in a sizeable amount of money. 'We made more money on the sidewalks than anywhere else,' John recalled.

'We were living together in a $30 a month apartment and we really didn't have any money,' Lou testified.

We used to eat oatmeal all day and all night and give blood among other things, or pose for these nickel or 15-cent tabloids they have every week. And when my picture came out it said I was a sex-maniac killer and that I had killed fourteen children and had tape-recorded it and played it in a barn in Kansas at midnight. And when John's picture came out in the paper, it said he had killed his lover because his lover was going to marry his sister, and he didn't want his sister to marry a fag.

At the same time as they struggled to stay alive, Lou was working on creating the myth of his own psychodrama. It had become a custom of Lou's to shock and astound his friends and associates with stories of his psychiatric treatment, drug use and run-ins with the law. This was the sort of image building Reed would, in a continuing search for a personality and voice to call his own, perfect in the coming years, culminating in a series of infamous personas in the 1970s. 'At that time Lou was relating to me the horrors of electric shock therapy, he was on medication,' Cale recounted.

I was really horrified. All his best work came from living with his parents. He told me his mother was some sort of ex-beauty queen and his father was a wealthy accountant. They'd put him in a hospital where he'd received shock treatments as a kid. Apparently he was at Syracuse and was given this compulsory choice to do either gym or ROTC. He claimed he couldn't do gym because he'd break his neck and when he did ROTC he threatened to kill his instructor. Then he put his fist through a window or something, and so he was put in a mental hospital. I don't know the full story. Every time Lou told me about it he'd change it slightly.

As their relationship solidified and their musical ideas coalesced, Lou and John resolved to form a band, orchestrate their material into a performable and recordable body of work, and venture out into the world to unleash their music. 'When we first started working together, it was on the basis that we were both interested in the same things,' said Cale.

We both needed a vehicle; Lou needed one to carry out his lyrical ideas and I needed one to carry out my musical ideas. It seemed to be a good idea to put a band together and go up on stage and do it, because everybody else seemed to be playing the same thing over and over. Anybody who had a rock-and-roll band in those days would just do a fixed set. I figured that was one way of getting on everybody's nerves – to have improvisation going on for any length of time.

*

While Lou was wrapping himself in the troubled dreams and screams of his music, elevating himself, as one friend saw it, to another level of anger and coolness, and becoming progressively weirder, he began to put some distance between himself and his past. True, he still borrowed his mother's car sometimes to go into dangerous parts of town to score drugs, and still made the occasional trip or phone call home, but he began to amputate those friends with whom he had maintained contact after leaving Syracuse. The first to go was the stalwart Allen Hyman. Living in Manhattan with his wife and going to law school, his former buddy had lost the ability to provide anything for Lou (save a free meal). Later, Allen said wistfully, 'I kind of lost touch with him.' Richard Mishkin still fulfilled a function in that he had a big space in Brooklyn where Lou sometimes rehearsed, and a yacht called the *Black Angel* tethered at the 79th Street Boat Basin where they sometimes socialized, but he was maintaining contact with Lou at a price. 'At that point he was putting me down more than he would have at Syracuse,' Ritchie recalled. 'He was definitely different than he was at Syracuse. He was on the way to what he became.' According to Schupak, 'Lou changed in a lot of ways. I think he became very controlled by the drug environment. He became a disciple.'

Parting ways is common among former schoolmates who move on to new jobs and allegiances. The breaks that cut more deeply and perhaps more definitively were made by Lou from the people who had been most influential, the ones who knew too much about him.

After a period in the nuthouse, Lincoln Swados had re-emerged on the New York scene and was living downtown in the East Village not far from Lou. For a short time he was making a reputation for himself as a comic-strip illustrator and stand-up comedian. But soon he beat Lou hands down in the lunatic sweepstakes by stepping in front of an oncoming subway train, saying, 'I am a very bad person, I am a very bad person . . .' Moving aside at the last minute, he survived – minus an arm and a leg. Subsequently, he became something of a fixture on the Lower

East Side as a crippled street performer. Lincoln's sister Elizabeth, who had gone on to a distinguished career as a playwright, was quite upset by the extent to which Lou, rather than opening up to Lincoln after this tragic episode, put even more distance between them. Lincoln, though, had a perceptive understanding of his friend's motives. 'Lou pretends to be like us,' he told his ex-girlfriend, the journalist Gretchen Berg, 'but he's really not, he's really someone else. He's really a businessman who has very definite goals and knows exactly what he wants.'

Interestingly, Delmore Schwartz, who was now in the final year of his own agonizing tragicomedy, had drawn a similar conclusion. A Syracuse classmate of Lou's who ran into Schwartz in Manhattan one day was astonished to discover that 'he looked really bad. He had on a black raincoat which looked like it was covered with toothpaste stains. He seemed to have been drinking, maybe he was drunk. And the only thing he was interested in discussing was his dislike for everyone at Syracuse; how Lou Reed and another student were spies paid by the Rockefellers.' When Lou discovered that Schwartz was living in the dilapidated fleabag Dixie Hotel on West 48th Street, he went up there and tried to make contact, but Delmore let him have it with both barrels, screaming, 'If you ever come here again, I'll kill you!', and frightening off a shaken Reed who later explained, 'He thought I'd been sent by the CIA to spy on him, and I was scared because he was big and he really would have killed me.'

The third mind in Lou's life at Syracuse, Shelley Albin, reversed the amputation process, cutting him out of her life when she married a man named Ronald Corwin who had been a big wheel on the Syracuse campus in 1963–65 as the head of the local chapter of CORE, and whom Lou subsequently characterized as an 'asshole airhead'. The marriage was a blow to Lou inasmuch as he still considered Shelley to be 'his' girlfriend, even though he had not seen nor made any attempt to contact her since the summer of 1964. Still, he had not carried on a romantic relationship with anyone else. Shelley would remain a thorn in his side at least until the end of the 1970s, inspiring in time some of his most poignant, if vicious, love songs.

The only people Lou seemed incapable of amputating were his parents, who were vividly remembered by friends as a pair of never seen but apparently ogrelike spectres threatening at any moment to have Lou committed (despite the fact that he was now twenty-three years old and legally beyond their reach).

About a month into his collaboration with Cale, one of those chance meetings that have often played a historic part in the formation of rock groups took place when Lou bumped into his friend from Syracuse, Sterling Morrison, walking in the West Village. Lou invited Sterling to Ludlow Street to play some music. By then Angus MacLise had become involved playing drums around Lou and John. The next time Tony Conrad dropped by, he discovered that the Reed–Cale relationship had blossomed with MacLise and Morrison into what they were beginning to call a group. They had even made a first stab at choosing a name, trying on for several months the Warlocks (which, coincidentally, was the name being used at the same time on the West Coast by the proto–Grateful Dead), and were taping their rehearsals. The music, heavily influenced by LaMonte Young via MacLise and Cale, but equally by the doo-wop and white rock favoured by Reed and Morrison, was ethereal and passionate.

'Our music evolved collectively,' Sterling reported.

> Lou would walk in with some sort of scratchy verse and we would all develop the music. It almost always worked like that. We'd all thrash it out into something very strong. John was trying to be a serious young composer, he had no background in rock music, which was terrific, he knew no clichés. You listen to his bass lines, he didn't know any of the usual riffs, it was totally eccentric. 'Waiting for My Man' was very weird. John was always exciting to work with.

Their original precepts were to dedicate themselves with an almost religious fervour to their collective calling, to sacrifice being immediately successful, to be different, to hold on to a personality of their own, never to try to please anyone but themselves, and never to play the same song the same way. The group discovered and exploited musical traditions lost to their contemporaries, rejecting outright the popular conventions of the day. 'We actually had a rule in the band,' Reed explained. 'If anybody played a blues lick, they would be fined.'

The consensus of opinion was that their first complete success in terms of arrangements was 'Venus in Furs'. When Cale initially added viola, grinding it against Reed's 'ostrich' guitar, illogically and without trepidation, a tingle of anticipation shot up his spine. They had, he knew, found their sound, and it was strong. Cale, who applied the mania to the sound, recalled that 'it wasn't until then that I thought we had discovered a really original, nasty style'. With the words of this song, wrote the British critic Richard Williams,

Lou Reed was to change the agenda of pop music once and for all. But it wasn't just the word either. 'Heroin' and 'Venus in Furs' were given music that fitted their themes, and that didn't sound like anything anybody had played before. Out went the blues tonality and the Afro-American rhythms, the basic components of all previous rock and roll. The prevailing sound was the grinding screech of Cale's electric viola and Reed's guitar feedback, while the tempo speeded up and slowed down according to the momentary requirements of the lyric.

According to the rock historian Robert Palmer, while working on a ten-part television history of rock and roll he came to see

in the overall picture of the music the fact that Lou's stuff has been such a major influence on people who sold so many more records and penetrated so much more deeply into the pop culture. I mean, it's hard to imagine a lot of Bowie without Lou Reed. And the whole of the last generation of rock, certainly since the mid-late seventies, there hasn't been a rock band that hasn't picked up on the Velvets thing. In so many cases it really shaped what they did. It was so influential. I hear Lou's kind of singing, I hear the guitar thing, certainly the whole approach to the drone thing. Plagal cadence is a one chord–four chord C to F to C to F. 'Heroin' is that. 'Waiting for the Man' is basically that. An awful lot of Velvets songs are basically that. Really Lou taught everyone to use the plagal cadence with a drone. Cale's influence with the drone is very obvious, but the fact that Lou was stringing the guitar all to one note shows that he was thinking along the same lines. With that kind of very, very simple chord progression, there are several notes that harmonize with both chords. So you can just keep that one drone note going, and have the skeletal chord changes over it. That particular harmonic cadence – that one chord–four chord thing – can be so evocative. I can't think of anybody else who was writing using that kind of simple cadence that got anything like what Lou got out of it. He just came up with this whole fresh approach to the whole idea of melody in rock and the whole relationship of melody to harmony – or lack of harmony. Lack of harmonic changes. Christ, he just influenced everybody.

The chemistry of Reed's and Cale's personalities was more unstable. On one occasion, Lou played a new song he had written and John immediately started adding an improvised viola part. Sterling muttered something about it being a good viola part. Lou looked up and snapped, 'Yeah, I know. I wrote the song just for that viola part. Every single note of it I knew in advance.' Although unable to outdo Lou verbally, John stuck to his guns through music. Several observers of the scene believed that John did more than that – he actually brought Lou Reed out of himself, completed him, as it were. Some believe that without John Cale, the Lou Reed who became a legend would not have been born.

'It's a fascinating relationship,' commented one friend.

That John worked with Cage and LaMonte Young would be interesting enough if his career ended there, but that he met Lou and saw something in Lou despite the fact that Lou did not have the same kind of training that he had. I think he recognized that and must have done much in his way to nurture it and allowed it also to change the course of his life.

Insecure about his playing, and in need of constant encouragement, Sterling stood in the background and tentatively muttered the choruses he was supposed to sing. One friend recalled that 'it was typical of Sterling to play a wonderful solo and pretend he didn't care. But then after an hour sidle up and ask, "How was the solo?"' Morrison hid this nervousness under a cloud of silence when anything went wrong. His personality often made him a useful buffer between Reed and Cale, but it could also cause problems when, without informing anybody that he was upset, he would simply clam up.

The linchpin in the operation was Angus MacLise. Not only did the band get their electricity from his apartment, but Angus was, by all accounts, a whimsical, gnomelike man, inspired, inspirational and a serious methedrine addict. As a drummer, he was intuitive and complex, pounding out an amazing variety of textures and licks culled from cultures around the world. He was influenced a lot by his travels, by the dervishes of the Middle East and people he had met in India and Nepal. A visionary poet and mystic who also belonged to LaMonte Young's coterie, MacLise believed in listening to the essence of sound and relating it to one's inner being. 'Angus had dreamy notions of art – I mean real dreamy,' Sterling said.

Both Cale and MacLise continued to play with the Theater of Eternal Music throughout 1965 in between rehearsing with the Warlocks, although this contravened Lou's need for total allegiance and commitment. This made LaMonte Young almost a third mind in the construction of the band's basic precepts. It was characteristic of that period and place – specifically the East Village – that certain figures, like LaMonte Young, Andy Warhol, Robert Rauschenberg and Allen Ginsberg, were ensconced within an adoring entourage of followers and fellow workers. It is significant that despite his two bandmates' close connections with one of the most charismatic figures of the period, Lou Reed never met LaMonte Young during his entire career with the Velvet Underground. Reed understood that people who really wanted to make it on their own – to be stars – had to keep their distance from the vortex of such strong groups.

In fact, the central paradox of Lou's career, particularly in the 1960s, was that by entering the highly competitive, fast-paced world of rock and roll he was by definition entering the one art form that relied completely and uniquely on intense, rapid, often nerve-racking collaboration – the one thing he had the least talent for. Soon his new bandmates would discover what the Eldorados had collided with at Syracuse – that Lou could be the sweetest, most charming companion, but that he was virtually always a motherfucker to work with. His biggest problem, apart from demanding complete control and having a Himalayan ego, was the matter of credit. Just as the Rolling Stones had done when creating their music, the Velvet Underground worked up almost all of their songs collectively from the simple, inspirational chord structures or sketchy lyrics composed by Lou. Reed was under the impression, however, that he had single-handedly crafted masterpieces like 'Heroin', 'Venus in Furs', 'Waiting for the Man' and 'Black Angel's Death Song'. In truth, although Reed undoubtedly supplied the brilliant lyrics and chord structures, the various and greater parts of the music – Cale's viola, Morrison's guitar, MacLise's drumming – were invented by each individually. In short, Reed could have shared the majority of his writing credits with other members of the band. At first, of course, before the question of signing any contract came up, everything was copacetic – since there was nothing to argue about. The group was also under the impression, due to the nature of the material, that no one would ever record or cover their music. In time, however, this vital subject of artistic collaboration, credit and, most importantly, of publishing rights (which is where the most money is made in rock and roll in the long run) would become the deepest wound in the band's history of battles.

Still, in early 1965 Angus became a devoted, if crazy, friend to Lou, in the tradition of Lincoln Swados. Angus turned Lou on to the easily available pharmaceutical methamphetamine hydrochloride, also known as methedrine, which was the drug of choice of a particularly intense group of visionary seekers centered around Jack Smith and, later, Andy Warhol. Amphetamine – speed – is a key to understanding what set Reed and Cale's sound aside from the mainstream of American pop in the second half of the 1960s, which was based on soft and hallucinogenic drugs. In fact, for a while one transient tenant was said to be mass-producing speed for the Mafia in the very Ludlow Street building John and Lou occupied. They were thus at the heart of the speed scene. Lou and Angus collaborated on an essay called 'Concerning the Rumor That Red China Has Cornered the Methedrine Market and is Busy Adding Paranoia Drops to Upset the Mental Balance of the United States', a manifesto of the band's basic precepts. It read, in part, 'Western music is based on death, violence and the pursuit of PROGRESS ... The root of universal music is sex. Western music is as violent as Western sex ... Our band is the Western equivalent to the cosmic dance of Shiva. Playing as Babylon goes up in flames.'

The tension between these four disparate personalities became the emotional engine of their music. Twenty years later, Reed would vigorously deny that the friction, particularly between himself and Cale, was constructive. But this was simply one of his many attempts to write or control his own history. Morrison remembered:

> I love Lou, but he has what must be a fragmented personality, so you're never too sure under any conditions what you're going to have to deal with. He'll be boyishly charming, naive – Lou is very charming when he wants to be. Or he will be vicious – and if he is you have to figure out what's stoking the fire. What drug is he on, or what mad diet? He had all sorts of strange dietary theories. He'd eat nothing, living on wheat husks. He was always trying to move mentally and spiritually to some place where no one had ever gone before. He was often very antisocial and difficult to work with but he was *interesting*, and people were *interested* in the conflict and some of the good things that came out of it.

Some of the good things that came out of it were the songs that began to soar out over the gritty, dangerous drug supermarkets that surrounded Ludlow Street from Eldridge to the Bowery. Lou, Sterling, Angus and John hammered away at songs day in and day out, honing down the ones that would appear on the first Velvet Underground album two years later. According to Cale:

> We actually worked very hard for about a year on the arrangements for the first album. I felt when we were doing those first arrangements back in Ludlow Street '65, that we had something that was going to last. What we did was unique, it was powerful. We spent our entire weekends going over and over and over the songs. We had no big problem with the work ethic; in fact, we were hanging on to the work ethic for dear life.

By the spring of 1965, the music began to soar. John Cale remembered these earliest days of playing as their best. Cale contributed his unique electric viola, Morrison his hauntingly beautiful electric guitar, MacLise his ethereal Far Eastern drumming and Reed his fresh, raw lyrics and his delivery of them. Apart from being the best songwriter in the band he was, Morrison pointed out, 'one of the great rock vocalists. He could do some amazing things with his voice.' Often the band would improvise a riff and Reed would simply make up the lyrics as he went along. 'He was amazing,' Cale said, 'one minute he'd be a Southern preacher, then he'd change character completely and be someone totally different'.

'In my head it would be great if I could sing like Al Green,' Reed said. 'But that's in my head. It wasn't true. I had to work out ways of dealing with my voice and its limitations. I wrote for a certain phrase and then bent the lyric to fit the melody. Figured out a way to make it fit.' In 1965 he was remarkably creative, carving a dark, macabre, Poe-like beauty out of Cale's orchestration of the band's musical chaos. 'We heard our screams turn into songs,' Reed later wrote, 'and back into screams again.'

Meanwhile Cale, travelling back and forth between London and New York on his classical scholarship funds, was bringing back the latest singles of the most exciting new British groups: the Who and the Kinks, with whom they felt they had some affinity. It was an intensely creative, highly energized time in rock history, and the band gorged themselves on everything they liked.

Drugs were both a catalyst and an inhibitor for the music. 'There were no heavy addictions or anything, but enough to get in our way, hepatitis and so on,' Sterling recalled.

I would take pills, amphetamines, not psychedelics, we were never into that. Drugs didn't inspire us for songs or anything like that. We took them for old-fashioned reasons – it made you feel good, braced you for criticism. It wasn't just drugs, there were vitamins, ginseng, experimental diets. Lou once went on a diet so radical there was no fat showing on his central nerve chart . . . his spinal column was raw!

We took a lot of downers – that's what I used to do. We did all sorts of junk. It took us a long time to get into speed. There was just so much going on, you had to keep up with it, that was all. I never got really A-headed out. But if you had two members of the band heavily sedated and the other on uppers, it is gonna affect your sensibilities. They wanted to do slow dirges and I wanted to do uptempo songs!

That summer two parallel events catapulted the Warlocks, who also occasionally used the in-your-face drug-innuendo name the Falling Spikes, out of the obscurity of Ludlow Street toward the limelight that would soon illuminate them.

First, through MacLise's connections on the Lower East Side underground film scene, the most potent movement of the moment embracing arguably the largest, most intelligent and creative audience in New York, they were invited to play their rehearsal tapes or sometimes perform live to accompany screenings of the mostly silent films by Jack Smith, Ron Rice, Andy Warhol, Stan Brakhage and Barbara Rubin that were making a big splash that season. 1965 was the climactic year of the Lower East Side art community and in particular the underground film scene. One of the scene's most outstanding, enigmatic figures, the poet and filmmaker Piero Heliczer, who often screened films at his enormous art-factory loft on Grand Street, three blocks from 56 Ludlow Street, first offered the group a venue to play. Soon they were playing regularly at Heliczer's and other artists' spaces, sitting behind the film screens or off to the side. The most popular underground film theatre space at the time was Jonas Mekas's Cinematheque, which became the band's most regular venue. Sterling recalled:

> Centre stage of the old Cinematheque was a movie screen, and between the screen and the audience a number of veils were spread out in different places. These were lit variously by slide projections and lights, as Piero's films shone through them onto the screen. Dancers and incense swirled around, poetry and song rose up while from behind the screen a strange music was generated by Lou Reed, John Cale, Angus and me, with Piero back there too playing his sax.

Occasionally they would play bare-chested with painted torsos or try to look outrageous in some other way. In the process they gained enthusiastic audiences, among whom Barbara Rubin would become their most influential fan.

Their second breakthrough came in July when they recorded a demo tape at 56 Ludlow Street which included early versions of 'Heroin', 'Venus in Furs', 'Black Angel's Death Song' and 'Wrap Your Troubles in Dreams'. '"Wrap Your Troubles in Dreams", that's relentless,' said John Cale. 'Lou's often said, "Hey, some of these songs are just *not worthy* of human endeavour, these things are best left alone." He may be right.' The tape also included a song which Morrison later recalled as 'Never Get Emotionally Involved with a Man, Woman, Beast or Child'. Cale took the tape over to London in the hope of securing a recording contract with one of the more adventurous British companies (after all, the Who and the Kinks used similar techniques), and there was considerable interest from, among others, Miles Copeland, who would go on to manage the Police.

By the autumn, with their music mature and their audience growing, they felt that something was happening. This seemed confirmed in November when they stumbled upon the name they would keep, the Velvet Underground, 'swiping it', as Lou put it, from the title of a paperback book about suburban sex Tony Conrad literally picked out of the gutter and brought to Ludlow Street. The Velvet Underground seemed perfectly to fit their affiliations and intentions. That same month they got their first media boost when filmed playing 'Venus in Furs' for a CBS documentary on New York underground film, featuring Piero Heliczer and narrated by Walter Cronkite. When the prestigious rock journalist Alfred G. Aronowitz offered to manage them, they accepted.

Al Aronowitz, who had an influential pop column in the *New York Post* and had written extensively about the Beatles, Stones and Dylan, was an important player on the New York rock secene. 'Aronowitz was famous,' wrote one onlooker.

> Aronowitz was the man who'd introduced Allen Ginsberg to Bob Dylan and Bob Dylan to the Beatles. He'd known Billie Holiday and Jack Kerouac and Paul Newman and Frank Sinatra. He could get Ahmet Ertegun, George Plimpton, Clive Davis, or Willem de Kooning on the phone. He'd been Brian Jones' American connection and Leon Russell's New York guru and the one who introduced Pete Hamill to Norman Mailer. Only Aronowitz could write a rock column in a daily newspaper that'd make the whole country snap to attention.

His interest in the Velvets was a sure sign of impending success.

Suddenly, however, their unorthodox background clashed with their progress. As soon as Aronowitz presented them with their first paying job, opening for another group he managed, the Myddle Class, Angus MacLise, as Lou recalled, 'asked a very intriguing question. He said, "Do you mean we have to show up at a certain time and start playing – and then end?"

'And we said, "Yes."

'And he said, "Well, I can't handle that!" And that was it. He was a great drummer . . .'

Lou, who put his beloved group before anything and anyone, never forgave MacLise. But as it developed, Angus's withdrawal set in motion one last chance meeting that would perfectly complete the band. With the Aronowitz date booked for 11 December, only days away, Lou and Sterling suddenly remembered that their Syracuse friend Jim Tucker had a sister who played drums, and wondered if she might be able to fill in. Cale, horrified by the mere suggestion that a 'chick' should play in their great group, had to be placated by the promise that it was strictly temporary. When he acquiesced, Lou shot out to the suburbs of Long Island to audition Moe Tucker. 'My brother had been telling me about Lou for a while, because he had known him for a few years before that,' Maureen recalled. 'I was nineteen at the time, living at home and had a job, keying stuff into computers. Lou came out to my house to see if I could really play the drums. He said, "OK, that's good."'

When she first went to John's apartment in New York to hear the band play their repertoire, Maureen, whose favourite drummer was Charlie Watts, was knocked out. She could see that Lou was a bona fide rock-and-roll freak, and the whole band was amazing. 'When they played "Heroin" I was really impressed. You could just tell that this was different.'

Maureen's drumming was a distillation of all the rock and roll that had gone before and yet, influenced by African musicians, she played with mallets on two kettledrums while standing up. 'I developed a really basic style,' she said, 'mainly because I didn't have any training – to this day I couldn't do a roll to save my life, or any of that other fancy stuff, nor have I any wish to. I always wanted to keep a simple but steady beat behind the band so no matter how wild John or Lou would get there would still be this low drone holding it together.' Methodical and steady as a person and a drummer, Maureen kept up the backbeat. Young as she was in comparison to her older brother's friends, she held her own, rarely keeping her opinions to herself when they mattered. Though bowled over by the Velvets' music, she was not always impressed by the lifestyle that went along with it. She thought it was crazy for John and Lou to go out and look for firewood to heat their apartment. 'It wasn't very romantic,' she commented later about the flat. 'It stank.'

The Velvet Underground's first job took place at Summit High School in Summit, New Jersey, on 11 December 1965. They were squeezed in between a band called 40 Fingers and the Myddle

Class. 'Nothing could have prepared the kids and parents assembled in the auditorium for what they were about to experience that night,' wrote Rob Norris, a Summit student. 'Our only clue was the small crowd of strange-looking people hanging around in front of the stage.'

What followed the gentle strains of 40 Fingers was a performance that would have shocked anyone outside the most avantgarde audiences of the Lower East Side. The curtain rose on the Velvet Underground, revealing four long-haired figures dressed in black and poised behind a strange variety of instruments. Maureen's tiny androgynous figure stood behind her kettledrums, making everyone immediately wonder uneasily whether she was a girl or a boy. Sterling's tall, angular frame shuffled nervously in the background. Lou and John, both in sunglasses, stared blankly at the astonished students, teachers and parents, Cale wielding his odd-looking viola. As they charged into the opening chords of the cacophonous 'Venus in Furs' louder than anyone in the room had ever heard music played, they rounded out an image aptly described as bizarre and terrifying. 'Everyone was hit by the screeching surge of sound, with a pounding beat louder than anything we'd ever heard,' Norris continued. 'About a minute into the second song, which the singer had introduced as "Heroin", the music began to get even more intense. It swelled and accelerated like a giant tidal wave which was threatening to engulf us all. At this point most of the audience retreated in horror for the safety of their homes, thoroughly convinced of the dangers of rock and roll music.' According to Sterling, 'The murmur of surprise that greeted our apperance as the curtain went up increased to a roar of disbelief once we started to play "Venus" and swelled to a mighty howl of outrage and bewilderment by the end of "Heroin".'

'Backstage after their set, the viola player was seen apologizing profusely to an outraged Myddle Class entourage for scaring away half the audience,' Norris concluded. 'Al Aronowitz was philosophical about it, though. He said, "at least you've given them a night to remember," and invited everyone to a party at his house after the show.'

Observing that the group seemed to have an oddly stimulating and polarizing effect on audiences, Aronowitz advised them to get some experience playing in public by doing a residency at a small club. Four days later they started a two-week stand at the Café Bizarre on MacDougal Street in New York's Greenwich Village. 'We played some covers – 'Little Queenie', 'Bright Lights, Big City', the black R&B songs Lou and I liked – and as many of our own songs as we had,' Sterling reported.

> We needed a lot more of our own material, so we sat around and worked, that's when we wrote 'Run Run Run', all those things. Lou usually would have some lyrics written, and something would grow out of that with us jamming. He was a terrific improvisational lyricist. I remember we had the Christmas tree up, but no decorations on it, we were sitting around busy writing songs, because we had to, we needed them that night!

This fortuitous opportunity was pivotal for their career. Firstly, since there was so little time between the two dates they decided to keep Maureen, initially much to Cale's chagrin. Moe remembered standing in the street with John, who kept saying, 'No chicks in the band. No chicks.' Secondly, at the very time they were playing at the Café Bizarre to unreceptive tourists twice a night for $5 apiece, the pop artist and entrepreneur Andy Warhol was looking around for a group to manage for a nightclub he had been asked to run by the theatrical impresario Michael Myerberg (who brought Beckett's *Waiting for Godot* to the USA in 1956). Barbara Rubin, for whose film *Christmas on Earth* the band had played in their previous incarnation, was spending a good deal of time at the Warhol studio, the famous Silver Factory, and thought the Velvets would be the perfect band for Warhol's upcoming discotheque. She took two of Warhol's leading talent scouts, the film director Paul Morrissey and the underground film star Gerard Malanga, to see them. Malanga, who had just starred in Warhol's version of *A Clockwork Orange, Vinyl*, was an outstandingly handsome

young man with a potent sexual aura. Combining the looks of
Elvis Presley and James Dean with the long hair of Mick Jagger,
Malanga dressed head to foot in black leather and wore, purely for
dramatic effect, a black leather bullwhip wrapped around the
shoulder of his jacket. During the Velvets' set, Gerard suddenly
leaped up from his table onto the empty dance floor. All of the
other customers were too terrified by the music to move. Making
ample use of his whip, he undulated in a sinister, erotic dance that
perfectly illustrated the visceral, throbbing music. The band was
dumbfounded by Gerard's mind-blowing performance. In the
intermission Lou and John went over to his table and told him to
come back and dance any time. Instantly spotting a starring role
for himself in the scenario, Malanga thought the group would be
perfect for Warhol.

The following night Malanga returned to the Café Bizarre with
Rubin, Warhol's business manager Paul Morrissey and Warhol
himself, accompanied by an entourage including his reigning
superstar Edie Sedgwick. They were thrilled by the weird and
raucous performance of the Velvet Underground. Not only did
the group do the same thing Warhol's films did – make people
uncomfortable – but their name and the fact that they sang about
taboo subjects perfectly fit Warhol's programme. To top it off,
Morrissey was intrigued by the band's androgynous drummer.
After the set Barbara brought the Velvets over to Andy's table.
The curly-haired Lou Reed, with his shy, gum-chewing smile, sat
next to the pop artist and the two of them immediately hit it off.
'Lou looked good and pubescent then,' Warhol recalled. 'Paul
thought the kids out on the Island would identify with that.'

Morrissey, who was the most influential person in Warhol's
world after Malanga, was fascinated:

John Cale had a wonderful appearance and he played the electric
viola, which was a real novelty; but best of all was Maureen Tucker,
the drummer. You couldn't take your eyes off her because you
couldn't work out if she was a boy or a girl. Nobody had ever had a
girl drummer before. She made no movement, she was so sedate. I

proposed that we sign a contract with them, we'd manage them and give them a place to play.'

'We looked at each other,' Lou Reed remembered, 'and said, "This sounds like really great fun."'

chapter six   **Fun at the**
                            Factory

                            ## 1966

                            [In which Lou and the Velvets
                            join forces with Andy Warhol
                            and Nico, create a new rock
                            performance format called the
                            Exploding Plastic Inevitable,
                            and record their first album.]

*The next step may be the electrification of all mankind by the
representation of a play that may be neither tragedy, comedy,
farce, opera, pantomime, melodrama nor spectacle, as we now
comprehend these terms, but which may retain some portion
of the idiosyncratic excellence of each, while it introduces a
new class of excellence as yet unnamed because as yet
undreamed of in the world.*

                            EDGAR ALLAN POE

When Lou and Andy met, Warhol was thirty-six, wealthy and in
control of his life and followers. Reed was twenty-three, strong as
stainless steel, confident and as ambitious as his mentor. In
Warhol, Reed found the all-permissive father-mother-protector-
catalyst-collaborator he had always craved. Warhol was curious
about Reed because he saw quite a bit of himself in Lou. They
were both isolated people who kept their innermost thoughts to
themselves. Each had had nervous breakdowns.

Lou Reed has been described by friends and enemies over the
years by sobriquets such as 'a control freak', 'a schizophrenic', 'an
asshole'. Not one of them was 'fun'. Andy Warhol has been

described over the years as 'a mad queen', 'a Zen warrior', 'a creep'. None of them was 'fun', either. And yet the truth of the matter is that over the next four months, from January to April 1966, *fun* is exactly what Lou and Andy had together. Their relationship can be seen in a photograph taken at the Factory that year. They stand facing each other with face-splitting grins in front of a life-size full-figure Warhol painting of Elvis Presley with a drawn six-gun. Andy, the lion-hearted Leo, his head cocked slightly to one side with its strong, high cheekbones and muscular jaw, betrays the Draculian power he possesses in the pencil-thin, sinewy body concealed beneath his trademark black outfit. He looks like Sylvester staring at Tweety Pie. Lou, the uncharacteristically shark-hearted Pisces, gazes in turn at Andy with all the gamin-like love he had been withholding from his father since he was twelve and discovered that he was bisexual and wanted to play the guitar and feel like a rock-and-roll star. He eyeballs him with the adoration and openness of a disciple who has just met the master who will open the gates of heaven and hell and let him in. Lou Reed fell in love with the *idea* of Andy Warhol, Andy completely seduced Lou by showering his prodigious ego with the highest compliments.

Andy told me that what we were doing with music was the same thing he was doing with movies and painting, i.e. not kidding around. To my mind, nobody in music was doing anything that even approximated the real thing, with the exception of us. We were doing a specific thing that was very, very real. It wasn't slick or a lie in any conceivable way, which was the only way we could work with him. Because the first thing I liked about Andy was that he was very real.

The real idea was to listen all the time. He had great ideas at the drop of a hat. But so did I. The thing was, he was there. There were a couple of people who were floating around who were there who always seemed to get in touch with one another one way or another. In other words, no other band could have been able to hold it up. It would have been overwhelmed by the lights or the movies. That's not, in fact, what happened. And that's because what we did was very strong.

'Lou learned a lot from Andy, mainly about becoming a successful public personality by selling your own private quirks to an audience greedy for more and more geeks,' wrote the rock critic Lester Bangs. 'The prime lesson he learned was that to succeed as this kind of mass-consumed nonentity you must expertly erect walls upon walls to reinforce the walls that your own quirky vulnerability has already put there.' Lou agreed with Lester, but put it in his own terms: 'Andy Warhol was an inspiration to me. I watched everything he did and how he did it. Some of these things serve me well to this day. For example, how to handle interviews, the press . . .'

'His ideas would stun me,' Lou affirmed. 'His way of looking at things would stop me dead in my tracks. Sometimes, I would go for days thinking about something he said.' Warhol taught Reed that an artist was a person who had to work hard and not waste time. Whenever Andy asked Lou how many songs he'd written that day, whatever the answer, he would urge, 'You should do more.' He taught Lou that work was everything and Lou came to believe that his music was so beautiful that people should be willing to die for it. It was the kind of effect Andy Warhol often had on his followers.

Lou, with his androgynous good looks, his slippery, rail-thin body, his hysterical cackle, romantic violence and demented will, seduced Andy into spending the next five months trying in part to turn Lou into a marketable persona that would make the most money in the shortest time – a rock-and-roll star. 'If Andy had been able to achieve the Walt Disney Hollywood status, Lou would have been able to change his persona to be like an Elvis,' the Factory manager Billy Name pointed out. 'Andy would have put out Lou Reed movies: Lou in Hawaii, Lou in the army, Lou as a half-breed trying to decide whether he should like the Comanches and stay with the family that raised him.' In many ways their relationship was no different from John Lennon's with Brian Epstein or Johnny Rotten's with Malcolm McLaren. One only has to figure out in the end who did what.

Lou would make a career out of finding mentors. He somehow

made himself completely available to Warhol – just as he had done with Delmore Schwartz at Syracuse – without selling him his soul. For a time he was able to drop his need to be the only genius in the room. For Lou it was a romantic, remarkable transition. One day he was a rockroach scavenging on the Lower East Side, the following week he was an honoured member of a charged hierarchial entourage combining some of the best minds and bodies in New York. To be with Warhol was to be willing to die for him. Indeed, a number of people who worked at the Factory did die before, during and after Lou's brief tenure as a Warhol superstar.

Surprisingly, when Warhol moved the musicians in the Velvet Underground around like mannequins in a store window to get the most striking effect, everyone, including Reed, intuitively accepted his moves. However, if Lou had known what was behind these machinations he would not have been so amenable. 'The problem is,' Paul Morrissey had warned Andy before taking him to see the Velvet Underground for the first time, 'these people have no singer. There's a guy who sings, but he's got no personality and nobody pays the slightest attention to him.' The first move Warhol made after securing a managerial contract in which he would receive 25 per cent of all their earnings (the average manager took 20 per cent, but Warhol was not average) was to tell the astonished band members they needed a chanteuse (he was careful not to say singer) to front the group. He had the perfect vehicle in a new girl in town whom he was going to make his next, biggest superstar: the tall, big-boned, awesomely beautiful blonde actress from Europe who went by the single name of Nico.

Stunned by this first move in the intricate chess game that would evolve between them, Lou stammered, 'Andy, c'mon, I mean, gimme a break . . .' But Warhol's will was as pliable as a steel girder. Moreover, Lou was swayed by Warhol's well-earned reputation for turning people overnight into exactly what Lou so wanted to be – a star! As a result, Lou quickly caved in with only two stipulations. The first was that Nico be kept separate from the band, her name – in the reverse of standard policy – tacked onto the end of the band's. Secondly, he wanted it understood that she was with the group only because Andy wanted her to be.

The arrangement was worked out under the convincing influence of Warhol's business manager, Paul Morrissey, who just didn't think Lou had enough personality to stand in front of the group and sing.

The collaboration between the Velvet Underground and Warhol hinged on the connection between Andy and Lou. It is almost inconceivable that the singer in a rock group enjoying its first flush of success would agree to bow into a background role at the very moment of his triumph. The fact that Lou did so emphasized his ambivalence about being in the spotlight and his fervent devotion to Andy Warhol. Not only did they share a number of characteristics, but the louche, homosexual atmosphere of Warhol's Silver Factory in the mid-1960s brought out Lou's gay side. According to John Cale, 'Lou was very full of himself and faggy in those days. We called him Lulu, I was Black Jack. He wanted to be queen bitch and spit out the sharpest rebukes of anyone around. Lou always ran with the pack and the Factory was full of queens to run with.' The combination of the connection between Andy and Lou, Lou's need for a mentor, and the spiritual, sexual, human home he found at the Factory, turned him into a disciple of Warhol's in a manner more extreme, open and complete than he would ever reach with another collaborator.

In every strong relationship with his superstars, Warhol found elements of himself. This was particularly evident in his work with Nico. Although he had come at times to look astonishingly like Edie Sedgwick, Warhol never came closer to finding a living embodiment of the beautiful woman a part of him wanted to be than Nico.

Another part of Andy wanted to be a pop star like Elvis Presley. In 1963 Andy had actually fooled around with the notion of being in his own rock band, rehearsing on several occasions with none other than LaMonte Young, Walter DeMaria and several other members of the downtown art community. In placing Nico like a chess piece in the vanguard of the VU, Andy became a member of the band by proxy.

With Reed coaxed into submission and Warhol living out his vicarious fantasy, the introduction of Nico might have gone smoothly, but neither she nor Lou liked being a puppet. The real trouble began when Nico announced that she wanted to sing all the songs Lou had written, especially her favourites. 'When I started with the Velvets, I wanted to sing Lou's song "I'm Waiting for the Man",' she admitted, 'but he wouldn't let me. I guess he thought I didn't understand its meaning, and he was right. And we had the song "Heroin", which I thought was a provocation. But I have to say that Lou and John took heroin, and those songs were songs of realism.'

Each of them dealt with the situation differently. Cale, at first, didn't know what to do with her. Sterling typically took the dismissive position that there was nothing wrong with Nico, she simply didn't understand English! Moe snorted that she was a schmuck with an enlarged ego who was irrelevant, until she started insisting on singing 'Heroin', at which point Moe put her foot down, firmly.

Then things started to happen so quickly that for the next six months very few of them kept their feet on the ground for a moment. Warhol had sixteen projects going on at once and he drew the Velvets into as many of them as possible, rehearsing them for the opening of his big nightclub in Queens that was going to be called Andy Warhol's Up, and upsetting as many people as he could. For example, in January he had an engagement to show his films and give a lecture at the prestigious Psychiatrists' Convention at the swank Delmonico's Hotel on Park Avenue. Instead, he unleashed on the convention his first multimedia performance. While the band and Nico played songs about drugs and S&M at ear-splitting volume in front of a screen on which some of his silent films like *Couch, Kiss* and *Blowjob* played, Gerard Malanga and Edie Sedgwick, arguably the two most sexually threatening figures in New York, danced erotically in front of the ensemble.

Meanwhile, Barbara Rubin ran from table to table shoving a movie camera and a harsh light into the psychiatrists' faces, screaming insulting questions like IS YOUR PENIS BIG ENOUGH? and DO YOU EAT HER OUT? As the flummoxed guests recoiled, she filmed their reactions. Half the audience leaped up from the tables, grabbing husbands and wives like passengers on a sinking ocean liner fighting their way to the lifeboats. The other half sat forward tentatively trying to 'understand' the performance. The event caused such an uproar it made the *New York Times* and the *Daily News* the next day. For Lou, the episode was a hilarious vindication of his childhood terror at the hands of his psychiatrist. What wasn't, in the glow of the moment, quite so obvious to Lou was the fact that the articles were about Andy and barely mentioned the band. The misdirected spotlight would be a source of frustration for years to come.

A few days later, working on a Warhol film called *A Symphony of Sound*, the band rehearsed their raucous cacophony at the Factory until puzzled cops showed up to stop the show, looking like the Three Stooges as they became part of the film. In the most telling scene of the sixty-minute film, Warhol skitters across the bottom of the screen, moving away from the policemen and grinning like Dennis the Menace.

In addition to working on *A Symphony of Sound*, the band also recorded soundtracks for two Warhol movies shot at the beginning of 1966, *Hedy* and *More Milk Yvette*.

While the Velvets were generally welcomed at the Factory, only Lou was treated like a star. Only Lou was asked to sit for a Warhol screen test (a three-minute film in which the subject is asked to sit completely still without moving a muscle staring straight into the camera, thus brutally revealing themselves by every little twitch). And even though John Cale was more attractive and charismatic and Sterling embodied the cooler-than-cool Keith Richards-style guitar hero, only Lou was treated like a sex symbol. The fragile, savvy Reed was apparently equally attractive to men and women, looking on the one hand like a pretty little girl with his curly brown hair and tentative smile, and exhibiting on the other hand an insouciant attitude to sex that presented an ambivalent challenge. Lou quickly abandoned the sweaters, casual jackets and loafers he'd worn since leaving Syracuse, and donned the Factory costume of Warhol-inspired black leather jacket, high-heeled boots and shades.

Of the Velvets, Lou was the only one who was wholeheartedly accepted by the upper echelons of the Factory hierarchy – Gerard, Billy and the Warhol superstar Ondine. Morrissey was the lone dissenter, feeling that Reed was a creep whose act was based on making people uncomfortable. For Lou, going to the Factory every day to rehearse, then going out every night with Andy and his colourful entourage was 'like landing in heaven'.

Before the Factory, Reed had created scenarios for his songs; now Warhol provided the cast and the telling details. 'Everyone was very campy,' Cale said. 'There was a lot of game playing. Lou felt at home in that environment.'

For the first time, Lou had found an institution that celebrated everything he had been rejected for and supplied him with everything he needed: intellectual and emotional sustenance, new equipment and drugs. The hard-core Factory queens favoured methedrine, to which Lou had already been turned on by Angus MacLise the previous year. This form of amphetamine radically changed his life and – so it seemed at first – solved a lot of his 'problems'.

According to the *Amphetamine Manifesto* by Harvey Cohen:

Amphetamine stimulates the central nervous system. Amphetamine is very much an overachiever's type of chemical.

Methedrine rolls back the stone from the mouth of the cave. It is the most profound of all drugs, the most unexplored and the freakiest. It can be so many things; there's always a place to go behind methedrine that you've never been before.

Methedrine is also a great aphrodisiac, giving a man an

erection that could break a plate, as well as Homeric duration in the act.

Amphetamine had two vital functions for Lou creatively. By allowing him to stay up for three to five days at a time without sleep, it altered the synapses of his brain, cutting off a lot of static that could stymie the flow of words, and gave him – particularly in writing – the energy to pursue each vision to its conclusion. One can see its effects in his great essay 'From the Bandstand', published in *Aspen* magazine, December 1966 or in songs like 'White Light/White Heat' and 'Murder Mystery'.

Being a favoured customer, Lou could buy a film canister of the powder, which he cooked up and shot, for as little as $5. He became drug buddies with the 'amphetamine glories' who gathered around Ondine at the Factory. They saw themselves as religious, heroic and immortal visionaries. They weren't, of course, and many of them, like the brillant Ondine, died sad deaths. But when they lived, they lived beyond the barriers of society. As Lou would write in the liner notes to *Metal Machine Music*, 'My weeks beat your year.'

Like Warhol, Reed was more interested in the idea of sex than in its execution. He enjoyed the voyeurism and role playing of transvestism and S&M and he had a number of sexual and platonic friendships with men and women at the factory. One of his best friends was Danny Fields, a young medical-school dropout with whom he developed a connection that would last over thirty years. 'When I first heard "Heroin" I thought it was beautiful music,' Fields recalled.

> But I was terrified of Lou. I was always trying to figure out things to say to him that would be sharp. Everybody was in love with him back then. Around 1966, he was the sexiest boy in town. I was ever so in love with Lou. Everyone was in love with him – me, Edie, Andy, everyone. I thought he was just the hottest-looking, sexiest person I ever had seen. He was a major sex object of everybody in New York in his years with the Velvet Underground.

'Lou's relationship with Danny was collegial,' explained Gerard Malanga.

They were in the same business and there was a lot of history between them. Lou and I crashed at Danny's on more than one occasion. He was living on East 20th Street between Fifth and Sixth Avenues above a coffee shop, which in those years was a very unfashionable place to live. Danny was a pioneer. He had a floor-through loft in a two-storey building. There were couches and pillows and mattresses on the floor with a few people staying there. It was basically a crash pad. Thank God for Danny. We would have been homeless. We always knew he could be relied on to put us up.

In the midst of all the ego collisions and role playing, screaming guitars and parties, Fields observed:

We all had this feeling about Lou – that he would bury us. He was much too smart to get sucked into the whirlpool. Others may have been too fragile, too beautiful to survive – but he knew what he was doing.

Gretchen Berg, who often visited the Factory to interview Warhol, noted that Reed maintained a strong position there:

I had the feeling that Mr Warhol created the atmosphere of a family around him and there was a certain amount of competition. You had the feeling that Lou was someone rather special. He was the brother who was away for many years and had to be caught when he came in. The father must now speak to Lewis who's just come in because Lewis will not speak to anyone else but father. It was exactly that feeling. No one else must speak to Lou. And then Lewis would speak to father and then leave.

   Lou was very quiet. He almost never spoke to anyone, and when addressed he would not answer. He would act as if you weren't there. I respected him. I saw that he was an artist of some kind and he had his group around him. They were always quite nice, but they always kept their distance. It was a bit snobbish. If you came up to him it was not as if he was rude exactly, but he would just look at you and take a puff of his cigarette. Lou was very much in the background, but he kept himself in the background. There was always something that was being created in the background. While everyone else was going through their thing and living and having all this attention, this in the background was going on very quietly and very steadily. He was like Paul Morrissey in a way. He had a lot of power with Andy on a one-on-one basis.

Morrissey resented the fact that Reed was given such a strong position of power at the Factory and was uptight about Lou's relationship not only with Andy but with Nico, with whom he was infatuated. 'Lou was always moody,' he thought. 'He was ill at ease as a performer, and that's what his act still is – a remote, ill-at-ease person.' Reed and Morrissey also shared a certain meanness, which led one observer to comment that Lou was 'like Paul Morrissey with a guitar'.

'There was tension between Paul and everyone,' agreed Gretchen Berg. 'I think he felt that he must not say anything about Lou Reed because he had no power over Lou. Lou Reed came in when he liked, left when he liked.'

No wonder Reed was seduced by the Factory and Warhol's offer of instant stardom, despite having to share the stage with the ultra-glamorous and charismatic Nico. No wonder he didn't complain when their first public booking that February – a week at the Cinematheque developing the multimedia concept first un-leashed at the Psychiatrists' Convention – was called Andy Warhol Uptight. It was fun to drive over to the Cinematheque every night, walk through the lobby that was full of enlarged contact sheets of fabulous pictures of the band taken in the previous weeks rehearsing at the Factory, and blow away a tiny audience of New York beatniks. He hardly minded that the band members didn't see any of the $12,000 the show earned (it was a benefit for the Cinematheque). Lou and the others received $5 per day each – providing they could wrangle the small sum from the tight-fisted Warhol, who knew how to turn everything into a game and keep everybody running around laughing so hard they hardly had time to ask questions.

Reed characterized the band's Manhattan debut at the Cinema-theque as 'a dogwhistle for all the freaks in the city'. According to one critical observer, these shows amounted to nothing more than 'ritual dances devised by dope fiends with nothing better to do'. According to another, 'Everybody hated them. The whole macho East Village group really hated the Velvets – just put-down after put-down – the hatred had nothing to do with their music; a lot of it had to do with the gay image. Also, Lou and John were really good musicians, whereas Ed Sanders and Tuli Kupferberg [of the Fugs] wouldn't have known music if it bit them on the ass.'

In March, the whole troupe went on the road, driving down to New Jersey's Rutgers University and then out to Ann Arbor, Michigan, where the act really came together, reaching its first climax. Returning to the city they all felt ready to make their big impact on New York at the opening of Andy Warhol's Up.

The format that Warhol choreographed for the first shows in January, February and March 1966 has been denounced by some other artists as a rip-off of ideas already explored and presented in 1965 by Piero Heliczer and LaMonte Young. However, forty years of rock and roll history has shown that the music and performances are not so much original works as they are, in the best instances, ingeniously appropriated and combined forms comprising a wide range of influences. Warhol was no more original than were the Beatles or Bob Dylan – but he was just as great in his inventiveness and impact. The shadow of Warhol's reputation as a rip-off artist nevertheless fell darkly over the Velvet Underground, and Lou Reed in particular, during the time they regularly played in New York City between 1966 and 1967. Its pall had a lasting and ambivalent effect upon their reputation. For years Reed would be written off by critics as a Warhol groupie and given little credit for his brilliant songs, great singing and seminal albums. Never has such an outstanding rock star, who can stand today on the same level as the other major figures of that period, been afforded so little recognition or been confronted with such hostile rejection as Lou Reed was between 1966 and 1970.

This hostility, which was a reflection of his association with Warhol, goes a long way towards accounting for the bitterness that would cloud Reed's solo career and his relationship with Warhol in the 1970s and 1980s. Although he is the only artist ever to emerge from the Factory and become an international superstar in his own right, Warhol was so omnipresent that ironically the very force that ultimately freed him from the fetters of his family would hold him prisoner of its own myth.

At the time, however, things could hardly have looked better for Lou than they did from January to April 1966. It was the single most outstanding creative period of Reed's entire career. To grasp its full significance is to understand Reed at his most enlightened. While there is no doubt that it was Warhol who engendered this creative streak, it was Reed's ability to receive the stimulus that is the paradigm of his career. Although he would never again engage so openly with such a strong artist at the zenith of his powers, Reed would, in fact, wittingly or not, base his career on finding the right person at the right moment to complete his work. From here on, the high points of his recording career are marked by the brilliant people he worked with, from John Cale through David Bowie to Bob Quine.

Lou, his penchant for large women intact, fell madly in love with Nico. For a short time he had a fantastic affair with her, which only seemed to confirm how right Andy had been all along in bringing her into the band. 'Nico's the kind of person that you meet, and you're not quite the same afterwards,' he said. 'She has an amazing mind. A close friend of mine always said that I bring out the idiocy in people, but I can also bring out something in them which is the best they've ever done. It was like that with Nico and John Cale. They were fantastic with the Velvet Underground. They helped produce a great sound. When I gave Nico a song of mine to sing, I knew she would totally understand what was being said and perform it from that standpoint.'

Nico remembered Lou as 'very soft and lovely. Not aggressive at all. You could just cuddle him like a sweet person when I first met him, and he always stayed that way. I used to make pancakes for him.' Lou, John and Sterling had all moved to Piero Heliczer's loft at 450 Grand Street at the end of 1965, but Lou often stayed at the apartment Nico was subletting on Jane Street in Greenwich Village. Not only were Lou and Nico lovers – his first love since Shelley – but she also became his muse.

When the band met Warhol they had already worked up the hard music that would appear on their first album. Now Andy and Nico replaced Cale as the catalysts who would draw forth some of Reed's greatest songs. To everybody's surprise these songs, written for Nico's voice, were radically different from anything else in their repertoire. While 'Heroin', 'Venus in Furs' and 'The Black Angel's Death Song' were born out of a raw, violent juxtaposition of instruments creating a squealing cacophony, the new songs, 'Femme Fatale', 'All Tomorrow's Parties' and 'I'll Be Your Mirror', were pretty, delicate ballads presenting sensitive emotions. 'Femme Fatale' was based on a request from Andy that Lou write a song about Edie Sedgwick because, he said, 'Don't you think she's a *femme fatale*, Lou?' 'All Tomorrow's Parties' was Warhol's favourite Velvet Underground song. Twenty years later he would tease Lou by saying he thought Nico wrote it. 'I'll Be Your Mirror', which grew out of Lou's relationship with Shelley, came together one day when Nico said, 'Oh, Lou, I'll be your mirror.'

Cale joked that the Lou–Nico affair was both 'consummated and constipated', but admitted that 'these psychological love songs gave the band a new dimension'. It was a magnificent, creative and, to all the Velvets, magic period. As they worked up the three new songs, Nico began to find a voice and place in the band.

Trouble was brewing, however, and it exploded on them without warning when the impresario Michael Myerberg, from whom they expected to receive $40,000 for a month's stand at Andy Warhol's Up in Queens, suddenly informed them that owing to what Morrissey tactfully called 'Italian influences', they were to be replaced by a group called the Young Rascals. This band, soon to have a national hit ('Good Lovin''), was led by Felix Cavalieri, who had been the most prominent musician at Syracuse during Lou's student years.

Despite losing the $40,000, the Warhol steamroller was not to be stopped. The same day Myerberg informed Morrissey that their services would not be required, Paul suggested to Andy that they rent their own place. He found a Polish meeting hall, the Dom, smack in the middle of St Marks Place in the East Village. Just like a bunch of kids in high school, he and Warhol determined to put on their own show! As a sure sign of Warhol's belief in their ultimate goal – to make a lot of money quickly like the Beatles – he put up $3,000 as a security deposit and first month's rent for April.

By now the act that had begun as Andy Warhol's Uptight had turned into the Exploding Plastic Inevitable (EPI). The medium was the same: the band, all dressed in black and wearing sunglasses, played before a backdrop of Warhol's films accompanied by Nico, stage centre, dressed from head to foot in white. But the other exciting embellishments had been developed considerably.

Gerard had a new partner, the fabulous Mary Woronov, who would shortly star as one of Warhol's *Chelsea Girls*. Between the two of them, the sexual resonance of the dances grew even more spectacular, deliberate and outré. As Gerard knelt to kiss her black leather boots, Mary whipped him. To enhance the mind-altering ambiance, Warhol had developed a light show as simple and complex as his paintings. Standing behind a battery of slide projectors in a balcony at the opposite end of the room, he was able to wash the whole ensemble, which was bathed in hot white strobe lights from either end of the stage, in patterns of different colours. A kaleidoscopic effect was created as the lights bounced in shattered shards off a spinning mirrored ball from the 1930s Warhol had found in an antique shop. The ball hung above and slightly in front of the stage, refracting the light to create an alarmingly disassociative effect, bombarding the audience as hard as the music bludgeoned it. In the coming years, Warhol's spinning mirrored ball would become a staple of discotheques across the country.

The writer Stephen Koch, whose *Stargazer* is among the best books about Warhol, described how the performance mirrored Reed and Warhol's artistic marriage.

The effort to create an exploding (more accurately, imploding) environment capable of shattering any conceivable focus on the senses was all too successful. It became virtually impossible to dance, or for that matter to do anything else but sit and be bombarded – 'stoned' as it were . . . it came home to me how the 'obliteration' of the ego was not the act of liberation it was advertised to be, but an act of complete revenge and resentment wholly entangled on the deepest levels with the knots of frustration. Liberation was turning out to be humiliation; peace was revealing itself as rage.

The media pundit of the age, Marshall McLuhan, found the EPI remarkable enough to include a double-page-spread photograph of their performance in his classic book *The Medium Is the Massage*, with the statement, '"time" has ceased, "space" has vanished. We now live in a global village . . . a simultaneous happening.' To which Lou responded in a poem, 'I'm an electric child / Of McLuhan. (Bullshit) / He's got no clue / To what's going on.'

'Andy created multimedia in New York,' Reed claimed.

Everything was affected by it. The whole complexion of the city changed, probably of the country. Nothing remained the same after that. Andy just had an incredible flair for publicity. We were all over the papers. For a while we were attracting surburban matrons . . . we used to think that if we stole just one coat, it would pay for a month's rent.

Some critics, jealous of Warhol's publicity and angered by his indulgence towards amphetamine use and homosexuality, attacked the EPI as nothing more than an untalented evening of noise and insults. Warhol, they charged, was ripping people off at six dollars a head just to make them feel uncomfortable. 'People would tell us it was violent, it was grotesque, it was perverted,' Lou recounted with amusement.

We said, 'What are you talking about? It's fun, look, all these people are having fun.' Right around the corner was Timothy Leary and some mixed-media event. He criticized us, saying, 'Those people are nothing but A-heads, speedfreaks.' So the people talking for Andy Warhol said, 'Those people take acid. How can you listen to anything those people say?' It was that insane and ridiculous. We were always astonished in the first place that people were shocked by us. Andy and us were cut from somewhat the same cloth, and we wanted to shake people up a little bit. Just so much fun. When confronted with a – quote – really straight audience, that's what we went for. We were never playing to make enemies; we were playing to make music.

On more than one occasion, however, members of the group were attacked by bottle-wielding malcontents as they left the building.

The *New York Times* mentioned the event, but placed it on the women's page. 'And it was all about Nico,' recalled Paul Morrissey. 'You can imagine how well that went down with Lou Reed.' In fact, the *Times* review was one of the kinder reactions to the performance. 'We were attacked constantly,' said Reed. 'No one ever wrote anything nice about us, or even looked at it very seriously, which was fine. But you got tired of being called obscene. It just seemed to go on and on and on and on and on. Our favourite quote was "the flowers of evil are in bloom. Someone has to stamp them out before they spread." '

The month-long spectacle was a huge hit, drawing a lot of press and celebrities, but most of them came on account of Warhol's notoriety. The names cropping up most often in the press were still not those of the Velvet Underground, but Andy, Nico and Gerard Malanga. Reed's acceptance of this demotion from front man to sideman, at least for a year and a half, showed an extraordinary faith in Warhol's judgment.

If Reed could not share the spotlight with Warhol, he began to fulfil his need for power at this point by taking more aggressive control of the band and Nico. In the interim between the February Uptight shows at the Cinematheque and the April shows at the Dom, tension fuelled the music. For one thing, Lou and Nico had broken up and developed an extremely uneasy relationship which poisoned the atmosphere both on and off stage. According to Cale, Lou was 'absolutely torn up by it all. When it fell apart, we really learned how Nico could be the mistress of the destructive one-liner.' He recalled one rehearsal at the Factory shortly thereafter: 'Nico came late, as usual. Lou said, "Hello," to her in a rather cold way, but just "Hello," or something. She simply stood there. You could see she was waiting to reply, in her own time. Ages later, out of the blue, came her first words: "I cannot make love to Jews any more."'

'Lou was absolutely magnificent, but we quarrelled a lot, he made me very sad then,' Nico explained.

Lou may have lost his lover, but when it came to the Velvet Underground, he tightened his control over every element, including Nico. 'Lou was the boss and he was very bossy,' she lamented. 'He wouldn't let me sing some of his songs because we'd split. Lou likes to manipulate women, like program them. He wanted to do that with me. He told me so. Like, computerize me.'

'He was mean to Nico,' Malanga attested. 'Lou could not stand to be around somebody who has a light equal to his or who shines more intensely.'

Reed's adoption of Warhol's aesthetic of conflict turned him, unwittingly, into a pawn of Warhol's. Warhol liked nothing better than to pit strong personalities against each other, and then sit back and watch the melee from the sidelines. He now looked on with amusement as Lou sparred not only with Morrissey and Nico, but with Cale as well. Reed's connection with Cale had turned from a partnership into a competition. Cale remembered:

To begin with, Lou and I had an almost religious fervour about what we were doing – like trying to figure ways to integrate some of LaMonte Young's and Andy Warhol's conceptions into rock and roll. It was exciting because what Lou did and what I did worked. What he put into words and what I put into music and what the band put together, the combination of everything and the mentality involved in it, was stunning.

And after four months of being near the top of Andy's list as Queen Bitch at the Factory, Lou was beginning to lose his footing. 'Warhol was a man of parts, most of them contradictory which accounts for his nickname, "Drella", composed equally of Dracula and Cinderella,' wrote Malanga. 'He was a person of much generosity and kindness – yet he could slice a person at a glance. He was possessed by the people he had gathered around him, yet he was habitually exploiting, betraying or otherwise mistreating those who were close, or seemed close to him.' Cale, who appreciated Warhol deeply but kept his distance from the camp game playing that was the emotional engine of the Factory, watched Lou compete with ironic detachment. 'Andy and Nico liked each other's company,' he explained.

As he saw it, Lou was confounded by the relationship between Warhol and Nico, who shared a European sensibility far removed from Lou's 'straight-up Jewish New York' background. Apart from being repeatedly caught out by their repartee, often even sharper than his own, Reed's basic problem in working at the Factory arose from a need to 'struggle alone, not as part of a group'.

'In some ways, if you're a protest writer like Lou is, then you need some spark of injustice to continue – and where one does not exist, then you find one,' John Cale pointed out. 'That makes one awfully close to being a malcontent. I think that's always been Lou's problem, he's always tried to find something which he can work off.'

Lou's first victim in the group became Nico, an easy target for his hatchet tongue. Everything she did in preparation for her performance irritated Lou. Then, when she finally got on stage, having held up the band lighting candles for good luck, she'd often come in at the wrong place and start singing off the beat. 'We know what we're doing, Nico!' Lou would hiss at her across the stage. Sometimes she would find her microphone unplugged or turned way down. There was a constant tension between Lou and everyone else in the band, except Moe, on one level or another, which sharpened the raw edge of the music.

One man who sat in on several shows when Cale got sick, the avant-garde violinist Henry Flynt, recalled:

Reed taught me their whole repertoire in about five minutes, because basically he just wanted me to be in the right key. At one point I got in a fight with him on stage because I was playing a very hillbilly-influenced style on the violin and that upset him very much. He wanted a very sophisticated sound, he didn't want rural references in what was supposed to be this very decadent S & M image that they were projecting.

Richard Mishkin, who kept in touch with Lou and occasionally sat in on bass at the Dom, thought Lou was making progress.

Anybody who could tolerate what he was tolerating in terms of lifestyle would have to be driven. I remember playing at the Dom in front of strobe lights, and I had never been exposed to strobe lights, and thinking, this is really hard, this is not playing music. Lou was doing what he had to do. He knew that he wasn't Paul McCartney or Elvis Presley. He was Lou Reed, and if he was going to do what he wanted to do and become a rock and roll star, he had to do it the Lou Reed way. That's what he was doing, he was creating his place in history, so to speak, by being so different.

April 1966 must stand as one of the climactic months of Lou Reed's professional life. Unfortunately, before it ended, one night when he was playing at the Dom a thief, leaving sneaker prints on his bed, broke into Lou's apartment, stealing his ostrich guitar and his entire record collection of singles that dated back to the beginning of his fascination with rock and roll when he was twelve. Moe recalled that Lou was heartbroken over the loss, but he was too busy to spend time grieving.

Reed found an outspoken vitality in performing at the Dom. 'Young people know where everything is at,' he told the writer Richard Goldstein backstage. 'Let 'em sing about going steady on the radio. Let 'em run their hootenannies. But it's in holes like this that the real stuff is being born. The universities and the radio kill everything, but around here, it's alive. The kids know that.'

'The music is all,' he wrote in an essay, 'From the Bandstand', that year. 'People should die for it. People are dying for everything else, so why not the music. It saves more lives.'

During April, while they were still playing at the Dom nightly, Warhol rented a recording studio where the band made their first album, *The Velvet Underground and Nico*, in three days for $2,500. Because he had been making records since he was fifteen, Lou seized the opportunity to act as engineer and producer. Cale, who had a limited knowledge of the recording studio, contributed significantly to the album's sound. His classical training and love of experimentation perfectly complemented Reed's songs. 'Basically, Lou would write these poppy little songs and my job was to slow them down, make them "slow 'n' sexy",' John explained. 'Everything was deeper, too. A song written in E would be played in D. Maureen used cymbals. I had a viola and Lou had his big drone guitar we called an "ostrich" guitar. It made a horrendous noise, and that's the sound on "All Tomorrow's Parties", for instance. In addition, Lou and Nico both had deep voices. All of this made the record entirely unique.'

The Reed–Cale collaboration reached a peak recording the album. Conflicts, however, quickly erupted. 'Everyone was nervous about it,' Cale recalled. 'Lou was paranoid and eventually he made everybody paranoid.' Lou didn't want Nico on the album, and she felt she didn't have enough material to sing. Then Nico kept insisting on singing 'I'll Be Your Mirror' in what Sterling described as a 'Götterdämmerung voice'.

'The whole time the album was being made,' Warhol wrote, 'nobody seemed happy with it.' Still, it was to be Reed's and Warhol's last great moment together, and Lou would never forget it. 'Andy was like an umbrella,' he recounted.

We would record something and Andy would say, 'What do you think?' We'd say, 'It's great!' and then he would say, 'Oh, it's great!' The record went out without anybody changing anything because Andy Warhol said it was OK. It was hilarious. He made it so we could do anything we wanted.

Andy made a point of trying to make sure that on our first album the language remained intact. He would say, 'Make sure you do the song with the dirty words, don't change the words just because it's a record.' That was an amazing freedom, a power, and once you've tasted that, you want it always.

chapter seven

Exit Warhol

1966–1967

[In which the EPI tours the
West Coast, Lou gets hepatitis,
*The Velvet Underground and
Nico* is released, then Lou
fires Andy.]

*Andy Warhol's studio became the equivalent to Walt Disney
studios. Lou was going to be Andy's Mickey Mouse, the
idol-hero. But originally, in the first Tugboat Mickey cartoon,
Mickey was a nasty guy. And so Lou in his Mickey Mouse
period was never able to achieve the lovable one, and had to
live underground like Tugboat Mickey.*

BILLY NAME

Warhol specialized in capturing young, as yet unformed,
eccentric, creative people on the edge of a nervous breakdown in a
painting or on film. Now he had done the same thing in music,
pulling out of Lou not only the three great songs that would
balance out the content of the first album, but pushing him so that
he played and sang like a man passing through the centre of a storm
of inner turmoil. However, there was one significant difference
between Lou Reed and anyone else who worked and played with
Warhol at the top of his game. And it was what would make Reed a
star in time and give him the duration so rare in rock and roll.
While remaining open to all of Warhol's input, and taking all the
death-defying trips he took during his season in 'hell' (one of
Reed's many descriptions of the Factory), Lou had, in fact,

retained an inner control. Essentially this was because he was there primarily as a writer. 'I watched Andy,' he explained. 'I watched Andy watching everybody. I would hear people say the most astonishing things, the craziest things, the funniest things, the saddest things. I used to write it down.' The voyeuristic medium gave him the distance of an observer and allowed him to maintain control of his own craft. It would in time allow him to escape traps and hells far worse than anything he experienced at Andy Warhol's Factory.

Andy Warhol, Paul Morrissey and even Lou Reed did not comprehend just how cutthroat and competitive the rock business was. They reached the zenith of their collaboration in April 1966 with the dual triumph of the Dom shows and the recording of the album (which would not be released until the following year) – only to have the rug pulled out from underneath them by a henchman of Dylan's manager Albert Grossman, Charlie Rothchild, who moved in on Morrissey with promises of helping them out by handling the booking end of the business. He immediately got them a May-long job at the Trip in Los Angeles. Despite the fact that the EPI was the hottest thing happening in rock and roll in New York that spring, it made sense to Reed and Warhol to go out to LA because major record companies had their headquarters there.

On 1 May, the entire EPI packed their guitars and drums, their whips and chains and their thirteen selves onto a jet plane and streaked across the continent. Brimming with enthusiasm, they were confident that the rock gods were on their side and that in Lala Land they would find an environment freaky enough to embrace their far-out sounds. After all, what could be more plastic, more California, more Hollywood, than Nico, Gerard Malanga, Andy Warhol and songs about sex, drugs and paranoia?

They were wrong. From the moment they landed at LA International, signs that they had made a disastrous mistake erupted like cockroaches out of the woodwork. Driving in from the airport, the first song they heard on the radio was a soupy ballad called 'Monday Monday' by a leading West Coast group, the Mamas and the Papas. According to Morrison, a chill ran through the group.

The truth was, everybody in the band despised the sixties West Coast sound. Nobody hated it more than Lou Reed, who proved himself a vituperative critic. 'We had vast objections to the whole San Francisco scene,' he said.

> It's just tedious, a lie and untalented. They can't play and they certainly can't write. I keep telling everybody and nobody cares. We used to be quiet, but I don't even care any more about not wanting to say negative things, 'cause somebody really should say something. Frank Zappa is the most untalented bore who ever lived. You know, people like Jefferson Airplane, Grateful Dead, all those people are just the most untalented bores that ever came up. Just look at them physically. I mean can you take Grace Slick seriously? It's a joke.

Asked what separated them apart from distance, he snapped, 'The West Coast bands were into soft drugs. We were into hard drugs.' 'Our attitude to the West Coast was one of hate and derision,' Cale concurred. 'We all hated hippies,' Morrison affirmed. 'We really despised all of the West Coast bands,' Tucker concluded.

Despite this out-and-out aggro, the EPI's engagement at the Trip got off to a big start when show-biz celebrities they hated – like John Phillips of the Mamas and Papas, Sonny and Cher – and movie stars like Ryan O'Neal showed up on opening night. Also in attandance was a host of unknowns, including a UCLA film student named Jim Morrison, who would shortly cop every inch of Malanga's act to turn himself into the Lizard King of rock and roll as the front man of the Doors. There was no question that Warhol's show had an enormous impact on the LA scene, but it was so intense it burned itself out in a record three days. Flouncing out of the club on the first night, a terrified Cher snapped that the music would replace nothing except, perhaps, suicide (a quote the Warhol people could not but relish). As soon as news spread that the Warhol gang was in town, every weirdo in LA gravitated towards them. Among them was the local sheriff, who rapidly found good reason to close down the club. His action left the thirteen musicians and workers who composed the Warhol entourage stranded in their $500-a-week residence, the Castle. According to Musicians' Union rules they had every right to collect their full fee as long as they remained in town for the duration of the booking.

Lou sat out the failed Trip engagement at the Castle, listening to the Velvets' record over and over again, and socializing with Gerard Malanga. Reed and Malanga filled the time in LA taking drugs and hanging out in the clubs. 'Lou was the first person, and the last, to turn me on to Placidyls,' recalled Gerard.

He said, 'Gerard, I want to turn you on to something,' and then we went out on the town that night. It was a tranquillizer. It was legal and you could buy it over the counter. Now you've got to get it by prescription. My system just couldn't take experimenting with these drugs. Placidyls is a funny name for a drug because it comes from the word placid or tranquil, and it just put me in a state that made me feel clumsily numb. But Lou obviously relished it.

One night, Gerard ran into two women he had met at the Trip and invited Lou to join in.

Lou and I were involved with these two babes, Linda Lawrence [the mother of Brian Jones's child, she would go on to marry Donovan] and Cathy Cozzi. They had beautiful bodies and blonde hair. Our initial situation took place in a motel room, and then continued on at the Castle. And we had a wild sex scene in the motel room. The four of us were taking a shower in the motel and I peed down Lou's leg.

Relations between Reed and Warhol soured during this frozen time in the spooky environs of the Castle. Reed began to be persuaded by the sharks circling the wounded enterprise that Andy was not, perhaps, the most focused of rock managers. And it was true. The rock business was growing rapidly. Millions of dollars were at stake. Andy and Paul, for all their perspicacity, simply didn't seem to know how to get down in the dirt with the real rock-and-roll swine and root around to suck up the cash. Not only did Andy lack the temperament for this unpleasant job, he was overextended. He was the most famous pop artist and underground filmmaker in the world, and he had an enormous number of personal and financial problems to deal with on a daily basis.

Lou, on the other hand, was devoting all his attention to the Velvet Underground. He was the only member of the group who saw what wasn't going on, with the Velvets' album. 'Lou had worked for his father's accounting firm, so he had a strong background in the business side of things and his feet never left the ground,' noted Cale. 'Mine definitely did.'

At first, the band's immediate future did not look as disastrous as it would turn out to be. After having their album turned down by every rock mogul they could contact in New York, in LA they finally encountered the record producer Tom Wilson, who had done wonders for the folk-rock sound of Bob Dylan and Simon and Garfunkel. Wilson realized that the quality of the Velvet Underground music was on a par with that of his other superstar clients. Explaining that he was about to move from Columbia to head an experimental label at MGM, Verve Records, he guaranteed them a deal if they would be patient. Warhol, Morrissey and the band were relieved to have encountered such a receptive and established producer.

Wilson suggested the best way to make the album more commercial would be by adding more songs by Nico, and releasing one of them as a single. Lou complied, writing the relatively commercial 'Sunday Morning'. 'Andy said, "Why don't you just make it a song about paranoia?"' Lou explained. 'I thought that was great so I came up with, "Watch out, the world's behind you, there's always someone watching you," which I feel is the ultimate paranoid statement in that the world even cares enough to watch you.'

'"Surn-day Mourning" sounded all right for Nico because she brought something weird to everything,' Morrissey recounted. 'Tom said OK, and we went into a studio paid for by MGM-Verve. Somehow, at the last minute, Lou didn't let her sing it.'

Lou then proceeded to sing the song in a voice that was so full of womanly qualities that you paused on first hearing it, wondering just who the hell *was* singing. Reed's ability to sound like different people could be spooky.

The terms of the Velvet Underground's contract with Warhol specified that all monies earned by them would be paid to Warvel (the corporation Warhol and Morrissey had created specifically for that purpose). Warhol and Morrissey were to keep 25 per cent and pass the rest on to the band. When it came time to sign the record contract, however, Lou refused to accept its terms unless it was revised to ensure that all monies went first to the Velvets, who would then pass on 25 per cent to Warhol and Morrissey. Reed was acting on his own in a show of remarkable determination and increasing leadership of the band, but he was also taking advice from several people who wanted to take over management of the VU.

Warhol grudgingly agreed to the demand over Morrissey's protestations. The contract was amended and the record deal signed. But Lou's victory over Warhol was short-sighted. The contract failed to stipulate the percentage of royalties the band would receive. As a result it would be many years before anybody in the band would receive any royalties from their first album. Warhol never received a penny from the sales of *The Velvet Underground and Nico*, though it sold steadily around the world for the twenty years between the time of its release and his death.

Even though they all believed that the album was going to be a great success and big moneymaker, the disagreement over the contract stripped the lustre off Andy's artistic love affair with Lou. 'I think at a certain point Andy didn't take Lou as seriously as Lou wanted Andy to take him,' Gerard Malanga observed.

> Because when you do something against Andy, Andy would cut you off. So that incident, in a sense, was a real cut-off point. I think Andy distanced himself from Lou, he'd be gracious to Lou in his presence or at a party or if Lou came to the Factory. But Andy never really involved Lou in anything that he was doing after that in any kind of direct way. There were no portraits of Lou, there was no type of that stellar involvement that Andy had.

*

The final debacle of the West Coast trip came in San Francisco. Begged by the rock impresario Bill Graham to play his Fillmore Ballroom, the EPI, who had by then been stranded in LA for three weeks, were loath to explore the West Coast further. Then, when they finally agreed, arriving in San Francisco on 26 May for a two-night stand with the Mothers of Invention and the early Jefferson Airplane, they were met with a hostility far more vicious than anything LA had thrown at them.

Before they even set foot on stage, the band had provoked the considerable ire of Graham. Perturbed by Morrissey's sarcastic air and bald-faced recommendation that all rock musicians take heroin, he was incensed by the insular aura of the Warhol entourage, who travelled everywhere by limousine, rejecting what they saw as the phony egalitarianism of hippy culture. Seconds before they went on stage Graham screamed, 'I hope you motherfuckers bomb!'

Ralph Gleason, who wrote a review of the show for the *San Francisco Chronicle*, was particularly scathing in his remarks. 'Gleason hated us,' said Sterling. 'He was our number-one enemy on the West Coast. When we first played San Francisco, he said it was an East Coast poison intended to corrupt, defile and destroy their pure innocence.'

Gleason's review went on in similar fashion:

Warhol's Exploding Plastic Inevitable Show was nothing more than a bad condensation of all the bum trips of the Trips Festival. Few people danced (the music was something of a dud, the Velvet Underground being a very dull group). It was all very campy and very Greenwich Village sick. If this is what America's waiting for, we are going to die of boredom because this is a celebration of the silliness of café society, way out in left field instead of far out, and joyless.

In their final set on the second night, when the band leaned their instruments up against their amplifiers and left the stage so that a barrage of sonic feedback blasted the audience to kingdom come, Graham finally pulled the plug.

To make matters worse, the San Francisco poet and playwright

Michael McClure refused to sign a release allowing Warhol to show a film he had made of McClure's play *The Beard*; Gerard was arrested in a restaurant for carrying his whip, labelled an offensive weapon, and spent a nervous night in jail; and Lou shot up a drug that seized up all his joints. He was diagnosed (incorrectly) as having a terminal case of lupus.

A shattered EPI, who had only four weeks earlier left New York in triumph, limped back across the continent separately, leaving behind one member, the lighting man Danny Williams, who would subsequently commit suicide. Back in New York, Lou checked into Beth Israel Hospital with a serious case of, as it turned out, hepatitis. Every time Lou got hepatitis he gave friends the impression his parents were waiting to seize him and lock him up. Sterling was always afraid of Lou's parents. Lou seemed to believe there was this constant threat of them seizing him and having him thrown in a mental hospital. Nico departed to Ibiza, her favourite island off the coast of Spain. The rest of the band rehearsed for a June booking in Chicago. Warhol, disappointed by the lack of money he had expected from his five-month investment in the group, returned to his first love, making films.

While he was laid up in the hospital undergoing a six-week course of treatment, Lou became paranoid about losing control of the group. Not only was he excluded from the one-week stint in Chicago, but the band covered his absence with relative ease. Angus MacLise was brought back in as drummer; Maureen switched to bass. According to Sterling, Angus realized what a mistake he had made in quitting the group and hoped to be allowed back in. Lou, however, still angry about MacLise's defection, was adamant about punishing Angus and maintaining his loyalty to Moe.

When Warhol, Malanga and MacLise stopped by Beth Israel Hospital to inform Reed of the alterations in the line-up, Gerard could see that he was disturbed. The reappearance of MacLise once again turned the power axis of the Velvet Underground against him. 'Lou was sitting on the edge of his bed in a bathrobe,' recalled Malanga.

Lou was yellow in the face and looked sickly – he always looked sickly. Sitting at the end of the bed having this discussion about what was happening with the Chicago gig. And I remember distinctly Lou turning to Angus and saying, 'Just remember, this is only temporary.' Like, 'don't think you're coming back into the group.' There was a real tug of war between Lou and John – not so much with John, but with Angus, which caused Angus to leave. Lou had a very specific agenda, and Angus was the antithesis of that agenda. Angus was too idealistic for Lou. Lou wanted the group to be rock and roll, and there was a real confrontation there.

The success of the band's Chicago dates at Poor Richard's provided a revealing glimpse into Reed's usually well-hidden insecurity. Despite the absence of its stellar members Nico, Warhol and Reed, the band pulled off such a successful stand they were held over for an extra week. Back in the hospital, everyone fed Lou's paranoia with catty gossip. Andy was calling Lou and saying, 'Oh, they got great reviews. Gee, it seems OK without you. Everyone's happy.' They were just trying to make Lou uptight, and he worked himself to a boil imagining what was going on without him.

As Lou reflected on his future, another blow struck from his past. In July Delmore Schwartz, to whom the Velvet Underground had dedicated 'European Son' on their first album, had a heart attack and died in New York at the age of fifty-three. Gerard called up Lou and told him that Delmore had died, suggesting that they go to the wake. Lou, who had been told by his doctors that he wouldn't be able to leave the hospital for three weeks, leaped out of bed, donned a pair of black jeans, black boots, a black T-shirt and a black jacket and headed off. 'We were very informal,' said Gerard. 'Lou was in jeans and a dungaree jacket. He just showed up like a slob. Lou didn't have much of a sense of sartorial splendour about him. I think Lou relished the idea of bad taste. Lou was into anything that had a disguise to it.' Later, Lou noted, 'I checked myself out of the hospital to go to Delmore's funeral and never went back.'

Malanga took Reed to the open-casket wake held at Sigmond

Schwartz Funeral Home, 152 Second Avenue. They arrived in the middle of the eulogy. After a number of readings, the assembly rose and filed past the body. The effects of alcoholism and drug addiction were evident on Schwartz's ravaged, puffy face. 'We went up to the coffin together,' Gerard remembered. 'Lou didn't react. He was silent and withdrawn. Outside afterward a former classmate of Lou's grabbed him and said, "Why don't you come to the burial?"'

In one of his more telling descriptions of the emotional lives of his mentors as they mirrored his, Lou said, 'Delmore Schwartz was the unhappiest man who I ever met in my life, and the smartest – till I met Andy Warhol.'

> He didn't use curse words until he was thirty. His mother wouldn't allow him. His worst fear was realized when they put him in a plot next to her. I'm just delighted I got to know him. It would have been tragic not to have met him. But things have occurred where Delmore's words float right across. Very few people do it to you. He was one.

In the summer of 1966 Lou was supposed to write the theme song for Warhol's new film *Chelsea Girls*; Nico was going to sing it. Yet he failed to deliver. For a man who wrote songs as regularly as he ate breakfast (he had, after all, trained at Pickwick, and preferred to write on assignment), his passive-aggressive act signalled a negation of his collaboration with the twin devils of Warhol and Nico. Lou saw here a dramatic point of departure.

The fact was that he simply didn't want Nico to sing the song. If he could have sung it himself you can be sure that he would have written it. But then Lou was not in the film, despite the fact that he and John eventually recorded part of its soundtrack.

Other factors that combined to create the split between Lou and Andy were everywhere. Morrissey, whose animosity towards Reed had not diminished, pushed Warhol towards supporting Nico's career, arguing that she was a more manageable and marketable star than the cantankerous, uncharismatic Lou.

When Morrissey arranged for Nico to sing solo in a small bar called Stanley's, underneath the Dom, Reed fumed with spite.

When Paul asked the band to provide a backup acoustic guitar player, he slammed into Reed's wall of resentment. 'Lou didn't want to do it,' said Morrissey. 'Lou said, "It's not good for the group's image." I replied, "This is awful. She needs work, she has some songs. Couldn't one of you help her?" Then Lou said, "We'll put it on tape."'

Lou most likely resented Nico for finding such a good performance space at a time when the band had just lost its own. Upon returning from California, the EPI had discovered that Bob Dylan's manager had stolen their idea for a nightclub and taken over the Dom, renaming it the Balloon Farm. It was a terrible blow with severe, lasting consequences. Not only was potentially significant revenue lost, but it would be years before the Velvets would find as good a venue in the city in which to perform. In fact, out of sheer frustration and paranoia, the band would soon boycott New York shows altogether.

Meanwhile, Lou, John, Sterling and Moe were working on their next album, *White Light/White Heat*, on which there were no songs for Nico. Hitting a creative roll, they made July and August highly productive months. Sterling, John and Lou moved into a building on West Third Street which they dubbed 'Sister Ray House', and devoted their time to working on the album. Unlike most rock stars who do a lot of writing on the road, Lou and John created their best songs in New York, when living either together or a few blocks from each other. It was while they were living in the same place that 'Sister Ray', for example, was worked up over an extended period of time. They reverted to their Ludlow Street routine, playing music all day together and going out at night. Their favourite haunt was the club that had become Warhol's social headquarters, Max's Kansas City, on Park Avenue South just above 17th Street.

Run by Mickey Ruskin, a restaurateur and club owner who catered specifically to the art world, Max's was divided into two sections. One was a standard bar-restaurant. The bar ran down the left-hand wall of the rectangular room, the rest of which was occupied by tables and chairs. The other was a smaller, square back room which was guarded, usually by Ruskin himself, and into which only the hip elite were allowed. The room was lit by a red light sculpture by Dan Flavin in one corner and furnished with a series of booths along the left- and right-hand walls. Its occupants encompassed visiting Hollywood aristocracy like Roger Vadim and his wife Jane Fonda, rock stars like the Rolling Stones, writers, top-of-the-line groupies, drug dealers and drag queens. The supercharged, Felliniesque atmosphere was dominated by the arrival, presence and departure of Warhol, who made a habit of going there every night between midnight and 2 a.m.

The artistic netherworld of Max's back room offered the perfect setting for Lou Reed's anthropological reports on the hell and heaven of the thriving underground. Girls like the up-and-coming Warhol starlet Andrea Feldman might leap up on a table and entertain the crowd with a song and a strip show while Eric Emerson, another Factory star, might piss into a glass and bolt down his bodily fluid claiming that it tasted good. Meanwhile, the half of the room held by the Warhol elite would be on speed while the other half, representing the anti-Warhol faction, would be on acid or other hallucinogenics. Many an affair was started, carried out and finished at Max's – often in the phone booths. The free-for-all atmosphere often created eruptions that would in time sound the death knell of the sixties. It was here that one could encounter Warhol's would-be assassin, Valerie Solanas, slumped at a corner table, or overhear the poet Gregory Corso snarling at Warhol, 'You and your faggots and rich women and Velvet Undergrounds, I don't understand!' only to be shushed into silence by the bardic presence of Allen Ginsberg. It really was an extension of the Factory. At Max's Lou was afforded all the attention due a star. Here he could be seen with his arm wrapped around a girl or a boy, or somebody of undetermined gender. Everybody was dressed to kill, and either blissfully content or raging with paranoia, lust, greed, hatred and contempt. The room vibrated with all the elements of the sixties as they were in New York.

*

In the autumn of 1966, Lou suffered a series of disappointments which brought him back to that place of despair he sank into when he felt powerless. The biggest disappointment was the non-appearance of *The Velvet Underground and Nico*. While Verve brought out the Mothers of Invention's first album, *Freak Out*, the Velvets' album appeared to be on eternal hold. The band was being told that MGM-Verve was having difficulties in reproducing Warhol's cover illustration of a banana that actually peeled, and that the company had temporarily mislaid one of the master tapes. Meanwhile, the Velvets found their extraordinary EPI performances transformed into a carnival freak show which hardly supported itself and which Warhol rarely had time to even attend. 'It wasn't very good when Andy started losing interest in the whole project,' said Cale.

> We were touring round the country and then he just wasn't interested any more, and there was a lot of backbiting going on in the band. For one thing, travelling with thirteen people and a light show and everything is a kind of mania if you don't get enough money. And the only reason we got a lot of money, probably, while we toured was because Andy was with us.
>
> We became a road band, which is why Andy dropped out of the picture. He'd often be too busy to come out and see us – and when that happened, a lot of people stopped being into us. Promoters actually wouldn't book us unless they were assured of Andy's presence, so we got people like Gerard Malanga to pretend to be Andy. I think we even got women to pretend to be Andy!

As they changed from an art-rock band into a touring band, Lou grew weary of the mundane experiences that greet all such entertainers.

In October and November the EPI did a short tour of the Midwest, playing in venues that sometimes paid less than $1,000 a night. A pall of bad humour hung over the whole event. Paul, acting as road manager, had to slog his way through an unglamorous Greyhound bus tour. To make matters worse, relations among members of the troupe soured. Nico was now close with Cale. The fact that Nico had emerged as the new superstar of *Chelsea Girls*, and become far more famous than both Reed and Cale, also grated on Lou's nerves. He took to attacking her in public. 'He had a reputation for being mean to women, but he was always very nice to me,' recalled Hope Ruff, a close friend of Danny Fields's.

> He was wild to Nico. I remember Lou talking to Nico like she was a pile of trash. I remember him yelling at her – she really couldn't sing and she couldn't play. At the Balloon Farm or in the back room at Max's, she'd say something stupid and he'd jump on her because he's very smart and he hated stupid. Put it this way, he was caustic with anybody who was weaker than he was. I don't think you just had to be female. I mean, there were dumb guys around too – dumb rock stars. Lou had a sharp mouth as far as they were concerned because he wasn't mainstream famous and he was very talented and way smarter and that's the way it goes. So I think if he sensed that someone was weak, as a lot of us did those days, he would sweep in for the kill because it was funny.

That summer Lou had had a brief affair with one of Gerard's girlfriends, creating more unspoken tension. Meanwhile, the continued delay in the release of the album aggravated everyone. On top of this, Lou ran into random violence more often than seemed coincidental. Driving downtown in a cab with Malanga he was in an accident that left him with cuts and bruises. Walking into Max's with Warhol he was hit by a table which some drunken freak heaved at Andy, screaming obscenities. Warhol was pushing everybody as close to the edge as he possibly could. Violence had begun to erupt around him constantly. Lou was close to the flames.

As the watershed year of 1966 – the year of Dylan's *Blonde on Blonde*, of the Stones' *Aftermath* and of the Beatles' *Revolver* – neared its end, it looked as if a great moment had been lost, perhaps for ever. Then, when Verve belatedly released two singles, 'All Tomorrow's Parties' / 'I'll Be Your Mirror' and 'Sunday Morning' / 'Femme Fatale', the company failed to give them the necessary promotion. 'Sunday Morning' stalled at number 103 on the Cashbox chart. It was a failure, despite its merits, and Lou had to live with that.

The poorly timed and little publicized release of *The Velvet Underground and Nico* finally came in March 1967. So little enthusiasm was left from the original Warhol collaboration, begun fifteen months earlier, that there were no celebrations. In fact, the event became fodder for even more negativity. First of all, the famous cover – consisting of a white field graced by a life-size bright yellow banana by Warhol, prominently signed with his trademark rubber-stamp signature in the bottom right-hand corner – did little to publicize the band. Warhol was also credited as producer on the spine of its gatefold sleeve. Those lucky enough to catch a glimpse of the poorly distributed record in stores were confused about its contents. Had Warhol embarked on a recording career? 'We thought it would seem better with his name on it,' Reed later explained. 'We were all having fun and didn't care about credits, and things like that. "Produced by Andy Warhol." It was like being a soup can.'

The cover contributed to the popular misapprehension that the Velvet Underground was Warhol's band, and therefore a put-on. 'And if you really got into the sticks, they thought Andy Warhol was the lead guitar player,' Lou would joke.

To top it all off, the album's appearance sparked the kind of critical backlash Andy had become used to, but that was new to Lou. The songs' controversial subject matter of drug use, sadomasochism and society's less savoury side drew universal criticism. The print media refused to run ads for the record, apart from Grove Press's *Evergreen Review*. For the same reason, the majority of radio stations refused to play it. One DJ who played it slammed the album, snapping, 'That was the Velvet Underground, a very New York sound. Let's hope it stays there.' The scattered reviews it received were dismissive, uninterested or condemning. As a result, MGM-Verve shrank from providing publicity and cut their already scant marketing budget.

The album's negative reception was among the worst

experiences of Lou's life. Although as a person who specialized in making people feel uncomfortable he may have wanted the album to elicit hostility, he asserted otherwise. 'The Velvet Underground very consciously set out to put themes common to movies, plays and novels into pop-song format,' he stated.

I thought we were doing something ambitious and I was taken aback that people were offended by it and thought I was causing some kids to become drug addicts. What happened to freedom of expression? At the worst, we were like the antedated realists. At the best, we just hit a little more home than some things.

In May, Warhol tried to recreate the heady nights at the Dom by renting a new hall, the Gymnasium, located on Manhattan's Upper East Side. But with attendance low, it became clear that the EPI's initial magic was gone. Furthermore, the fact that EPI's shock value had diminished became evident when people started to focus on the music, criticizing the band's unorthodox playing. The DJ Terry Noel, who had a considerable influence on the club circuit, vividly recalled the Gymnasium shows.

We went because it was a big deal and people were talking about the Velvets. Because of Andy. Normally I never went to any Andy Warhol things, but I was interested in new things and this was a new thing going on and it was hot. We all went there, and *oh, my God!* None of them can play instruments. They're all off key. It wasn't like today, today they're all off key because they mean to be – it was so bad I couldn't believe it. Nobody could believe it.

They had a light show, but it was unbelievably primitive. We're talking a few light bulbs on the side of the stage that went off and on. There was nothing. Andy sat in the back in all black leather from head to toe. Once was all I could handle, because it was horrible, I couldn't believe how horrible it was. The music was unbelievably bad. Everyone thought it was a joke. Andy thought it was a joke. Andy was throwing it in the face of everybody – bad books, bad art, bad music, bad everything. And the badder the better. And not in the sense of bad today – down dirty and good – but bad in the old-fashioned sense of the word: bad. It was bad.

Recognizing yet another failure on the growing list, The Velvets decided they had had enough of the EPI.

When the album started to make some headway on the charts – despite bad reviews – a maverick Warhol superstar, Eric Emerson, sued MGM for putting his picture on the back cover without getting a release. Rather than paying him off or getting Warhol to shut him up, the company withdrew the album from the stores for six weeks while they had Emerson's face airbrushed off the cover. Embittered by the lack of support from both MGM-Verve and Warhol, who, like the record company, hadn't lifted a finger to dissuade Emerson from his legal action, Lou flicked his switchblade tongue. If he wasn't attacking Frank Zappa in public, he was having a go at the Beatles. Years later he recalled his initial reaction to *Sgt Pepper*, which was released that summer:

> Let me tell you, it didn't have any effect on me. I don't even own it. I thought it had some of the worst songs I've ever heard in my life on it. 'Mr Kite' – absolutely unbearable. I didn't like it then, and I don't like it now. I don't know how people can even think of it seriously when you compare it to, like, the Velvet Underground's first album. No comparison. I think that, perhaps, if people listen to it in retrospect now, they might find it a little more ridiculous, the way I did then. It was like gooey pap. On top of that it was cute.

Perhaps the worst thing that happened to Lou as a result of the banana album was the extent to which he was compared to Bob Dylan. 'Bob Dylan did more to make Lou miserable,' explained Sterling.

> Early critics of the Velvet Underground always compared Lou to Bob Dylan – eccentric phrasing. When I first met Lou he liked to play guitar and harmonica together. He liked to play Jimmy Reed harmonica, and he was very good. But he stopped because of the Dylan comparison. He wouldn't do it even on songs that cried out for it – you should hear 'Waiting for My Man' with harmonica. Lou always defended Dylan – but I said I hated him. He was always chasing an audience. I remember Lou's quote on Bob, 'Dylan gets on my nerves. If you were at a party with him I think you'd tell him to shut up.'

Asked, 'What's so great about rock and roll?' Lou replied, 'Because it's up front, and nothing more than what it's supposed to be. Until you hit Dylan, which was a really unfortunate period, it doesn't get didactic. That's why I really like teenybop a lot – "ooh, ooh, sugar, sugar!"' For the next twenty years Lou would have to live with the fact that Dylan completely overshadowed him although they were creative equals.

In retrospect, Robert Palmer, having studied both Reed's and Dylan's careers for twenty-five years, had this to say:

Of course everyone in the Velvet Underground was always dissing Dylan. They thought Dylan was absurd, and a lot of Dylan during that period was absurd. The thing about Dylan as a songwriter to me is he went through his folk thing, and then he started writing songs, but it was more like he was doing the drugs and letting it come through. Sitting there jotting it down as fast as he could. Certainly he didn't have an editing process for all that. Whereas Lou may ramble in his guitar solos, but not in his lyrics. There's a certain purity of vision there. Dylan's done so much stuff, obviously if you add it all up it's very important, but there are weaknesses in the Dylan thing. Like, everybody is trying to find meaning in this stuff – there isn't any meaning in this stuff. I love *Highway 61 Revisited, Blonde on Blonde*. But to me, personally, none of it holds a candle to the first VU album.

I often wondered how much of his vocal resemblance to Lou is influence and how much is cultural background. And it's a dicey area. Because with black people we have no problem at all saying, This guy sounds like he's from Mississippi. But once you get to Lou and Bob Dylan, you say, Well, these guys sound like middle-class Jewish college . . . and people would go Wha? Dylan's vocal style showed how to sing rock and roll without being able to sing, quote unquote. And if you've got that kind of voice and that kind of cultural background it's inescapable.

Lou decided that in response to his album's rejection in New York, the band should no longer play in the city but instead tour the sticks. Indeed, they did not play NY publicly again until 1970. 'The New York radio scene is so awful,' he snapped. 'A record won't be played unless it's already number seven all over. All over has phenomenal records no one in NY gets to hear. There's great music in the hills.' Thus, totally unappreciative teenagers at, for example, Le Cave on Euclid Avenue in Cleveland were able to see them. The writer Glenn O'Brien, then a student in Ohio, recalled the first time he ever saw them just after the release of *The Velvet Underground and Nico*:

> That spring the Velvet Underground were on tour and they were coming to this club, Le Cave, which I went to all the time to see people like Caroline Hester or Ian and Sylvia. It was a Saturday night and the club was full. They came out one at a time. John came out first and he looked so fucking weird. He had this really long hair and this diamond rhinestone collar which you'd never seen anything like. And then Moe came out and you couldn't tell what sex she was. The first song took about twenty minutes and Lou was the last one to come out. He just looked amazing. His neck looked so muscular and he had this weird kind of Roman haircut. It was hip to have long hair then, but he had pretty short hair and these amazing sunglasses and a hollow-bodied Gibson guitar. We were all sitting there thinking, 'These are really junkies!'

In fact, by this time the Velvets, at a performing peak, were an astonishing act to see live. The audiences who managed to discover the band experienced something they had never before witnessed in another rock band. Togged out in mean-looking black outfits, the Velvets ground out a wailing symphony of invention and power while standing rigidly stock still. As Moe explained:

> We were never a moving-type group. Sterling was like a ridgepole. He didn't budge. Lou would move a little. He never danced like Mick Jagger, or moved that much, but if he was playing something, he'd get a little more movement than Sterling. In fact, we were probably at first, extremely sinister-looking. We all, through no mutual decision, always wore black. Maybe we were all in bad periods of our lives, or something. And sunglasses. I always wore sunglasses, and so did everybody else. I'm sure everybody thinks that was our scheme, so we'd look eerie and sinister. But that's just the way we were anyway.

Several discerning critics and musicians, particularly in

England, recognized the importance of the Velvets' music, not least among them the lead singer of the Rolling Stones, Mick Jagger, who was later quoted as saying:

> 'Ere, but listen, I know who started all that! Lou Reed. Lou Reed started everything about that style of music, the whole sound and the way you play it. I mean, even we've been influenced by the Velvet Underground. I'll tell you exactly what we pinched from him, too. You know 'Stray Cat Blues'? [On *Beggars Banquet*, 1968.] The whole sound and the way it's played, we pinched from the very first Velvet Underground album. You know the sound on 'Heroin'. Honest to God, we did.

Although by now the Velvet Underground had put some distance between themselves and Andy Warhol, they remained open to the possibility of continuing the arrangement if Warhol would only turn his attention once again in their direction. However, in the aftermath of the album's commercial failure, raw nerves in the relationship grated. One point of contention between Warhol and the Velvet Underground had been his refusal to take them to Europe despite numerous offers from European promoters to set up tours. Among other offers, the Italian director Antonioni wanted to film them for a nightclub sequence in his famous movie *Blow-Up*, and Barbara Rubin wanted to put them on at the Royal Albert Hall in London. At the end of May when Warhol took an entourage with him to the Cannes Film Festival in France to show *Chelsea Girls*, he excluded the Velvets. Not only did he choose to leave them home but, in a move typical of the perverse way in which he often operated, he included among his entourage the renegade Eric Emerson, who had caused them so much trouble only a month earlier.

With Warhol away for a month, along with the majority of the prominent people from the Factory, Lou was left with some time to start seriously looking for a new manager. Clearly, the Velvet Underground needed fresh, professional business help. There were an increasing number of managers on the expanding rock scene with the resources to make things happen. A number of them had approached Reed soon after he and the Velvets achieved their initial success at the Dom, whispering in his ear that he could be making more money. One of these go-getters was a young Bostonian by the name of Steve Sesnick, who had part ownership of a popular club in that city called the Boston Tea Party. Sesnick had known Warhol and had been involved in discussions about Andy's multimedia performance ideas. He was well connected and friendly with Brian Epstein's lawyer Nat Weiss in New York. Sesnick had been watching the progress of the Velvets in New York with great interest. Unlike Warhol, who was unresponsive to Reed's questions on business matters, Sesnick made himself available to explain the machinations of the music business. He virtually promised to deliver the Velvets success on a silver platter.

When Warhol returned, Lou got a minor, but symbolic, opportunity for retaliation. The night he got back from Europe, Warhol took Nico to Boston so she could join the VU on stage during a concert at the Boston Tea Party. In typical Warhol fashion, the two arrived late. Surprising both Andy and Nico, Lou refused to let her on stage. Nico blamed Lou's enlarged ego for the incident. 'Everybody wanted to be the star,' she said. 'Of course Lou always was. But the newspapers came to me all the time. That's how I got fired – he couldn't take that any more. He fired me.' Reed's refusal to let Nico come on stage could have been excused by the fact that the band had only two more songs to go and they weren't songs that she could sing. But Andy did not see it that way and took Lou's action badly.

These incidents prompted a meeting between Warhol and Reed. Warhol wanted to decide what kind of financial and time commitment to make to the EPI, if any at all. He had many plans in the works, most of which centred on making films. He also had a number of art shows coming up. Andy said to Lou, 'Look, you have to make a decision, do you want to continue presenting your music in art museums and at colleges – those are the only venues we can present to you. Don't you think that you should be moving into the Fillmores and the rock theatres of America?' Billy Name, who was at the meeting, recalled:

Andy said this to everybody who worked with him: 'You have to start developing your own career and not just be dependent on what's going on here.' He had no problem with it because Andy was an artist. Lou was trying to get into the straight music scene and not be the puppet of an artist. So in a sense it was good. He wanted to have a real manager in the music business. There were no problems about leaving Andy.

However, as Lou remembered it, when he told Warhol, without consulting Cale, that he judged it best they move on, or, as Lou later said, fired him, Warhol 'was furious. I'd never seen Andy angry, but I did that day. He was really mad. He turned bright red and called me a rat. That was the worst thing he could think of. This was like leaving the nest.'

Lou was shaken by Andy's uncharacteristic display of emotion. The extraordinary thing, and one of the examples of Andy's generosity, was the fact that he let Lou out of the contract with no argument. Nonetheless, he still presumed that Lou would honour the arrangement that they had made in California, namely, that he would receive 25 per cent of all earnings from the Velvet Underground's music created under his management. The record had been produced under his management, and Andy even put up some of his own money to pay for the production of it and contributed the artwork. He really wanted the Velvet Underground to be successful, so he let them go. Asked to explain this uncharacteristic financial laxity years later, Warhol replied:

I don't know. I liked them so much, we might have had a contract but it didn't matter . . . they just decided to find some other manager. Well, it was just too hard going around. It was fun to go around for a few months. And then we could have gotten another nightclub, and it would have meant staying up until seven every morning and it was just too hard to worry about that.

chapter eight   *Exit Cale*

1967–1968

[In which Lou replaces Warhol
with Steve Sesnick, the band
records and releases *White
Light/White Heat*, tours the US,
and then Lou fires John Cale.]

*The relationship between John and Lou was symbiotic. They
loved each other, but they also hated each other.*

LYNNE TILLMAN

By the spring of 1967, Reed's growing hunger for control
threatened to destroy the Velvet Underground. Heading increasingly opposing camps were Lou, who counted on Moe's
support, and John, who looked to Sterling as his ally. Reed
wielded enough power to fire Warhol and replace him with his
own man, Steve Sesnick. Sesnick, with his allegiance to Reed,
swayed the balance of power even more resolutely against Cale.
John meanwhile, admitting that Lou had more experience in
business matters, allowed Reed this liberty in return for a stonger
position as musical arranger. Unfortunately, though, once Lou
gained managerial control there was no stopping him from trying
to usurp absolute control.

In the summer of 1967, despite these behind-the-scenes
manoeuvres, the band was charged with the enthusiasn of a fresh
start. Instead of dwelling on the poor response to *The Velvet
Underground and Nico*, and the possibly adverse effects of
breaking with Warhol, everyone had great expectations for Steve
Sesnick and the new material they were working up for a second

Lewis Reed, 17, 1959. 'I don't have a personality.'

Creedmore State Mental hospital. *(Victor Bockris)*

Above: Reed playing in one of his highschool bands, the C.H.D. or, backwards, Dry Hump Club.

Left: The house in Brooklyn where Lou was born. *(Victor Bockris)*

Below: Reed playing in his Syracuse college band, L.A. and The Eldorados, with (left) Richard Mishkin. *(Archives Malanga)*

Bottom: Where Lou spent his troubled teen years in Freeport. *(Victor Bockris)*

ilm frame enlargement from *Screen Tests* by Gerald Malanga and Andy Warhol. *(Archives Malanga)*

The E.P.I. core group in 1966 at The Castle, Los Angeles. From left to right: Andy Warhol, Nico, Danny Williams, Sterling Morrison, Mary Woronov, Paul Morrissey, Lou Reed, John Cale. In front: Maureen 'Moe' Tucker. Kneeling: Gerald Malanga. *(Archives Malanga)*

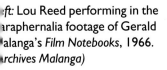

ɔu at Loaded sessions, 1970. *(Jim ummins/Star File)*

ft: Lou Reed performing in the araphernalia footage of Gerald ʾalanga's *Film Notebooks*, 1966. *rchives Malanga)*

Mickey Ruskin visiting Lou Reed and Barbara Falk prior to Lou's concert at the Music Inn, Lennox, in the Massachusetts Berkshires where Mickey maintained a country home. Summer, 1973. *(Gerald Malanga)*

Bettye and Lou in Florida 1973.
(Barbara Wilkinson)

performing in New York, December 1973. *(Chuck Pulin)*

Lou with Barbara Hodes in New York, 1974. *(Bob Gruen)*

Danny Fields with Rachel and Lou in New York, 1976. *(Bob Gruen)*

album. In turn, Sesnick had his own expectations for the group. 'He was honestly convinced that we could be the next Beatles,' said Maureen. 'He always talked up – never down. Of course, even I realized he was in it to get rich. He had such high, high hopes.'

The dissenting opinion about Sesnick came from Cale, who instinctively distrusted the fast-talking, cigar-smoking bullshit artist who managed to manipulate everybody in the group as well as the record company with a smokescreen of promises, laughter and exaggerations. 'Steven just drove a wedge right between Lou and me,' said Cale. 'That was his main concern to say, "Look, Lou's the star, you're just the sideman." Wrong, Steve.' John also found himself constantly arguing with Lou about arrangements for the new songs. Lou, who continued writing more commercial tunes, was pushing the band to appeal to a wider audience. John was resisting with all his might. 'There were pressures building up, and we were all getting very frustrated,' Cale recalled. 'After the first record we lost our patience and diligence. We couldn't even remember what our original precepts were.'

Although not yet officially their manager, Sesnick immediately got to work on a number of Velvets projects behind the scenes. One of the first things he did was send a copy of *The Velvet Underground and Nico* to the Beatles' manager, Brian Epstein, with an eye to making a publishing deal with Epstein's company, Nemperor. The deal, backed by an Epstein-produced European tour, could have elevated them to international stardom.

One night that spring Danny Fields found himself at Max's with the British impresario and looked for an opportunity to encourage the deal. 'I wanted Brian to manage them, or promote them, or get them to Europe, or something!' Danny recalled. Spotting Lou in the crowded back room, he scooted over and whispered, 'Pretend you have to go uptown and I'll get you a ride with Brian Epstein!' Although he was in the midst of an intense conversation, Lou complied.

In the car, Brian, who had just returned from Acapulco, leaned over and, fondling Lou's arm, murmured, 'My lover and I spent our whole vacation listening to your record.'

'Oh?'

'Well, I like it very much,' Brian continued.

'Why, thank you,' Lou answered.

'Everybody thinks we homosexuals are wanton perverts, but as a matter of fact we're all quite straight and selective,' Reed sniffed dismissively to a friend afterwards.

Sesnick continued to pursue a deal with Epstein in the ensuing months, cashing in on his personal relationship with Epstein's lawyer in New York, Nat Weiss. Tragically, Epstein died of a drug overdose six months later, without having done anything about the VU.

In July, John helped produce and arrange Nico's first solo album, *Chelsea Girl*. It was an unlikely collaboration, containing three songs by Lou (who seemed much more willing to collaborate with Nico from a distance), as well as tracks by Dylan, Cale, Morrison and Jackson Browne.

Jackson recalled meeting Lou during the sessions: 'Lou, who always had this incredible menacing scowl on his face, wouldn't say more than one or two syllables because that was how Andy was. But he was a sweetheart underneath.' Impressed by Jackson, Lou took the seventeen-year-old singer-songwriter under his wing. At one point he told Jackson about the recent 'be-in' hippie celebration in San Francisco, and revealed that he'd been to the simultaneous event in New York.

> The way he described it, you realized there was a place for all that inside of him. He loved seeing Central Park full of people all just high and loving each other. Afterwards he took me for a big Chinese meal and then on to see the Murray the K Show at RKO. There was Wilson Pickett, the Blues Project, the Who, Etta James. What a day!

Unfortunately, when *Chelsea Girl* was released in October of that year, almost everybody, especially Lou, John and Nico, was disappointed by its production. 'If they'd just have allowed Cale to arrange it and let me do some more stuff on it,' Reed exclaimed.

I mean that song, 'Chelsea Girl'. Everything on it, those strings, that flute, should have defeated it. But the lyrics, Nico's voice. It managed somehow to survive. We still got 'It Was a Pleasure Then'; they couldn't stop us. We'd been doing a song like that in our beloved show, it didn't really have a title. Just all of us following the drone. And there it sits in the middle of that album.

As a result, Lou became more determined to make the next Velvets album a success no matter what the cost.

Despite this ambition, in a psychological reaction against his father, Lou refused throughout the Velvet Underground's career to pay much attention to the business end of the group. In fact, it is extraordinary how passive he appeared to be, even when it came to collecting royalties on his songs. Danny Fields's friend Hope Ruff stepped into the breach, writing the requisite lead sheets of musical notation for each song and registering the 'E Forms' without which Lou would not have been able to earn any money from the songs – these have, in time, become his most valuable possession. 'John was certainly capable of it but I think he was really strung out a lot,' she said.

I don't think Lou could do it. It's a real pain in the ass for most people. But it was nothing to me. I would write it as fast as they'd play it. Lou was not as crazy as he pretended to be. Danny would say, 'Oh, Lou, he did this, he did that,' and I always said to him, 'He is just a kid from Long Island.' He calls his mother up to make sure she fed the dog. And that's how I always thought of him. He'd say, 'I have to go make a phone call,' and I'd say, 'Who are you calling?' He'd say, 'I have to call my mother to find out how my dog is.' When you're really crazy you don't worry about that kind of stuff. But everybody saw what they wanted to see. I thought he was a nice person. And Danny would look at me like . . . That was a big insult in the 1960s. You don't say that about someone: 'He was a nice guy.' But he was. And I had great respect for him.

The Velvet Underground recorded their second album, *White Light/White Heat*, in September. They had been working up the material since the previous summer, and took very little time to complete it in the studio. The short, intense sessions lent the music a feeling of spontaneity.

Nowhere was this more evident than on 'Sister Ray', which Reed had written on a train coming back to New York from Connecticut. The lyrics echoed scenes from *Last Exit to Brooklyn* by Hubert Selby, one of Lou's favourite writers. ' "Sister Ray" has eight characters in it and this guy gets killed and nobody does anything. The situation is a bunch of drag queens taking a bunch of sailors home with them, shooting up on smack and having this orgy when the police appear.'

> The album's great set piece [the critic Richard Williams wrote] – a classic of sixties musical ambition to stand with Dylan's 'Sad-Eyed Lady of the Lowlands', Riley's 'In C' and Ornette Coleman's Free Jazz – was the 17½-minute 'Sister Ray', in which a song structure no more demanding than that of dumb punk classics like '96 Tears' or 'Woolly Bully' was made to serve the demands of the avant-garde. Musically, 'Sister Ray' offered none of the familiar blues-derived comforts of a lengthy jam by, say, Cream or the Grateful Dead. It was harsh, barbed, unwelcoming, built on the nagging buzz and drone of Cale's cheap electric organ, the chop and squeal of the guitars, and the relentless clatter of Tucker's garbage-can drumming. Reed wrote its lyric to match, diving into the netherworld with the conviction of a long-term resident. Barely piercing the din, the words of 'Sister Ray' dealt strictly with drugs. This time, though, there was a difference. 'Sister Ray' wasn't a carefully arranged art-song about drugs and sex: in its rush and incoherence and desperation, it was drugs and sex, done together in absolute extremis.

White Light/White Heat was the most manic, abrasive and powerful artefact of the Velvet Underground. According to one critic, it reflected the internal tensions of a band ascending into prominence and 'at each other's throats', as Cale said. The desperate feedback and distortion gave an immediacy to the music that sounded like a backstage brawl. The intelligence in the band, however, could not offset the daily antagonism of differing musical ideas. Some observers insisted that Lou, at this point, realized he wanted to make it as a solo performer, regarding a band as a necessary but supportive evil.

'I Heard Her Call My Name', which opened side two of the record, played a decisive role in the intensifying Reed–Cale battle. Lou, in an extraordinary move, went into the studio without telling any of the others, and remixed the track so that he would appear prominent on it. According to the normally restrained Moe Tucker, ' "I Heard Her Call My Name" was ruined by the mix – the energy. You can't hear anything but Lou. He was the mixer in there, so he, having a little ego trip at the time, turned himself so far up that there's no rhythm, there's no nothing.'

In the autumn of 1967 the band split up their communal living. Sterling moved in with Martha Dargan and her brother Tom on East Second Street. John moved into the Chelsea Hotel with his girlfriend Betsey Johnson. Moe was living on Fifth Avenue and Ninth Street. Lou bounced from place to place, staying mostly on Perry Street and later in a loft on Seventh Avenue and 31st Street. Lou's loft was 'just me, a bed and our stuff, five or six huge amplifiers and guitars'. Despite this separation, the band still spent most of their time hanging out together. 'We'd come flying in at five in the morning and play "Sister Ray" through them,' Lou continued.

> I was the only guy living in the building, except for this big black guy upstairs who had a gun. When it got too loud he'd start jumping up and down on the floor; you knew when the ceiling started buckling that things were getting serious. Then he'd come down and start pounding on the door. That was it: rehearsal cancelled due to gun.

The biggest shift in the group came, however, not from the recording of *White Light/White Heat* or from the break-up of their living situation, but rather from their having signed a managerial contract with Steve Sesnick. Cale's predictions were beginning to play themselves out with catastrophic consequences. 'Lou was starting to act funny,' said John.

He brought in Sesnick – who I thought was a real snake – to be our manager, and all this intrigue started to take place. Lou was calling us 'his band' while Sesnick was trying to get him to go solo. Maybe it was the drugs he was doing at the time. They certainly didn't help. It was maddening, just maddening. Before, it had always been easy to talk to Lou. Now you had to go through Sesnick, who seemed pretty practised in the art of miscommunication.

Cale later claimed that it was at this point, after the recording of *White Light/White Heat* in the autumn of 1967, that he first thought of leaving the band. He realized that they weren't going to progress any further on the path that he and Lou had embarked on in early 1965. Lou was beginning to introduce to the group a light, pop style of playing. The songs he was writing that autumn signalled a clear backing-away from the material typified by 'Sister Ray', and towards an increasing emphasis on his lyrics.

Cale's original idea – to create an orchestral chaos in which Lou could spontaneously create lyrics – was being lost, because Lou was looking for a group that would follow his directions to create pop songs. Sesnick was also playing a large role in this, because Sesnick was supporting Lou's approach towards what he imagined to be a more popular and commercial form.

Making matters worse for John was the fact that Lou, who demanded 100 per cent allegiance and attention from his collaborators, resented his close relationship with Betsey Johnson. Betsey had a great belief in John and encouraged him to step out of Lou's shadow and make his own music, write his own songs and sing them himself. A fashion designer of international fame who had recently been written up in *Time* magazine, Johnson had a shop called Paraphernalia which was said to be the hippest clothes shop in America. John was very photogenic, and Betsey enhanced this greatly by designing clothes for him. She also designed clothes for the rest of the band, but John's tastes and style became increasingly flamboyant. In one instance, he wanted her to make special gloves for him so that his hands looked as if they were on fire when he was playing guitar. Sometimes he wore dramatic masks on stage. Sterling recalled that after being dressed by Betsey

Johnson, John became astonishing to look at and even more charismatic on stage next to the diminutive, uncomfortable Lou.

With the rock field expanding rapidly, the stage was set for a successful debut of *White Light/White Heat* on 30 January 1968. But, to everyone's dismay, it too was banned on the radio. Lou was still confident that they would succeed, and, if anything, took this rejection as a sign that he was right to move further into the mainstream.

At least one critic, Richard Mortifoglio, agreed with him:

> *White Light/White Heat* is the most resolutely anti-melodic rock ever recorded before punk, a truly 'black' record, from the colour of the cover to the crackling electronic burp closing 'Sister Ray', that monster opus that summarizes the album's high anarchy and takes seventeen minutes to end it. It's an extreme record, and this very extremity marks it for the kind of failed brilliance most 'experiments' suffer in time.

Among the high points of the album, he singled out Lou's guitar playing. 'What Reed's guitar work most resembles is the sour rhythmic fill-ins that a blues rocker like John Lee Hooker specialized in,' he continued.

> *White Light/White Heat* is nothing less than a violently strung-out urban blues. Reed's singing is also bluesier than before. With honky-tonk piano in tow, he glides through 'White Light/White Heat' in a giggly, black-faced voice, sounding like he's getting goosed by Cale's bass-neck.

White Light/White Heat turned out to be another severe commercial disappointment, receiving an even harsher response than the first album. Because of the lyrics, there was almost a complete blackout on the radio. Moreover, the lack of association with Warhol limited their channels of publicity. With no Warhol or Nico publicity boosting it, the record had to rely on the standard conduits for rock music, where *White Light/White Heat* was largely ignored. Even *Rolling Stone* magazine refused to review the album. 'Most of our singles were never distributed,' noted Morrison. 'However, where they appeared on jukeboxes, people have really liked them. 'White Light/White Heat' as a single is nice. That single was banned every place. When it was banned in San Francisco we said, the hell with it. That's as far as it ever got.' Aside from neglect, the album faced competition from an enormous pop market that was being flooded with all sorts of flash-in-the-pan product, soaking up the teenagers' dollars. As the rock-and-roll industry came into its own, alternative groups like the Velvets found it increasingly difficult to break in. Making matters worse was the fact that the band was still being put down for being Warhol acolytes – drug-taking, homosexual, S&M devotees – without the advantage of Warhol's umbrella protection and buoyant encouragement.

The Velvet Underground, though, knew how good they were, and maintained a positive outlook despite the reviews. Fortunately, by the end of January, their financial situation had improved. When managed by Warhol, the Velvets had lived on paltry per diem handouts from the Factory. But after Sesnick was able to renegotiate their situation with MGM-Verve, they actually began to make a little money. Lou especially, as the songwriter and lead singer, got enough money to rent an Upper East Side apartment.

Most of their money came from touring. In one bright moment of an otherwise terrible relationship with MGM-Verve, Sesnick was able to persuade the company to take the money that they would have used in publicity and devote it to the expenses of the Velvets' touring. As a result, they flew first class, stayed in the best hotels and ate in nice restaurants. Moreover, they were sure they would sell out and get a great response at several of their regular venues – Le Cave in Cleveland, the Tea Party in Boston, the Second Fret in Philadelphia, and a number of other places on the West Coast and in Texas.

'We never did tour Europe, but it vexed us beyond imagining that we never made inroads in the US,' said Sterling.

The band, who received no royalties from their albums, earned $600 one week, $2,500 the next on the road. It was the only way they could make money, and they liked to play, but the pressures of touring did little to assuage the developing tensions.

Like any rock group spending large amounts of time on the road, they had problems getting along with each other. Whenever they got to a hotel, for example, Sterling would virtually knock everyone over in his attempt to get himself the best room in the suite. He usually shared a room with John, while Maureen would team up with Lou. Cale and Reed fought about the musical direction, and Sesnick's manipulative involvement made matters worse between them. According to Morrison:

> One time in Chicago the club had a circular stage. I was playing the solo on 'Pale Blue Eyes', Cale was lurching around on bass and stepped on a distorter which quadrupled my volume. It was an accident. Everybody staggered back. John shuts it off and kicks the box across the stage. I look over at Lou and Lou's eyes are saying 'What an asshole.' But for Cale, offence is the best defence, so when confronted he attacks. I said, 'John, I wish you wouldn't come lurching over, bla bla bla, Oh, forget it.' Cale was really getting into it. On one occasion he drank nineteen whisky sours. They had a big argument in Chicago. They may have thrown a few punches at each other. The first time they did that in California I was horrified. I wasn't alarmed by the fighting, I was enraged. Sesnick and I felt like throttling the both of them.

Indeed, Cale found himself fighting more than Reed and Sesnick about maintaining the band's radical sound. Facing the extreme counter-avant-garde while touring the Midwest, he found that an element of compromise crept into their original precepts. 'To make audiences feel comfortable,' John explained, 'we ended up putting a backbeat on everything, as if to say, "We may be crazy but we're still rock and roll."'

During the early months of 1968, with Steve Sesnick egging him on, Lou Reed chipped away at the Velvets' democratic foundations. Sesnick and Reed decided where the band should play, setting up a surfeit of gigs at the Boston Tea Party, broken by occasional visits to California, Cleveland and Canada. They also masterminded a subtle shift in the band's musical axis, away from the explorations of sound towards an emphasis on lyrics. Lou stepped into the forefront with his poetic investigations of a human spirit burdened by obsession and guilt.

John recalled it as an unhappy time.

> Lou and I couldn't see eye to eye any more. We weren't rehearsing, we weren't working, we were flying all over the place and we couldn't concentrate on anything long enough to work. It was a result of touring day in and day out – which can be a detrimental influence. In terms of emotional balance, there was no more room in the band for anyone else – Lou and I did enough fighting for all. We weren't very compatible writing together, but we did turn out a number of songs.

In 1968, in two recording sessions that served to harvest the seeds of their breakdown, they attempted to cut a single. During the first session they recorded 'Ferryboat Bill' and 'The Bottom of Your Heart', poppy, crowd-pleasing rock-and-roll songs that indicated the direction Lou wanted to take. In the second session they produced 'Mr Rain', Cale's recording swan song with the Velvets, a return to the prominent drone and viola. None of these songs was particularly inspired. Whereas they had previously gone into a recording studio and recorded an album in a day or two, they were now hacking around for days getting nowhere just trying to record a single.

In defending his turf musically, John went to extremes that even Sterling found intolerable. He recalled how John drove them all crazy:

> One thing that really rankled was John insisting on building this bass amp of his with band money. Something to do with acoustic suspension speakers producing this great wall of sound. Thousands were spent on these goddamn things – and then they didn't work. Meanwhile, we were on endorsement to Acoustic Amplifiers, who made this fabulous bass amp, the Acoustic 360. John refused even to accept a free one from the factory. Later on, John found out that if he'd only had a pre-amp, it would have worked. All this money for what I called the Tower of Babble. There was a general dissatisfaction with his free-spiriting – and free spending. It really did piss everybody

off. What the hell was he up to? Ha ha ha! But it was an ugly business, stupid and counterproductive.

According to John:

Because there was less and less finesse of anything we were doing on stage, we lost sight of the music. There were a lot of soft songs and I didn't want that many soft songs. I was into trying to develop these really grand orchestral bass parts, I was trying to get something big and grand and Lou was fighting against that, he wanted pretty songs. I said, 'Let's make them grand pretty songs then.' All of that was just irritating, it was a source of a lot of friction. It was unresolved, it was a constant fight of who was gonna play what. They were creative conflicts. I think egos were getting bruised.

Even Moe was feeling the frustration with Lou.

Louie is really hard – it's hard to tell when you see him, is he gonna be, 'Hey, great to see you,' or is he gonna be down on the ground. He has always been like that. You can't tell what his reaction is going to be at any given point. As long as you can understand that and deal with it, it's fine. Sterling couldn't handle that. He couldn't handle a lot of Lou too well. Lou is a kind of sad person; not sad himself – I feel sad about him sometimes, that he isn't happy, that he's very influenced, I think so, anyway, by the people immediately surrounding him. If he's in the drug store, and those people are reacting to him in a certain way, he gets right into that, and reacts back the way they want to see him. Then you get back to the hotel, and it's just us, and he's different. It didn't bother me, 'cos that's Lou. I always loved Lou. I feel kind of sorry for him, as I said. I'd like to see him be a real happy-go-lucky little thing. I feel sad when I think he's sad. Because I love him, and I want him to be happy.

In February, a radio interviewer asked Lou and John what their plans were. Reed's enthusiastic reply gave no suggestion of the mounting tensions. 'We wanted to ultimately work on a tape that would take up every minute of every hour of every day for the entire year!'

That same month, John and Betsey announced that they planned to be married. Lou, she realized, 'was not happy that John was getting married. Period. To me. Period.'

'When you're in a band,' Cale explained, 'you're married to the band.'

The wedding was postponed when Cale came down with hepatitis and spent several weeks in hospital, but John and Betsey finally got married in April. Lou attended the ceremony, but the Reed–Cale relationship was clearly under siege.

If the Velvet Underground was a family and Lou was the husband, it raises the question of whether Lou had a personal life beyond the band. Mary Woronov, who saw him occasionally through the speed circle that centered on Ondine, recalled that Lou did not date and other friends had the impression that Lou was no longer that interested in sex. However, the truth is that from 1966 onward, when Shelley Albin moved to New York City with her husband, Ronald Corwin, Lou continued to have a relationship with her. It was a small world. The Corwins were living nearby at Bleecker Street and Broadway. Unfortunately, while giving him at times intense satisfaction and inspiring a number of outstanding songs, the relationship continued to torture Lou who felt that she possessed everything he wanted but could not keep.

At first Shelley hoped that she could maintain an open, honest friendship with Lou which would have included her husband, but when Corwin rejected the notion of having anything to do with Reed, saying he was a bad influence, she found herself having to reject Lou's overtures since she could not imagine being dishonest. Consequently, during 1966–67 they rarely met. However, by 1968 she crossed the border and entered into a secret affair with Lou. 'Are you going to come and spend your life with me?' Lou would ask, 'or are you going to stay with that asshole?'

Shelley felt ambivalent about the situation. Part of her was so relieved to be with an intelligent and real person with whom she could have a conversation, but another, overriding part was scared by Lou's lifestyle and all that it entailed. 'You're more interested in security than love,' Lou would often chide her, and Shelley reluctantly had to admit he was right.

'Leave Ron,' Lou would urge her. 'What are you doing with

him? Why don't you just come out the door and stay out the door?' Hard-pressed to answer this challenge, Shelley would have to reject Lou over and over again, reverting to her last-ditch defence: 'I don't care if you're unhappy and miserable and dying. I don't give a shit if you die.' What kept the relationship alive for Lou as much as the effect her presence had on him was the challenge. Shelley, who still knew him better than anybody, was quite sure that if she had agreed to move in with him, Lou would have made her life a living hell as he had done at Syracuse and pushed her out again. That was the curse of being Lou. He was, she was convinced, miserable throughout the sixties and obsessive about his misery to boot.

One striking difference Shelley found in Lou was that wherever he was with her, walking down the street, sitting at a lunchroom counter, he appeared to be constantly composing music in his head. Suddenly out of the blue he'd bark out, 'You beat on the Coke glass boop boop de boop. You sing woo wah doo.' In other words, either help me write this song or shut up. Actually, Shelley reflected, nothing had really changed. If you were with Lou you had to resign yourself to being an instrument. You were always at his service.

Months would pass in which they would not see each other. Then they would get together in the simplest way, meeting for a Coke or a walk in the Central Park Zoo. In order to protect herself from being seduced against her will, Shelley had as early as 1965 stopped listening to the radio altogether, and through the second half of the sixties and all of the seventies (during which time she constantly missed Lou and had to work at staying away from him) she never heard any of Lou's music for fear that it would have had the effect upon her that the sirens had on Ulysses.

That summer the band toured the West Coast. Lou had hardly recovered from John's wedding when one morning in Los Angeles, riding down to breakfast in the elevator with Sesnick at the exclusive Beverly Wilshire Hotel, he glanced at a stack of newspapers piled on the floor to see a glaring headline announcing that on the previous day, 3 June, Andy Warhol had been shot at the Factory and had less than a 50:50 chance of surviving. Badly shaken, Lou found his jumbled emotions difficult to sort out. Part of him wanted to call New York to find out what the diagnosis was, while another part of him was frightened of being rejected by Warhol.

Shortly after Warhol was shot, Lou, back in New York, met Shelley at Max's and told her he was hiding out because Warhol's would-be assassin, a radical feminist writer named Valerie Solanas who had penned the manifesto of the Society for Cutting Up Men (scum), was after him. 'I can certainly understand why,' Shelley recalled. 'I don't know why he wasn't the first. We were having this discussion and he was rolling because the people next to him realized who he was and were having a wonderful time listening to our conversation, so he went into his whole production about how women are supposed to be subservient.'

Before the end of the month, Lou mustered the courage to call Warhol in the hospital. 'I was scared to call him,' he remembered, 'and in the end I did and he asked me, "Lou, Lou, why didn't you come?"' Reed felt terrible, but after a few minutes Andy started to gossip, and Lou realized he would be all right. Already tinged with guilt, Reed's relationship with his former mentor grew even more complex after the attempted assassination. Father figures weren't meant to be mortal. 'I really love him,' Lou confessed on many occasions, and the emotion was always reciprocated by Andy. But there was also an inhibition on both sides, an awareness that some boundary of behaviour had been breached.

In his song about the assassination attempt on *Songs for Drella*, written twenty years later, Reed concluded that he wanted to execute Valerie Solanas. In an extensive interview with the British writer John Wilcock, who compiled a book of interviews with Warhol's friends in the wake of the tragedy, Lou spoke about his feelings for the man who was – after Cale – perhaps the most important influence on his life.

'Andy's gone through the most incredible suffering. They let her [Solanas] off with three years. You get more for stealing a car. It's just unbelievable. But the point is the hatred directed at him by society was really reflected.' He also revealed his own fears about the relationship between success and persecution. 'I had to learn certain things the hard way. But one of those things I learned was work is the whole story. Work is literally everything. Most very big people seem to have enemies, and seem to be getting shot, which is something a lot of people should keep in mind. There is a lot to be said for not being in the limelight.'

It was after the Warhol shooting that Lou decided to take extreme measures to get rid of Cale. The question of who was really in command of the Velvet Underground had to be definitively settled. John felt strongly that they'd worked constructively to capture something rare on the first two albums, but that the motivating spirit was gone. By the summer Reed and Cale had lost sight of the original precepts and were blocking each other's progress. Cale felt the problem could be solved; the more aggressive, business-minded Reed did not.

Once again their conflict centred on Sesnick's role. Reed, of course, wanted Sesnick in, whereas Cale continued to find his presence unbearable. 'Whenever a new song came around, it was like picking at sores. It was very badly handled and exacerbated constantly by Steve Sesnick. Sesnick built up a barrier between Lou and the rest of the band. Lou and I were very close and running the band, and gradually Sesnick came along and said, Lou's the songwriter, he's the star.' After a year with Sesnick at the helm, Cale admitted, 'I felt like a sideman, more or less. It was a mishandling of the situation.' However, although Cale felt demoralized, he did not think things were irreconcilable. He wanted to go on.

Conflicts like the Reed–Cale one were as common in the rock world as the clap. Most partners resolved it in some manner that allowed them to continue. Undoubtedly the VU's commercial failure added to the tension. Whatever the case, Reed suddenly struck.

In September, Lou called a meeting of the band at the Riviera

Café on Sheridan Square in the middle of Greenwich Village. When Sterling arrived he found Maureen and Lou waiting, but no John. 'Lou announced that John was out of the band,' Morrison recalled. 'I said, "You mean out for today, or for this week?" And Lou said, "No, he's out." I said that we were a band and it was graven on the tablets. A long and agonizing argument ensued, with much banging on tables, and finally Lou said, "You don't go for it? All right, the band is dissolved."'

'I could say that it was more important to keep the band together than to worry about Cale,' Sterling admitted.

What upset John most was the way Lou handled the situation. It fell to Sterling to deliver the news to John, who remembered:

We were supposed to be going to Cleveland for a gig and Sterling showed up at my apartment and effectively told me that I was no longer in the band. Lou always got other people to do his dirty work for him. I don't think I'm blameless about what happened, but Lou never confronted me, saying, 'I don't want you around any more.' It was all done by sleight of hand. As for resentment, I dunno. Things had been pushed pretty far between us and I can't say I was entirely blameless in that situation. But I felt that was treason.

Disgusted with Lou, and creatively frustrated, John stormed off, claiming, 'I left because the music was getting redundant, we weren't really working on the music any more – and I decided I was going to find another career.'

In retrospect, Reed laid the blame for the split on 'foul and disgusting management'. At the time, however, he felt triumphant enough to say, 'I only hope that one day John will be recognized as . . . the Beethoven of his day.'

As a result of the brutal betrayal of the man who had offered him his home and introduced him into a world he had only benefited from, in collaboration with Steve Sesnick, Lou gained complete control of the Velvet Underground, but became at the same time alienated from Sterling Morrison. When he would need Sterling's support in the year to come, Sterl would not be there.

John's comments about the episode were dismissive and bitter.

'It was just a flash in the pan,' he reflected on his four-year investment in the Velvet Underground.

It came and it went, and all of it had gone on without anybody really noticing that it had been there. We never really fulfilled our potential. With tracks like 'Heroin', 'Venus in Furs', 'All Tomorrow's Parties' and 'Sister Ray' we defined a completely new way of working. It was without precedent. Drugs, and the fact that no one gave a damn about us, meant we gave up on it too soon.

chapter nine

The Deformation of the Velvet Underground

1968–1970

[In which Lou replaces Cale with Doug Yule, the band records and releases *The Velvet Underground* and *Loaded*, and slowly disintegrates under the pressures of the road.]

It became less fun when we had a manager. I think he destroyed the group. He took two or three years but he destroyed it and made it so it wasn't any fun.

LOU REED

If the first half of the Velvet Underground's career had been devoted to pure musical experiments, the second half, resulting in *The Velvet Underground* and their fourth studio album, *Loaded*, would focus upon Lou's struggle to find a reason to keep living. During this period, the band degenerated from a group of travellers exploring uncharted terrain into Lou Reed's backup band trying to swim into the pop mainstream. 'After the glamour died down,' said Danny Fields, 'it was Lou Reed and a backup band. It was like any other rock group on the road.' Nothing made this transition clearer than the musican Reed chose to replace Cale.

Lou might have chosen any number of outstanding musicians from the ranks of the avant-garde, inventive rock or jazz, but chose a journeyman bass player who he felt confident would have no ego problems at all – somebody who would be happy to live permanently in his shadow.

Doug Yule grew up in Great Neck, Long Island. Living in Boston, where he had been a member of the Glass Menagerie, Doug had socialized with the Velvets during their frequent visits, occasionally putting Morrison up at his River Street flat. He was a big fan. Consequently, when he received a phone call from Steve Sesnick requesting that he drop everything and entrain to New York to audition for Lou, Doug left Boston the same day.

One of the few constants in Lou's character was the method by which he seduced people he could make use of. Seizing upon those aspects of their personality that were at once their strongest and weakest, he instantly set about singing their praises so intensely that within no time they had come to rely upon him for their self-image. In the process, he amputated them from almost everyone they had known before meeting him by demanding, in exchange for his insights and time, their full attention twenty-four hours a day. The reverse side of this operation was, of course, Lou's ability to withdraw his support, leaving his adoptees like blind junkies in search of the 'man'. It was one of the things he had learned from Warhol.

Doug was particularly susceptible. An attractive, bouncy young man who wanted to be a great guitar player, he did not have a well-defined personality or sense of direction. Lou picked up on Doug's amorphous identity and bent it towards his own ends. Reflecting back upon the early days of their relationship, he commented, rather derisively, 'I was working with Doug's innocence. I'm sure he never understood a word of what he was singing. He doesn't know what it's about.' Ironically, Lou then went on to reveal his own lack of personality by speaking in the voice of Andy Warhol: 'I mean, I thought it was cute. I adore people like that, they're so cute.'

The rest of the band had mixed feelings about Yule. Sterling was in a permanent snit for the next three years. 'It was never the same for me after John left,' he complained. 'He was not easy to replace. Dougie was a good bass player, and I liked him, but we moved more towards unanimity of opinion. I don't think that's a good thing. I always thought that what made us good were the tensions and oppositions. Bands that fight together make better music.'

Maureen valued Doug less as a bass player than as a positive complement to the group. Doug wasn't about to make waves. For a while she thought Lou was just glad to have somebody in the group that he didn't have to worry about.

Yule, for his part, was snowed by the whole experience. He came down to New York on the Wednesday after Cale's departure and met the band at Max's. They jammed on songs until Friday and played their first date at Le Cave in Cleveland on 2 October, one week after he joined them. A week after that, he was catapulted into the jet-set lifestyle of a rock-and-roll band, flying first class to San Francisco and checking into the exclusive Ritz Carlton under the auspices of Steve Sesnick.

The second phase of the Velvet Underground, covering late 1968 through August 1970, is known to some as the Lou Reed and his backup band phase. It was a productive time – in two years Lou recorded two studio albums (and two others which wouldn't be released for twenty years), as well as two live albums – not unlike the previous four years. There, however, the comparison ends. Whereas 1965 to 1968 represented a period of artistic creativity, 1968 to 1970 represented its flipside, a time of rock-and-roll commercialism as exemplified by groups like the Monkees. But while some forty other bands prospered fantastically in this period, the Velvet Underground, despite a schedule packed with tours and recording sessions, continued to languish in the commercial doldrums, selling few records and being restricted to playing mostly small clubs in their strongholds of Cleveland, Boston, Philadelphia, etc.

From 18 to 20 October they played the Avalon Ballroom in San

Francisco, the city that had two years earlier sent them packing with hostile reviews and bum drugs. Far from missing Cale, the audience applauded the band's poppier sound. One long-time fan, Tim Robbins, who had seen the Summit High School show three years earlier, managed to get backstage and met a charming Lou.

I went into a big back room where Lou Reed sat, all by himself, eating what looked to be sawdust out of a jar. I was speechless. After sizing me up for a few seconds, Lou said, 'What are you on, amphetamine or something?' I mumbled that I was not and asked what it was that he was eating. I was informed that it was high-protein wheat-germ mixture that he always ate before playing. This was followed by a brief lecture on drug abuse. I blurted out something about how much I loved their music and that I had seen them at Summit High School three years earlier. Lou broke into a huge grin and took me into the other room to meet the rest of the band. Everyone was amazed that I'd seen the show (except Doug, of course) so we sat around and reminisced until it was time for them to go back on stage. I was really impressed by how intelligent, articulate and polite they were: it changed my whole impression of rock-and-roll stars. They were real people like you and me after all.

Robbins was a typical fan of the Velvet Underground in that he was fiercely dedicated to the group, its music and lifestyle. Unlike many rock groups of the era, the Velvets maintained a small but dedicated number of followers, many of whom became friends or associates of the band. 'After that show,' continued Robbins,

I saw the Velvets a lot and every time I did, I'd go back and see Lou holding court answering fans' questions, giving his opinion on just about every topic imaginable. My favourite nights were those when I could sit and listen. They would discuss the most amazing things; angels, saints, the universe, diet, yoga, meditation, Jesus, healing with music, cosmic rays and astrology.

Lester Bangs, who also first met Lou during this tour, recalled:

When I met them, I thought to come on cool, so when the subject of drugs came up, I smiled knowingly. 'Well, I think you can take any drug, just as long as you don't take it too often.' And Lou blandly replied, 'Well, yeah, if you want to be a smorgasbord schmuck.'

Doug Yule had only good memories of his early days with the band. As he said, 'In the late sixties everything was rock and roll, and that was the best place to be. Basically we were just touring and playing and smoking pot when we could get it. It was a responsibility-free environment.' Even Sterling, who more than anyone held on to their original precepts and saw himself in the guise of a crusader, had to admit that 1968 was their best year, noting, 'our touring was successful, our playing was excellent'.

Looking back at this period, though, Morrison pointed out that at the very moment they reached the position they had been struggling towards since their inception, they lost their innocence and embarked upon a road to megalomania and ruin. 'Our struggles to succeed on our own terms, once directed outwards towards the audiences, record execs, radio stations and what not, perhaps turned inward towards the group, with unfortunate consequences.' With the return to the recording studio, there surfaced the problems that had been simmering beneath the camaraderie of touring.

They were booked to make their next album at TT&G Studios in LA in November 1968. The sessions would test the new band's mettle. Challenged to come up with an album that would go beyond *White Light/White Heat*, Reed sidestepped the issue by making its polar opposite. The only continuity was the level of the lyrics.

From the outset the recording presented technical and personal problems. According to Sterling, 'Right before we went into the studio all of our electronic gear was stolen in their ammunition boxes at the airport. So we didn't have fuzzers and expressers and compressors. We were left with amps and guitars, so we made a straightforward record.' Lou's voice, never strong under any circumstances, was ragged from constant touring. Furthermore, Morrison got his back up when presented with the soulful 'Pale Blue Eyes'.

Why do you think that happened on the third album? 'Pale Blue Eyes' is about Lou's old girlfriend in Syracuse. I said, 'Lou, if I wrote a song like that I wouldn't make you play it.' He was very vain about his gifts as a lyricist. He didn't want them swept by the wayside. I didn't argue hotly about this or that feature on the album. My contribution was as much as ever, probably even more, but I didn't try and get my own way all the time. Perhaps the Cale business left me all argued out, or perhaps I didn't feel that strongly about the material one way or the other. I tried to maintain some tension by instigating a tremendous paranoia because I was still hanging around with Cale.

Lou was clearly in the driver's seat. With Maureen, Doug and Sesnick deferring to his every wish, he cut a series of songs that fit into one of the first concept albums in rock and stand today as among some of his most durable and beautiful. The music, almost folklike in its simplicity, was a realization of Reed's view of the rock record as a unified whole. Like a book of connected short stories, the libretto followed the adventures of Candy (based on the Warhol superstar and drag queen Candy Darling) and her junkie boyfriend. It also mirrored Lou's ongoing relationship with Shelley.

Reed described the story's progress as:

All this unintelligible stuff. You know, but the intent was really noble. I just meant finally after seeing the light, explaining everything and getting things right, and finally saying now I got it right, *bam*, what happens? A whole new series of problems, y'know, new level, new problems.

Lou's use of Doug as a puppet came into play as he divided the vocal chores effectively between them. Happy to be part of the Velvet Underground, Doug was impressed by Lou:

He could make you laugh or cry, depending on what he wanted. The best and the worst thing about Lou as a person to work with is he has a lot of creative willpower and drive. He gets an idea and he does it. I deferred more to Lou than to Sterling or Moe. In that he was the strongest personality. Also, he was five years older than I was. Lou's someone who is real good with words. He was a brilliant person with words.

The album was a more commercial effort than their previous recordings, not only because of Reed's writing, but because of Yule's contribution on a number of vocal tracks. 'Doug had a sweet little voice, and he could sing certain ones better than Lou,' said Tucker. 'But the main reason Doug did the vocals was that Lou's voice wasn't up to it when we were in the studio,' explained Sterling.

> Lou never had a durable voice, which was one of the reasons why we tried not to play too often – a long series of one-nighters would be out of the question. Lou had used up his voice at the Whiskey, where we played during the time we were making the album. Since we wanted to get the album finished and Doug could sing, he got the nod.

Yule sounded so much like Reed, it was hard to tell their recorded voices apart.

There were continuing tensions and arguments in the studio between Reed and Morrison, and in many cases Sterling picked up where John had left off. Maureen believed that:

> Sesnick always handled Lou as if he had this underlying mental affiliation with him. I always accepted his treatment of Lou, because Lou was special and different. He can't handle a lot of shit that I can handle, and that Sterling should be able to handle. But instead of saying, 'Well, OK, that's Lou,' Sterling would start digging, and there'd be all this baby shit. Ego, I suppose. I guess it was because they were guys. You have three guys competing in the same group for the best riff, whatever. I never had that kind of problem like they had. No fights, just a lot of underlying shit. Which is extremely tedious, and used to infuriate me because there was no reason for it. Lou, being sort of a special person, I would think Sterl could bend a little to deal with things. I was closer to him than Sterling was. Lou and I used to share rooms, and be more social than Sterling. Sterling would never go out and eat with us.

The final straw for Lou's backup band came when, in the kind of underhanded move which sows more dissent among bands than almost anything else in the studio, Lou remixed the whole album behind their backs in order to bring his own playing to the fore.

Even the loyal Yule was puzzled by this move. 'I felt that the mix was not as even when Lou did it,' he said. 'It reflected more of his own viewpoint. His personal view as a songwriter as opposed to a producer. It's very hard to separate yourself from things. If you wrote the song and then you played on it, when you go in to mix it you're going to have certain biases.'

Despite these conflicts, or perhaps because of them, the album was a victory for Reed, revealing his developing abilities as a writer as well as his willingness to take risks that set him, once again, apart from his peers. '"The Murder Mystery" was intended as a kind of application of modern literary techniques to rock and roll, like Burroughs and his fold-ins,' he explained. 'I'd fired John from the band and was having fun wondering if you could cause two opposing emotions to occur at the same time.'

As soon as the album was completed, the band was back on the road. Not only was touring virtually their only source of publicity, but they were facing more and more competition in the alternative-music category. Another pressure Lou had to contend with in the wake of Cale's departure came from such developments outside the group. When the Velvets had entered the arena in 1966 there were few bands working in their vein, which made them stand out in the US. By 1968, however, a generation who had been inspired in part by the VU were emerging to compete with them as the coolest band in the land. Iggy Pop, the MC5 and the Modern Lovers, to name three, were waiting in the wings.

In fact, that December the Velvet Underground were challenged for their crown by the rowdy Detroit-based MC5. Returning to their favourite venue, Sesnick's Boston Tea Party, they found themselves on the same bill with the Detroit band, who were were performing a kind of rabble-rousing *faux*-revolutionary rock inspired by a movement called the White Panthers. After screaming at the Velvets in their dressing room that they were going to blow them off stage, the MC5 performed a dynamite set and then, with typical 'revolutionary' logic, exhorted the audience to burn down the hall, because it was not large enough to hold their energies, and rush out into the street! When the Velvets came on, Lou calmed the crowd, saying, 'I'd just like to make one thing clear. We have nothing to do with what went on earlier and in fact we consider it very stupid. This is our favourite place in the country to play and we would hate to see anyone even *try* to destroy it!' The Detroit contingent was stunned by this remark and the thunderous applause that followed it. The Velvets played well that night. 'Live at this time, the band was incredible,' wrote Tim Robbins. 'Super-tight, confident, very powerful and loads of fun.'

Each year of the 1960s was characterized by one form or another of social upheaval. 1969 was marked by the surfacing of both the women's liberation movement and the gay liberation movement. Both had a particular effect upon Lou. Apart from his affair with Nico and his lingering involvement with Shelley, he had confined his sex life to the occasional one-night stand with either a woman or a man. Inasmuch as it had not been cool to be gay until now, he had kept the latter under wraps, confining his experiences primarily to hustlers in Greenwich Village afterhours clubs. In step with the gay liberation movement he engaged in sexual games with his long-time friend Billy Name.

In 1968 Warhol had moved out of the Silver Factory to a suite of rooms downtown on Union Square that resembled, with their polished surfaces and organized desks, the offices of an artistic corporation. Morrissey was the number-one man after Warhol, but a new collaborator, Fred Hughes, brought a sleek and elegant style that seemed to suit the post-shooting Warhol better than the free-for-all of the previous setup. The only holdover from the hard-core gay amphetamine group was Billy Name. However, by 1969 Name had withdrawn into a small darkroom at the back of the new Factory where he locked himself up in silent protest against Hughes's influence. The only people who visited him were Lou and Ondine. 'They would come over and all three of us were doing amphetamine so we had that bond,' Billy recalled. 'But we were all three into Alice Bailey books too, the white magic and esotericism. We would just get off talking about that stuff.'

According to Billy, he and Lou became not so much lovers as sexual comrades. That summer, Lou would stop by the Factory at night, pick up Billy and cruise the downtown gay bars, epitomized by the later to become legendary Stonewall on Christopher Street. Returning to Warhol's studio, if they had not found partners, Lou and Billy drifted into a series of sexual encounters.

We would go to a gay dance bar and gravitate towards getting our rocks off. Lou would stay with somebody from the afterhours bars or we would walk down Eighth Street and I would say, 'Well, come over to the Factory.' The more intimate relationship happened only because of the afterhours bars. We wouldn't have had a relationship if we hadn't gone out to that type of place and got blasted and there was a place at the Factory for us to go back to. It was strictly a result of the cultural theme going on. We weren't lovers or anything. And we weren't necessarily intimate. We were making out and we were closely bonded.

My favourite remembrance of Lou was at the second Factory. Lou came and everything and was getting ready to go and I said, 'Wait a minute, I didn't come.' So I made him sit on my face and he said grudgingly, 'OK,' so I could get off. So it was a playful type of relationship. But he could turn it off. I would never turn it off. He had that little streak of his own mentality operating where he'll just say no where I would never say no. It really pissed me off one time I said, 'Come over to the Factory,' he said, 'No.' He could do that after being very close and very friendly. He was a brat. Other than that the relationship was purely bonding, real friends, love and respectful, really into art and esoteric literature and very young-type things. I think that whole mean streak was in there, though.

On the other hand, as Lou pointed out, Billy also told him he was a lesbian.

'Another important person to Lou was Mary Woronov,' Billy recalled of one of the former EPI dancers. 'Me, Lou and Mary used to go to the Stonewall a lot when it first opened. I remember one time they stopped Mary from going in, they said, 'No women allowed,' and Lou got so pissed he wouldn't go in. I wanted to go in, but she was that important that he would not go in. Lou really loved and respected her.'

Billy, Mary and Lou formed a vigorous threesome. 'Lou used to like queers, and I used to hang out with queers, so we went to gay bars,' Mary recounted.

He liked sleazy drag queens. We were crazy about drag queens like Jackie and Holly and Candy. We knew them as very funny people. Lou had a loyalty towards me not as a girlfriend or as a fuckable person, but in the same way as he had a loyalty to a person like Maureen. I was a girl he liked. In other words, he never made a pass at me. Once I brought him home to my parents' apartment in Brooklyn Heights. My parents were freaked out because he looked so strange. He looked horrible. He was kind of strong about his health. He could take major drug abuse and not be bothered at all. But he looked skinny and he always slouched. And his hair was always that wiry conk stuff. He wasn't a good-looking guy. He never dated. No one would touch him with a ten-foot pole.

Lou's affair with Shelley reached something of a climax from the spring through the autumn of 1969, as is reflected in a number of songs on the third and fourth VU albums, and albeit fleetingly they really did have some wonderful times together. Lou had a charming ability to reveal an encouraging interest in what she was doing. At the time Shelley was seriously into pottery and although this seemed far removed from anything in Lou's world, he would apply his mind to it as if she were another Warhol, encouraging her to get an angle and go with it. He was, she recalled, heavily into his injections of methedrine from the Dr Feelgood so many celebrities went to in the late sixties, subsisting otherwise on health foods – bee pollen, wheat husks and other natural substances – way before it became fashionable.

In January 1969, Nico released her second solo album, *The Marble Index*, produced by John Cale, who recalled, 'When we finished it, I grabbed Lou and said, "Listen to this: this is what we could have done!" He was speechless.'

In March 1969, the band's third album, *The Velvet Under-*

ground, with a black-and-white cover photo by Billy Name, was released. For the first time no individual songwriting credits were listed. On a melodic level some of Lou Reed's finest moments occurred on the album. It was as if a rocking, rowdy part of his character had flamed out on *White Light/White Heat*, leaving the Lou Reed who'd penned 'I'll Be Your Mirror' and 'Sunday Morning' to blossom.

Once again, the demarcation between the two musical brothers was staked out by the two works which could hardly have been more disparate. Lou was certainly criticized in some quarters, particularly by Cale, for having sold out to light pop material as opposed to the awesome vision and power of the Cale–Nico collaboration.

The third album offered hints of the path Reed would eventually follow to personal survival. The album, like the band itself, had moved out of anarchy into a balance.

> I've gotten to where I like 'pretty' stuff better than drive and distortion because you can be more subtle, really say something and sort of soothe, which is what a lot of people seem to need right now [he explained]. Like, I think if you came in after a really hard day at work and played the third album, it might really do you good. A calmative, some people might even call it muzak, but I think it can function on both that and the intellectual or artistic levels at the same time. Like when I wrote 'Jesus', I said, 'My God, a hymn!' and 'Candy Says', which is probably the best song I've written, which describes a sort of person who's special, except that I think that all of us have been through that in a way – young, confused, with the feeling that other people, or older people, know something you don't.

As it turned out, Lou's choice of drag queens for subject matter had been prescient. The gay men who impersonated movie stars and other glamorous women were emerging in the wake of gay liberation as among the most striking new characters in the American media circus. The album met with good reviews from the more discerning critics for both its musical and lyrical content.

By this time, however, Lou was exhausted by his battle with MGM. As the VU continued to tour to ever increasing and appreciative audiences, they were constantly disappointed to find their album was unavailable outside the major cities on the two coasts.

The band and their manager maintained high spirits. They held on to Sesnick's belief that success, fame and wealth, and all the rewards being culled by the Grateful Dead, the Jefferson Airplane and all the West Coast bands Lou despised, would soon be theirs. Lou had already moved into an expensive Upper East Side apartment. When Morrison visited him to check it out, he was stunned by the glimpse of his colleague's private life.

> He was paying an outrageous amount of money for it, so I thought I'd go over and see what this palace looked like. Well, you know how those high-rise apartments are – they're real barren. And this was totally unfurnished, nothing except some kind of pallet that he had pushed up against one corner. And a tape recorder and some old tapes and I guess a notebook, and an acoustic guitar. There was nothing in the fridge except a half-empty container of papaya juice. I mean nothing, not even vitamins. It was just the picture of isolation and despair. He is the despairing type. So maybe it helps him.

Lou had occasionally stopped using speed over the previous two years in order to regain some balance to his system, but in the second half of 1969 through the summer of 1970, he appeared to return to it with a passion. It was a prolific period. In order to get out of the MGM contract the band had to deliver two more albums. In the summer of 1969 they made what for years was referred to as the Lost Album – since MGM never released it – under the most pleasant conditions they had ever recorded.

> That was the best session, with Gary Kellgran at the Record Plant [Maureen remembered]. Young guy, extremely helpful, a real nice guy, engineer, producer. We recorded in New York, six or eight days, tremendous. That was our best recording session, and we had no intention of releasing it, which was pretty absurd. That whole album is just gone with the wind. The one I really regret not having is 'Mr Rain'. Lou decided that it would actually rain when we did that song – because it did.

(This material would be released in the mid-1980s on *VU* and *Another View*.)

Lou was on a roll. Not only did he knock off the Lost Album, he also wrote 'Sweet Jane' and 'Rock & Roll' that year – both of which would appear on *Loaded* – trying them out on the road the very days he wrote them as they continued touring.

Despite the good work, Lou was isolating himself. His relationship with Sesnick began to break down as the manager, finding Lou endlessly demanding and difficult to control, switched his allegiance to the malleable Yule. And in light of this, Yule, who had been in the band long enough not to feel he automatically had to defer to Lou, began to exercise his own ego. When Doug Yule first came to the band at the end of 1968, 'we all thought he was great – a great guitar player, bass player, singer,' Maureen recalled. 'But within a year he'd become an asshole . . . in my eyes and, I believe, in Lou and Sterling's.'

Meanwhile, relations between Sterling and Lou stood at low ebb, characterized by an incident that took place at the Chateau Marmont in LA while the band was on tour. Sterling had taken some coke and went to get a blueberry yoghurt from the fridge in the band's suite. When he discovered that Lou had eaten it, he went ballistic. 'What are you on?' Lou exclaimed. 'OK, I ate your blueberry yoghurt, I don't deserve to die!'

Sesnick's influence on the Velvets was increasingly destructive. Lou, who had prided himself on displaying little emotion on stage, was reduced to being Sesnick's puppet. In an attempt to broaden their appeal, Steve insisted he wiggle his ass like a blank Mick Jagger.

That November, the guitarist Bob Quine, who would work with Lou in the 1980s, met him during the band's visit to San Francisco.

> You could see the relationship during the rehearsals. Lou seemed to be closer with Doug Yule than with Sterling. Sterling seemed to be a little detached from things. When Lou was working on arrangements he would direct more comments to Doug Yule. Doug Yule did a good job – he didn't get in the way of songs. Like 'Sister Ray', and

sometimes they would whip off a version of 'Black Angel's Death Song'. I don't think they were pleased to be in San Francisco, and they knew what awaited them. They were regarded as Andy Warhol's death-rock band. It was still the height of clichéd hippiedom – flowers and everything. I saw them at the Family Dog the first week and they were great. But it was fairly tragic. Hordes of hippies would just go there regardless of who was playing. They had their tambourines and harmonicas and they were all playing along with the band, who they didn't know, of course. At one point Maureen was laughing. Lou said, 'She's laughing because the tambourine players can't keep time.' He was doing amazing choreography – stuff that would make Chuck Berry look like a cripple – way beyond the duck-walk types of things and amazing guitar solos.

Then they did this long thing at the Matrix club. They were there two or three weeks and I saw them every night. The most inspiring thing for me was that Lou was writing a lot of songs like 'Sweet Jane', 'Sweet Bonnie Brown' and 'New Age', some of which would show up on *Loaded*. And they would change from night to night. He would improvise lyrics on 'Sweet Jane' and they were different each night. Sometimes they would be funny and sometimes very, very scary. One night they did a version of 'Waiting for My Man' and instead of that up-tempo thing it was very slow and bluesy. Instead of taking any guitar solos he'd whistle. He was making up whole new verses: 'Standing on the corner waiting for the sun to rise, Miss Gina and Miss Ann said that they had a surprise. It's no mystery, it's no mistake, I guess that I'll just have to wait. I'm waiting for my man.' He would go on and on and on. Two or three 'Sister Ray's where he would really cut loose on guitar.

But they knew they were up against it. Mike Curb was at MGM. He was bubblegum mentality at best and they knew they had to get out. I had overheard a conversation in the spring of '69 where Lou was saying they were enthusiastic and were making a fourth album. Then I asked them about it in November and he just canned it: no comment. Lou would occasionally give them little talks, like, 'If we just stick together I know we'll make it.' It's hard for people to imagine now how totally ignored they were. Then they had this image – despite songs on the third album that anybody should have been able to like, like 'Pale Blue Eyes', 'Candy Says' – the image worked against them.

In the autumn of 1969, the Velvets and MGM finally parted ways. 'Hard-drug groups come into your office, wipe out your secretary, waste the time of your promotion people, abuse the people in your organization, show no concern in the recording studio, abuse the equipment, and then to top things off, they break up,' said the MGM president Mike Curb, who was praised by the vigilant antidrug President Nixon for his 'forthright stand against drug abuse'.

The staff at MGM toed this party line. One representative told Lester Bangs in an interview:

> The lead singer is absolutely the most spaced out person I have ever met in my entire life. I think he was on speed all the time they were here. And on top of that, he had the nerve to tell me what a fucked-up company MGM is, and how much he hates the way we're handling them, and why don't we give them promotion – he's sitting there running down the people who are giving me a paycheck every week! What am I supposed to do, agree with him?

As 1969 drew to a close, dark omens appeared. Warhol, who was worried about the fate of Billy Name, surprised Reed by asking him for some methedrine. Lou thought Andy wanted it for himself, only later realizing that he had been trying to get it to help Billy propel himself out of his darkroom, and felt embarrassed for doubting his good heart.

The next time Lou visited Billy at the Factory, in November, he too became concerned about what was happening to his friend. 'By November 1969, Billy Name had kept himself locked inside a closet for nearly a year,' Warhol wrote. 'But then one day Lou Reed came by and spent three whole hours in the darkroom with Billy. When he came out he looked really spooked. "I should never have given him that book last year," Lou said, shaking his head.' Lou had given Billy a stack of books on white magic. 'I'm a channel. I bring things to other people, things people have given me,' boasted the singer.

> I brought the books to Billy not as a gift, but so he could learn what the information was, understand it and tell me and then I could talk

about it to others. The next thing I know, he was in the closet and not coming out. He's shaved his head completely – he said the hairs were growing in, not out – and he's only eating wholewheat wafers and rice crackers. He's following the white-magic book that shows you how to rebuild your cell structure – you play with the cell centres and eat, like, this yoghurt. I asked him to tell me how to do it, and he said it could be really dangerous, that he'd only tell me part of it because if I made a mistake and did something wrong, I could end up like him.

Not only were Lou's friends showing signs of methedrine psychosis, but all around him he saw the erosion that the drug had caused as it became more widespread. 'Who can you talk to on the road?' Reed wrote in an essay about the hardships of being a rock star. 'Long-haired dirty drug people wherever you look.' This brought him face to face with the charge that he had played some role in encouraging drug use. That December, when the band checked into the Second Fret in Philadelphia, he announced that he was no longer going to perform 'Heroin'. 'That track tears me apart, I don't want to know it any more,' he explained. So when the Velvet Underground settled in for a New Year season at the Second Fret, 'Heroin' was gone, and in its place was a set of new songs, including early versions of 'Oh, Jim' and 'Sad Song'.

Coincidentally, one of the waitresses at the club turned out to be the daughter of Michael Leigh, the author of the book from which Lou and John had swiped their name. At first Lou was amused, but when she told him that her father had recently died, he felt another nail had been pounded into the coffin. Despite his knowledge of drugs and the care he took when using them, he began to fear that pressures of the road, the endless problems, and his isolation might some day soon do him in if he could not bring his work to fruition. The Rolling Stone Brian Jones's death in July 1969 stuck like a mug shot on the rock world and stayed in Lou's mind like a suicide on a pavement.

The year 1970 started well when the band signed a recording contract with the legendary Ahmet Ertegun at Atlantic Records, which also represented the Buffalo Springfield and Felix Cavaliere's the Young Rascals. Sesnick had been negotiating with Atlantic for some time in the hopes of at long last obtaining some record company support. But for Lou, the euphoria was short-lived as they returned to the road with the same problems they had endured through most of 1969. First of all, it turned out that they owed MGM $30,000. Like most rock bands, they couldn't figure out what their manager had done with all the money they had earned. Their albums sold steadily and they toured endlessly, yet they had seen none of the profits. At times they were making ends meet on as little as two dollars a day.

But the most irritating problem for Lou was the blossoming ego of Doug Yule. 'Sesnick began to push Doug,' Maureen recalled.

'I was young and arrogant and naive and believed everything Steve Sesnick said,' Yule later admitted. 'When I found out that he did deals, got advances and kept the money from the band and practised divide and rule, I would have gladly killed him.'

'We were running around pretty much out on the coast there, and in Chicago, and down in Texas,' added Moe.

We all wondered why Lou would put up with Yule, for years. It seemed like he pissed Lou off in certain ways. Why didn't he just say, 'I want him out of the band?' We were all so damn sick of him, we would've jumped on it. But he just lets it build up. I asked Lou, 'Why the hell don't we just throw Doug out? What the hell are you bothering with this fool if he bothers you so much?' I can't remember if he ever answered. Maybe he just didn't like any of us.

Another blow to Lou came when Maureen, who was his only supportive friend in the band now, got pregnant and took a sabbatical in March to prepare for the delivery of the baby due that summer.

At the same time Maureen was having her first baby, Shelley Corwin became pregnant by her husband. Lou finally had to accept that Shelley had chosen her family over him. 'It drove us apart in many ways,' she said. 'I consciously went a different way, I chose my child over Lou. He had too many places to go, he was very narcissistic, and I knew he could never pay attention to a child.'

The last act of the tragedy of Lou Reed and the Velvet Underground took place, fittingly enough, in New York City where they had not played for the public since 1967. The rock world was in a state of flux. In July the Beatles' US single 'The Long and Winding Road' and the Bob Dylan double album *Self Portrait* represented reflective views of those who had been undisputed leaders. It was obvious that something new was going to come along soon and surprise everyone, but in the summer of 1970 there was little indication of what it might be or where it would come from. Lou was working from his own complex, paranoid and, some would say, drug-addled mind. He told Moe that he had been levitating several feet above his bed.

According to Richard Meltzer, 'Lou went out of his skull and ended up with a warped sense of time and space that lasted several weeks (reached out at insects only he could see, stuff like that) and the band had been internally bickering up to then anyway.'

Between June and August 1970, the VU were booked to record their first album for Atlantic and simultaneously play a ten-week residency at the club that had been the social centre of their lives in New York since 1966 – Max's Kansas City. The Max's contract required that they play twice nightly from Wednesday to Sunday; Mondays and Tuesdays were left for work on what was to become *Loaded*. Doug Yule's brother Billy, who was still in high school, sat in on drums. The band was in such a terrible financial situation that Billy was offered a flat $60 for the complete ten weeks, although he ended up making about $25 per week because he was paid for his daily return fare from Long Island plus food. The group began to fall apart and Lou was especially unhappy. By the time they started work on *Loaded*, he was exhausted, frail and paranoid. On amphetamine again, he averaged six hours of sleep a week.

Once again, Lou's paranoia had some reasonable ground: behind the scenes Sesnick was taking over control of the production of *Loaded*. In time, he would even lift Reed's name off the song credits and replace Lou's productions with his own mixes. Richard Meltzer remembered going up to the Atlantic offices where he overheard Steve Sesnick, in an adjacent office, talking about removing Lou's voice from the album altogether. 'You have to be very careful with these manager people, some of them are very sick,' Reed recalled. 'I thought we could still continue in some way, but he made it impossible. Those were terrible times.'

Lou had once again come up with an inspired batch of songs and he threw himself into the recordings with all the gusto and drive he had brought to every record they had ever made. The recording went well, although Sterling was miffed by the extent to which Yule had taken on Cale's role as the band's arranger. He stormed out of the studio on more than one occasion as Lou and Doug fought at the sound board, driving one producer, and then his replacement, crazy.

'The role that I played on *Loaded* was basically a facilitator for Lou in that he would start with some material and I would sometimes help him formulate them into songs,' Yule explained. 'And sometimes I would do the arranging. *Loaded* was basically Lou and I and Sterling was there occasionally. Basically I was having a good time. We were in the studio and I would just cut loose and do all the things I always wanted to do.'

Meanwhile, they began the Max's residency. On the surface everything looked smooth. The Max's audiences were enthusiastic and the band, by all accounts, gave a series of excellent shows. At first, like someone who has decided to kill himself and feels the euphoria of a lifted burden, Lou put on a good front. 'I'd never seen Lou so happy,' remembered Billy Altman. 'He was cracking jokes and dancing!'

'No other band could possibly have opened up Max's for live music and no other ambiance could possibly have served so well in reintroducing this by-now-legendary group to the city of its origin,' wrote Richard Meltzer. 'But more important is the whole thing actually worked (whole summer of them playing real good almost every night), one of those rare times when anything that rock-predictable was actually worth the bother.'

'Everybody is trying to do it in their own way and we just play some rock and roll and people dance and get some rocks off to it,' Reed told a reporter from the *New York Times*. 'Fabulous! That's enough, that's enough.'

Signs that Lou was not himself, however, became evident when he continued jumping around the stage, executing classic rock-star moves, trying to satisfy Sesnick. 'We were always anti-performers, and Lou was leaping around and making all those gestures he does now,' said Sterling. 'But Sesnick had often exhorted us all to be more dynamic on stage; I guess he had been working on Lou in particular. I didn't realize until Lou told me later on.'

Although outwardly enjoying himself, Reed despised his role as a puppet to Sesnick's machinations. Not only was Sesnick aiming for a more dance-oriented commercial show, he was pulling everyone's emotional strings in order to achieve it. 'I would say that Steve was running everything,' said Yule. 'He basically manipulated everyone. A pattern emerged of separating people and talking to them about other members. Sesnick pitched me against Lou, but I couldn't see that at the time.'

Later, Reed realized he was losing his grip on his identity. 'I hated playing at Max's,' he said.

Because I couldn't do the songs I wanted to do and I was under a lot of pressure to do things I didn't want to and it finally reached a crescendo. I never in my life thought I would not do what I believed in and there I was, not doing what I believed in, that's all, and it made me sick. It dawned on me that I was doing what somebody else was telling me to do supposedly for my own good because they're supposed to be so smart. But only one person can write it and only that one person should know what it's about. I'm not a machine that gets up there and parrots off these songs. And I was giving out interviews at the time saying yes, I wanted the group to be a dance band, I wanted to do that, but there was a large part of me that wanted to do something else. I was talking as if I was programmed. That part of me that wanted to do something else wasn't allowed to express itself, in fact was being cancelled out. And it turned out that that was the part that made up 90 per cent of Lou.

'There was that comment by that guy that I became unplugged from objective reality,' Reed recalled. 'Well, that's not what happened. I plugged into objective reality, and I got very sick at what I saw, what I was doing to myself. I didn't belong there. *I didn't want to be a mass pop national hit group with followers.*'

The final falling-out came in a fight between Steve and Lou in which the manager, echoing Shelley's leitmotif, told his fragile star, 'I don't care if you live or die.'

'Lou couldn't face this, to be very suddenly slapped in the face by someone he trusted,' said Sterling. 'My impression of Lou then was that he prized loyalty,' said Doug. 'And that if you didn't do anything against him he would accept you on that basis. But if he felt someone sold him out, they were the enemy.'

Quietly, without informing anybody in the band, Lou made a big decision. Not only was he going to leave the group as soon as the Max's contract was fulfilled, but he had contacted his parents, asking them if he could move back to Freeport in order, as he put it, to realign his life. Sid and Toby made plans to pick Lewis up at Max's after the final set of the last show.

Thoroughly burned out, Reed soldiered on for the last few performances. By the kind of magic coincidence that regularly marked Reed's passage, Andy Warhol's superstar Brigid Polk came to the VU's last show, on the night of 23 August, with Gerard Malanga and a tape recorder, and caught Lou in his farewell performance. 'The last night I was there, when Brigid Polk made that tape, that was the only night I really enjoyed myself,' he remembered. 'I did all the songs I wanted – a lot of them were ballads. High energy does not necessarily mean fast; high energy has to do with heart.'

After the show, Lou told Sesnick that he was leaving the Velvet Underground. 'Lou loves to dramatize,' explained Ronnie Cutrone, one of Lou's Factory friends. 'He loves to be the orphaned child, the orphaned genius.'

'His leaving the group came as a complete surprise to me,' said Doug Yule, who got the news from Steve Sesnick.

The reason Lou left the band was a personal thing between him and Sesnick. Sesnick kept everybody separate so Lou didn't confide in me about what he was feeling. So the fact that he was going to leave came down very suddenly. We were going along fine, we were playing at Max's, we finished up the album, and we mixed it and stuff – things were going great. And then boom!

The most heartbroken by Lou's decision was Maureen, who had come in from Long Island to see the last show. 'The night I went was the last night Lou played,' she remembered. 'He said he felt bad about it, but he had thought about it for a long time and he had just decided that he had to go on his own.'

The last person to be informed was Sterling, who got the news while relaxing after the show.

It was my contention that he left the band when the magazine *Gay Power* reviewed the show and said I was the sexiest lead guitarist since Keith Richards, and Dougie was just as cute as a Christmas present under the tree. And this is supposed to be Lou's constituency! I said to Steve Sesnick, 'Boy, will Lou be hot when he reads this.' That night I'm sitting in a booth upstairs at Max's eating a cheeseburger and Lou comes up and says, 'Sterling, I'd like you to meet my parents.' I was astonished. Lou always had an extremely troubled relationship with his parents. So I was thinking, 'What in the world can this portend?'

'There were a lot of things going on that summer,' Reed concluded. 'Internally, within the band, the situation, the milieu and especially the management. Words can't do justice to the way I got worked over with the money. But I'm not a businessman. I always said, "I don't care about it," and generally I've gotten fucked as a result of that attitude.'

chapter ten

Fallen Knight

1970–1971

[In which Lou exiles himself
to his parents' home, meets
his first wife, and begins a
physical and emotional
recovery.]

*I'd harboured the hope that the intelligence that once
inhabited novels and films would ingest rock. I was, perhaps,
wrong.*

Lou Reed

For Lou, returning to Freeport involved shedding one skin and
growing another. It was not an easy transition, but Lou's
multifaceted personality enabled him to fade into the leafy green
streets where time stood still and kids still played baseball or
cowboys and Indians. Lou had first come to Freeport when he was
eleven, barely months before he first turned on the radio and
suddenly discovered the exhilarating world of rock and roll. Here
he could transport himself back to his rock roots and figure out
where he had gone astray.

The Reeds had moved from an apartment in Brooklyn to their
house in Freeport back in 1953 – the year before rock began.
Number 35 Oakfield Avenue, on the corner of Oakfield and
Maxon, was a modern single-storey house in a middle-class
subsection called the Village. Most of the houses in the neighbourhood were built in colonial or ranch style, but Lewis's parents

owned a house that, in the 1950s, friends referred to as 'the chicken coop' because of its modern, angular, single-floor design. Though squat and odd from the outside, it was a very beautifully laid-out and comfortable house. It also had a two-car garage and a front lawn perfect for children to play on. The wide, quiet streets doubled as baseball diamonds and football fields when the local kids got together for a pick-up game. Freeport, a town of just under 30,000 inhabitants at the time, lay on the Atlantic coast, on the Freeport and Middle Bays, protected from the ocean by the thin expanse of Long Beach. The town, one of a thousand spanning the length of Long Island, was designed and operated around the requirements of large, middle-class families. With parks, beaches, social centres and well-funded schools, Freeport was suburban utopia. Though just forty-five minutes from Manhattan by car or train, it could have been a lifetime away from Brooklyn, the city the family had just deserted.

Lewis was surrounded by boys of his age who came from the same social and economic background. His closest childhood friend, Allen Hyman, who often used to eat at the Reeds' and lived only a block and a half away, remembered, 'The inside of their house was decorated modern. It was fifties modern, living room and den. At least from sixth grade on my view of his upbringing was very, very suburban middle class.'

After graduating from Carolyn G. Atkinson Elementary and then Freeport Junior High, in the autumn of 1956, Lewis and his friends began attending Freeport High School (now replaced by a bunkerlike junior high). A large stone structure with a carved façade and an expanse of lawn, located on the corner of Pine and South Grove, the school resembled an old English boarding school like Eton or Rugby. It was a ten-minute walk from Oakfield and Maxon through the tree-lined neighbourhood of Freeport Village and just over the busy Sunrise Highway.

Long Island has a history of nurturing some markedly unstable individuals who lash out against their surroundings. This phenomenon, as exemplified by numerous satanic and drug-related murders, renegade teenagers and creative but troubled artists and entertainers, offers one explanation for Lou's obsession with alternative lifestyles from the artistic to the criminal.

'I started out in the Brooklyn Public School System,' said Reed of his time at PS 197 and beyond, 'and have hated all forms of school and authority ever since.'

'My main memory of Lou was that he had a tremendous sense of satire,' recalled his high-school friend John Shebar. 'He had a certain irreverence that was a little out of the ordinary. Mostly he would be making fun of the teacher or doing an impersonation of some ridiculous situation in school.'

Lewis and his friends were also drawn to athletics. Freeport High was a football school. Under the superlative coaching of Bill Ashley, the Freeport High Red Devils were the pride of the town. Lou would claim in 'Coney Island Baby' that he wanted to play football for the coach, 'the straightest dude I ever knew'. But he had neither the size nor the athletic ability, and never even tried out. Instead, during his junior year Lou joined the varsity track team. He was a good runner, and was strong enough to become a pole vaulter. Although he preferred individual events to team sports, he was known around Freeport as a good basketball player. 'Lou Reed was not only funny but he was a good athlete,' recalled Hyman. 'He was always kind of thin and lanky. There was a park right near our house and we used to go down and play basketball. He was very competitive and driven in most things he did. He would like to do something that didn't involve a team or require anybody else. And he was exceptionally moody all the time.'

Lou's moodiness was but one indication that he was developing a vivid interior world. He was an enthusiastic reader of science fiction and wrote stories and poems as well as songs. 'By junior year in high school, he was always experimenting with his writing,' Hyman reported. 'He did a lot of writing. He had notebooks filled with poems and short stories, and they were always on the dark side. I mean, they were not about flowers and stuff.' Having managed to convince his parents to buy him a motorcycle, he would spend much of his time riding around the streets of Freeport in imitation of Marlon Brando. His friend and neighbour Eddie, however, would often surprise even Lou. 'Eddie was a real wacko,' commented another neighbour, Carol Wood, 'and he only lived about four houses away from Lou. He had all these weird ideas about outer-space Martians landing and this and that. During that time there was also a group in town that was robbing houses. They were called the Malefactors. It turned out that Eddie was one of them.'

Lou demonstrated from the first that he was interested in people who lacked regard for the norms of society and who were willing to live outside the law. It was the one thing that had attracted him to the crowd at Ludlow Street, to Warhol's Factory, and later – in the mid-seventies – to the New York amphetamine circuit. 'Eddie was friendly with Lou and with me, but Eddie was a lunatic,' agreed Allen Hyman.

> He was the first certifiable person I have ever known. He was one of those kids who your mother would never want or allow you to hang out with because he was always getting into trouble. He had a BB gun and he would sit up in his attic and shoot people walking down the street. Lou loved him because he was as outrageous as he was, maybe more. He used to get arrested, he was insane.

Allen's brother Andy recalled that it was typical of Lou to maintain a number of mutually exclusive friendships which served different purposes. Allen was Lewis's conservative friend, while Eddie allowed him to exercise quite a different aspect of his personality. 'There was a desire on Lewis's part – of course I didn't know this at the time – to be accepted by the regular kinds of guys, and on the other hand he was very attracted to the degenerates,' Andy recalled. 'Eddie was kind of a crazy guy who was into petty theft, smoking dope at a very early age and into all kinds of strange stuff with girls. And Lewis was into all that kind of stuff with Eddie while he was involved with my brother in another scene.'

Throughout his teens, Lou would try anything to break the tedium of life in Freeport, especially if it was considered outside the conventional. Lou managed to find other characters desperate to elude boredom. One such moment came about indirectly through his interest in music. Every evening, the better part of the high-school population of Freeport and its neighbouring towns would tune into WGBB Radio to hear the latest sounds, make requests and dedicate songs. Often the volume of telephone calls to the station would be so great that the wires would get crossed, creating a kind of teenage party line over which friendships developed. On one occasion, Lou became friendly with a caller. 'There was this girl who lived in Merrick,' said Allen Hyman.

> She was fairly advanced for her time, and Lou ended up going out on a date with her. He came back from the date, and he called me up and he said, 'I've just had the most amazing experience. I took this girl to the Valley Stream drive-in and she took out a reefer.' And I said, 'Is she addicted to marijuana?' Because in those days we thought if you smoked marijuana you were an addict. He said, 'No, it was cool. I smoked this reefer, it was really great.'

According to his own testimony, what made Lewis different from the all-American boys in Freeport was a hypersensitivity to the fairly common homosexual feelings he experienced as he went through puberty. In his adult sexual life, it would be fair to say that Lou has been a practising bisexual with heterosexuality his stronger suit. He is also a person who reacts extremely to the smallest ruffle on the surface. The sudden rush of, at the time, inexplicable erotic fantasies about boys, would have badly unsettled him, and there was no way he could discuss them with anybody, because of the prejudices of mid-fifties America. Instead, he turned his raging romantic emotions inwards, affecting the rest of his life negatively.

By the time Lou emerged from his room, two days after the Velvets' final show at Max's Kansas City in August 1970, he had reverted to the spoiled little domestic tyrant who had left for Syracuse University a decade earlier.

Lou was clearly shaken, and this initial period in exile was painful. He stopped taking speed and all other drugs and dragged through the hours and weeks feeling dull and listless. Like many artists who get unplugged from their drugs and from their work, Lou went into a deep hole of despair. He described his 'sad and moody self . . . spellbound by the possibilities and amazed at my own dullness'.

In late 1970, as Lou experienced the bends of withdrawal, the rock world was going through its own difficult passage. Elvis Presley embarked on his first tour since 1958, Elton John began his first US tour in Los Angeles, and Jimi Hendrix played his last concert at the Isle of Wight Pop Festival.

One reason Lou left the Velvet Underground was that he was afraid of dying. He had good reason to believe that he might. On 18 September, Hendrix died in London, at age twenty-seven. The period 1970–71, covering Lou's exile to Freeport, took an inordinate toll on the rock-and-roll industry. Following Hendrix, Janis Joplin, Jim Morrison, Gene Vincent, Slim Harpo, Duane Allman, Junior Parker, Alan Wilson, Tammi Terrell, Otis Spann and King Curtis, who had played on Reed's first recorded single, 'So Blue', met their deaths through disease, drug overdoses or, as in the case of Curtis, violence.

In the month following Lou's resignation, the authorities turned their attention to the very music he was most associated with. Vice President Spiro Agnew gave a series of speeches in the autumn attacking liberal Democrats as 'troglodyte leftists', charging them with 'pusillanimous pussyfooting', with an emphasis on music and media as promoters of drugs. In November, President Nixon proposed that all pro-drug lyrics be banned. In response, the president of the Velvets' first label, MGM, cancelled the recording contracts of eighteen artists accused of promoting drugs, including Judy Garland (posthumously) and Connie Francis. The permissive era was coming to an end.

Meanwhile, fans, rock critics and members of the Velvets were left trying to figure out just why Reed had deserted them. Strange rumours floated around the New York rock scene, such as: Lou really was dead and his manager murdered him; he had cracked under pressure and split for parts unknown; he had finally succumbed to the lure of heroin . . . When the more mundane truth, that he had gone home to Long Island to live with his parents, emerged, one cynic quipped, 'Oh, well, he writes all his best songs on Long Island,' echoing Cale's sentiment that Lou wrote best in reaction to his parents.

Home cooking and a healthy lifestyle did not really provide the answers Lou was looking for. His torment went deeper. Lou had to piece together from his many selves a sense of who he was. He knew he couldn't rely on the reflected image of himself thrown back at him by his audiences. Indeed, his role as a performer made his search for self almost impossible. One of his greatest fans, the up-and-coming David Bowie, recognized the problem when he said, 'I was David Jones from Brixton who wanted to do something artistically worthwhile. But I hadn't the courage to face the audience as myself.' In some ways Lou's audience had become a many-headed monster to confront. He was at times able to find an identity in the adulation of his fans, but he could not rely on such a response. Not only did the audience lack an identity of its own, it could not offer a performer any degree of consistency in its love. 'There is no son more delinquent, no family more in chaos than the audience which comes to sit at the table of rock,' Reed wrote.

While Lou was grappling with the conundrum of his self and trying to decide which direction he should take, Sesnick and the Velvet Underground – or the 'Velveteen Undergound', as Danny Fields dubbed them – continued touring in support of *Loaded*, publicizing the new record as if there had been no significant change in the line-up.

This was enough to make Lou uptight, but to make matters worse, Steve Sesnick engaged in some rewriting of history that virtually erased all traces of Reed's influence on the band and the new album. 'As soon as Lou left, Sesnick started going around making statements to the effect that they were gonna have a great band now that the Problem (which was his interpretation of Lou) was out of the way,' reported Lester Bangs. 'According to Danny Fields, Sesnick even had the balls to start claiming that he wrote some of the songs himself!'

Coincidentally, Lou had retreated to Freeport the same week *Loaded* was released. Taking advantage of the fact that Reed wasn't around, Sesnick had packaged the album to make it appear as if Lou had barely been involved, and Doug Yule was chiefly responsible for its creation. The front cover, an illustration that looked like a cheap ad in a hippy paper of some steps leading to the subway, was a stupid image Reed would never have accepted. The back cover was even worse. Stretched across the top was a black-and-white photograph of a brooding musician (identified as Yule in the rock press), sitting alone in a recording studio amid a melange of musical instruments, which could be taken to imply that Yule had not only composed and arranged the album, but played most of the instruments on it.

Below the photograph, the band members were listed in telling order: Yule, Morrison, Reed, Tucker. Moreover, despite the fact that Lou had done all the songwriting, credits were awarded, as they had been on *The Velvet Underground*, to the whole band collectively. 'The song credits on the grey album was an effort to present a united front,' Doug Yule explained. 'In a sense a lot of it was a whole-group project, but the lyrical content all came from Lou. On *Loaded* it was Sesnick's ploy to discredit Lou. His idea was to disperse as much of the credit as possible to the rest of the band, because Lou had already left. He wanted to keep his meal ticket going.' Incidentally, Yule later claimed to have had no prior knowledge of the sleeve design and said he hadn't seen it until after it was printed. Sesnick continued to deceive and manipulate the whole band.

Reed was dismayed that the album had been remixed in his absence. Abbreviating his arrangements of 'Sweet Jane' and 'New Age' had, in his opinion, destroyed the tracks. 'The end of "Sweet

Jane" was cut off, the end of "New Age" was cut off, the guitar solo on "Train Coming Round the Bend" was fucked around with and inserted,' he said. 'How could anyone be that stupid? They took all the power out of those songs.' Looking at the song listings, he realized that their sequence had been changed so that the thematic structure of the album, an element Lou considered vital to the presentation of material, was entirely missing. 'Secondly, I wasn't there to put the songs in order,' he complained later. 'The songs are out of order. They don't form a cohesive unit, they just leap about. If I could have stood it I would have stayed with them and showed them what to do.'

Lou's criticism, however, was dismissed by Sterling Morrison, who, along with the rest of the band, cited the success of the album as proof that they hadn't conspired to undermine Lou's masterpiece. '*Loaded* is incomparably the best mix of any of our albums,' he asserted. 'Lou had no control over the mix, and if [the recording and remix engineers] Geoffrey Haslam and Adrian Barber were involved in such a "conspiracy", why did the work come out sounding better than anything else?'

In fact, *Loaded* met with almost universal critical approval. For the first time in the history of the band, the singles received radio play and the album sold well and got good reviews.

Still tied emotionally to the Velvet Underground and heartened by the positive reviews of *Loaded*, Lou apparently had second thoughts about leaving the band. In late September he visited Sterling, proposing that his former guitar partner quit the Velveteens and start anew with him. It was a hasty, ill-timed move prompted, perhaps, more by emotion than foresight. 'I had hardly talked to Lou for months and I said, "Man, I just don't want to talk,"' Sterling recalled.

He said that as long as I'd played with him I'd never told him he'd played well. This was quite possibly true. I said, 'I didn't need to, because other people told you.' And he said, 'Who do you think I wanted to tell me?' It pointed out to me a real failing in me – I didn't think he needed me to tell him. I was dumbfounded. But I was so mad at him I just didn't want to talk. I would never tell him why. Which is a strange way to behave. You know 'The Poison Tree' by Blake? Like that. 'I was angry with my friend / I told it not . . . ' I don't tell you and that's your punishment.

Sterling had been on a slow burn ever since 1968 when Lou had forced John out of the band. He had virtually refused to talk to Lou since. By pleading with Morrison from a weak position, Lou had begged to be rejected. And Sterling, who had an understandable if misplaced sense of revenge, snapped at the opportunity. 'He was saying, "Oh, it was this diet I was on. Wheat husks,"' Morrison continued. 'He said, "I take responsibility for all that. You and me, we'll put together some new band." So I said, "Lou, from what I see, it will take at least two years to get right back to where we are today." I was right: it took him at least that long.'

Reed's identity crisis was exacerbated by the undaunted progress of the Velvet Underground, but there also emerged a second factor which both depressed and motivated him. During 1970–71, as Lou sat on the sidelines of the music scene, Cale came out with his first solo album, *Vintage Violence*; Nico released her third, *Desert Shore*; and Warhol produced *Trash*, a commercially successful (partially Lou Reed–inspired) film about a heroin addict and a drag queen.

Forced to embark upon a solo flight, Lou began quietly to reconnoitre New York. Meeting with old friends and checking on his connections, many of whom were shocked by Reed's confused state, Lou tentatively tried to re-establish himself. 'He was living with his parents,' recalled the writer Glenn O'Brien, who was working for Andy Warhol's *Interview* magazine.

He came around the Factory and he was really pathetic. I don't know what he was on, but he was really out of it. He was my hero, but it was like his life was over. So I thought, He's a great poet and a great writer. I'll get him to write for *Interview*. And he turned in this thing that was so embarrassing that I was really shocked. I had suspected that he had been on psychiatric drugs when I met him. It was like it was written by somebody on Thorazine. It just didn't make any sense at all. Then I had to call him up and say, 'Maybe you really didn't want to do this.' He was kind of apologetic. 'Well, oh yeah, you know I knew it really wasn't good . . . ' It was horrible.

Lou set himself up for another rejection when he called Shelley in November to congratulate her on the birth of her daughter Sascha, and she hung up on him. 'My mother was sitting next to me when he called,' she explained.

I said, 'You have the wrong number.' He said, 'It's me,' and I said, 'I know.' He said, 'It's Lou!' He was absolutely devastated. I can still hear his voice today. He was crushed. It was such an awful thing to do, but I was just not duplicitous by nature and it was not in my ability to carry on a conversation and not have her know that this was Lou. But he was really astounded and shocked and hurt. It was a terrible time in his life and I think the end came for Lou and me when I hung up on him. It was as if I was saying once again, 'I understand how rotten you feel, but I've done it so go fuck yourself and die! And I'll watch quietly.' I completely lost my best friend when I did that, and I have just been sorry about it ever since.

Towards the end of 1970, Reed was asked to contribute an essay to a book called *No One Waved Goodbye* about the deaths of Brian Epstein, Brian Jones, Jimi Hendrix, Janis Joplin and Jim Morrison. Lou penned a sober reflection full of images of himself. It was a much more successful piece than he had done for *Interview*, and good therapy too. 'One cannot get to the top and switch masks,' it read in part. 'Your lover demands consistency, and unless you've established variance as your norm a priori you will be called an adulterer.' His essay followed the course of his exile full circle, from anguish and surrender to hope for the future. 'Does one pore endlessly over monstrous manuscripts praying to find the sacred words, to resurrect once again the excitement, the glory and the power?' he asked, suggesting, 'Perhaps I should die. After all, they all (the great blues singers) did die, didn't they? But life is getting better now, I don't want to die. Do I?'

*

When the novelty of Lou's presence at their home in Freeport wore off, his parents nagged him into taking a full-time job at his father's firm in Garden City. 'I became a typist for my old man, $40 a week,' he said. 'He really wanted me to be in the family business. But that was a real impossibility. I never said I was smart. I don't want to be the company man.' Reed would later claim also to have had a second job, collecting rubbish off nearby Jones beach. Like a character in a novel by Samuel Beckett, Lou wandered across the sand with a stick, spiking pieces of trash and sticking them in a bin. 'It lasted one day. A guy threw an orange peel down near the trash bin. I said, "You gotta be kidding, man."'

One day he received a phone call from 'these very intense fortyish Italian hippies with grey hair and a Park Avenue apartment', who told him they thought that after Ray Davies he was the most literate rock songwriter and the perfect person to turn Nelson Algren's book *Walk on the Wild Side* into a Broadway musical. Expressing comic disbelief, Lou riposted that he was now a typist. After some consideration, however, Lou concluded that it beat trash collecting, and might even lead somewhere. At their request he bought a paperback copy of the book and proceeded to try and make an X where he thought the songs might go. Lou didn't get very far with the score before the show's producers backed out in favour of another play, but he did end up with the theme song for the piece, 'Walk on the Wild Side', and figured he would save the title 'for the day I decide to assault the world'.

At the end of 1970, Lou began to pull himself back together. The bulk of 1971 would be spent not so much in retreat as in reappraisal.

The first thing he did was launch a lawsuit against Sesnick to win back songwriting credits and copyrights on *Loaded*. Reed eventually won the lengthy battle to gain sole copyrights to the songs on the two albums, *The Velvet Underground* and *Loaded*, that listed the credits to the band collectively. 'Lou really did want to have a whole lot of credit for the songs, so on nearly all of the albums we gave it to him,' Sterling Morrison commented a decade later.

> It kept him happy. He got the rights to all the songs on *Loaded* so now he's credited for being the absolute and singular genius of the Underground, which is not true. There are a lot of songs I should have co-authorship on, and the same holds true for John Cale. The publishing company was called Three Prong because there were three of us involved. I'm the last person to deny Lou's immense contribution and he's the best songwriter of the three of us. But he wanted all the credit, he wanted it more than we did, and he got it, to keep the peace.

However, Lou found moral justification in the decision of the court. 'Every song on the album was written by me,' said Lou. 'And no ifs and buts, nothing about it. But I had to go to legal lengths to establish it.' He was also able to free himself from his management contract with Sesnick, although in the process he lost the rights to the name Velvet Underground.

In January 1971, John Lennon, whose own group had only just broken up, released a single called 'Mother'. It had a big influence on Lou, who was particularly struck by the subject matter, the opening church bells and the raw, honest emotion of the song. It would soon have Lou constructing his first solo album in his head. The foundations were now laid for Reed's re-emergence into the world, and it was clear that it was going to be on his own terms. Reed realized that in order to embark on a solo career he had to take the reins himself and not let them slip into the hands of power-hungry managers. 'It was just obvious that whatever it was, *I had to have control*,' he concluded. Control became his mantra over the course of his solo career.

Meanwhile, with the commercial success of *Loaded*, more and more fans and fellow artists were coming to appreciate Reed's work. Everyone from Alice Cooper to Iggy Pop spoke of Reed with reverence, and many incorporated aspects of his image into their own performances. The Rolling Stones borrowed several Velvet Underground themes for their album *Sticky Fingers*, complete with an Andy Warhol cover. Reed dismissed the parallel with a shrug. 'Our references were upfront. I laid it out on the line with those songs. No one has come out with a statement that strong. The first album was five years ahead of its time – if it was to be released now it would get the recognition it deserved then.'

The most significant development in Lou's life that year came when, shopping in a department store, he met a straight, attractive, aspiring actress named Bettye Kronstadt. Anybody who had known Shelley Albin would have been struck by how similar Bettye Kronstadt looked. She had the same colouring, build, face. They could have been sisters. But there the comparison ended. Lou was infatuated with her. By his own admission he decided the time was right to become heterosexual again. 'He got together with Bettye soon after I had my daughter,' Shelley remembered. 'This was the definite marker along the way. It was like, that's that. It's the end of us.'

The affair reeked of the same duplicity that was tearing Reed apart. On the one hand there was the proper, traditional woman of Sidney and Toby's dreams, and on the other the impulse to homosexuality, unrestrained emotional expression and violence. 'I met Bettye once,' recalled Gerard Malanga. 'She was a very sexy-looking Jewish babe, but quiet. And Lou kept her in the background. She wasn't voluptuous, she was very thin and taller than Lou, at least five foot nine. She was a stylish babe, she knew how to dress.' With her conservatively styled hair, string of pearls and elegant clothes, Bettye lived in a different world from the violent landscape of Reed's writing. She reminded Lou's more sceptical friends of Betty in the Archie comic books. 'Some part of Lou really does like stability and the old cozy kitchen and homey living rooms,' concluded Sterling Morrison.

'Bettye,' Lou announced in the trendy magazine *Fusion*, 'is not hip at all, and I want to keep her that way. I believe in pretty princesses.' He underscored the sentiment in a poem he published in the same magazine, but worried that he might sound like a 'bisexual chauvinist pig'. In his most poignant image of Bettye, Lou wrote that she looked like Mary Queen of Scots.'

'I think I am in love,' Lou announced in a poem called 'Bettye'. 'I seem to have the symptoms (ignore past failure in human relations / I think of Bettye all the time).' Another piece, 'He Couldn't Find a Voice to Speak With', began, 'I am sorry, princess, I am so slow in loving / Believe me, it is inexperience / This inability to show affection / The long minutes without words / and then a clumsy pinch perhaps.'

In addition to pouring his heart into the relationship with Bettye, Lou also channelled his dark energy into poetry and music. In the early months of 1971, he completed a substantial body of work. In March, Gerard Malanga arranged for him, along with Jim Carroll, to give a poetry reading at St Mark's Church in Manhattan, only a block from the Dom, where the Exploding Plastic Inevitable had played so brilliantly five years earlier. In front of an avant-garde audience of rock writers and poets, including Allen Ginsberg, Lou rose to the occasion, leading off with 'Heroin' and going on to read 'Sister Ray', 'Lady Godiva's Operation' and 'The Black Angel's Death Song' to considerable acclaim.

Carried away by the audience's response, he announced he'd never sing again, because he was now a poet. He went on to say that if he ever did anything as silly as returning to rock and roll the ghost of Delmore Schwartz would surely haunt him.

According to Lou's favourite writer on the downtown scene, Richard Meltzer, 'Finally he read a series of gay poems he had written just for the occasion. Pro-gay rather than anti-gay was the way he explained it. "Anti-gay is too easy," he declared. This brought a warm response from Danny Fields, because of their modest militant sensibility.'

Lou was trying to reconcile his duplicitous feelings about sex and love and his relationship with Bettye. In the process he worked out his view of being gay:

Just because you're gay doesn't mean you have to camp around in make-up. That's just like platform shoes. You just can't fake being gay. If they claim they're gay, they're just going to have to make love in a gay style, and most of these people aren't capable of making that commitment. You can't fake being gay, because being gay means you're going to have to suck cock, or get fucked. I think there's a very basic thing in a guy if he's straight where he's just going to say no. 'I'll act gay, I'll do this and I'll do that, but I can't do that.' Just like a gay person if they wanted to act straight and everything, but if you said 'Okay, go ahead, go to bed with a girl,' they're going to have to get an erection first.

Lou started to needle Bettye constantly about his 'gay past', and drive her nuts by telling her how much he liked sucking cock. Now, he lashed out at her violently on the slightest provocation. Friends recalled the bruises and black eyes Bettye hid behind dark glasses.

Meeting up with his old friend Allen Hyman, Lou demonstrated just how far he had drifted from the sensibility of his parents and his own Freeport self. 'We hadn't seen each other in a couple of years and he called me up and said it was time we got together again,' Allen recalled.

So we met for a drink in a restaurant over in Garden City because he was spending some time doing some work for his father, whose office was there. We met in the afternoon and had a drink and spent seven or eight hours having beers and talking about what was going on with him. I was very fascinated because the Velvet Underground was one of my favourite rock-and-roll bands, and I wanted to know about 'Heroin' and how he had come to write this music. He communicated to me how he had been addicted to heroin at the time, and I had no idea that he had been. We were talking about his obsession with drag queens. It was like he was more attracted to the lifestyle, rather than being involved. It sounded so outrageous.

When a visit to Allen's house followed, it became clear to Hyman that Lou's outrageous lifestyle still lurked beneath a brittle surface calm.

So he came out to the house with this girl, Bettye, and we were sitting in the living room and my brother Andy was there also, because Lou and Andy were very friendly. Lou and Andy were jamming and we were having a good time. Then suddenly his girlfriend said something to him and he started beating her up, slapping her around. And Suzanne, my wife, got so upset, she said, 'Stop this, what are you doing?' And it was clear that he wasn't kidding around. She'd interrupted a song or something like that, and he started smacking her around. My son, who was maybe four or five years old, was really upset by this whole thing going on, and Suzanne said to Lou, 'You're going to have to leave.'

The incident ended Lou's relationship with Allen, and signalled the end of his exile. Andy Hyman agreed: 'Lewis rejected my brother because Allen wasn't going to further him in any way. I think he was looking for relationships that were going to further his career and notoriety and image, or else he just wasn't interested.'

In 1971, many of the more vital young writers in the US were rock writers – poets like Patti Smith and Richard Hell, commentators like Richard Meltzer and Lester Bangs, journalists like David Dalton and Henry Edwards. Some of them were members of a loosely formed group, Collective Conscience, centred on the husband-and-wife team of Richard and Lisa Robinson, comic-book versions of Leonard and Virginia Woolf. Richard was a staff producer at RCA, Lisa a rock journalist specializing in gossip columns, whose favourite singer was Frank Sinatra. 'We thought,' she recalled, 'we were going to change the world.'

Lou was introduced into the group by Danny Fields, and soon found himself being offered a worshipful reception at their soirees in the Robinsons' apartment. According to Richard Meltzer, Lisa Robinson used to throw parties for Lou,

mainly so she could hype him on making a rock-and-roll comeback with her husband Richard as producer (all he'd done up to this point was obscure stuff like the Flamin' Groovies and Hackmore Brick so a reactivated Lou Reed would be quite a feather in his cap). A discreet respectability was maintained at all times. Lou was down on dope and most drugs, so no grass was allowed at these get-togethers (guests were quietly warned on the way in so Lou wouldn't hear).

With the support of the Robinsons and their coterie, Reed regained much of the confidence he had missed since his days with the Velvets. Before long he was holding court.

'Richard Robinson made a videotape of Lou singing his solo songs,' another friend remembered. 'Lou was kind of drunk, sitting there playing beautiful folk guitar that really gets that whole person. You can really see he's so cool. I think Lou was in love with Richard, who was a very good-looking guy with long hair. When he sings his songs he's singing to the camera and he's singing it to Richard.'

The Robinsons' coterie had their own rigid hierarchy and rules of etiquette. 'It was a worshipful scene,' Edwards recalled. 'There were certain presences before which you weren't supposed to do too much talking – like the arrival of Patti Smith and Sam Shepard, Jackie Curtis or Lou Reed.' By entertaining and promoting such people, the Robinsons aimed to establish a power base in the rock industry. 'The pop press that grew up around the Robinsons had the job of creating newness and of creating an ersatz demand for newness so that they could prove that they could sell things, thereby justifying their existence,' explained Edwards. 'The seventies was an amazing manufacturing of the style of style as an attempt to replace the style of authenticity.'

These Robinson blowouts allowed Lou to mingle with music's movers and shakers. At one such event he met an unusual combination of corporate lawyer, rock rat and literary scholar, Dennis Katz, who had just become vice president of artists and repertoire at RCA. 'I was musically oriented and had the ability to negotiate and structure deals that would give them an A&R head with both backgrounds,' Katz explained. 'An A&R head must be able to do more than evaluate acts and listen to tapes. He must have a feeling for an act's commercial potential, to know what they'll be worth.' Once again it looked as if everybody was in the right place at the right time. Having just signed the hottest new rock star in the UK, David Bowie, Katz soon persuaded dubious RCA executives that Lou Reed would be another perfect star for the new rock era. RCA had been living off Elvis Presley since the mid-1950s and done little since then to consolidate their position. Katz was a bright light in an otherwise lacklustre company. Other RCA artists during Lou's RCA years were John Denver, Harry Nilsson, Hall & Oates and Alabama. Lou signed a two-album solo contract with the company and immediately set to work with his new mentor.

Once Lou got back in touch with Danny Fields and found himself a star in the Robinsons' coterie, things moved forward rapidly. In September he met a man who was to play a vital supporting role in his career, David Bowie. Bowie was on the verge of taking off into superstardom. He was already making a big point of how much he thought of Lou. He came to New York with his wife Angie, guitar player Mick Ronson and manager Tony DeFries, to sign his RCA contract and meet Lou. Tony Zanetta, an American actor who had recently starred as Warhol in Warhol's play *Pork*, was the go-between. 'To celebrate the signing Dennis Katz arranged for this party at the Ginger Man,' Zanetta recalled.

It was like going to a bar mitzvah. There were twelve to fifteen people, Richard and Lisa Robinson, Bob Ring who was A&R at RCA, Dennis and other record company people. Lou took Bettye and David had Angie with him. Ronson, Tony and David thought of me as his entree to Lou and Andy. I didn't know Lou. I was very intimidated by Reed. That amphetamine cutting humour frightened me so I sat there quietly, smiling. David was also not used to the biting, caustic humour. David was flirtatious and coy. He was in his Lauren Bacall phase with his Veronica Lake hairdo and eye shadow. So he let Lou take the driver's seat conversationally. Plus Lou was one of David's idols from the Velvet Underground. David was very shy.

I remember Lou being in jeans and a denim jacket. No coloured fingernails or any of that. He didn't even have long hair. And no one knew how to take Bettye. We all thought she was an airline stewardess. Very vapid. She didn't have much to say. She wasn't very hip-looking. She was in pantsuits. Lisa Robinson was the social centre of all of this, she was pivotal in terms of conversation at the dinner. After the dinner, we went down to Max's so David could meet Iggy. It was in the back room seated at the big booth in the corner on the right when you went in. Danny Fields was officiating over the introductions.

Dennis Katz saw an outstanding potential in Lou Reed: 'Up to that point he was basically a songwriter. I really liked the Velvet Underground, even if I became familiar with their work only after they disbanded. The original group with John Cale had a much wider effect on other artists, but the later band was much more commercial, in my opinion.' He also found a personal connection to his new artist. 'Dennis was straight,' recalled one observer, 'but he had a few kinky things about him. He was into Nazi paraphernalia and collected Nazi flags.' Both appreciated music, poetry and maintained a strong work ethic. Katz and Reed formed the core of a team that would prepare the way for Reed's solo career.

It was taken for granted that Richard Robinson, who had become obsessed with reviving Lou's career, would share production credits with Reed. 'To date,' he said, 'he has not been recorded in a way that enables him to communicate easily with those who want to listen. And he's written the best rock-and-roll songs I've ever heard.'

As 1971 drew to a close, Reed looked around for a manager. The first person he approached was Danny Fields, who declined, explaining, 'Lou was making me crazy. So at a party at the Robinsons' I went over and I told him, "Lou, I love you but this won't work. I just want to be your friend." This was best left to professionals who weren't so emotionally or aesthetically involved, who weren't so enraptured of him.' Next, Lou turned to Fred Heller, who managed Blood, Sweat and Tears, whose guitarist was Dennis's brother. Dennis was clearly having a strong influence on Lou, who hired Fred on his advice. The perspicacity of this choice was sublimated by a buoyant, optimistic mood.

Heller's inventive motto was: 'Lewis is going to be big in the business.'

Everything looked good. Lou had a two-album contract with the same company that was launching David Bowie. He had Dennis Katz in his corner who would act as an inspiration and catalyst. Richard Robinson was willing to bend over backwards for him. Fred Heller was optimistic. Bettye Kronstadt was willing to tend to his every desire.

Lou began dusting off a collection of songs he had written for the Velvets in preparation for the upcoming recording sessions. Remarkably, during his one-and-a-half year break he had written few new songs. He had always put conflict, and particularly conflict with his parents, to creative use. But now he had to fall back on recycled material, resuscitating Velvets songs that either hadn't been recorded, or had been recorded but not released. None of them had the power of his great works.

London, meanwhile, was being primed for Reed's arrival. An article in *Melody Maker* on 18 September hailed the UK re-release of *The Velvet Underground and Nico* and *The Velvet Underground*: 'The first of these albums, recorded in 1966, is one of the most important and influential rock records ever made. The second, made two years later, is the most organic and interesting extended work in rock.'

chapter eleven

The Phantom of Rock

1972

[In which Lou puts out *Lou Reed* and almost destroys his solo career before it gets off the ground.]

I'm a ball of confusion, mentally, physically . . . everything about me is confused, and Lou is very much the same way.

DAVID BOWIE

Lou's arrival in London on 28 December 1971 was as perfectly timed as his entrance into the Factory six years earlier. Glitter rock arrived, releasing sexual forces as potent as the British pop explosion of 1964. The glam or glitter-rock movement was based on blurring the line between genders by its male stars adopting elements of the costumes and styles of camp movie icons of the 1930s like Lupe Velez and Mae West strained through Warhol's pastiche of them in his late sixties to early seventies trilogy of films, *Flesh*, *Trash* and *Heat*. Exemplified in England by David Bowie with his 1971 album *Hunky Dory* and hit single 'Changes', and in the US by Alice Cooper, who had just released his album *Killer*, glitter rock changed rock's look and sound, blowing open the doors for a number of new groups and movements.

Glitter rock was a visually loud mix of extremes that would eventually envelop Lou in its confusion. With its vamping and camp borrowed from stage and film stars, glitter rock became the first large-scale demonstration of a new creative surge brought into the open by the gay liberation movement. Using Warhol's drag queens as early role models, glitter rockers smashed open gender barriers by wearing jewellery, make-up, high-heeled platform shoes and sequined outfits. Yet, despite the feminine trappings, the male glitter rocker acted just as macho and adolescent as groups like the Rolling Stones, strutting and preening like little red roosters. (In New York the trend was exemplified by the New York Dolls.) Reed would have been hard-pressed to compete in this burlesque had he too not donned an attention-getting image. Though at times during the decade losing sight of the thin line separating persona from person, Lou would become a master of the seventies pageant.

Lou hated everything about Alice Cooper. He hated his glitzy outfits and he hated Cooper's dazzling stage histrionics, which included such attention-getting routines as wrapping a snake around his neck and spattering himself with blood. Bowie, on the other hand, had a smart, cool demeanour that appealed to Lou. Moreover, with his paler-than-pale skin, sensitive eyes and floppy hair, Bowie looked appropriately androgynous. In Bowie, Reed would find an ally as important as Warhol – only much more commercial.

Reed and his entourage checked into what was London's most popular hotel for top-of-the-line rock stars, the Inn on the Park. An ultramodern American-style hotel, it was located on the same block as the London Hilton overlooking Hyde Park. Throughout January, Lou and Bettye and Richard and Lisa lived in a world of their own focused on the making of the solo album and little else.

Lou had often used the metaphor of a chess game to describe his various moves. One of his most daring moves on the comeback board was to record in London instead of New York. For a man who was proud of being a control freak he was taking an enormous risk in choosing to work in a scenario he knew nothing about and could not therefore easily manipulate. There are any number of possible reasons for this decision. He was better known in Britain than in the US. If he had recorded at RCA Studios in New York, RCA would have legally owned the master tapes. By recording in

London, Reed could maintain control of his own product.

Reed's strategy of starting his campaign in London was smart. It would have been a mistake to launch his return anywhere in America where his association with Warhol and the Velvet Underground was the kiss of death. Not only was his work better appreciated in Britain, but the new generation of rock stars, spearheaded by Bowie, welcomed him like a hero and gave him the red-carpet treatment he had never had in America. The atmosphere in London was tolerant. Moreover, England had a long history of fondness for eccentrics and cross-dressers, who often played starring roles in music-hall and pantomime. In 1972, London offered a hospitable atmosphere for Lou Reed to work in.

However, despite appearing to be well prepared, Lou walked into a situation in which he was leaving himself wide open, and gave up almost complete control of the project from the word go. Despite five years of experience and a fifteen-month furlough to prepare himself for the next stage, Lou seems to have been totally unprepared for his first solo recording sessions. Instead of emerging into the spotlight with a strong and carefully prepared portfolio of the new works to stake his claim on the 1970s, Lou showed up with a motley collection of old VU tracks along with several castoffs from other aborted projects. But nothing really explains the lack of attention Lou paid to preparing for the recording sessions unless he anticipated that serendipity was to play a strong role, or was so besotted by Bettye he wasn't paying full attention, or he was smashed out of his mind. When Lou emerged from realigning himself in Freeport, he had not only picked up a few pounds, he had become a drinker of some renown and was using a variety of drugs.

This was the most blatant of many signs that indicated an ambivalence on Reed's part to the task at hand. For a man who had created an image at the Factory based upon being pencil-thin and virtually hidden behind sunglasses and black leather, the chubby, shaggy-haired thirty-something who presented himself to British customs officers at Heathrow Airport as a musician on 28

December 1971 did not look anything like a rock star, let alone the glitter rocker who would soon be the world-famous standard bearer of a powerful new movement.

Lou, who delighted in parading around with Bettye on his right flank and Richard on his left and introducing them as 'my boyfriend and my girlfriend', could hardly have been more pleased with himself than he was during this period. However, the basic problem lay in his choice of comrades. Whereas when he had stepped out on the stage with the Velvet Underground he took with him the powerful support, balance and intelligence of John Cale, Sterling Morrison and Moe Tucker, now he was surrounded by a decidedly B list of characters. Bettye, despite resembling her, was no Shelley Albin. She did not have the mind or the strength to be a real partner of Lou's. Richard Robinson was certainly no John Cale. And it gets worse as the list goes on. Lou was not only taking on the whole burden that had been shared with the VU, but, as he would soon discover, he was carrying a lot of useless baggage. With no Jiminy Cricket whispering in his ear, with no one to joust with, he was surrounded by people who agreed with him. These were not collaborators, they were enablers. Any real collaborator would have spoken up on the first day of the recording sessions and brought a halt to the farce as soon as they saw the musicians who had been chosen by RCA to play with Lou.

When Lou arrived in the studio, unpacked his guitar and turned towards the microphone he was astonished to discover, peering at him from behind their instruments, two keyboard players from the progressive rock band Yes, Rick Wakeman and Tony Kaye; Caleb Quaye from Elton John's band; as well as Steve Howe and Paul Keogh on guitars, Les Hurdle and Brian Odgers on bass and Clem Cattini on drums. These men were orthodox professionals who knew how to play their instruments. However, as session musicians they brought little spirit to the music. Since spirit was what Lou was all about – it was all he brought to the sessions – he simply could not play with them. Consequently Lou Reed, whose guitar playing had won praise for a rarely praised band and who was, in John Cale's words, 'a wild man on the guitar', did not play a single note of music on his first solo album. In fact, Lou's guitar was one of the biggest props missing from his whole early solo period. Throughout the Velvets' reign, the guitar had been an extension of Lou, but now that third arm was amputated. 'I thought of it like starting at ground zero,' he recalled.

> I didn't particularly know any musicians so it didn't matter who you got. If they played what I told them to play then it might be OK and if they didn't then it wouldn't. Making a really good record is very, very difficult and it's a matter of control. If you don't have the right musicians and you don't have the right engineer it's very hard. But you have to start some place. The situation is not always one where you can call all the shots or even half the shots.

Amazingly Lou, who was either on some mighty powerful sedative or had been warned by Dennis Katz not to complain, expressed no ire with this development and proceeded efficiently. It was as if he was bending over backwards to show the RCA people how professional and easy to work with he could be.

Having crossed that bridge, however, he encountered another, more harrowing problem. It turned out that Robinson, who had scant experience as a producer, found himself confused by some of the more sophisticated British technology. Having nobody he could really fess up to about this unfortunate development, he proceeded to fake it. Richard gave the impression that everything was under control, assuring Katz's assistant, Barbara Falk, in a letter that month, 'We are into technical cutting stages. As far as I can tell it is the best album I've done to date. Lou is in ecstasy.'

Richard videotaped a number of scenes with Lou in London, including one with Ray Davies and Lou sitting drinking and talking in the Portobello Hotel. But Lou did not make a big social splash in London during his first visit. He saw David Bowie, who had recently stated in *Rolling Stone*, 'Lou Reed is the most important person in rock and roll in America.'

'David was very smart,' noted his wife Angie Bowie. 'He'd been evaluating the market for his work, calculating his moves and monitoring his competition. And the only really serious competition in his market niche, he'd concluded, consisted of Lou Reed and (maybe) Iggy Pop. So what did David do? He coopted them. He brought them into his circle. He talked them up in interviews, spreading their legend in Britain.'

'A lot of what I do is intuitive,' Reed said about making the album. 'I just go where it takes me and I don't question it.' This admission about his lack of direction, combined with the weak raw material of the album, cried out for a strong collaborator. 'I'm not consulting anybody this time, it's a solo effort with my producer, Richard Robinson,' Lou avowed publicly. However, in private he kept saying to Richard, 'This is not the way it's supposed to sound. The album is not defined enough.' But Robinson, was not ready to hear Lou's complaints, and, according to Reed's own account, he too felt confident that despite the lack of definition, 'this was the closest realization to what I heard in my head that I ever did. It was a real rock-and-roll album, and my direction had always been rock and roll – I saw it as a life force.'

'Writing songs is like making a play and you give yourself the lead part,' Reed said in an interview about making the album.

> And you write yourself the best lines that you could. And you're your own director. And they're short plays. And you get to play all kinds of different characters. It's fun. I write through the eyes of somebody else. I'm always checking out people I know I'm going to write songs about. Then I become them. That's why when I'm not doing that I'm kind of empty. I don't have a personality of my own. I just pick up other people's personalities.

Just how ambivalent Reed felt about his solo career was emphasized near the end of the month when John Cale blew through London and invited Lou to join him and Nico in Paris at the Bataclan Club on 29 January. Lou, who abhorred rehearsing, threw himself into the project. He spent two days rehearsing with John in London and another whole day with Nico in Paris. The show, filmed for French television, seems to have been one of his happiest performing experiences.

I always wanted to do a song like on the album – 'Berlin' – that's like a Barbra Streisand kind of thing. A real nightclub torch thing. Like, if you were Frank Sinatra you'd loosen your tie and light a cigarette. And when I was in Paris that's how I performed it. I didn't play at all. I had John play the piano and I sat on a stool with my legs crossed. And during the instrumental break I lit a cigarette and I puffed it and said, 'It was paradise.' It was heaven. It was really bliss. I was just doing that Billie Holiday trip. She was really . . . her phrasing. I mean that's singing; I think I'm acting.

The experience was marred, however, by Nico's and Cale's rejection of Lou's overtures to get back together. At the time, Nico had already released two solo albums with considerable critical success, and Cale had made some real headway as a producer and solo artist. They were both in a better position than Lou.

During January 1972 Lou had lived inside a bubble: waited on hand and foot in a luxurious hotel; at the centre of a circle of people whose sole reason to be there was he; and doing what he liked best, writing and singing and recording. However, as soon as he returned to New York on 30 January, the bubble burst and he dropped into a hell of doubt and insecurity about his future.

Dennis Katz was appalled by how bad his album was. 'The production did not come out the way I'd anticipated it,' Katz explained; 'it was much too sparse.' Everybody in New York's management organization was drop-dead shocked by how terrible *Lou Reed* was. 'What are we doing wasting our time with this schlemiel?' the sales people at RCA were screaming at Dennis Katz. 'They made it clear that they were disappointed in Lou,' he recalled. 'They rejected the direction – and specifically the production – of the first album.' By the middle of the year, RCA would come up with a handle for their new product. They would call him the Phantom of Rock. Ironically, this pointed at Lou's greatest weakness. Lou Reed was the Phantom of Rock in the sense that the figure he presented to the public didn't really exist. The character was made up of a patchwork of other people's personalities. He somehow let himself be made over in the image of what people, especially English people, imagined he was – a sexy wolverine, homosexual junkie hustler and advocate of S & M.

Andy Warhol, a man who had an eye for these things, once pointed out, 'When John Cale and Lou were in the Velvets, they really had style. But when Lou went solo he got bad and was copying people.'

The album was to be released in May. Between now and then it was Lou's job to put together a band and tour the US, drumming up interest in his new work. Now Lou found himself in a confusing place with nobody he could really talk to. He was trying on different disguises. Money was tight. Lou and Bettye squeezed into a cubicle-like studio apartment in what was popularly known as the airline-stewardess ghetto, on East 78th Street on Manhattan's Upper East Side. His close friend Ed McCormack, who edited *Fusion*, a magazine that had published a number of his poems, remembered Lou sitting in his apartment at midnight wearing a pair of sunglasses, keeping his fears at bay by bolting down copious quantities of booze, joined by an equally nervous and battered Bettye. 'His life with Bettye and his apartment seemed to provide a kind of domestic security that Lou needed to sustain him in his transition from cult-group figure to solo artist,' Ed reported.

'He had the most horrible apartment,' recalled Glenn O'Brien, another writer he socialized with.

With shag carpeting going up the walls and really bad furniture. And Lou was boozing really heavy. He was a little bit more together, he didn't seem so pathetic, but he must have been doing a lot of booze and pills. He was the first person I ever saw who was really shaky like that, having double bloody Marys at noon. The first time I met Bettye she had a black eye. She was kind of cute, but I remember her always having a black eye.

Lou faced the question, whom do you choose to play with when you've played in one of the greatest rock-and-roll bands of all time? Lou chose an unknown and unacclaimed band whose name, the Tots, said just about everything you had to know about them. Not only were they pedestrian musicians, but, according to Lester Bangs, they were also 'the ugliest creatures assembled on one stage' and 'an intentionally asexual band'. But the Tots provided Lou with exactly what he wanted. The audience's attention would be focused exclusively on him. No member of the band would question any orders or arrangements and he would have total control. He also figured that teaching them his repertoire would be no problem since the majority of his songs were the same songs written over and over again, and stemmed from the same three chords. Lou said they were the greatest band. He thought it was good that they were young and unknown. Later he would say they were the worst band.

Reed's initial foray onto the solo stage during a short tour of colleges in the US that April revealed how ambivalent he felt about his role. The ensemble made a nervous debut at the Millard Fillmore Room of the University of Buffalo. Togged out in black leather trousers, a black leather jacket and wearing his long, stringy hair in a halo of ringlets around a face covered in a layer of clown-white pancake make-up accompanied by lipstick and eye shadow, Lou looked like a cross between the hamburger clown Ronald McDonald and Frankenstein's monster. To make matters worse, Lou had abandoned his guitar and found himself thrust into the spotlight without the natural or planned series of stage moves that are a vital part of the lead singer's repertoire. According to the student who arranged the show, Billy Altman, Lou's performance was uptight, rigid and tentative. The overall effect of the band was nervous. Lou seemed trapped between personalities. At one moment he would be parodying Mick Jagger, clapping his hands over his head; the next he would turn into a performing seal. In between songs he recited polite introductions. When Altman, who had published a glowing review of the concert in the local paper, visited him the following day, Lou was curt to the point of obnoxiousness and made the five minutes they spent together excruciating. Lou was immensely impressed by the suicide that month of the British actor George Saunders, who had left a note containing the explanation, 'I'm so bored.'

When Lou's album *Lou Reed* and two singles, 'Going Down'/'I Can't Stand It' and 'Walk and Talk It'/'Wild Child', were released in May, Dennis Katz's worst fears were realized. Damned with mediocre reviews, *Lou Reed* sold around 7,000 copies, an embarrassing number in an industry where 50,000–100,000 was considered reasonable.

It was a telling moment for the Robinsons and their coterie. Lou was the mascot of the New York underground whose inhabitants would have done anything to see him succeed. Critics like Donald Lyons wrote in *Interview* magazine that Lou was 'a classic romantic – the smell of his work is the smell of Baudelaire's Paris – grappling, tempted and sometimes happy, always human. It's a wonderful album.' And Robert Christgau gave it a B+ in the *Village Voice*, but added that it was 'hard to know what to make of this. Certainly it's less committed – less rhythmically monolithic and staunchly weird – than the Velvets. Not that Reed is shying away from rock and roll or the demimonde. But when I'm feeling contrary he sounds not just "decadent" but jaded, fagged out.'

Most reviewers lambasted the results. 'The comeback album – the resurrection of the Phantom of Rock itself – was one of the more disappointing releases of 1972,' wrote Nick Kent in the *New Musical Express*.

> Reed's songwriting style had deteriorated – his dalliance with whimsical little love ballads was at best mildly amusing, at worst quite embarrassing, and always out of context.

Lou's defence was lukewarm. 'There's just too many things wrong with it,' he lamented. 'I was in dandy form, and so was everybody else. I'm just aware of all the things that are missing and all the things that shouldn't have been there.' It was decidedly not music that anyone would be willing to die for. 'Edith Piaf he ain't,' noted a disappointed Lester Bangs.

Nobody claimed to be more surprised and upset than Sterling Morrison. 'I really felt sad,' he recalled. 'I thought, "Oh, man, you have blown it!" He used to be one of the great rock vocalists but either his voice had seriously deteriorated or he can't or won't sing any more.' Cale explained that the seemingly out-of-character lyric Lou sang at the end of 'Berlin', 'don't forget / hire a vet,' was deadly serious. He noted that Lou would often get passionate about something everybody else found funny, then be offended by their laughter. But, particularly in light of the bad production of Velvets leftovers, he found the album a poor approximation of the great band the Velvets had once been.

To make matters worse, no sooner had Lou come rushing out of the gate with his first solo effort than he was unhorsed by the same hurdle the individual Beatles had came up against – the spectre of previous work. In Reed's case the invidious comparison between his earlier and current work was made painfully obvious when his last night with the Velvet Underground at Max's was released the same month. *Live at Max's Kansas City* enjoyed far better reviews and sales than *Lou Reed*.

At this juncture, Lou put into play one of the elements that would always set him apart from the pack. He had an ability at crucial times to charm and attract powerful people who really believed in him and were willing to go to bat for him. Dennis Katz, Lou's lawyer during the first half of 1972, who was now in the process of leaving RCA, began to make overtures to become Lou's manager, replacing Fred Heller.

Katz's offer to become Reed's manager coincided with increasingly tumultuous relations between Reed and Heller. Bettye complained about Fred pushing her around at Lou's shows. Lou and Fred had a big personality conflict. Finally, Lou told Fred he was going to be replaced by Dennis. A lawsuit ensued, from which Lou extricated himself at considerable financial cost.

Free of Heller, Lou now seized upon Dennis as a father figure, even though the two were roughly the same age. Poised, literate, happily married and devoted to his career, Dennis represented a guiding strength. Everyone around the two recalled their friendship with awe, largely because Lou never contradicted or challenged Dennis.

'I think Dennis liked the fact that Lou needed him and depended on him,' said Katz's assistant Barbara Falk.

He really thought that Lou was fantastic. David [Bowie] was just starting to take off at RCA right after Dennis left. Now Dennis swung totally to Lou. I remember Dennis's wife saying that Lou was so much better than David Bowie, he wasn't all the frills and glitter and he was stark and black, he was the street poet. Being of the literary bent, one of the things that attracted Dennis to artists were the lyrics.

Simultaneously, Andy Warhol, thriving in a particularly dramatic period of his comeback from the 1968 attempted assassination, asked Reed to write some songs for a proposed Broadway musical by Warhol and Yves Saint-Laurent. Lou always responded well to assignments. Andy said, 'Why don't you write a song called "Vicious"?' Lou recalled. 'And I said, "Well, Andy, what kind of vicious?" "Oh, you know, like, I hit you with a flower." And I wrote it down, literally. Because I kept a notebook in those days. I used it for poetry, things people said.'

Additional help for Lou arrived when David Bowie returned to London after his triumphant American tour, bathed in the success of *The Rise and Fall of Ziggy Stardust*, which came out in June. Bowie wasted no time in proposing to RCA that he produce Lou's second album. According to Dennis Katz, 'They had a lot of faith in Bowie because he produced both *Hunky Dory* and *Ziggy Stardust*. So they were then willing to take another shot at an album – assuming he was working with Lou.'

Tony Zanetta attended 'another bar-mitzvah dinner' for David Bowie and Lou in New York. That's when they started talking about doing *Transformer*. Plans were made fast. David was still doing gigs and planning on coming back to New York in September and they were planning to record in July and August. 'They wanted to work with Lou because they didn't like the first album and didn't think that's what he should be doing,' said Tony

Zanetta. 'But it was a sensitive issue because of Richard Robinson.'

According to Barbara Falk:

Dennis started getting more interested in Lou, and when David Bowie expressed an interest in producing Lou, Dennis got even more involved. Dennis got more protective and there was more contact and a relationship developed.

It was odd because Dennis was so different from Lou. He was an attorney, right then when we were at RCA he had bought his house in Chappaqua, he had a little child. He was very home-oriented and private, he didn't like to go out at night, he wasn't your typical rock-and-roller. He collected autographs and first editions. And he was very, very literary in his interests. That part of Lou interested Dennis, the fact that he had been published in the *Paris Review*, and the fact that they both read, which very few people in the rock world did. So they developed this strange relationship where they were both fascinated by each other's lifestyle and they kidded each other about them and joked and put each other down. But Dennis's allegiance was totally with Lou. Lou loved the fact that Dennis was eccentric. He found that it was cool. He said, He's not like all the other guys, he's got something in here. And there was this strange symbiosis between them. They got along really well, but then I could never picture Lou staying overnight in Chappaqua. With his hours . . . But he used to stay over in this really nice house. And Dennis got up at seven, he fell asleep at eleven o'clock. I can also remember going out with the two of them to some gay bar and Dennis refused to go to the men's room. He was fastidious. When they got along they were a funny pair. And Dennis was always a placater and a builder-upper. He was articulate and he could speak to Lou. He would get frustrated with Lou, but, let's face it, everybody would get frustrated with Lou. But Dennis always tried to make sure that Lou was aware of everything going on.

Lou's father came up to the office and wanted an accounting or reporting – because Lou had had problems with the guy who came before. He was a quiet, nondescript, businesslike fellow. He came on his own and he and Dennis went to lunch across the street. Mr Reed was concerned and Dennis was trying to assure him that he was in good hands.

Lou's decision to have Bowie produce his next album was a shock to Richard Robinson, who had been the only member of Lou's entourage to question Bowie's motives earlier that year. Richard had taken it for granted that he would be producing Lou's second album, especially since Lou told one interviewer, 'Richard had the same goals I had. We knew we wanted the album to come out this way. We had it all plotted out before we even went to London.' But once Lou became aware that Richard's involvement would doom him to oblivion, he agreed to cut him from the team. 'The Robinsons were rather possessive of him,' Glenn O'Brien recalled. 'They had a big problem because they thought he should have been eternally grateful to Richard for giving him his big break.' The Robinsons, who felt that they had brought Lou out of retirement, saw the move as the ultimate betrayal.

When Richard was informed over the phone from Katz's office that his services would no longer be required, he exploded, screaming that Lou was an 'aging queen'.

'I can understand it,' said Barbara Falk.

Richard thought, I brought him in and it was my thing and nobody wanted him, and part of my deal was that I would continue on. He thought he had an understanding. Lisa actually didn't speak to the Bowies for some time because of that – it was a big rift. Lou looked on her as the high priestess of the current rock scene. After the breach when they weren't speaking he'd say they're little pop people, but he probably still read her religiously.

Lou suddenly found himself closed out of Lisa's collective. 'I still love Richard,' Lou told Ed McCormack,

but I'm not so sure he loves me any more. But then, I wouldn't really know what people think of me. I hardly see anyone any more. There are dear friends who I no longer see, not because I don't love them, but because I can no longer be a part of that whole hip scene. These nights I hardly go out at all, except down to the liquor store to buy another fifth. Sometimes I have this horrible nightmare that I'm not really what I think I am . . . That I'm just a completely decadent egoist . . . Do you have any idea what it's like to be in my shoes?

chapter twelve

The Transformation

1972–1973

[In which Lou records and
releases his second solo album,
Transformer, with David Bowie,
has his first hit single, goes on
tour and gets married.]

*My goal is to play Vegas . . . be a lounge act . . . be like Eddie
Fisher . . . get divorced . . . have a scandal . . . go
bankrupt . . . end up in Mexico, marry Connie Stevens and
read about myself in the* National Enquirer.

LOU REED

Lou returned to London at the beginning of July to take up with
his saviour of the moment, David Bowie. Their collaboration
allowed Bowie to pay an artistic debt to the Lou Reed of Warhol's
Velvet Underground. David would return to Lou the work and
ideas of which Bowie was born, distilled into the cock-rock
format dominating the European pop charts. For Reed, this was a
godsend.

'David is a seductive person and that is his MO,' Tony Zanetta
explained.

And he used that with Lou because he wanted something from Lou.
He looks you right in the eye and no one exists but you. But that's
only for a few minutes. We all went for it and I'm sure Lou did. And
I'm sure Lou was ignored – not out of a lack of interest, but because

David was so busy. David was interested in Lou, but he wanted everybody. That's what Ziggy was.

David put himself at Lou's disposal in any way he could, instructing Angie Bowie for example, to help Lou and Bettye find a flat. According to Zanetta:

Lou was pawned off on Angie. Angie took care of him, she was the human contact who would take care of things David didn't want to deal with. And Lou was one of those things. I don't know how involved David was with the record, I think it was mostly Ronson. He had a lot of things going on, gigs, touring, shows coming up and recording. And the Mott the Hoople thing.

Angela Bowie, who remembered, 'we felt extra special, intensely alive, incredibly alert,' was highly amused by Lou.

David introduced us and we shook hands, kind of – Lou's greeting was a rather odd cross between a dead trout and a paranoid butterfly. My first clear impression of him was of a man honour-bound to act as fey and as human as he could. He was wearing heavy mascara and jet-black lipstick with matching nail polish, plus a tight little Errol-Flynn-as-Robin-Hood bodyshirt that must have lit up every queen for acres around him.

Though he had very little money, Lou soon settled uncomfortably into a furnished duplex apartment in the London suburb of Wimbledon. At the time, Bowie was rehearsing for an upcoming tour, recording a new album and working his way rapidly towards international success. David introduced Lou to people who would be useful to him. One such contact, the writer and photographer Mick Rock, became his long-term friend. Everyone in Bowie's set thought that Mick was brilliant and they loved his work. 'Mick,' one friend commented, 'was a lot of fun because he was in the ozone.' Mick Rock was the perfect receiver for Lou Reed. Full of the good humour of the typical working-class Englishman out of a Charles Dickens novel, he possessed a mind that worked as fast as a camera, a charm that made people around him feel alive and at ease, and a detailed knowledge of Lou's work. Rock became

Reed's primary connection in London during the first half of the 1970s.

'Reed was staying in Wimbledon, a smart suburb of London favoured by businessmen, film stars and respectable hoodlums, and hating it there,' Mick Rock revealed of his first visit with Reed.

> He was a man who waited. 'People always come to me. They have to because I have the power on them. I like to make believe I'm a gun. I calculate. I look for a spot where I can really do it. Then they suddenly know I'm really a person . . . '
>
> Not that he always had such a high opinion of himself. Later he would say, 'I'm so dull really. That's why I don't write about myself. That's why I need other people. I need New York City to feed off.'

Very few artists are capable of the generosity David Bowie extended to Lou Reed in the summer of 1972. As proof of his devotion, Bowie invited Reed to guest star at his headlining show at the Royal Festival Hall on 8 July, a benefit for Friends of the Earth. At the end of the set David brought Lou Reed, dressed in black, on stage to perform 'White Light/White Heat', 'I'm Waiting for My Man' and 'Sweet Jane'. It turned out to be not only the most important, but the greatest concert of Bowie's career. Writing under the accurate, if corny, headline 'A Star Is Born!', Ray Coleman noted that 'when a shooting star is heading for the peak there is usually one concert at which it is possible to declare, "That's it. He's made it."'

After Bowie chaperoned Lou's introduction to British audiences, he held a day of press interviews at the Dorchester Hotel meant to forward the music and personas of them both. It was at this gala that Lou minced into glitter rock proper, appearing in his new, Bowie-influenced Phantom of Rock persona, fully made-up and resplendent in designer clothes, six-inch platforms and black nail polish. With studied deliberation, the Phantom wasted no time in putting his two cents into the gay-liberation kitty by tottering across La Bowie's suite and firmly planting a kiss on David's mouth. Announcing that Bowie, 'a genius', would be producing his next album, he withdrew.

'People like Lou and I are probably predicting the end of an era and I mean that catastrophically,' Bowie declared. 'Any society that allows people like Lou and me to become rampant is pretty well lost. We're both very mixed up, paranoid people – absolute walking messes. I don't really know what we're doing. If we're the spearhead of anything, we're not necessarily the spearhead of anything good.'

For a few weeks Reed soaked up the influence of his charismatic friend, much as he had done with Warhol. 'I had a lot of fun,' Reed recalled in 1973, 'and I think David did. He seemed really quick and facile. I was very isolated. Why were people talking about him so much? What did he do? What did he do that I could learn? A lot of it reminded me of when I was with Warhol.

The two of them cruised London's seamy side. 'Lou loved Soho, especially at night,' Bowie said.

> He thought it was quaint compared to New York. He liked it because he could have a good time here and still be safe. It was all drunks and tramps and whores and strip clubs and afterhours bars, but no one was going to mug you or beat you up. It was very twilight.

A week after the Dorchester press conference, Lou and the Tots set out on their first British tour with a show at the Kings Cross Sound in London. Reed's performances in the summer of 1972 made apparent the influence of Bowie's theatrical, sexually ambiguous aesthetic. Lou wore black eye make-up, black lipstick and a black velvet suit with rhinestone trimmings. 'I did three or four shows like that, and then it was back to leather,' Lou commented after the tour. 'We were just kidding around – I'm not into make-up.' These tentative forays into the glam scene were merely the beginning, however. Reed relished the fact that he was being grabbed on stage by both girls and boys.

Lou had an enthusiastic response from audiences in Britain, but it was clear that he would have to work up some new songs to match his stage act. The press reaction was often critical of his material. 'I've rearranged my old songs and slowed some of them down, and the press brand the new versions as travesties of the originals,' Lou protested. 'They're *my* songs, surely I can do what I like with them. And I like them slower now.'

Although he was accused of aping David Bowie in his appearance and stage act, Lou was still putting the finishing touches on the Phantom of Rock.

I'm *not* going in the same direction as David [Lou insisted]. He's into the mime thing and that's not me at all. I know I have a good hard rock act, I just wanted to try doing something more – to push it right over the edge. I wanted to try that heavy eye make-up and dance about a bit. And how could anyone say I was letting my guitarist upstage me? He was doing it on my instructions. I told him to get up and wiggle his ass about and he did. Anyway, I've done it all now and stopped it. We all stand still and I don't wear make-up any more.

As an afterthought he added lugubriously, 'They don't want me to have any fun.'

At the beginning of August, Bowie and his guitarist Mick Ronson took Lou into Trident Studios in London to commence work on *Transformer*. All three men were under a lot of pressure. Bowie and Ronson, who were also recording with Mott the Hoople, were due to play concerts that month in London and New York. Their time was split between rehearsing and recording. For Reed, whose career depended on the outcome, every moment in the studio was a vital one. The fast, furious, drug-induced pace of their collaboration would have a lot to do with the album's ultimate success.

Lou was dazzled by David, his management machine and his popularity. Reed soaked up elements of Bowie's character, adding them to his own, evolving day to day. When David took his Ziggy Stardust act into the Rainbow, a huge former cinema in London, on 19 August, Lou described the show as 'amazing, stupendous, incredible, the greatest thing I've ever seen'.

As for Lou and David, they were bound to attempt to outdo each other in their tortured, creative artist's roles. Angie Bowie, who frequently visited the studio, was confronted with the sight of David curled into a foetal ball beneath the toilet bowl in deep depression, or Reedian tantrums so violent that she fled the studio before their velocity blew her out of the room. These exercises in nostalgia for childhood did not, however, faze the musical partners. Whenever David retreated to the John, Lou claimed he knew exactly how he felt and insisted that nobody disturb him. David in turn often pulled Lou out of deep depressions just by being there and talking to him in exactly the right way.

If *Lou Reed* had been a failure from its inception, *Transformer* was the opposite. Lou had written a batch of songs which reflected the new times – the seventies – and the new Lou. 'Last time they were all love songs,' he snapped, 'this time they're all hate songs.' Reed would play Bowie and Ronson the bare bones of the song, and they would craft the song's eventual setting. Bowie and Ronson were attuned to what Lou's songs needed and their arrangements reinforced his material. 'Mick Ronson was really instrumental in doing the album,' one observer confided.

Whereas Cale had drawn together the lyrics of 'Heroin' and all the great songs on the first album, that task now fell to Ronson. Ronson wrapped the lyrics in confident, sparring music that leaped out of the speakers and grabbed you around the throat, just as the Velvets' music had. Ronson described their approach: 'We are concentrating on the feeling rather than the technical side of the music. He's an interesting person but I never know what he's thinking. However, as long as we can reach him musically it's all right.'

David was characteristically modest about his intentions. 'All that I can do is make a few definitions on some of the concepts of some of the songs and help arrange things the way Lou wants them,' he said. 'I'm just trying to do exactly as Lou wants.' Bowie was at the core of the production: it was his encouragement, like Warhol's, that brought Reed to the fore as a solo artist. Bowie drew the songs out of Reed with his enthusiasm and got him to sing them at the top of his form. Enjoying himself, Reed was able to invent different attitudes and personalities for the album that found their way into the songs 'Vicious' and 'Walk on the Wild Side'. 'I always thought it would be kinda fun to introduce people to characters they maybe hadn't met before, or hadn't wanted to meet, y'know,' Lou joked. 'The kind of people you sometimes see at parties but don't dare approach. That's one of the motivations for me writing all those songs in the first place.'

'What you have to worry about is insanity,' Lou mused to friends later. 'All the people I've known who were fabulous have either died, or flipped or gone to India, Nepal and studied and gave it all up, y'know, the whole trip. Either that, or else they concentrated it on one focal point, which is what I'm doing, which is what I think David is doing.'

'*Transformer* was a very beautiful, very widely accepted album that David did out of love for Lou,' concluded Bowie's friend Cherry Vanilla. Reed's reaction to the collaboration with Bowie and Ronson was ecstatic. '*Transformer* is easily my best-produced album,' he exclaimed. 'Together as a team they're terrific.'

The completion of the album marked the end of the Bowie-Reed relationship for all intents and purposes. 'David was always hot and cold with people,' said Tony Zanetta. 'I think he was always intimidated by Lou. Because Lou was sharp and David wasn't. David never pursued Lou the way he pursued Iggy. He would come and go with Lou. Once that album was done I don't remember David ever mentioning Lou. Or wanting to go see Lou or wanting Lou to come see this.'

As Bowie flew off into his own orbit, Lou took the Tots back on the road. In October they toured Britain before returning to the US. Reed dressed, as one observer put it, 'in leather and charisma', delivering a series of devastating performances to rapt audiences. His Bowie-influenced stage act, combined with his new material, propelled him into the pop limelight. 'I'm the biggest joker in the business,' he said. 'But there's something behind every joke.'

Before Lou left London, Mick Rock did a photo session with him that would supply Lou with his first successful solo publicity image. The picture, in which Lou stared past the camera with haunted eyes heavily underlined with black kohl, presented a startling remake. The Lou Reed who had previously worn the black jeans, T-shirt and rumpled corduroy jacket of a man uninterested in frills and stripped for hard-core action, now appeared in the guise of a bisexual glitter rocker. Lou's face was heavily made-up with a mask of deathly white pancake. Black lipstick delineated his Cupid's-bow mouth. His jet-black hair was worn in a stylish semi-Afro similar to Marc Bolan's. Dressed from head to foot in a black jumpsuit, he also sported black nail polish on his chubby fingers. The whole ensemble was made all the more mawkish by the fact that the skinny rocker of the sixties was carrying a little more weight than was normally affected by glamorous rock stars. The extra pounds were culled from his mother's and now Bettye's ample meals, heavily laced with cakes and pastries. In this respect he joined Gary Glitter in a neo-Elvis camp self-parody. Despite his paunch, he was, in fact, on his way to creating the image that would shortly take him to the highest commercial peak of his entire career. His new image so perfectly captured the era that it later got hijacked by Tim Curry, who put it to use in his starring role in the 1975 cult musical and movie *The Rocky Horror Picture Show*.

RCA and Katz were also ecstatic. They had found a formula and a team. It was presumed that for his next album Lou would return to work with David, creating a perfect follow-up to *Transformer*.

When Dennis Katz and the people at RCA heard *Transformer*, they knew they had made the right decision in entrusting Reed to David Bowie. Convinced it would be a success, and perhaps even yield a hit single, they prepared the way for its release and a subsequent tour by the artist. The album, with a great cover photo by Mick Rock, was due out in November 1972.

Transformer was an enormous success and opened up a new world for Lou Reed.

Bowie had insisted that RCA release 'Walk on the Wild Side' as the single – against Lou's wishes. Reed was sure it would be banned on the radio and didn't want to repeat the pattern he had had with the great Velvets albums that were never heard. Fortunately, Lou relented and, as the record company predicted, the single emerged from the album and began to climb the charts, peaking at number 16 on the US charts in late winter of 1973. The song remains Lou's only charted single in a career spanning thirty years.

The Bowie and Ronson influence was considered paramount in the direction of the work. 'Thanks to their intelligence and taste,' Tim Jurgens wrote in *Fusion*, 'Lou Reed has found the perfect accompaniment to such flights of fancy that he's been lacking since John Cale went his own way.' The *Village Voice* noted that 'you can cut the atmosphere surrounding each song with a knife . . . and the clue to this album's appeal lies in . . . a mix that has a chance of startling the listener and touching our common humanity'.

Not everyone bought this new act quite so unquestioningly. When *Transformer* was released in the US, Lisa Robinson got everybody in her group of writers to give it a negative review. 'As long as he played ball with Lisa and Richard everybody supported him,' explained Henry Edwards.

> But if you pull the reviews of *Transformer* you have a little story, because she single-handedly turned the press against him. And she got everyone to pan his album, including me. And that's a good story, I think. No one thought at that moment he had a future. Everyone thought that he was a pop artefact to be manipulated – he was almost a golden oldie in a very short period of time. And he was desperate . . . I do feel guilty about writing a bad review of his album for the *Times*. I did what everybody else did – we fucked the album.

'What's the matter with Lou Reed? Transformer is terrible – lame, pseudo-decadent lyrics, lame, pseudo-something-or-other singing, and a just plain lame band,' wrote Ellen Wills in the *New Yorker*. 'Part of Reed's problem is that he needs a band he can interact with, a band that will give him some direction, as the Velvets did, instead of simply backing him up – in other words, not just a band but a group.'

The album rode the wave of gay liberation and the sexually ecstatic awakening of the early seventies, and Lou became a spokesman for the burgeoning gay community. 'What I've always thought is that I'm doing rock and roll in drag. If you just listen to the songs cursorily, they come off like rock and roll, but if you really pay attention, then they are in a way the quintessence of the rock and roll song, except they're not rock and roll.'

Referring to another song, 'Make Up', he commented, 'The gay life at the moment isn't that great. I wanted to write a song which made it terrific, something that you'd enjoy. But that's just one song. But I know if I do that, I'll be accused of being a fag, but that's all right, it doesn't matter. I like those people, and I don't like what's going down, and I wanted to make it happy.'

Andy Warhol realized that 'Walk on the Wild Side' was the single strongest piece of publicity for his trilogy of films starring various drag queens and Joe Dallesandro – *Flesh*, *Heat* and *Trash*. 'Walk on the Wild Side' would become the number-one jukebox hit in America in 1973, and every time it played in a restaurant or bar, or came wafting out of an apartment or car, it reminded everybody that Warhol's movies were playing nearby. Warhol was certainly happy about that, but on the other hand, he could not help thinking that Lou had now twice tapped into the Factory for material – where was the money Lou owed him from the first album? Thus, while embracing Lou publicly in his democracy of success, Andy harboured a hard-boiled resentment. Lou, however, was travelling too fast to notice.

In fact, by the end of 1972, Lou was forging ahead in his new identity as the Phantom of Rock with such ferocity that he had little time for his old friends. That December he had an uncomfortable brush with the past when Richard Sigal, who had sung with him in the Jades in Freeport, visited him unexpectedly. Allen Hyman recalled:

Just before New Year's Eve I got a phone call from him, and he said that our old friend Richard Sigal had shown up at his apartment. Richard was teaching school somewhere in Virginia. Lou got on the telephone and said, 'I want you to do me a favour, I haven't asked you to do me a favour in a long time. I want you to speak to Richard and tell him to get out of my house and to never speak to me again as long as he lives. And I want you to do whatever you can to make this happen. I can't stand him any more, he's making me crazy.'

I said, 'Lou, what's going on? I haven't talked to you in years . . .'

And Lou said, 'He's totally insane, he told me that he blames me for all the bad things that ever happened in his life, he said that I abandoned him, that I was responsible for all his upset and misery and he's written a song that he wants me to sing and record – listen to the lyrics.' And he read me the lyrics, the lyrics were so insane.

I said, 'Sounds like the man does have a problem.'

He said, 'Here, talk to him.' And he put Richard on the phone.

I said, 'Richard, I haven't spoken to you in years, how are you?'

And he said, 'Terrible!'

I said, 'What's wrong?'

He said, 'You fucking guys abandoned me.'

I was so taken aback.

'You and Lou.' It was like, 'You don't write, you don't call . . .'

I said, 'I have no idea where you were.'

'The two of you, you were my best friends. Lou won't talk to me.'

I said, 'Come on out, I'll talk to you.' He never came out. But that was vintage Lou.'

The year 1973 would be one of the greatest of Lou Reed's career. As *Transformer's* sales mounted – it would take six months to peak – Dennis Katz and the RCA machine swung into action, sending Lou out on a seemingly endless tour that winter. In January, at his first New York solo show at Alice Tully Hall, he wore black leather jeans and jacket and was, by all accounts, electrifying. By March 1973, Lou had reached a high level of success with his barnstorming tours turning into chaotic rock events. Although he had never possessed the charisma of Bowie or Jagger, Reed played a great rock-and-roll show.

In January, to everyone's surprise, the sexually ambiguous Reed married his ever faithful sidekick, Bettye Kronstadt. David Bowie was married, Mick Jagger was married. Maybe it was the hip thing to do. It was something to do. And so Lou Reed, who thought of himself as a knight who believed in pretty princesses and sparrows, married the woman another part of him already looked upon as a Stepford wife. 'Yes, he's got the princess, she's Jewish, she likes making homey things,' noted one sceptical friend,

> and I was glad that he was happy, he needed a companion tucked away to be there when he needed them. But Bettye really didn't understand him *at all*. He needed a person he could joust with, and ultimately Bettye really couldn't play the game. She'd be very boring. That's why he always ended up hitting her. He would never hit anybody who would smack him back.

Dennis Katz used the occasion to make the erroneous claim that Bettye was taking great care of Lou's health, keeping him from drinking and trifling with drugs. But the marriage raised a number of questions concerning his motivations. Lou readily admitted that he had no idea how to handle money or take care of himself. He was of that school of rock stars who, from their late teens, had lived in a world in which their music was the only vital factor. In everything else they needed to be led or to follow somebody's orders. Meanwhile, some of Lou's lifelong supporters were affronted that he would do something so bourgeois and they continued to raise questions about his sex life, to which he blithely replied that he did not believe in bisexuality. His different personalities switched back and forth so fast Bettye never really knew what happened. They were so drunk and stoned most of the time that not much of what happened registered. And they were exhausted from the combination of touring, drinking, drugging, partying and fighting. *Transformer* kept them pinned to the road for the next four months.

Katz, who saw that Bettye encouraged Lou's drinking more than she discouraged it, soon added to Reed's team his assistant Barbara Falk, who would be Lou's road manager through the mid-seventies and an indispensable member of his support team. In those days it was unusual for a woman to have such a powerful role and Barbara suffered from both the macho businessmen who ran the rock concert scene and Lou's wife, who was understandably jealous of another woman usurping her role as Lou's babysitter. However, Barbara Falk, who possessed seemingly unlimited energy and a tough sense of humour, found herself enjoying the wild ride that was Lou's life in those intense, successful years.

They played three to five concerts a week, for fees ranging from $6,000 to $7,000. Dennis Katz took 20 per cent off the top. William Morris took 10 per cent off the top. Barbara Falk, who collected and distributed the money, recalled that she was paying twelve people per diems of $100 per week.

> There must have been money owed – rehearsal money to be paid. Guitars. It never seemed to me that there was enough. I used to do these budgets. There were as many expenses as there were receipts and then some. Rent-a-car or limos, hotels. In Europe and Asia sometimes the promoter would pay hotels and cars. In Australia we would get maybe $5,000 a gig. And not very many of them. They paid flights. I never got paid all my salary. Then there was the accountant and the IRS. The accountant dealt with them, we never put money aside for them. And Lou could spend a lot on the road. I was doling it out, very petty cash. He'd come up to me with his little hand full of receipts. I used to have Lou sign things like, 'Before money is paid to Lou such and such amounts must be paid to Transformer Inc.' He read what was written and he could usually quote it back to me. I remember thinking of Lou, it was so sad that here was this guy with records and fans and all this, and he was living in this little sublet of a place with rented furniture . . . And coffee ice cream.

To begin with she genuinely adored Lou, who 'had a great sense of humour. He joked a lot. He would make fun of politicians, audiences, promoters, record-company people, imitate accents, DJs. All were targets.' She also quickly learned to get along with and respect Bettye who was so obviously devoted to Lou. For a while Bettye helped him to stop using speed, but her willingness to match him drink for drink was his ongoing problem. Still, it was evident that Bettye was 100 per cent for Lou, seeing him more as an actor than a singer, and on the early tours even running the lights for the shows.

Above all, despite the chaos, the pressures and the tight

budgets, they managed for the most part to have fun. One of Barbara's favourite memories of the *Transformer* tour was the occasion on which Lou was arrested on stage in Miami for singing 'sucking on my ding dong' while tapping the helmets of the policemen guarding the front of the stage with his microphone. As Lou was lead away by a big cop with a serious expression intoning, 'This man is going to jail', Lou could barely control his hysterical laughter.

On 24 March, Reed was bitten on the bum by a fan screaming 'Leather!' at a show in Buffalo, New York. 'America seems to breed real animals,' Reed commented afterwards. 'The glitter people know where I'm at, the gay people know where I'm at,' he explained. 'I make songs up for them; I was doing things like that in '66 except people were a lot more uptight then.'

chapter thirteen   # Rock 'n' Roll Animal

1973–1974

[In which Lou records and releases *Berlin* and is devastated by the reaction. Lou tours the world, gets divorced, becomes an amphetamine addict, and records and releases *Rock 'n' Roll Animal*.]

God isn't a Christian or a Muslim. He's the victim of cult followings. He's a bit like Lou Reed.

KARL WALLINGER, WORLD PARTY

The zenith of Lou's commercial success came during the spring and summer of 1973 between April and June when *Transformer* and its single 'Walk on the Wild Side' peaked, first in the US, then on the UK charts. Lou finally took a firm hold on the reins of his public image and above all his music. 'Walk on the Wild Side' placed Reed alongside the most established artists on the music scene, competing with 'Frankenstein' (the Edgar Winter Group), 'Midnight Train to Georgia' (Gladys Knight), 'Angie' (the Rolling Stones), and 'Love Train' (the O'Jays) as the most popular singles of the year. He was living in New York with Bettye, and for a brief moment, success was sweet. As the initial excitement of success waned, Reed considered the cost of stardom. He was trapped in the Bowie-inspired Phantom persona, and much of his celebrity was tempered by comparisons between the two – many of which attributed the acclaimed work directly to David. Ever since *Transformer*, Lou's audiences had come to expect the 'Son of Andy Warhol', a manufactured cartoon character Reed had never been comfortable with, but had nonetheless used to resurrect his flagging career. 'It did what it was supposed to,' stated the Phantom of Rock. 'Like I say, I wanted to get popular so I could be the biggest schlock around, and I turned out really big schlock, because my shit's better than other people's diamonds. But it's really boring being the best show in town. I took it as far as I could possibly go and then o-u-t.'

Common business sense dictated that this was the time for Lou Reed to solidify his place among these groups by maintaining a high profile and continuing to tour. But Lou, who had a habit of going against the grain, chose instead to duck back into the studio and record a depressing album that would destroy his happiness and commercial credibility.

Convincing the record company to finance the project was not easy. 'There was this big fight with RCA,' Lou recalled. 'I talked them into the veracity of the whole thing, of how astute it would be to follow up "Walk on the Wild Side" with not just another hit single, but with a magnificent whatever. So I shoved it through.'

To gain artistic control of the project, once again Reed entered into a Faustian agreement with RCA that would undermine the first half of the seventies for him. In exchange for being allowed to make a tortured and poetic album, *Berlin*, exactly as he wanted it, he promised that he would deliver two commercial products – one live and one studio album in the style of *Transformer*. Lou's management team and friends were against his taking this direction. Lou himself knew that after a hit single his best move would have been to, as he put it, hand them down a boogie album. 'But I had to do *Berlin*,' he said. 'If I hadn't done it, I'd have gone crazy.'

Much to the consternation of the RCA executives, Reed cut David Bowie, along with his glitter-rock overtones, out of the equation. Reed and Bowie had put much distance between them by the autumn of 1972. As the media continued to compare them even after Lou's North American tour, Reed started to criticize and even insult Bowie as a way of escaping the stigma of dependency on his collaborators. Each rock star hinted in the press that the other was exploiting the relationship. Bowie, for example, insinuated that Lou was borrowing too much of his identity, and Lou retaliated by calling him, in *Circus* magazine, 'a very nasty person, actually'.

Reed was fighting on several fronts to maintain control of his professional life in the spring of 1973. In the process he sacrificed many of the personal relationships that had sustained him along the way. His marriage to Bettye was collapsing. 'For a while,' his friend Ed McCormack reported, 'the nuptial plan seemed like self-preservation, but eventually Lou realized it was the worst thing in the world. The girl he had married wasn't trying to save him – she was trying to housebreak him.'

Reed responded to the disintegration and chaos with strong material. In ten songs he dramatized the breakdown of his marriage with Bettye by telling the story of two American drug addicts living in Berlin. The song sequence, which eventually became *Berlin*, revealed a darker, more introspective side of Lou than his first two solo albums.

Lou's writing had never been better. He had mastered a lot of what he had acquired in Delmore Schwartz's classes. 'That's deciding to take the approach you would use in poetry,' Lou explained.

> Instead of making a division between pop songs and a real story or a real poem, merging them so the separation didn't exist any more. So the fun you had in trying to write a really good short story or poem wasn't separate from writing a song. You put the two together and then you have the whole thing going on at once. It makes perfect sense if you think about it.

Despite the new, downbeat songs and his split with David Bowie, Lou was still a long way from transforming himself from the Phantom of Rock to his next incarnation, the Rock 'n' Roll

Animal. The essential thing was to find a collaborator who could translate and develop his material as well as Cale, Warhol and Bowie had.

Fortunately, since Lou was at his commercial peak, all the doors in the rock world were open to him, particularly those of the emerging new generation. After Bowie, Reed and Iggy Pop, the most striking player on the scene was Alice Cooper, whose comic-book translations of Reed's more serious themes, combined with brilliant management, had turned him into the biggest-selling rock star of the early seventies. Lou hated Alice, and attacked him with the same vituperative humour he had directed at Zappa. This did not, however, stop him from borrowing Alice's twenty-four-year-old producer, Bob Ezrin, the whiz kid responsible for Cooper's classic albums *Love it to Death*, *Killer*, *School's Out* and *Billion Dollar Babies*. Ezrin had also produced an album by Mitch Ryder's group Detroit, which included a cover of Reed's Velvet paean 'Rock & Roll'.

Reviewing the material Lou had already written, Ezrin suggested he weave the songs into a story, 'a film for the ear' (as the album was eventually marketed), building the album entirely around movie images. 'It was thought of as a concept right from the top,' Lou explained. 'It was an adult album meant for adults – by adults for adults.' With this in mind, Reed and Ezrin flew to London in April.

The London Ezrin and Reed found themselves in during the summer of 1973 was a city crackling with rock energy, and Lou, who had received more votes than Mick Jagger in a music fans' popularity poll, could have had the world at his feet. But, rather than continuing with Phantom of Rock posturing and ego trips, Reed totally committed himself to getting his artistic self-portrait down on vinyl. Since he and Ezrin were playing at the top of their respective games, they had their pick of the top musicians on the London rock scene. They put together Lou's best recording band since the early Velvets. On bass, Jack Bruce; on keyboards, Steve Winwood; on guitars two top-flight Detroit players who had worked on Alice Cooper's records, Steve Hunter and Dick

Wagner. B. J. Wilson, of the psychedelic band Procol Harum, played drums on two tracks before being replaced by the blues-based Aynsley Dunbar. Finding Lou's enthusiasm infectious, the musicians took the recording as seriously as Reed. Unlike many other studio musicians Lou worked with during the first part of his solo career, Jack Bruce paid enough attention to Reed's work to read the song lyrics and thereby construct an accordingly empathetic musical part. 'Jack Bruce,' Lou recalled, 'wasn't supposed to be on the whole thing, but he went through the whole trip because he liked it a lot.'

As he started burrowing into the dark tunnel of some of his greatest compositions, the harder, colder Lou Reed emerged. Their central motif was addiction and self-destruction. 'It explains the whole motivation for the girl in *Berlin*,' Lou concluded. 'It's a central theme for almost everything I do.'

On Berlin, Lou wrenched up the dark side of his personal life and slapped it down on vinyl at almost exactly the same time it was happening. He had cut Bettye off from contact with anybody and isolated her in his world. Consequently, she was far removed from reality and crushed like an insect (one of Lou's favourite poetic images) by Lou's indomitable weirdness. 'My old lady was a real asshole,' he bragged to an astonished interviewer. 'But I needed a female asshole around to bolster me up, I needed a sycophant who I could bounce around and she fitted the bill . . . but she called it love, ha!' Poor Bettye, who was completely out of her depth with Lou, and is happily married with children today, unable to conceive of how she got so deeply involved with him, ended up, according to Reed, trying to cut her wrists in a pathetic and futile cry for help. 'She tried to commit suicide in a bathtub in the hotel.' Lou, who appeared to wear other people's tortured lives as a badge of courage, laughed mirthlessly. 'It was someone standing there holding a razor blade. She looks like she might kill you but instead she starts cutting away at her wrists and there's blood everywhere . . .

'She lived,' he complained, 'but we had to have a roadie there with her from then on.'

Reed poured his feelings into work. Each song seemed to tear away another layer of bandages from the wounded mummy of Lou Reed. And with the exposure of each cut he challenged his audience to wonder how it felt to him – staying up for five days straight on speed and booze, lonely, cold, miserable and terrified of going to sleep because he could not stand to encounter himself in the world of his dreams. What made Lou's work stand out was that despite portraying himself as a basket case, he was also portraying himself as a pioneer of pain, willing to take extreme risks in order to bring back the pictures of his explorations. For example, despite showing, like Warhol, an extreme fascination with suicide, he claimed that he wouldn't consider committing it for a second: 'It's so easy a way – the actual process. I mean, I've seen so many people like that. You either do it or you don't. And I know where I want to go. I'm in control. I know that there's this level and then there's this level. And I've seen over that level and I'm not even going to go near it. Ever.

'I'm in control, that's for sure.'

According to at least one musician, though, at the *Berlin* recording sessions Lou was far from being in control. Blue Weaver recounted how Lou was brought into the studio to record the vocal track over the instruments: 'He couldn't do it straight, he had to go down to the bar and then have a snort of this or that, and then they'd prop him up in a chair and let him start singing. It was supposed to be great, but something went wrong somewhere.' Clearly, Reed was feeling the strain as the recording drew to a close, and he reacted violently to criticism. 'Blue Weaver is an asshole,' Lou snapped. 'He's a schmuck, a fucking ass. Blue Weaver ought to keep his fucking mouth shut, because he can't fucking play.' But in fact, Lou had such difficulty laying down the vocal tracks that he finally had to overdub them later in New York.

After that, Dennis Katz spirited Lou off to Portugal for a much needed respite. Lou was joined by two friends from Amsterdam, with whom, according to friends, Lou had a tryst. In a postcard to Barbara Falk in New York, Lou wrote that both he and Portugal were divine, signing off, 'Ha! Ha!'

Berlin was originally planned as a double album with a gatefold sleeve and a booklet inside consisting of 'film stills' of the story and their lyrics. However, one week before Ezrin, strung out on heroin and exhausted, was due to deliver the final mix, RCA informed him that on second thoughts they would not accept a double album. They didn't think the product merited that kind of outlay. Consequently, while Lou lay back, his job completed, Bob Ezrin was reduced to snipping fourteen minutes off the opus – a horrible job that was bound to leave him feeling that the beautifully constructed work had been butchered. With his famous last words, 'Awright, wrap up this turkey before I puke,' he checked into a hospital suffering from withdrawal from both the intensity of the project and his lack of experience with heroin, which was cheap, strong and easily available in London. 'I would rather have had a nervous breakdown,' he explained later. 'I didn't know what heroin was till I went to England on this gig. We were all seriously ill.'

Lou, who prided himself on being able to take more pain, aggravation, drugs, alcohol – more everything – than everyone else, recalled:

> Doing that album did have its effect on Bobby. We killed ourselves psychologically on that album. We went so far into it that it was kinda hard to get out. It was a very painful album to make. And only me and Bobby really knew what we had there, what it did to us. When Bobby Ezrin gave me the master, he said, 'Don't even listen to it, just put it in a drawer.' He went back to Canada and flipped out.

However, according to a close friend of Ezrin's, Bob's collapse had as much to do with rebounding from such an intense involvement with Lou as with heroin or his music: 'Bob played the wrong game with Lou – he tried to be brilliant, to be his match. Nobody could ever be as brilliant as Lou. The only way to survive is to be the best you can and care for him deeply and hope nothing goes horribly wrong.'

*

RCA released the album first in the UK, that July, because it was Reed's strongest market. Lou flew to London for the release. While he was there he attended David Bowie's retirement party at the Café Royale. By July 1973, David had been working solidly since January 1972. 'We were touring all the time; he did three albums, Lou's album, Iggy's album, Mott the Hoople's album; and we weren't doing drugs,' Tony Zanetta recalled.

> Drugs came in when we stopped. So the party was part of the promotion. We flew Don Pennebaker over to film at the Hammersmith Odeon. And we planned this party at the Café Royale and invited every celebrity we could think of. And a lot of them came. The famous result was Mick Rock's picture of Lou, Mick Jagger and David. But how involved were Lou and David? They were ships in the night. David's attention span is short. And it was an intense period in his career. David didn't have a social scene. Maybe they had a chummy reunion that night, but that was the extent of it.

Berlin was released in the US in September. The album was undoubtedly Reed's first solo masterpiece, but, at the time, it attached itself to him like a limpet mine. Despite the notable exceptions, *Berlin* drew predominantly negative reviews, of which 'the worst album by a major artist in 1973' was one of the more restrained. *Rolling Stone* pronounced it 'a disaster'. The *New Musical Express* found it a sleazefest 'that will culminate in a breathtakingly vulgar pair of concerts at London's Rainbow'. William Gurvitch noted in the *Village Voice*, 'It is heterosexual, but about a druggy bi slut who gets her children taken away.' Even Lester Bangs, devoted to Lou all his adult life, could pronounce it only 'a gargantuan slab of maggoty rancour that may well be the most depressed album ever made'. Another critic lamented, 'I have difficulty caring about Reed's maladjustment,' while Bruce Malamut considered it 'the most naked exorcism of manic depression ever to be committed to vinyl'. David Downing wrote in *Future Rock* that it contained 'no hope . . . [The protagonists] stare straight into each other's eyes, and find only emptiness.' And Roger Klorese regretted the range of Lou's vocals, 'which sound, typically, like the heat-howl of the dying otter'.

Its critical reception twisted Lou into knots of resentment and anger of Warholian proportions. In interviews for *Berlin*, Lou developed a hard-line stance with rock journalists. 'When he talks, he's polite but distant, never allowing those with him the privilege of feeling quite comfortable in his presence,' one writer observed. 'He also enjoyed drinking particularly fearsome alcoholic concoctions and forcing writers to partake with him.' During this period in public he maintained a fixed, sinister glare and rarely smiled. For the most part, his speech was abrupt and evasive. 'Who cares about critics?' he told one reporter. '*Berlin* was an album for adults.'

In his defence, Reed claimed:

> Before *Berlin* came out, *Rolling Stone* said it was going to be the *Sgt Pepper* of the seventies, and afterward they wrote a pan and then they had a huge article criticizing the pan. It won all kinds of awards . . . it won the Thomas Edison award, and the best album of the year in *Stereo and Hi-Fi*. So critically it did not get panned, not in my book. Not unless you look at some jerk-off magazine, a tit-and-ass magazine disguised as some junior hippy kind of thing. But outside of those morons – who are illiterate little savages anyway – it did really well.
>
> If people don't like *Berlin*, it's because it's too real. It's not like a TV programme where all the bad things that happen to people are tolerable. Life isn't like that. And neither is the album.

John Rockwell, who would excel as a rock critic throughout the decade and become an important supporter of Lou Reed's, wrote one of the very few perceptive reviews in the *New York Times*. Rockwell pinned both the dramatic, filmlike quality of the piece and its complex sexual overtones as important departures from the run-of-the-mill rock record. 'The backings are clothed in rock dress, but the form is more operatic and cinematic than strictly musical in the traditional pop sense, and the sentiments are entirely personal,' he wrote.

> While others prance and play at provoking an aura of sexual aberrance, Reed is coldly real. *Berlin* is a typically dream-like saga of a

sado-masochistic love affair in contemporary Berlin. But the contemporary is enriched by a subtle acknowledgment of Brecht and Weill, and the potential sensationalism of the subject is calmly defused by a sort of hopeless matter-of-factness. It is strikingly and unexpectedly one of the strongest, most original rock records in years.

Every major event in Reed's life from 1973 to 1975 can be seen as stemming from the failure of *Berlin*, which stalled at 98 on the US charts. 'The record sales, compared to *Transformer*, were a disaster for a normal person, but for me it was a total disaster,' Reed said. 'The record company did a quick scurry round like little bunnies, but I went somnambulant. It wasn't brain rot like some people think. I just kinda did no more.'

Lou's nastiness protected his sensitive inner self. While being as hard as stainless steel on the outside, he could also be easily hurt. To his friends he cried, 'Can you think of another rock star who inspires so much hatred?' Some of them thought *Berlin* marked the major turning point in his solo career. 'I think Lou's power probably ended after *Berlin*,' stated a new friend of Reed's, Jim Jacobs. 'He had poetry and he had something to say and he said it and then he was finished saying it. It was an extraordinary moment but he never went beyond it.'

Berlin, however, would live a long life full of redemption and rebirth, and the first of a long line of reconsiderations appeared in the press within a year. In an eloquent defence of the record in *Rolling Stone*, Timothy Ferris shot back at Reed's critics, noting:

> Stephen Davis, writing in this magazine, characterized the record as 'a distorted and degenerate demimonde of paranoia, schizophrenia, degradation, pill-induced violence and suicide'. Which it is. But I fail to see how that makes a bad record. *Berlin* is bitter, uncompromising and one of the most fully realized concept albums. Prettiness has nothing to do with art, nor does good taste, good manners or good morals. Reed is one of the handful of serious artists working in a popular music today, and you'd think by now people would stop preaching at him.

In August 1973, Lou and a new band moved up to Stockbridge, Massachusetts, where they rented a set of rooms at the Music Inn and set about rehearsing for American and European legs of a tour in support of *Berlin*. 'Lou created quite a row there,' recalled Jim Jacobs, the man who would design and run the stage throughout the epic tour. 'He was drug-induced all the time. He hated rehearsing. He resented everyone and everything. He's not a nice guy and he can't help himself.'

During the rehearsals Reed drunkenly stumbled around the stage, smashing equipment and barking orders at the road crew. Acting as if he didn't give a shit about the endeavour, he fomented strife among his musicians, staff, management and friends at every opportunity. 'Lou's very good theatrically, he's very good at staging,' recalled one observer.

> He was always a great director. I noticed on several occasions he would be in the middle of a situation and without saying anything, or really doing anything, he had everyone around him fighting. He started some big chaos or commotion. And unless you were watching very, very carefully or from a distance, you would never have known that he was responsible for it.

Reed was nonetheless deadly serious about delivering a professional show. In this sense he managed to combine the Rock 'n' Roll Animal image with his unique performing style. 'I enjoyed listening to his music every night, because he was so crazy and so out of tune all the time,' remarked a philosophical Jacobs. 'Lou really preceded punk rock by ten years.'

The European leg of the tour had twelve scheduled dates, stopping in Paris, Copenhagen, Amsterdam, Brussels and a handful of cities in the UK. Despite receiving a plethora of bad and/or puzzled reviews and going down in history as a commercial disaster, *Berlin* did well in Britain, rising to number seven on the album charts by November and winning him a silver record. And *Transformer* was still on the charts. Reed thought of *Berlin* as his version of *Hamlet*, dubbing himself 'the Hamlet of Electricity'. The comparison applied particularly well to the European dates on the 1973 *Berlin* tour, which Lou and his people called the Rock 'n' Roll Animal tour. The ecstatic but exhausted Lou, skirting his own drug and alcohol madness after touring continually for over a year and a half, took the lead. Joining the royal-size entourage of twenty-three, Bettye, who was still holding on by her fingernails, was cast in the dual role of Ophelia and Gertrude. Dennis, who was beginning to look and sound to Lou like his parents, played Claudius; and the two young men who were hired to run the lights and act as his bodyguards, Jim Jacobs and his partner Bernie Gelb, became Lou's Rosencrantz and Guildenstern.

Reed and his entourage flew into Europe and then drove from country to country. They played a different city every night, often driving on to the next venue after a show. Lou spent most of his time with Jim Jacobs and Bernie Gelb, who took close and possessive care of him. Jim immediately connected with Lou, finding him wonderful to be with, bright and witty. 'I thought that he was a first-rate intellect and a qualified and very fine American poet,' Jacobs said. 'He was also very ambitious. And I cared about him.' Gelb, a lighting expert officially on the payroll as Lou Reed's bodyguard for the European shows, had similarly strong feelings for his charge. 'I carried Lou offstage, I walked him to his dressing room and got him to the shows and I drove his car. Lou and Jim and I travelled separately from the band. And thus there was some jealousy from the other members of the entourage. But we were having a good time.'

Before going on tour, Lou had gone to see Andy at the Factory to ask advice on how to do the lights for the shows while sticking to his limited budget. Warhol advised Lou to use the simple, stark, raw lighting device Albert Speer designed for Adolf Hitler's speeches: intense white spotlights against a black background, setting the whole spectacle in high contrast. 'On the European tour the lighting design involved a black stage and, for the most part, straight white spots right in Lou's face,' Gelb remembered. 'He was the centre of the illumination on the stage and anything else you saw was reflected light. There were some other small coloured effects but basically the band on that tour wore all black and stood at the back of the stage and Lou was front and centre with the lights shining on him.' The effect was simple, as Lou Reed stared down his audience. 'I've seen Lou perform over the years and that was close to the top of his performance peak, his stage personality,' Gelb summed up. 'He had it all together. Europe was just incredible. The whole tour was sold out.'

Uncharacteristically, Lou paid little attention to what was going on around him. Spending his time sleeping in the car, he allowed everything to be done for him. 'He had no control and he didn't want it,' said Gelb.

> He was totally uninterested. He just wanted to show up, he wasn't interested in the opening act, didn't want to sit around too long before or after the gig. I think by the time we got to Europe we didn't even use him for sound checks. Lou would just show up, walk on, do the set and split. Then he'd chill out and get in the car and go back to the hotel. He never asked a question or got involved with anything and was very cooperative. He did whatever we asked him.

The three-week tour met with universal success thanks, to a degree, to the supercharged band led by the guitarists Steve Hunter and Dick Wagner. Their twin guitar riffs gave Lou's music a heavy-metal sound it had not had before, and perfectly accented the Rock 'n' Roll Animal on stage. Many Reed classics, such as 'Sweet Jane', 'Rock & Roll', 'Waiting for the Man' and 'Heroin', became current again. 'The band cooked,' Gelb agreed. 'They were fabulous. When I say Lou wasn't in control and he didn't pay attention to the details, that was true for everything except for on stage.'

Reed painted his face a stark white, blackened his lips, eyes and hair, donned a black-on-black costume and employed a number of props such as sunglasses and a leather jacket. His jerky, stumbling movements were combined with a catalogue of rock clichés borrowed from classic performers like Jagger, Bowie and Iggy Pop. Every show was sold out, and the crush of fans caused riot conditions.

The consensus of opinion was that Lou's shows were either

brilliant or terrible, depending on how stoned he was. He had no rhythm, no flow. When he was off he just stuttered and stopped. When he was on and it moved from song to song he was a brilliant performer with energy. But sometimes his timing would be completely off. One moment he would be standing stock still at the microphone and the next he'd career across the stage on a collision course with the amplifiers. The more outrageous Reed became on stage, the more the audience applauded him. One Dutch journalist who interviewed Lou a number of times in the 1970s, Bert van der Kamp, commented, 'There were people in awe of him, and he would act the part. He could hardly stand on his feet and they had to push him out on stage. People were very fascinated by this over here.'

In a moment of lucidity and honesty, Lou announced to his audience in a packed theatre, '*Berlin* was a big flop, and it made me very sad. The way that album was overlooked was probably the biggest disappointment I ever faced. I pulled the blinds *shut* at that point. And they've remained closed.'

In Paris they played the Odéon. 'By then Lou could barely show up to the concert,' Jacobs reported. 'You just never knew if he was going to trip on the stage. He's not athletic, he's uncomfortable. It was very exciting to be involved on that total level.' In contrast to his previous European tours, the shows rarely disintegrated into complete riots with fans storming the stage, pitched battles with police and mass arrests. In fact, Gelb maintained a very good record of keeping the fans away from Reed, who hated to be touched by them. 'Only one fan was able to get to him on the whole tour,' Bernie Gelb recalled. 'That was in Paris. One crazy young girl who jumped on stage and wrapped her arms around Lou. I got to her three seconds after she got to Lou. I grabbed her, pulled her off stage, ripped her shirt off in the process and threw her out in the back alley topless and slammed the door.'

When the tour reached Paris, Bettye emerged briefly from the background in order to play out her final tragic scene. During the first part of the European leg of the tour her presence was subdued, but when Lou's attention finally turned to her the effect was devastating. Bettye made a desperate overture towards Lou; Jacobs and Gelb gave their allegiance to Lou, steadfastly ignoring Bettye, and Lou managed to rouse himself to action. 'Bettye made it a third of the way through,' Gelb remembered.

But then I saw the day that he turned on her. It was in Paris. Nico came to visit. He turned on Bettye and the next day she was a nobody, a stranger to him. He had the ability to turn on you so completely and quickly as if he was turning it on and off. It was amazing. I have never seen anyone else cut someone out of their life so efficiently.

'I think the sexual thing was not important to Lou,' Jacobs commented. 'It wasn't the real issue. He didn't want anyone else to be getting sex, but it was more like not getting his fair share. I don't think he really cared.'

In Amsterdam, Lou picked up his relationship with a man, with whom he shared a number of interests. 'One night in Amsterdam was the only night on the tour that he managed to get away from us,' said Gelb. 'He went out with this guy there who was a speedfreak.'

'He would do any drug that was available,' said Jacobs. 'Coke, speed, pot, Quaaludes, and a lot of booze. Speed and booze were his favourite drugs. He shot a lot of speed.' The repercussions of this particular night, however, threatened the next tour date in Brussels. Although Gelb and Jacobs managed to locate and transport Reed to the gig, his physical health and state of mind were significantly compromised.

They stayed up all night doing really awful speed. The next day Lou was in the worst mood I had ever seen him in my life, and that's truly an awful thing to say. I had to dress him. I finally got all of his clothes on. We played some games together and I finally got him into a better mood. His time came and I literally shoved him on stage. He could barely walk, he stumbled around and sang, and this audience just loved him.

Unfortunately, drugs were just part of the problem in Brussels. 'At one point he did some very odd manoeuvre and his leather pants ripped up the centre,' Jacobs recalled. 'He wasn't wearing any underwear and he was standing on stage with his balls hanging out. Bernie ran out onto the stage with some silver gaffer tape and taped him right around the crotch. Lou was so pissed because this tape was around his balls. He sang one more song and he left.'

'We didn't know, but just before he went on stage in Brussels he did a massive dose of meth,' Gelb added.

About a half hour into the show he started going into spasms, tachycardia, and he came over to the side of the stage and he said, 'Get me off the stage.' So I told everyone to shut it down. Then I picked him up over my shoulder and carried him up to the dressing room and locked the door. I laid him down and managed to bring him down to a state where I wasn't afraid he was going to die. And he was really fucked up. It was one of those things where he was saying, 'Don't let anyone see me, I can't talk to anyone. Don't let anyone in the room.' When I felt comfortable enough that he wasn't going to die, I stood outside the door for the next hour telling Dennis Katz, 'Yes, I understand you are his manager, but he doesn't want to see you now.'

'And he would not do an encore,' said Jacobs. 'They destroyed the theatre. They ripped the seats up and they threw everything at the stage and they even loved that! Because he was being such a bad boy.'

Realizing that Lou was seriously endangering his health and thereby compromising the tour, and that he was losing touch with his meal ticket, Dennis Katz, who seldom joined the touring, once more assigned his most trusted assistant, Barbara Falk, to the task of tour manager and Lou baby-sitter. It was a relationship that would last through the most hard-core mid-seventies touring, and that would also become one of the most significant of Reed's professional life. 'Lou was getting more and more difficult to handle,' recalled Barbara Falk, who had known and worked with Lou for some time.

You could never get enough for Lou. And Dennis wasn't perfect either. He didn't do what Lou thought he should do. Lou resented that Dennis didn't show up. Every once in a while Dennis would have to come to a gig somewhere, but he wasn't there hovering, saying 'What can I do, what can I do?' Actually, Lou didn't like it when he came to gigs. Because we had a routine, and I had to pamper him. The rider said, 'Johnny Walker Black. Don't give to Lou Reed, give to Barbara Falk' – and I would dole out one drink before he went on. I had to practically carry him onto the stage. But when Dennis would come, he would be jolly hockey sticks and all of this stuff. And it grated – it didn't help. Lou thought they were on totally different wavelengths altogether.

Lou was feeling more and more alienated – as if Dennis didn't care enough about him. Dennis was getting paid and we weren't. He had a Bentley and a this and that. And we owed everybody. Band members were always knocking at my door because they had family at home and they weren't getting paid. It was always borrow from Peter to pay Paul, and who can I put off the longest. But Dennis always got paid. And I think Lou started to resent that.

Actually, Dennis Katz was the least of Lou's worries. In order to maintain the ferocious pace of touring, he resorted to a wide variety of pharmaceuticals. 'He was like Lenny Bruce,' recalled Falk, who was astounded by the extent of Lou's involvement with drugs.

He had an enormous sense of fun and wit and chumminess. But he was usually coming up, down or sideways. We had this mother–son thing, but it was also like a twisted marriage. He thought it was cool to have a girl – they didn't have girls on the road back then. I used to have to carry him around. He was very light. I would drag him through immigration; I could have sworn he was asleep behind the shades a couple of times.

The combined efforts of Gelb, Jacobs and Falk aided greatly in the struggle to keep Reed sober. The trio's greatest success, in fact, was in convincing him to swear off booze for the bulk of the European tour. 'At the beginning of the tour in the States he was drinking really heavily,' Gelb remembered.

At shows, at rehearsals – always bottles of Scotch or bourbon hidden in the amps and the PA. And one day we put our foot down – he was smashing equipment, breaking things, being a jerk: the alcohol did terrible things to Lou – and somehow we convinced him. It seems incredible that he would agree to stop drinking, but it was necessary. We were ready to drop him. He's a real survivor. He had good sense. He partied, met friends, got high. But he didn't get drunk for the rest of the tour.

By the time the show found its way to Britain towards the end of the tour, Lou was relatively clean and the show had honed itself into an excellent performance. After the Brussels show he had learned his lesson and the English tour, where they were doing a city a night, demanded everyone's undivided attention. 'He drove the fans nuts,' Bernie Gelb said.

The Liverpool show – Jesus, that was the hardest show I ever had to get out of. The fans surrounded the hall, and they were tough there: every time we tried to leave they would throw rocks at us. We were pinned in the back alley, there was an IRA bomb threat. There were twenty steps up to the front of the building and I ended up driving the car up the steps, slipping out the front and driving back down the steps. It was like a movie, like driving on the stairs in Rome or something. It was really insane.

Audiences across the country reacted in much the same way, making it manifestly clear that Lou Reed had become a major solo rock-and-roll star.

Reed's success in Europe, especially the UK, where *Berlin* was in the chart's top ten and *Transformer* remained a large seller, may have been obvious to the fans, but to many journalists and celebrities, incuding the icons of mainstream rock, the Rock 'n' Roll Animal persona relegated Lou to second-class status. Feeling that he had done his time in the trenches and had been an extraordinary influence on younger bands, Reed resented being eclipsed by rock stars of the stature of Bowie and Jagger. 'He never got over the idea that he wasn't Mick Jagger or he wasn't David Bowie,' said Jacobs.

He was always overshadowed because they were better performers. Lou was not a good performer. He doesn't have a good voice. What Lou has is a devoted following of people who appreciate and love his work. That's saying something. But we did a concert at the Crystal Palace in England with James Taylor. I had known James quite well. James and Lou crossed paths and James said to me, 'What are you doing with Lou Reed?' I said, 'Well, you can't always eat white bread.'

The Rock 'n' Roll Animal tour continued playing across the US through the summer. As Lou's popularity soared, however, the aggression of his audiences followed. The primarily male audience erupted at each concert in chants of obscenities and endorsements ranging from 'Lou Reed motherfucker!' to 'It's your life, cocksucker!' Reed began to act out in an increasingly crazed manner. 'He was drinking so heavily again, he would go piss in the corner of the room and just drive you crazy,' recounted Barbara Falk. 'He did it up against the wall in some place in Canada. I think he pissed under the table one time on drummer Prakash John's foot. And Prakash was fastidious.'

'I know why you're all here,' he yelled at a bunch of friends, fans, entourage members, fellow musicians and journalists in a hotel bar late one night. 'You just want to get the headline story, "Lou Reed ODs in Holiday Inn," don't you?'

'Lou was the mascot of people who liked to get down and dirty,' Jim Jacobs summed up. 'It was very difficult with Lou. He was on speed at the time and his sexual ambiguity was always difficult. You didn't know whether he would get drunk and be with a man one night or get drunk and be with . . . But it was always very exciting to be involved on that total level.'

'Lou is brilliant', concluded Bernie Gelb.

He's as highly intelligent as any musician I have ever met. He can talk about any subject you want to talk about. But like all great stars, Lou had a great ego. At the end of the day, for all the good times and all the time spent watching him operate, Lou just isn't the nicest guy to ever walk the face of the earth. But he lived a very dramatic lifestyle.

In the autumn of 1973, Lou finally obtained a divorce from Bettye. The details were worked out by Dennis Katz. Lou later complained to friends that no sooner had he started earning money than he started losing it. Everyone who had ever spent any time with Bettye knew of her sweetness and emotional generosity. But Lou, who had moved into a whole new realm of existence, had come to resent her. The marriage, he said, had been 'kind of a pessimistic act' that 'kept me off the streets. And that's when I really started gaining weight. Then one day it dawned on me that it was all like a movie, and the thing about movies is that if you don't like 'em you can always walk out. And as soon as that became clear, it was all very simple. Now I don't get headaches any more and I'm poorer.'

Untying the knot with Bettye appeared to be the desperate act of someone about to become unhinged. After the break-up, Lou went into self-destructive overdrive. His physical and mental breakdown was in part accelerated by his resuming the steady use of meth amphetamine (back in the US, he had little problem acquiring it). One strong reconnection came about as a result of a chance meeting between Lou and his old Syracuse friend and Eldorado bandmate Richard Mishkin. Mishkin introduced him into a speed circle that centred on a man who would become a major influence on Lou in the 1970s, Ed Lister. 'I remember when I introduced them, it was a Sunday morning and I drove him down to Ed's house,' Mishkin recalled. 'Lister was one weird mother-fucker. He was the largest user of speed that I had ever encountered. He would use needles meant for horses, deep vein stuff so that he could get more in and just would use so much it was unbelievable.'

Ed Lister came from an upper-middle-class family in upstate New York. He lived in and owned a brownstone in Manhattan, which doubled as a shooting gallery. Lister, an accomplished thief, also used the house to store and fence stolen merchandise in order to fund his lifestyle. 'He would go steal cars and drive through the suburbs,' Mishkin recalled,

and he'd have a long pole with a grasper on it which he'd use to open people's mail boxes and steal credit cards. Then he would dress up in a priest's outfit – Lister was a master of disguises – and go round to the department stores and buy everything. So he was a fence. If you wanted something you could buy it from him. I couldn't understand why Lou had become enamoured of this guy.

Ed Lister was the leading member of a large New York speed scene made up of a bizarre cast of characters with whom Lou fit right in. There was another user, whom everyone called Turtle, who went to Columbia University. He was the Allen Ginsberg figure of the group in that he was loving, gentle and maternal. Turtle's apartment was a popular spot for the others to go to sit and talk for six or eight hours of amphetamine use. He had a lot of records and books, he was always interested in everyone and he was a complete junkie. Turtle distinguished himself by frequently getting arrested and spending more time in jail than anyone else. Bob Jones, who was also on the speed scene, and unlike most of the others had an appreciation of Lou's music, described Lou and Turtle's relationship.

> I don't think he liked Lou very much, although Lou sort of liked him. He was too gentle for Lou. He didn't have any of these macho pretences, but he would shake his head in great sadness and say, 'Mike was shot the other day at Eddie's apartment.' He had a way of saying it that was very gentle. I think Lou wrote a song or two about the Turtle. Another thing that was interesting was Turtle was gay and everyone around him was gay.

Marty, another member of the group, had a lot of scar tissue on his body. He had lost all his veins through shooting up, and was thus forced to inject himself in the most unlikely places. He distinguished himself by shooting up in his cock, for example, because it was one of the few veins he had left. One woman on the scene was Barbara, whom everyone called the Queen of Crime. Barbara was introduced to the scene through Lister, with whom she had had an affair, and her chief source of notoriety was in constant brushes with the law. 'Barbara would show up with a missing tooth or two, having been beaten up by some guy,' Jones commented. 'She was quite pretty, potentially, but she had a bad drug habit. She was always getting caught. I remember a story about a police roadblock she drove right through.'

Reed and Lister immediately hit it off, primarily because Lou was fascinated by him. 'Lou had a very romantic view of Lister,' Jones explained.

Lister came from a very rich family. Lister was a very educated man. Lister was godlike. Lister, for his part, treated Lou abysmally. He said that Lou couldn't sing, that nobody liked his music and that he could understand why. He said the guy was tone deaf, and who would listen to this shit? No wonder his records never sell. He liked people like John Denver.

In fact, none of the people in this litle crowd had any interest in Lou's music, and this put him on a social par with them. Lister, rather than Reed, was the big deal in that scene. 'Everyone just thought Lou was a bad singer and a pain in the neck,' concluded Bob Jones. 'He was only a big shot to me, and I think he liked to have me around because he recognized that kind of adulation. I was the only person who would both bring him drugs, shoot up with him and let him talk about rock and roll without sort of walking out of the room.'

'Lou spent quite a lot of time proselytizing shooting up,' said Jones. 'He said, "You're not really taking speed unless you're shooting up. You think you're taking speed, but you're not taking speed."' Somehow, though, Reed managed to retain a semblance of control. 'Lou, for the most part, used drugs very wisely,' commented another friend.

The man really knew his own capacity. He would take pure methamphetamine hydrochloride and grind it down, and include the whole experience in his music. Then after a month or two he'd decide to clean out his system. He'd stop entirely and move on to health foods and lifting weights. He knew exactly how to gauge the limits of his tolerance.

The popular sentiment in many amphetamine circles at the time was that speed was good, that it didn't harm one's health, and that the euphoric effects were perfectly natural. The only draw-backs, they argued, came through vitamin deficiency. As a result, Reed and the rest of the group would regularly ingest fistfuls of vitamins while shooting up – without, however, bothering to eat. The effects of chronic speed use and poor diet had particularly strong consequences for Lou, whose hands would become so dry that his fingers and fingernails cracked and bled. This made playing the guitar a near impossibility. He also experienced what the speed group called 'a wandering jaw', where his mouth would unconsciously open and his jaw would hang loosely.

Lou used the long hours and increased concentration afforded him by amphetamine use to compose a number of new songs.

Although he managed to cope with speed's physical assault, Reed succumbed to the radical personality changes it induced. He would go from being a nice boy from Long Island to a paranoid maniac, hallucinating about Machiavellian plots. Real and imagined slights elicited violent reactions. He took his reviews seriously and wanted to kill the writers, no matter how much they adored him. His free-floating hostility reduced most communication to the basics, even to the point of threatening old and dear friendships. According to Mishkin, ever since they had left Syracuse, 'Lou was never nice to me, and now he was more extreme. It was a straight line of development. But that was the speed, it made everyone awful. Your life loses meaning outside of the drug. Everything has to do with getting high and then getting more of it and then getting down without going crazy and then getting high again.'

In between speed binges and his divorce, Lou Reed and the Rock 'n' Roll Animal tour continued their assault on cities across America through the end of 1973. According to Lester Bangs, 'He'd poke his arm so full of vigorating vitamins that he lost all the fat overnight, then cartwheeled on stage in spastic epic(ene) colitic fits looking like some bizarre crossbreed of Jerry Lewis of idiot movie fame and a monkey on cantharides.' By this point Lou had stopped playing guitar at all on stage as well as in the studio. Instead, he had become a spindly-thin stand-up lead singer, whose eyes bulged out of his near-shaven bullet head as if they were plugged into an electric socket. His body was a shivering sack of anaemic skin and bones clothed in a black T-shirt and jeans. He moved in the short, clipped, violent motions of a speedfreak. A permanent cigarette distorted his hostile face. According to Cale, 'Steady doses of amphetamine changed the muscle structure of Lou's face so he can't smile any more. When he smiles his face gets limp and sags. It looks like a weird Frankenstein grimace.'

Reed continued to function as an artist, whether he was master of his senses or not. Working in an idiom where success was measured by commercial acceptance, however, he found himself marginalized. His devoted, if maniacal, public wanted a freak show. One reviewer described a show in Boston where Lou 'clumsily lurch[ed] about the Orpheum stage, violently yanking his frame downward at exactly the wrong times (rhythmically speaking) and crouched frog-like to serenade the front row as his band droned on'. It was an uncomfortable spectacle, and one which, for all its appeal to the audience, brought Lou dangerously close to the edge. 'They wanted to see me die,' Reed claimed.

Around the end of his tour and the beginning of his speed run, Lou became acquainted with Dennis Katz's brother Steve Katz, a star guitarist with Blood, Sweat & Tears. Lou and Steve became acquainted as guitar players, and as they developed an exciting musical relationship it was obvious that the collaboration could be expanded. 'Working with him,' recalled Steve, 'eased me out of the unhappiness with my own band. When he asked me to produce his next album, I went for it.' Dennis and Steve discussed the fate of *Berlin*. It was, Steve thought, 'a beautifully crafted album that was bombing . . . I think it sold maybe 20,000 copies. I told Lou we'd have to get rid of this old mystique and put out his songs to new people. He had a great band now and he could become a star with a hot live album.' Lou accepted the strategy.

At the end of the US leg of the Rock 'n' Roll Animal Tour, the burning, relentless drive that had produced two of his greatest solo works in a single year paid off when Lou recorded a concert in New York at Howard Stein's Academy of Music on 14th Street on 21 December. Guiding a Record Plant mobile unit, Steve Katz watched a capacity crowd explode into frenzy. A lot of fans still think it was one of the most spectacular concerts of their lifetime. Lou later characterized the performance as 'manic'.

Lou and the Katz brothers realized that the Academy concerts would make the great live album they had been searching for and set about mixing the tracks to get the record out as quickly as possible to capture Lou's moment.

According to Reed, who maintained the principles of recording *The Velvet Underground and Nico*, 'It was a perfect sound. Because I mixed it. The engineer just left. He didn't know how to record it. I couldn't stand what they were doing. Cleaning it up! And I went, "Oh, no!" and there was another big fight.'

In late December, Lou was arrested in Riverhead, Long Island, for attempting to obtain drugs from a pharmacy with a forged prescription. 'The game never ended,' said Barbara Falk. 'On Christmas Eve 1973, in the middle of Long Island, I had to scrape up $500 of my own money to get him out of jail – some misunderstanding about a scrip for guess what.'

Lou had been arrested for writing phony doctor's prescriptions in order to obtain speed. According to Lou, he had been sold out by another member of the speed scene. 'He was pissed off, but in a humorous kind of a way,' Falk recalled. 'Almost as if it was part of his image and act. Famous people get busted – that sort of thing. He wasn't scared or miffed about it, except that he was inconvenienced. He was miffed that Dennis didn't come. He said, "You come through for me, he never comes through . . . blah blah blah." He started kvetching a little bit.' Lou got through the minor scrape with the law, but it was obvious that his drug habits were getting the better of him.

*

In early 1974, Lou moved in with a new girlfriend named Barbara Hodes, at 45 Fifth Avenue, and immersed himself anew in the New York scene.

He prided himself on knowing more hot-dog places than anyone else.

In New York I can pick up a phone and have anything I want delivered to the door. I can step a foot outside the door and get into a fight immediately. All the energy, people going crazy, guys with no legs on roller skates. It's very intense, the energy level is incredible. It's nice at five in the morning to be stoned on THC and go down to Hong Fows, have some watercress soup, then you take a taxi uptown with some maniac and say, 'Go ahead, drive fast, wise guy,' and you just zip around. When you go up Park Avenue there's a very funny turn and it's always fun to wonder if they'll make it.

Bob Colacello recounted a January 1974 meeting between Reed and Andy Warhol where they discussed the possibility of making *Berlin* into a Broadway musical. Reed, Warhol and entourage went to dinner at Reno Sweeney's, a cabaret-style restaurant in Greenwich Village that had just opened.

Lou's opener was, 'I want you, Andy, your ideas – not Paul's or Brigid's.' It was a very difficult dinner, with Lou hesitant to tell too much about his ideas, afraid Andy would steal them. He did explain the psychology of the lead character a bit: he only shows emotion when he's out of speed, Lou said, and when his drug dealer makes it with his girlfriend but not him. When his girlfriend commits suicide, he can only describe and feels nothing.

In the wake of the Rock 'n' Roll Animal tour publicity, Andy Warhol seemed to take a renewed interest in Reed. Warhol was doing a series of videotape interviews for a projected TV show in which he'd usually sit silently staring into space or hiding behind a newspaper while the hapless interview victim was subjected to a series of banal questions by one of Warhol's minions, such as Colacello. Reed had agreed to be videoed on the stipulation that the interview be conducted solely by Warhol. Andy sat with his overcoat on, ready to split at any moment, making it obvious that he couldn't think of anything to ask, while Lou, heavily made up and looking as sick as one could without being locked up, made phone calls trying to find drugs in between trying to get a rise out of Warhol. The artist merely responded with an occasional mirthless laugh that meant he was bored and thought you were corny. The experience was excruciatingly uncomfortable. 'It was very sad,' Lou recalled, 'because he said while we were doing it, "You know, it can never happen again." And he was right.'

The new live album, *Rock 'n' Roll Animal*, was released at the end of February to universal acclaim. '*Rock 'n' Roll Animal*, an album of Reed's standards, opens with "Sweet Jane" and a jam by the band before Reed takes the stage, which establishes that, unlike some of his past back-up groups, this one is first-rate,' wrote Timothy Ferris in *Rolling Stone* that March.

> The rest of the side is devoted to a towering, unsettling version of 'Heroin'. It is sinister and stunning, rooted in a treacherous organ and strung tautly on a set of vaulting guitar riffs. The piece has the atmosphere of a cathedral at black mass, where heroin is God. *Rock 'n' Roll Animal* is much less claustrophobic and oppressive than *Berlin*, but many people will probably loathe it anyway. Faggots, junkies and sadists are not very pleasant, but theirs are the sensibilities Reed draws upon. His songs offer little hope. Nothing changes, nothing gets better.

The reviews for *Rock 'n' Roll Animal* were among the best ever. For the first time in his solo career he was being praised for his Velvet Underground as well as his solo material. 'At its best, Reed's live album brought the Velvets into the arena in a clean redefinition of heavy metal, thrilling without threatening to stupefy,' wrote Robert Christgau. ' "Lady Day", the slow one here, would pass for uptempo at many concerts, the made-in-Detroit guitars of Steve Hunter and Dick Wagner mesh naturally with the unnatural rhythms, and Reed shouts with no sacrifice of wit. This is a live album with a reason for living.'

In *Zoo World* Wayne Robins wrote that Lou might look like 'a cross between a mad executioner and an overgrown rodent', but he had become, finally, 'a rocker and not a chanteuse'.

John Cale, however, was not impressed.

I'm amazed at just how different Lou and I were in our ideas now that I've heard everything he's done since that time. It all sounds just like weak representations of tunes and nothing more. I mean, some of his songs in the Velvets really made a point. Now he just appears to be going round in circles, singing about transvestites and the like. The only thing I've heard him do since where he put up a good performance was on 'Sweet Jane'.

By the end of March 1974, *Rock 'n' Roll Animal* had soared to number 45 in the US, remaining in the hot 100 for twenty-seven weeks. Steve Katz was ecstatic with the success of his first production efforts.

The success of *Rock 'n' Roll Animal* redeemed Lou and gave him added confidence. Bowie was in town in February preparing for his Diamond Dogs tour. According to numerous sources, when they spent a night together the competition between them erupted. Lou was wired; they were both very stoned. Lou threw a drink or a table and there was a big fight between them. 'Bowie was successful and Lou would denigrate that,' Barbara Falk recalled. 'He was jealous, but he also said he was the cool, underground, credible one. David stomped out screaming.'

In February to March 1974 Lou hit the publicity trail doing interviews and photo sessions, even making a TV ad in which, emulating a Warhol screen test, he stared blankly at the camera for fifteen seconds before blinking, making the startled viewer realize they were not looking at a photograph.

To the press, Lou spouted the kind of contradictory reactions to the album that were his trademark, telling one journalist. 'It was like a walking time warp to me . . . but I had to get popular.' The live album, according to Reed, was payback for the deal he had made with RCA in order to get *Berlin* released. Now, he said, he was paying his dues. '*Berlin* being a failure and *Rock 'n' Roll Animal* being a smash was very hard to take. What I really liked was *Berlin. Rock 'n' Roll Animal*, what a degrading thing that was.'

To an interviewer from *Playboy*, Lou said he was having a good time by taking the road of least resistance and going with things that annoyed him rather than fighting them.

Ironically, for a man who was famous for wanting to kill his critics, Lou befriended a number of rock writers. He used them to sharpen his wits and keep abreast of what was happening in the rock world beyond his horizons. However, even when Lou was at his most charming, he could not help but exude an eerie quality in the key of Poe.

'He's a control freak and he's also very disrespectful, I mean he has no respect really for anyone, which is interesting,' said Glenn O'Brien. 'He's like Stalin in that he loves the people, he's filled with generosity for the human race, but not for any one person in particular. That's what he's all about to me. He loves being kind, but he hates your fucking guts.'

One scribe, who wishes to remain anonymous, recalled that talking with Reed was the weirdest interviewing experience he ever had:

Lou resembled the young Frank Sinatra slightly. When I pointed this out to him he seemed surprisingly pleased, joking, 'Don't say that to Frank.'

'Are you interested in Frank Sinatra, Lou?'

'Sinatra's fantastic. If somebody really gave him a really good song, with real lyrics, coming from him, and at this point he certainly could do it, you know, I mean, what the hell, come on, Frank.'

'Would you like to work with him?'

'I'd like to write for him. I would love to get to know him, then put lyrics in his mouth, then all he'd have to do would be sing them, wouldn't matter if he understood them. Can you imagine if Sinatra laid down 'Heroin' in Vegas at the Sands with Nelson Riddle conducting?'

As he spoke, the mask of the young Sinatra superimposed itself on his face like a ghost image, and for a split second Lou looked exactly like Frank! The transformation was so abrupt it made me nauseous. I ran to the bathroom to be sick. I recovered enough to conclude the interview. Before leaving, Lou invited me over his apartment the following day so he could teach me what I evidently didn't know about rock and roll.

Barbara Hodes's apartment, where he was staying, was an elegant one-bedroom, tastefully furnished in fashion-designer chic. Lou seemed comfortable there, joking with the Jamaican maid who was dusting the European issues of *Vogue*. When she left, Lou proceeded to take me through the history of rock, playing singles, explaining their significance, meanwhile exulting in the music, punching the air with a clenched fist, grinning from ear to ear at certain notes. He was an intensely alive person who certainly knew what he was talking about. He delivered the whole lecture with a great deal of passion. However, I thought even then when Lou was at his most serious, he could not help but stir up humour in his interlocutors to such an extent that it was hard to get people to take him seriously. In many ways, at least on the surface, Lou was an extremely funny man. Like his mentor Andy Warhol, he was constantly laughing and exulting in life.

As I got to know him, he turned at times into a fascinating bunch of guys. Once I was talking to him backstage at the Bottom Line when, in much the same fashion he had turned into Frank Sinatra, he suddenly metamorphosed into Jerry Lewis. However, on this occasion he was not so pleased when I commented on the resemblance. 'Enough with the cheap shots!' he snapped, turning abruptly back into Lou Reed. And I'll never forget the scene at Barbara's apartment the night I went to pick him up to go out for a drink. She was slouched in a chair looking very beautiful and very sad, begging Lou to let her have some Valium. Tottering around the room on his pencil-thin legs and high heels, Lou was clearly enjoying torturing her, saying that he didn't have enough to spare, then grudgingly giving her one. As we headed out the door, he launched into a story about fucking a groupie who kept asking him, 'How come when you're inside me I can really feel it, but whenever Mick Jagger's inside me I can't feel anything?' To which a bug-eyed Lou said he complained, 'Why are you telling *me* this?'

chapter fourteen

The Fall of the Rock 'n' Roll Animal

1974–1975

[In which Lou records and releases *Sally Can't Dance*, tours Europe, Australia and the US and releases the Velvets *Live 1969*. He also dumps Barbara Hodes for a drag queen named Rachel. Lou then begins work on *Coney Island Baby*, returns to Europe for a riot-torn tour and releases *Lou Reed Live*.]

The idea was to be always on stage. It was always showtime. One night we were at Max's and he ordered a Singapore sling. He sat there behind his sunglasses and for four hours he did not take a sip. Finally, I said, 'Uh . . . Lou . . .' and he said, 'That's just the point. It's very hip to order a drink and never touch it.'

DAVE HICKEY

In the spring of 1974, Lou had his frizzy locks sculpted into a military crew cut, bleached blond with Iron Crosses cut into each side of his scalp. Despite his own collection of Nazi memorabilia, Dennis Katz was perturbed when his recalcitrant star showed up thus shorn. Barbara Falk, who made Lou wear a hat whenever they went out, recalled, 'Dennis and Lou did have a fall-out when Lewis appeared with those Nazi crosses in his hair. We were worried when we first saw him like that, but what can you do? Lewis is such an extremist.'

Lester Bangs had a friend working as a bus boy at Max's Kansas City.

> The guy called me up one day: 'Your boy was in again last night . . . Jesus, he looks like an insect . . . or like something that belongs in an intensive-care ward . . . almost no flesh on the bones, all the flesh that's there's sort of dead and sallow and hanging, his eyes are always darting all over the place, his skull is shaved and you can see the pallor under the bristles, it looks like he's got iron plates implanted in his head . . .'

The crosses, which made it hard for Lou to walk to the liquor store to acquire another fifth, were gone within weeks, but they left their mark. While *Rock 'n' Roll Animal* climbed the international pop charts and Reed's image became popular, he embarked upon another harrowing recording session.

In March 1974, Reed went into Jimi Hendrix's Electric Ladyland Studios on West Eighth Street in New York's Greenwich Village to work on his next album, *Sally Can't Dance*. Lou had claimed to be a better guitar player than Hendrix back in the sixties, but he also thought Hendrix's 'Star-Spangled Banner' was the greatest rock record ever made. They had met during the sixties. Jimi had seen him at the Dom. Lou had inherited one of his shirts, which he wore on special occasions.

Once again, Steve Katz was lined up to produce. He brought an eclectic, often contrary catalogue of influences to the recording. Reed deferred to Katz's overall direction, letting him take over the most crucial stages of the music's development. As he worked up each of Lou's ideas into recognizable tunes, Katz emerged as a collaborator.

The single, notable exception to the recording process was 'Kill Your Sons', which dated back to the Velvets era. Chronicling his electroshock therapy and delivered with the vitriol of his childhood, it was the album's naked show of emotion. Another off-the-wall gem was the satiric 'I Wanna Be Black', in which Lou plays the part of a fucked-up middle-class college student who yearns to be his imagined black opposite, a pimp with an enormous dick, a gilded Cadillac and a stable of foxy whores. Even Reed would not dare to release this ditty until 1977.

According to Steve Katz, Lou spent the majority of his time in the studio in the bathroom. Katz was pretty sure he was taking drugs and becoming increasingly impatient. One weekend when Lou was staying at Katz's house in Westchester, Steve 'accidentally' walked into the bathroom and caught Lou in the act of injecting methedrine. Like his brother Dennis, Steve genuinely liked and respected Lou, but began to see that even though Lou would regularly stop taking speed to clean out his system and followed a rigorous diet and course of exercise, the drug was taking over his personality and negatively affecting his work.

Katz took control of the project. He took a supportive attitude towards Lou, but what he could not supply was the creative foil that Cale, Warhol, Bowie and Ezrin had. Steven echoed Blue Weaver. 'As an artist, Lou was not totally there. He had to be propped up like a baby with things done for him and around him.' Clearly, this was the situation he wanted. 'I slept through *Sally Can't Dance*,' Reed boasted. 'I did the vocals in one take, in twenty minutes, and then it was goodbye. They'd make a suggestion and I'd say, "Oh, all right." I just can't write songs you can dance to. I sound terrible, but I was singing about the worst shit in the world.'

After the album came out Lou denigrated it and the musicians and producer. However, as Katz pointed out, Lou would work with some of them for years. '*We all loved him* and understood him and tried to help him. But he simply refused to be there. The drugs were becoming just too much for me to deal with.'

Lou had been unhappy with his keyboard player on the Animal tour and asked Michael Fonfara to replace him in his band. 'The way Steve Katz produced that album was basically to take input from people and go on their word that things were going to be OK,' Fonfara explained.

To make matters worse, during the sessions Lou was so uptight for money he constantly hit up friends for cab fares and restaurant bills. For a man who had two international hit albums and a single still on the charts, it seemed too extreme to be believed. The truth was that Lou's separation from Heller, divorce from Bettye, drug bill and profligate spending habits had wiped him out. Never one to tackle financial matters like an accountant, Lou blamed the man who was handling his money, Dennis Katz. Their relationship had been amazingly smooth until now, but when Lou turned on somebody, particularly somebody who he thought betrayed him, there was no way back. As Barbara Falk saw it:

> Lou felt that *Sally Can't Dance* was a totally mistaken album. Lou would say, 'Dennis doesn't get it and he's got to have all the money.' And then he became even more paranoid, there was a conspiracy to manipulate him and his money . . . Full blown.
>
> By then Dennis saw the handwriting on the wall, because that last year [1974–75] he was very particular about everything. And I remember when Dennis negotiated the publishing agreement with RCA where it was a lot of money, and they got 20 per cent, then there were taxes, and there was very little left for Lou. The man had no real assets.

Reed felt RCA had him up against a wall. As he saw it, the company heads were in cahoots with the Katz brothers to milk him for what he was still good for. Lou was increasingly uncomfortable with the results of *Sally Can't Dance*. They were trying to make him sound like Elton John!

In another attempt to backpedal out of the trap, Lou tried first to reignite his relationship with John Cale. However, negotiations soon collapsed. Meanwhile, Lou had been writing to Nico. His attempt to rekindle his collaboration with her demonstrated just how much he had changed since what would now look like the halcyon 1967 period. At first, enchanted by her replies, Lou appeared to fall in love with Nico all over again. Waving one five-page scrawled letter in the faces of his friends in between tugging on a fifth of whisky, his face enlightened by her spiritual presence, Lou explained that she was magnificent. That she was everything. That *Berlin* was all about her. He adored her. Once again Nico was a genius.

To journalists Lou raved about Nico. 'The Marble Index, Desert Shore, The End are the most incredible albums ever made. Nico doing 'The End' is unbelievable. She's a whole galaxy unto herself. Nico is a true star.'

Flying across the Atlantic in March at Lou's expense, Nico must have felt that her dodgy career was once again going to be resurrected by the most brilliant songwriter she had ever worked with. Nico still loved Lou in her way. In fact, they were so close that Lou, uncharacteristically, invited her to stay with him and Barbara Hodes in his new Upper East Side apartment. As soon as he had her at his mercy, totally dependent on him, the manic Reed cavorted around Nico like a cat around a wounded mouse, taking little swipes, then sitting back studiously contemplating her reactions with that sliver of ice that is in the heart of every writer.

Within forty-eight hours Nico, who was not in particularly good shape and needed a steady supply of drugs and alcohol to keep her nerves afloat, was breaking down sobbing incoherently. She still emanated an aura of defenceless beauty that begged to be destroyed and Lou, taking his fantasies of ultimate control to the tenth degree, tortured her around the clock by withholding the drugs she needed, then allowing her a little bit before snatching the vial away at the last moment, whispering taunts. Not only did Lou slowly take her apart, he invited an audience of loutish electricians, roadies and journalists to observe his every dissecting snip.

Within three days he was done with his game and the bewildered, exhausted Nico found herself locked out of the apartment with her suitcase, her candles and her cigarettes, a harmonium grimly stashed beneath one sick arm, and not a penny in her purse. Finding her sitting mournfully on her doorstep that night, the generous Barbara Falk graciously took her in. There was, needless to say, no record. In fact, there was no mention of Nico's name around Lou. She was not given another audience. There would be no songs for her from Lou, ever again.

Cale was saddened by the wasted opportunity. Nico would remain a bone of contention between them throughout the decade. In 1974 alone they had several vicious spats about her over the phone, hanging up on each other frequently. 'Right through the seventies I hoped Lou would write her another song like "All Tomorrow's Parties", "Femme Fatale" or "I'll Be Your Mirror", but he never did,' Cale said. 'I'd tell him I was working with Nico on her new LP, whichever it was, and he'd just say, "Really?", nothing more, not a flicker of interest. He could have written wonderful songs for her. It's a shame and I regret it very much.'

In April, seeking friendship elsewhere, Lou took a brief trip to Amsterdam. However, he returned three days later deeply disappointed, his anger and frustration flashing on dangerous levels. He had, he told one friend bitterly, made another mistake. Even his relationship with Barbara Hodes began to wither. He had known the beautiful and artistic blonde since 1966. He never forgot how she had sought him out during his 1971 exile and encouraged him to make a comeback. Since early 1974, Barbara had intermittently lived with him. She was a sexy, intelligent woman in the fashion business who offered him everything and was much closer to his level than Bettye had been. Now he started seeing how close to the edge he could push her.

By making his life a battlefield, Lou made the rock-and-roll stage the only place he could really unleash himself. He brought the full force of his personality to the stage that year. In May and June, accompanied by an entourage of twenty-four people, including the disenchanted Hodes, Reed embarked on a tour of Europe that would take him through Sweden, Denmark, the Netherlands, Britain, Belgium, France, and back to Britain.

The climax of each show was reached with Lou's legendary rendition of 'Heroin'. Only now he added a theatrical twist to the performance. Extracting a syringe from his trouser pocket, then lashing the microphone chord around his arm, he mimed the ritual of injecting heroin. Although this was a total act, Reed made it seem so convincing that some members of the audience were sickened by the sight while others feared for his life. The image of a skeletally thin, cropped peroxide-blond Reed shooting up on stage became one of the classic images of rock in the 1970s and naturally only served to strengthen his image of a drug addict.

Lou was moving through people at an unhealthy rate. In order to keep balanced in between tours and recording sessions, he desperately needed a companion who could keep up with him. That autumn, back in New York, Lou met a tall, exotic hairdresser drag queen from Philadelphia named Rachel (né Tommy), who would become an ace nursemaid and muse through the mid-seventies. 'It was in a late-night club in Greenwich Village,' Reed later rhapsodized to Mick Rock.

> I'd been up for days as usual, and everything was at that super-real, glowing stage. I walked in and there was this amazing person, this incredible head kind of vibrating out of it all. Rachel was wearing this amazing make-up and dress, and was absolutely in a different world to anyone in the place. Eventually I spoke and she came home with me. I rapped for hours and hours, while Rachel just sat there looking at me, saying nothing. At the time I was living with a girl, a crazy blonde lady [Barbara Hodes], and I kind of wanted us all three to live together, but somehow it was too heavy for her. Rachel just stayed on and the girl moved out. Rachel was completely disinterested in who I was and what I did. Nothing could impress her. He'd hardly heard my music and didn't like it all that much when he did.

Rachel was a beautiful, half-Mexican transsexual raised in reformatories and prisons and on the streets since childhood. 'Imagine,' urged Steve Katz, 'a woman in a man's body, getting by as a juvenile delinquent. Understanding Rachel was a question of understanding a person's orientation. I found her wonderful, and very quiet. That whole thing about, was Lou a homosexual, was he straight – Rachel was physically gorgeous for any sex. Straight men were coming on to her all the time.'

However, Lou's sexual preferences had become important to his fans. Reed's roadies were constantly asked if their leader was bi. 'Bi? The fucker's quad!' one joked in a bon mot that bounced around the rock world. 'In my experience,' a friend, Dave Hickey, wrote,

and we spent a lot of time together, all these supposed 'digressions from the norm' were just bullshit. Anyway, if you took that much speed for that many years, you don't know what the hell you are. Physically, you cannot get an erection. Whenever he'd start talking about his prowess, I'd know for sure he wasn't getting it up, and therefore going to extremes. Psychologically I don't think he's oriented one way or the other. But he had the brilliance to dip in and out of deviance, and play with it, make an illusion of it.

He was on all the time, but he could be objective, and he had a real sense of humour about it. He was careful to observe all the feedback the 'Lou Reed persona' got in the press; he read an enormous amount of magazines. He knew he was carrying the weight of the image of the Velvet Underground; he knew Lou Reed had to be Lou Reed. If Lou Reed is supposed to take drugs and have a weird sex life – well, then, it has to be.

By the time he met Rachel, Lou had moved to an Upper East Side airline-stewardess apartment in the East 50s. The place was furnished with the basic hotel-suite look, a couch before a coffee table opposite an armchair with mirrors on the walls lit by floor lamps. The bedroom looked like a Howard Johnson's motel. The only signs of Lou's presence were the guitars leaning up against the walls, the musical equipment and stacks of tapes, and the perennial pint of coffee ice cream which lived in the fridge.

When he wasn't in the studio, rehearsing for a tour or voyaging around the city in search of characters or material, Lou spent his time here, writing songs, playing music and receiving a steady stream of visitors ranging from his drug dealers through recording engineers and journalists to guitar players and assorted drug buddies. When he had the right dose of speed in him and a bottle of

Scotch around, Lou loved nothing better than to while away the hours in this manner with his music. Rachel looked on protectively, and made sure there was enough coffee ice cream and Marlboros.

From Shelley Albin through Nico, Bettye and Barbara Hodes, there is a distinct pattern of gorgeous, alluring blondes with theatrical or artistic personalities. Rachel introduced an abrupt change in direction. Not only was this a guy – and, by the way, very evidently a guy when he would stay up for a couple of days, forget to shave and be drinking – but Rachel's colouring was dark and brooding. What Rachel had in common with her predecessors was a complete acceptance of Lou Reed, an adoration of the little boy in him and, most importantly of all, stamina. With Rachel around, Lou never had to be alone. She did not speak much, but when she did she put it across. Lou knew how to use her and benefited enormously from the relationship, although at first his motivation may have been a little unclear. 'I think Andy's fascination with drag queens was behind Lou's interest in Rachel,' said one close friend. 'The thing that Lou comically got wrong was that Rachel wasn't a Warhol drag-queen type. The Warhol drag queens had a feminine side, or a drag-queen side. Rachel was sort of Native American, there was a very stone-faced-Indian aspect to Rachel. Rachel didn't really have a woman's attitude.'

According to Bob Jones:

Lou was having a sexual relationship with Rachel. Rachel would come out of the bedroom with just a wrap around her and Lou would have just come out. They slept in the same bed, Rachel slept naked in the bed. Speed is the biggest aphrodisiac. Also, you can go for hours. It is very tactile and very erotic. You make out for two hours without coming, and you want to fuck daily. So I think Lou was having sex. There was never any talk about having sex, but it would be inconceivable that he would go three weeks without sex. In fact, it would be inconceivable to go a week without sex. Inconceivable.

Sally Can't Dance was released in August 1974 and got a lot of good press.

'"Billy", finally, is unusual even for unusual Lou,' wrote Paul Williams in the *SoHo Weekly News*, New York's hippest downtown paper.

It's a ballad about an old school friend and what became of him – and, by extension, about what became of Lou as well. It works. This album, with 'Kill Your Sons' and 'Billy', is among other things an acknowledgment of Lou's middle-class Long Island roots. Paradoxically, this adds a depth to his recorded persona. When he says, 'I often wonder which one of us was the fool,' I take it literally: he does wonder, he does sometimes try to evaluate his life in terms of his parents' values.

'Lou sure is adept at figuring out new ways to shit on people,' chimed in Robert Christgau in the *Voice*.

I mean, what else are we to make of this grotesque hodgepodge of soul horns, flash guitar, deadpan song-speech, and indifferent rhymes? I don't know, and Lou probably doesn't either – even as he shits on us he can't staunch his own cleverness. So the hodgepodge produces juxtapositions that are funny and interesting, the title tune is as deadly accurate as it is simply mean-spirited, and 'Billy' is simply moving, indifferent rhymes and all. B+.

Sally Can't Dance was Reed's biggest-selling album and stayed in the charts for fourteen weeks, becoming the only top-ten LP of his career.

Lou was disillusioned with the charade his career had become, exhibiting a new level of raw loathing. Interviews at the time more often than not degenerated into verbal war. Lou's cynicism perhaps reached its apogee when he told Danny Fields in *Gig* magazine, 'This is fantastic – the worse I am, the more it sells. If I wasn't on the record at all next time around, it would probably go to number one.'

According to Lou:

Sally Can't Dance wasn't a parody, that was what was happening. It was produced in the slimiest way possible. I like leakage. I wish all the Dolbys were just ripped out of the studio. I've spent more time getting rid of all that fucking shit. I hate that album. *Sally Can't Dance* is tedious. Could you imagine putting out *Sally Can't Dance* with your name on it? Dying my hair and all that shit? That's what they wanted, that's what they got. *Sally Can't Dance* went into the top ten without a single, and I said, 'Ah, what a piece of shit.'

While Reed played at indifference, he unleashed statements of contempt for his career, his public and ultimately himself. He also attempted to salvage his pose by a Warholian protestation of innocence. 'I'm passive and people just don't understand that. They talk and I just sit and I don't react and that makes them uncomfortable. I just empty myself out so what people see is a projection of their own needs.'

In an open letter in *Hit Parader*, Richard Robinson showed an unexpected sympathy, calling Katz's production 'admirable' and telling Lou that it's 'the closest thing you've been to being heard in some time'. But he regretted *Sally*'s lack of depth, energy and rock-and-roll craziness, which had him virtually unable to distinguish one track from another.

In retrospect, while betraying his two most commercial RCA albums, Lou insisted that he made them in order to get the Velvet Underground albums back into print, claiming, 'I kept going with *Rock 'n' Roll Animal* because it did what it was supposed to do. It got MGM to repackage all those Velvets things, and it got the *1969 Live* album out.'

However much this may reek of rationalization, his strategy was successful. Sterling Morrison, who had cut himself off from the music world, recalled with some annoyance that in early 1974 he began

> getting these calls from Steve Sesnick, and I thought, 'What is this bullshit?' Then Lou even called. Apparently his lawyer had told him to turn on the charm. They wanted me to sign the release for the *1969 Velvet Underground Live* album. I did not want it released. There is a certain clean feeling that comes from not dealing with the people you'd have to, to collect royalties on anything like that. And I'd listened to the tapes and I thought, Oh, man! I can't see this selling ten copies! Musically I much preferred *Live at Max's Kansas City* – it has

much more energy. I said I was not going along with it. Then Steve Sesnick finally convinced me. I signed the release for a pittance because he told me he needed the money. I'm sure he was in cahoots with Lou in some strange way.

That September, the double Velvet Underground album *Live 1969* was released in the US. Several other Velvet Underground compilations were released in Europe. Patti Smith, on the verge of her entrance into the rock world as the high priestess of punk, reviewed the album in *Creem*. She liked it because it was oppressive. By releasing the older albums Lou was able to service the audiences who had come with him out of the sixties as well as the younger fans who were attending his concerts in droves. A salesman in a record store in Cambridge, Massachusetts, described the people who were buying Lou Reed records: 'You get like these twenty-eight-year-old straight divorcee types, asking for *Transformer* and *The Velvet Underground*, but the amazing thing is that suddenly there's all these fourteen-year-olds, coming in all wide-eyed: 'Hey, uh, do you have any Lou Reed records?'

If Lou's London sessions had climaxed with *Berlin*, Lou's Rock 'n' Roll Animal period climaxed in his autumn–winter 1974 tour of the US. 'He was very big in New York, New Jersey, Los Angeles and parts of the Midwest,' explained Barbara Falk. Rachel accompanied Lou on the tour, officially listed as his 'baby-sitter'.

Those who met Rachel were amazed to find a tall, elegant person, embodying a compelling mix of male and female qualities. Mick Rock took a smashing photograph for *Penthouse* that captured their relationship: clad in matching black leather, tottering on pencil-thin legs, the couple embrace – Lou in front facing the camera with a stoned smile on his face, while Rachel, with her long black hank of hair hanging down to her shoulder blades, supports him from behind, her hands cupped possessively over his cricket set, with a look of serene possession.

To dramatize his self-destructive motif, Lou kept 'Heroin' in the tour repertory, pushing it for all it was worth. In *Melody Maker* of 7 December 1974, Todd Tolces described a 'gory Guignol' before 5,000 raving fans in San Francisco. Lou 'pulled a hypodermic needle out of his boot . . . as the crowd erupted into cheers and calls for, "Kill, Kill!" he tied off with the microphone cord, bringing up his vein. As the writer ran for the gentlemen's toilet, Lou handed the syringe to a howling fan.' No one could be certain what had really happened, but the image lingered on, and added fuel to the talk that these were Reed's final shows, that he would be unlikely to live beyond Christmas. For even if he wasn't actually shooting up on stage, it was clear to everyone that he was shooting up somewhere, and that the drugs and lifestyle were rapidly killing him. Along with the Rolling Stones' guitarist Keith Richards, Reed began to be fingered as an imminent rock-and-roll casualty.

'The Stanley Theater was the perfect setting for rock's king of decadence – Lou Reed – and he knocked them dead last night,' wrote Peter Bishop in Andy Warhol's hometown of Pittsburgh.

He fit right into the creaking old showplace, the civic arena would have been too refined for this little man with the blond hair, sleeveless black T-shirt, paste-pale skin and sunglasses, who looked more like a reprobate from around the corner on Liberty Avenue than a rock legend.

Once he got on stage, the crowd already standing on the seats applauding, he proved himself a star, embellishing the glitter-language lyrics with a choreographic blend of go-go, jitterbug, free-form and street-fighting moves that threatened to shake the painted-on jeans from his scrawny hips. And how the audience loved it when he made the raunchy lyrics of 'Walk on the Wild Side' even raunchier. This song and Reed himself are definite vestiges of the decadent movement of the late 1800s, and how Oscar Wilde and Aubrey Beardsley would have loved to hear and illustrate that song. He gives you more than your money's worth of music and show; he's what rock and roll is all about.'

One reason for Lou's success in 1974, as he often pointed out, was the rock-schlock horror prevalent in the culture. After being way out ahead of his times for the last half of the sixties, in the mid-seventies Lou was hitting the headlines smack on the nose day after day. He was as ugly, violent, vicious and stupid as the time. He was the time.

RCA got 13 September proclaimed Lou Reed Day in Cleveland; Lou celebrated by ripping free records off every radio station he visited and making his hosts play banned records over the air. A couple of weeks later RCA proclaimed Lou Reed Impact Day in New York; Lou played shows at the Felt Forum.

'Other stars admired him greatly,' recalled Barbara Falk.

> He never came out and said it, but I think he was touched when they found him pretty nifty. I'll never forget Mick Jagger crouching down behind the amps at the Felt Forum so he didn't detract from Lou's performance. I would bring him little glasses of champagne. Mick wanted to come right back into the dressing room and tell him how fabulous he was.

However, for the most part, Lou was not able to receive backstage guests after his shows. He was more often than not so profoundly moved by the emotional impact of the music and audience that Barbara Falk would find him alone in his dressing room, sobbing uncontrollably and unable to face anyone but her. As Barbara described it:

> He'd be wrung out, drenched, shaking and sometimes crying from sheer release of all this pent-up emotion. Especially if it was a good audience. Or if there was a really bad audience and he'd be upset that there wasn't anybody there. It was a physical and emotional release. After a while I would leave him alone to help pack up and then he wouldn't want to leave. And he'd talk about it – he'd say, 'Did you see these moves or that step?' I think he fancied himself a good dancer but he was terrible. He was best with just the cigarette.
>
> At the end of the year, he was more erratic. Dennis suggested that he go to his own doctor. Lou looked up to him so much that he trotted off. I can't imagine his doing this for anyone else. The doctor reported that Lou had . . . slightly elevated cholesterol. Ha! Lou never let Dennis forget this. His idea of a real doctor, of course, was the notorious Dr Feelgood. Sometimes he'd be waiting on that doctor's steps at 6 a.m.

By the end of 1974, rock, as personified by the sixties dinosaurs, was looking all too complacent. On 13 December, the former Beatle George Harrison had lunch with President Gerald Ford in the White House. The time had come for Lou to contemplate a radical move that would wipe out any attempt on the part of the record company or the critics to classify Lou Reed in the middle of the road.

In January 1975, Lou went into a New York studio with a stripped-down band and recorded 'Kicks', 'Coney Island Baby', 'She's My Best Friend' and 'Dirt' in four days. Behind him lay the ruined relationship with Dennis Katz, and the slithering Rock 'n' Roll Animal, whose skin he was painfully shedding. Reed was desperate to find a new image that would free him from the prison of any image. For the time being, the only reality that Lou could hold on to apart from his music was Rachel.

Dennis Katz, who feared that he was losing control of his most valuable asset, listened to the new tapes and told Lou flatly there was no way this music could be released. Apart from the fact that 'Dirt' was an obvious and brutal put-down of Katz, the songs were, in his opinion, too raw and negative to be commercially successful. The planned album, *Coney Island Baby* was temporarily shelved. Meanwhile, Lou was informed that he was broke and had to go back on the road to earn some money. It was an insensitive and self-interested move by Katz. Sending the unstable Reed out on an international tour was likely to push him over an edge he had been teetering on all year.

Accompanied by Rachel, the loyal Falk and a surprise addition to the band, Doug Yule, Reed launched this tour in Milan. Totally unbeknown to Lou, Italy was in violent political turmoil. On 13 February, a Dada-influenced gang called Masters of Creative Situations disrupted his first concert. As Barbara explained, 'These riots had nothing to do with Lou; they just chose our arena as their battle site, because there were so many people there. The fascists and the communists were trying to influence the elections, so they threw tear gas at the stage. The riot police were all over the place with big shields.' Throwing bolts and screwdrivers at the band, the rioters leaped on stage and denounced Reed as a 'decadent dirty Jew'. Lou left the stage in tears.

After this inauspicious start, Lou refused to proceed with the tour. Barbara cancelled the next show in Bologna and took him to Switzerland. Once he was in a neutral country, Lou demanded that somebody from the Katz managerial team fly over and consult with him immediately. Both Katz brothers declined the invitation. The bushy-eyed manager of David Bowie, Tony DeFries, who had been trying to manage Lou since 1972, went in their stead. 'Dennis was furious when DeFries came to Switzerland, that Lou would even consider talking to DeFries,' said Barbara Falk. 'We were holed up in this very modern hotel in Switzerland and Lou called DeFries. Lou said Dennis should have been there, Daddy should have held my hand.'

However, instead of grabbing the opportunity to switch his allegiance from Katz to DeFries and possibly reap the benefits Bowie had, in typically ambivalent fashion Lou holed up in a Zurich hotel suite refusing even to have a cup of coffee with Tony in the lobby. DeFries flew back to New York without so much as clapping eyes on Reed. Nonetheless, his point had been made, and both Reed and Katz knew that he was serious. The next concert in Frankfurt was also aborted. The promoter claimed Reed had a nervous breakdown. Another riot ensued, though this time Lou was not there to act as target for the bricks.

In these hectic circumstances the tour staggered on. In France, a fan jumped on stage and pulled a knife on Lou. In England, a fan bit him on the bum. Clearly things were not going well for Lewis. Then, Katz suddenly yanked Barbara Falk off the tour, replacing her with an antique-car mechanic named Alec. Now Lou went ballistic. First, he smashed up Coca-Cola bottles and stuffed the shards of glass in the hapless road manager's pockets. Alec severely cut his hand. Then Lou smashed up an RCA tour car that did not please him. Barbara Falk returned. Yule saw how desperately Lou needed Barbara, recalling:

There is a tendency to bitch and moan, but as a matter of fact, when I was touring with Lou in '75 it struck me that it is like being a child because you get food, you get taken to the airport, you're taken to the hotel, you play. It's very idyllic. You have someone taking care of you and all you have to do is show up. I guess when your handlers fall down, that's when it gets chaotic.

Barbara's return did not stop Lou from injecting speed. In fact, the turmoil contributed to his use of the drug. Barbara had put the fear of God into the band about carrying drugs since they were bound to be strip-searched as they crossed borders daily. 'Europe, of course, is famous for easy prescriptions, so Lou would go to a different speed doctor in every country,' she recalled. 'He truly believed in it! He was for ever proselytizing, trying to get me to take some. On tour he'd actually go to medical bookstores, he'd literally carry around written justification for amphetamine. Not only that, but he knew how to pronounce it correctly, in every language.'

By now, however, Lou had been injecting strong doses of methamphetamine steadily for two years, mixing it with alcohol and a wide variety of other drugs. 'Lou was not stupid,' said Barbara Falk. 'But with all his knowledge, he could not realise that he was not immune from the effects of the drug. It became a whole vicious cycle. European drug stores give you syringes instead of pill prescriptions.' Like most rockers, he found it almost impossible to sleep after the ecstatic adrenaline high he received from being on stage. He often stayed up for days at a time. Despite his protestations, it was not a healthy life. In Europe that winter, as a result of clinical fatigue, he collapsed in convulsions on several occasions. His favourite cousin, Judy, who was travelling in Europe, joined them for a few shows, helping Lou through the ritual of preparing for his nightly performance. 'He listened to her because he was going through a difficult time,' said Barbara Falk. 'She said he'd listen to a strong woman.'

At the beginning of March 1975, Lou returned to the US in time for the release of *Lou Reed Live*, a second album culled from the December 1973 shows which produced *Rock 'n' Roll Animal*.

'Satellite of Love', 'Sad Song' and 'Vicious' placed him in the mainstream of rock between Elton John and the Rolling Stones. Lou had insisted that the producers keep the clear hollow ring of a youth's voice screaming out from the bleachers, 'Lou Reed sucks!' at the very end of the second side. *Lou Reed Live* was yet another commercial success, reaching number 62 on the LP charts, where it hovered for several months. The trilogy of *Rock 'n' Roll Animal*, *Sally Can't Dance*, and *Lou Reed Live* vaulted Reed from the hesitant commercial start of the early seventies to a position on the rock mountaintop. His distinct following of the most fucked-up people in each country gave him a higher profile than he might otherwise have had. Lou Reed fans were loud and exhibitionistic.

As the graph of his record sales now rose steadily, the graph of his emotional state went plummeting in a series of jagged falls. The break with Bettye, the rejection of *Berlin*, the struggle with the Katz brothers, the riot-torn tour, and the success of *Lou Reed Live*, which he professed to loathe, reduced him to a shambling wreck. The more he stumbled, the less capable he became of singing, the more audiences goaded him on. Pinned by the spotlight to the stage, he saw himself as a sacrificial victim.

At this midway point in the middle-of-the-road decade, Lou's interview slugfest with Lester Bangs reached its climax. Ever since the Velvet Underground played San Diego in 1968, Bangs had set himself up as the conscience of Lou Reed and the Velvet Underground. After celebrating the Velvets during their last two years, he had remained true to them through the first half of the seventies, continually writing about their influence and keeping tabs on the activities of Cale, Nico and Reed. When he met Reed during the US tour, Lester wrote, 'Lou Reed is a completely depraved pervert and pathetic death dwarf and everything else you want to think he is.'

'I always thought when he was being interviewed by Lester Bangs was the peak of his career,' said the cartoonist and journalist John Holmstrom. 'Lou hated Lester. They really hated each other. Lester had the love-hate thing. Lou just had the hate.'

A basic personality trait a person would need to survive as a rock star would be the ability in the very worst situation to respond at the top of their game. With everything against him, by the time he returned to New York, Lou was delivering a gripping set. 'He was such a romantic figure at that point,' said one drug buddy. 'He was as good as you could be. He was very much a Rimbaud figure.'

When Lou was at loose ends in New York, rather than taking a vacation or looking for some way to turn off his ever-buzzing brain, he continued what amounted to an ongoing anthropological survey of the natives. Lou would scoot around the city solo from Times Square to the Factory, where he would often receive a chilly reception, to friends' apartments, to his doctor's office, to another bar. He rarely seemed satisfied and still suffered from a permanent case of *shpilkes*.

That spring, a complete and utter wreck, Lou retreated into the drug world, finding refuge and solace in the group of addicts that centred on Ed Lister. Bob Jones, his only fan in the group, spent a lot of time with Lou in 1975. Bob became Lou's on-again, off-again drug supplier as well as playmate throughout that long, hot summer.

> One of my biggest clients right away was Lou. I would get prescriptions from Lister, from Turtle, from Rita, from Marty, and I had a network of pharmacies I would go to. And another thing that was always difficult was getting syringes, I used to be the big syringe man. You had to go to the Upper West Side for syringes. You'd go to a drug store and buy them by the box.

Standard practice for the group was to shoot up first thing in the morning and then at some other point late in the day. The shots were as strong as to be considered lethal by conventional medical standards. A forged prescription of Desoxyn, for example, would consist of a bottle of 100 yellow pills, each of the highest (15 milligram) potency. The ordinary recommended dosage, adjusted, of course, to meet the needs of the individual, was 15 to 25 milligrams orally per day. The Lister amphetamine circle, on the other hand, would habitually take ten or twenty 15-mg pills at once and inject them directly into the bloodstream.

In order to inject the prescription pills, the amphetamine group employed a complicated series of chemical processes that prepared the intravenous solution. Essentially they put the pills in a pan on the stove and boiled them. Very quickly, the water would turn yellow from the methedrine as it was released from the tablets. Once the drug was successfully diluted into the water, as much as 300 milligrams of methamphetamine hydrochloride, it could be drawn into a smaller syringe in order to be injected into the vein. 'It was enough to take the top of your head off,' remarked Bob Jones. 'I'd take a shot and the first thing that would happen would be a hot rush through my nose and I'd sort of flinch.'

The effects of such intense speed consumption were severe. Lou would frequently be awake for from three to five days during which he would spend his time writing songs, talking and investigating the underbelly of New York. Over a long period of time the amphetamine caused the ends of his fingers to crack making it impossible to play the guitar. The drug went a long way in explaining Reed's often temperamental states of being. 'We never ate,' stated Jones.

We were very, very wired. Everyone's weight went right down. Lou weighed nothing. I lost 40 pounds. And we never slept. The effect of having no REM, rapid eye movement sleep, was that we were deprived of dreams. So we would literally go for months without dreaming. The effect of this is that we would begin to have dreams in our waking state, which accounts for the paranoia and the delusionary style of the amphetamine addict.

The first soaking of the pills produced a dark yellow in the water, representing a very strong dose. When, for one reason or another, the Lister group became low on pills – which happened a few times in the course of the two years Reed was involved with that scene – they would pour more water on the used pills, in what they called a second soak. After the same process, the result would be a faint yellowing of the water. Shooting this diluted mixture produced a weaker effect and a limited amphetamine high. It was enough, however, to hold them for a few hours while they went looking for more pills.

Despite thus seeming to open new vistas of creativity, in reality Lou was accelerating his spiralling decline. As his health deteriorated, his mental state suffered, and his professional responsibilities were compromised. When amphetamine could not be found and things got desperate, members of the Lister group would convince themselves that putting sixty twice-used pills in a tube and boiling them up would result in some small amount of speed. However, the third soaking of pills failed to yellow the water. Deceiving themselves into believing that there was some speed in there, they would end up shooting water into their veins. Of course, impurities would go into their veins along with the water, which wasn't such a good idea.

> What would happen [Jones explained] was that your temperature would go through the roof almost immediately, within five minutes; you would feel a strange aching in your body and the next thing you'd know is your temperature would be about 103. You'd be drenched in sweat and in terrible, terrible pain in all of your joints. Appalling pain. And you would take your clothes off because it was too painful to keep them on, and lie down on the bed racked with shivers and diarrhoea and agony, drenched in sweat. That was called a 'bone crusher'. You would lie there with your knees drawn up to your chest and retch and cry out in pain. And this would go on for five or six hours. At the end of Lou's involvement with the amphetamine scene, this was happening three or four times a week. Everyone got bone crushers. Lou used to reserve time in a studio, then he'd get a bone crusher and couldn't record. It was hopeless.

Jones recalled that not only did the drug create the fodder for songs, but the drug lifestyle was the ideal atmosphere for Lou's work. Lou's needs were few, and Bob could provide for most of them. After taking their shots, Reed and Jones would often sit around the former's apartment.

There was nothing but drugs at Lou's place. There was never any eating. I guess in the course of time I gravitated towards Lou because I was interested in the way he spent his time in between shooting up, which was more interesting than what the rest of the group was doing. He was an international star at the time, it must have been hard to maintain his humility. Especially if you're whacked out on drugs all the time. There would be acts of friendship, but Lou was very selfish. Lou probably had a few real relationships and then he had a series of symbolic relationships, which would fulfil some kind of purpose. And I think in a funny sort of way the relationship he had with Rachel was a symbolic relationship. The relationship I had with him didn't really exist except in the supplying him with drugs and with a pair of ears to listen to his speed rap about music and the drug world and crime. And someone who shared his interest in Warhol and was literate. There was a lot of strung-out, camp talk.

The two devoted a lot of time to listening to music and discussing their ideas of what was interesting about a particular piece. Lou showed Jones, who was the perfect sounding board, the new, speed-induced lyrics he was working on and he would also play the songs in draft. Lou was constantly playing, trying out songs, playing little riffs and working the words into the music. He experimented with all sorts of different styles. On one occasion he did a whole cassette tape of parodies of Bob Dylan. Lou also incorporated many of his experiences on the speed scene into quite a few songs of the period. 'All of those songs on *Coney Island Baby* and *Rock and Roll Heart*, actually, if you analyse them, are about this little crowd and its comings and goings,' said Jones. 'Having an attitude was a big thing for Lou. Attitude was the sort of drug equivalent of what is called in the black world signifying. Talking from the sides of your mouth.'

According to Jones, Lou's social life outside this speed scene was limited. Although he was seeing some people in the music business, like the singer Robert Palmer, his peculiar habits and long, erratic hours made it difficult for many friends to relate. 'He'd see guitarists, they'd come around and be moronic,' said Bob. 'He was very interested. They'd talk about music. He'd get interviewed and go into these big riffs about lawyers. Outside of that he'd see Rotten Rita, a real character from Warhol's novel *A*, about whom he would write *Magic and Loss* fifteen years later.

Rita was about six foot two, a hundred and ninety pounds. He lived under the elevated subway tracks in Queens. He was two stops away on the train, in an absolutely terrible apartment. He had recently gotten out of jail in Bermuda which he loved, and he had tapes of himself singing opera there. They were pretty funny, actually. He was very wild, campy, and lonely in a way. A very funny, potentially quite dangerous character, but at the same time quite sweet. You felt that he could tip a little bit and be capable of murder. And it was that side of him that was appealing to Lou. He was very much an outré camp figure who loved Callas, there was a lot of talk of Callas, there was a lot of playing of Callas albums, always opera, opera. He also became one of the main dealers.

For Lou, one of the most appealing aspects of taking amphetamine in such large doses was the effect it had of making the most horrible, chilling experiences, as well as horrible, chilling people, interesting. For a writer, the drug was an effective tool. According to Bob Jones:

There seems to be some kind of deprivation of the normal blocks against the macabre. There was a big police book that I bought at Barnes & Noble about gunshot wounds. And it showed people who had put shotguns in their mouths and pulled the trigger, in colour. It showed people cut up, shot, all kinds of wounds, and in large colour photographs. You'd see their brains spilling out all over the place. And it was very much that attitude that Lou was involved in at the time and that I became involved in, and I think understood as he did. It was that kind of erotic fascination with death.

chapter fifteen

The Chemical Man

1975–1976

[In which Lou records and
releases *Metal Machine Music*,
tours Japan and Australia,
breaks with Dennis Katz,
records and releases *Coney
Island Baby*. He then leavs RCA
for Arista, records and releases
Rock and Roll Heart and tours
the world.]

*If you look at Lou as an artist, and you said, 'OK, during this
period he was on drugs and during this period he was off
drugs,' by far his greatest work was composed when he was
on drugs.*

GLENN O'BRIEN

In the spring of 1975, after years of relentless, amphetamine-
fuelled touring behind his most commercially successful albums,
Reed faced the demand of his product- and profit-hungry record
company that he deliver a new studio album.

The album Lou came up with was a screeching cacophony of
feedback and electronic noise that lasted for sixty-four minutes.
'As soon as he came walking into my office I could see this guy was

not too well connected with reality,' recalled an RCA representative. 'If he was a person walking in off the street with this shit I woulda threw him out. But I hadda handle him with kid gloves, because he was an artist in whom the company had a long-term commitment. He's not my artist, I couldn't get his hackles up, I couldn't tell him it was just a buncha shit.'

The only thing the RCA executives knew for sure was that Lou's last three albums, *Sally Can't Dance*, *Rock 'n' Roll Animal* and *Lou Reed Live*, had been moneymakers, and in 1975 the company had high hopes that he would deliver another. Consequently, they let Lou walk all over them. On getting home he told friends he had had to run to the men's room, after presenting this highly unusual product to the RCA people, in order to explode with laughter.

'So I told him it was a "violent assault on the senses",' continued the RCA executive.

> Jesus Christ, it was fuckin' torture music! There were a few interesting cadences, but he was ready to read anything into anything I said. I led him to believe it was not too bad a work, because I couldn't commit myself. I said, 'I'm gonna put it out on the Red Seal label,' and then I gave him a lot of classical records in the hope that he'd write better stuff next time.

As might be expected, everybody at the company was completely horrified by this weirdness. One marketing executive, Frank O'Donnell, recalled:

> About twenty of us were seated around a vast mahogany conference table for a monthly new-release album meeting. The A&R representative at the meeting put on the tape and the room was filled with this bizarre noise. Everyone was looking at everyone else; people were saying, 'What the hell is that?' Somebody voiced that question and the answer came back, 'That's Lou Reed's new album, *Metal Machine Music*. His contract says we've got to put it out.'
>
> One day a middle-aged, very conservatively dressed and coiffed executive secretary asked me what I knew about 'this recording artist Lou Reed'. I told her, 'Well, I know he was involved with Andy Warhol and the Velvet Underground. One of his songs is called

"Heroin", so I believe he has a pretty big following in the drug culture. He's kind of in the David Bowie groove – you know, eye make-up and lipstick and all that, so the homosexuals like him. His brand of rock and roll is pretty wild . . . why do you ask?' The lady looked side to side, warily. Then, sotto voce, she said, 'He's my nephew. But if you don't tell, I won't tell.'

After much gnashing of teeth and pulling of hair on the part of RCA's top brass, the album was released in July. The company had wanted to issue it on their Red Seal classical label, but Lou demurred, arguing that that would be pretentious. Instead, they disguised the music within a record jacket showing Lou looking very cool on stage, which clearly suggested that this was another live heavy-metal concert. Included on the jacket was a list of the equipment putatively utilized in the recording, along with a bunch of supposed scientific symbols that Lou had copied out of a stereo magazine. 'I made up the equipment on the back of the album,' he admitted. 'It's all bullshit.' Those not prepared for what lurked beneath the cover of *Metal Machine Music* were in for a big surprise. According to Lou, 'They were supposed to put out a disclaimer: "Warning – No vocals. Best cut: none. Sounds like: static on a car radio",' but did not. The double album, subtitled 'An Electronic Instrumental Composition', was mixed so that each side was exactly 16:01 in length – except that side four was pressed so the final groove would stick, repeating grating static screeches over and over until the needle was physically removed from the record.

Lou often said that he thought *Metal Machine Music* should be the soundtrack for that summer's hit horror movie, *The Texas Chainsaw Massacre*. He took an aggressive stance when conducting interviews about *Metal Machine Music*, and his humour-laced bravado perfectly complemented the temper of the record. 'That album should have sold for $70.99,' he told one interviewer. 'If they think it's a rip-off, yeah, and I'll rip them off some more. I'm not gonna apologize to anybody! They should be grateful I put that fucking thing out, and if they don't like it, they can go eat rat shit. I make records for me.'

For the most part, the press and public's reaction was outrage and contempt. *Rolling Stone* voted it the worst album of the year. Even John Rockwell, who had been a champion of Reed's since *Berlin*, questioned the wisdom of its release. 'One would like to see rock stars take the risk to stretch their art in ways that might jeopardize the affection of their fans,' he wrote in the *New York Times*. 'But one can't help fearing that in this instance, Mr Reed may have gone farther than his audience will willingly follow.'

Beneath the furore at RCA and between the lines of Lou's cutting jokes and insults, however, lay another side of *Metal Machine Music*. The record, which would come to be seen as the ultimate conceptual punk album and a progenitor of New York punk rock, harkened back to the work of LaMonte Young and the Velvet Underground's experimental track 'Loop' (1966).

Reed presented the album as a grand artistic statement, claiming that he had spent six years to make the record, weaving classical and poetic themes into the noise. If one listened attentively, he promised, one could hear a number of classical themes making their way in and out of the feedback fury. 'That record was the closest I've ever come to perfection,' he stated.

> It's the only record I know that attacks the listener. Even when it gets to the end of the last side it still won't stop. You have to get up and remove it yourself. It's impossible to even think when the thing is on. It destroys you. You can't complete a thought. You can't even comprehend what it's doing to you. You're literally driven to take the miserable thing off. *You can't control that record.*

One impetus behind the project had been to break his managerial links with Dennis Katz as well as the contractual hold his record company had over him. Reed also anticipated a strong reaction to his statement from his fans, who would reject not only the Reed of *Metal Machine Music*, but also the Reed of previous incarnations. Reed knew that once it hit the stores, *Metal Machine Music* might destroy everything he had worked for. Yet jokes, insults and revenge aside, the album allowed Lou to throw off the yoke of his manager, record company and fans, and at the same time make a pure artistic statement. 'I put out *Metal Machine Music* precisely to put a stop to all of it,' he insisted.

> It wasn't ill-advised at all. It did what it was supposed to do. I really believed in it also. That could be ill-advised, I suppose, but I just think it's one of the most remarkable pieces of music ever done by anybody, anywhere. In time, it will prove itself.
>
> I put out *Metal Machine Music* to clear the air and get rid of all those fucking assholes who show up at the show and yell 'Vicious' and 'Walk on the Wild Side'. It was a giant fuck you.

'The key word was "control",' Lou concluded in his liner notes. In a conscious effort to present *Metal Machine Music* as a single, unified composition, Reed not only left the individual sides untitled, but offered a parody of classical liner notes. His first piece of published prose since his essay in *No One Waved Goodbye*, the *Metal Machine Music* 'Notation' was a combination of arrogance, bluster and inadvertent confessional. The writing was punk. Its subject shifted from Reed's complaints about the tedium of most heavy metal, through the symmetrical genius of his creation, to puns on his own album titles and insights into the gap between drug 'professionals' and 'those for whom the needle is no more than a tooth brush'.

'No one I know has listened to it all the way through including myself . . . I love and adore it. I'm sorry, but not especially, if it turns you off . . . Most of you won't like this, and I don't blame you at all. It's not meant for you.'

In the end, almost 100,000 copies sold. 'The classical reviews were fabulous,' Lou crowed. 'In Japan, they greeted me by blaring the fucking thing at top volume in the airport.'

In August, leaving his critics and fans with an unpleasant ringing in their ears, he went on another gruelling tour of Japan and Australia. Joining the tour on bass was Doug Yule, back with Lou since the *Sally Can't Dance* sessions. 'When we travelled as the VU we travelled as a group,' Doug recalled. 'But here he and

Rachel travelled together – they were like the VIPs – and everybody else travelled behind. It was nice, it was fun. He was a little more mercurial.'

In fact, much distance had come between Reed and the rest of his entourage, including the ever-present Barbara Falk – now replaced, in most capacities, by Rachel. Unfortunately, this was not an altogether healthy change, resulting in one of the few times Lou was incapable of overcoming his drug-induced exhaustion to make it to a show. 'In New Zealand he couldn't perform,' said Doug Yule.

> So there was an announcement that Lou wasn't going to play but the band was going to play. Anyone who wanted their money back could have their money back. We went out and played and I sang. The audience liked it a lot. But it was not an attempt (as had been reported) to present it as if I were Lou, nor were the people told I was Lou.

This set alarm bells ringing with Lou, his entourage and across the Pacific to his management team. In a series of frantic phone calls between New Zealand and New York, Reed was given the impression that Katz was rapidly moving to take control of his finances and tie up his recordings. The first casualty of this escalating battle was Barbara Falk. Exhausted after three years of baby-sitting Lou on 24-hours-a-day call, she left the tour after Lou accused her once too many times of being in cahoots with Katz to cheat him. Extremely agitated by thoughts of betrayal, Lou found himself unable to go on with the tour.

Returning to New York, Reed found himself, as it were, back at square one. While he had been touring, Dennis Katz had marshalled his pieces and presented Reed with what amounted to a *fait accompli*. According to Reed, the Transformer office had cut off his support payments. He discovered that he no longer had an apartment or money in the bank. At the same time, he was informed that he was $600,000 in debt to his record company. Furthermore, RCA did not intend to proceed with his next album as planned.

Lou believed that the only way to face a storm was to drive right through its centre at breakneck speed. Employing his considerable powers of charm and persuasion, Lou went to the heart of the matter. Approaching RCA president Ken Glancy, he talked him into supporting him long enough to show them what he could do in the way of coming up with a commercial album. Glancy, who knew Reed personally and believed in him in the same way that Katz once had, agreed to put him up in a suite at the Gramercy Park Hotel, a somewhat seedy establishment that had seen better days but now exuded a kind of louche charm as home for travelling rock bands and European tourists. Its suites were among the cheapest in New York, costing a mere $90 per day. The hotel's restaurant had the air of a department-store canteen and served abominable food. The bar, however, was something else, often pulsing with beautiful girls waiting for the appearance of a rock star. While Lou stayed there, Bob Dylan's entourage was using it as a base for their forthcoming Rolling Thunder tour, and in fact invited Lou to join them. Unfortunately, he had to decline the offer due to more pressing needs. Lou fit into the hotel's subculture and seemed more than comfortable there. RCA agreed to pick up his room and restaurant bills and pay him $15 per day in cash.

The stripped-down setup helped Lou to focus singularly on making his next album, *Coney Island Baby*. Strapped for cash as he was, there was little else he could do. He couldn't even afford to go and see a movie, let alone buy the instruments he would have liked for the recording. Otherwise, he continued living in almost exactly the same way as he had been before the Australian tour. In between writing songs and recording, he met with his lawyers to discuss three lawsuits against the Katz brothers. For entertainment, he listened to tapes of the comedian Richard Pryor and entertained visitors, but kept a low profile. Rachel whiled away the hours, in between listening to Lou's raps, playing Monopoly. During his stay at the hotel, a friend brought a grateful Lou a copy of the manuscript of his book of poems, *All the Pretty People*, he had been working on and mislaid during his recent change of address. He was thinking about getting it published.

An important ingredient in the success of *Coney Island Baby* was the amphetamine that was being delivered to Lou regularly by Bob Jones. According to Jones:

> The speed albums were *Coney Island Baby* and *Rock and Roll Heart*. There's a whole thing of emotional deadening that happened with amphetamine. One could have done an act of terrible violence without understanding the implications of it. You could have actually shot someone. There were guns around and ammunition. It was part of a whole aura of the time. You were constantly breaking the law every day, you were committing felonies, looking at photographs of corpses and cracking macabre jokes.

'There are different parts to everybody's personality, you just amplify one,' Lou said of the album. 'A lot of stuff is inevitably a reflection of whatever group I was hanging out with. At the time I was hanging around the criminally inclined.'

'I would bring him speed and we would shoot up and we would talk,' said Jones. 'A lot of it was Lou talking and me just sitting there. But a lot of it was just speed chat which had to do with catty gossip, a lot of macho posing. Staying up for two, three days at a time. You talk a mile a minute. You feel immortal, the way you do when you're young.'

Lou's next step was to find the right collaborator to make the album with. It seems incredible, but is nonetheless the case that he began it with Steve Katz producing. However, no sooner had they begun than it became obvious that this combination was not going to work. Lou took the opportunity to act out a lot of his resentment towards the Katz brothers in the studio.

Lou used conflict to get in the right frame of mind to work. To write anything good Lou had to make himself uncomfortable by going to some place in his head where he would not necessarily have chosen to go. The music on the album reflected this. 'Kicks', for example, was absolutely the dead heart of the speed scene – a cold, nihilistic song of contempt and hatred. This was juxtaposed to the heart-wrenching ballad 'Coney Island Baby', full of passion, nostalgia and tenderness.

Steve concluded that the drugs had finally driven Lou crazy and decided to bail out. 'Each day was a new head trip,' he said. 'Finally I said to him, right in front of all the musicians who'd gone through this, "I give up! If you're gonna play these games, I know you're gonna outwit me. I'm just your producer. I acknowledge that you're much smarter than I am – there's no point in playing these games."' Informing RCA that it would not be possible for him to deliver an album with this artist, Katz withdrew.

Lou knew he was on the right track. In October he met the man who would help bring the songs to fruition. One night at the hip club of the moment, Ashley's, on lower Fifth Avenue Lou met Godfrey Diamond, a talented young engineer in his eartly twenties who would become his next producer. Diamond, who was working at Media Sound at the time, recalled that he 'really wasn't a huge fan of his up to that point. I guess I was too young. But I really loved the banana album and *Transformer*. "Satellite of Love" was a work of art.' Diamond returned to the Gramercy Park Hotel with Lou to listen to his new songs.

It was an exciting job, and Reed and Diamond achieved a good connection. Diamond recalled, 'One thing that really impressed me is that you simply can't put anything over on him. He's always fully aware. I thought he was a real warrior, with such courage. He always goes for the tough edge, the risky stuff.'

'I was a bit erratic before,' Reed admitted.

You get tired of fighting with people sometimes. And to avoid going through all of that, I mastered the art of recording known as 'capture the spontaneous moment and leave it at that'. *Coney Island Baby* is like that. You go into the studio with zero, write it on the spot, and make the lyrics up as the tape's running and that's it. What I wanna get on my records, since everyone else is so slick and dull, is that moment.

The straitened circumstances strengthened the bond between Rachel and Lou. More than anything, she was a protective presence. Like so many high-strung people, Lou could not be alone. He acted as if, like a child, he didn't know how and would harm himself if left to his own devices. Though it is easy to make fun of rock stars as infantile, in fact the reason musicians often seem so helpless as human beings is that they cut themselves off from practical life in favour of living in their heads with their music. Rachel was the perfect companion for Lou because she let him ignore her and protected his way of being. She accepted it and didn't need him constantly paying attention to her. The stone-faced calm and patience on her face was a comforting presence. According to Lou, 'Rachel's a street kid and very tough underneath it all.'

Lou and Rachel also had a lot of fun together. Lou never tired of shocking people. One day a maid came into their suite unaware that they were in bed. When she walked into the bedroom she was astonished to see 'Mrs Reed' lying uncovered and naked, displaying an unexpected appendage. Lou, who was awake and witnessed the shocked expression on her face and the little cry of fear as she fled, was in stitches for days over the sight.

Around five o'clock on the morning they finished *Coney Island Baby*, Lou took Diamond over to Danny Fields's apartment for an immediate judgement. Fields had become an important critic and authority on the downtown scene and Lou regularly sought his opinion. As soon as they got there, they plugged in the record and took a seat in Fields's living room. To Diamond's dismay Danny pulled out a newspaper and appeared to be engrossed in it, but Lou whispered to him that Danny always did this so you could not see the expression on his face while he listened to your record. After a tense forty-five minutes Fields snapped shut his paper and declared, 'Great! Not one bad song.' They stayed there until 8 a.m. when Diamond had to go to work.

All that remained was for Mick Rock to do a photo session for the cover, and Lou had completed one of his finer solo recordings. RCA were as pleased with the results as he was. Before the end of the year, Lou's life was back on track and he could move out of the hotel back to the Upper East Side.

Boasting a uniformed doorman, Lou's new apartment building seemed worlds away from the shaky economic edge he had been living on downtown at the Gramercy Park. Greta Garbo owned an apartment at 450 East 52nd Street, on the same block. He soon was referring to his new place as the Garbo apartment, pointing out to friends her building at the end of the block. In reality, the flat consisted of two boxlike rooms containing nothing more than basic furnishings, Lou's electronic equipment, his books, two clocks – both permanently telling the wrong time – and a plastic plant he insisted on watering. Ed Lister and Bob Jones would go around to see him and shoot speed. Lou was always afraid that the police would come to his place looking for Lister – and on one occasion they did, because Lister had left a stolen car in Lou's parking space.

It was while he was living here that Lou acquired a new dog, Baron, who bore a resemblance to Seymour. Lou, admitting that 'underneath it all I'm just a sentimentalist', expressed the same kind of gentle, obsessive feelings towards him. 'The Baron is a miniature dachshund with a forceful personality,' wrote a friend who visited Reed in January.

> He justifies his name by his great ability to corner great chunks of the apartment in which he resides, and subjects all those who enter, including his coinhabitants, to the random exhibition of his caprices. Mr Reed, one of his coinhabitants, is enamoured of him. They have an excellent relationship based on Mr Reed's acceptance of his menial role in Baron's life.

Reed explained, 'I'm here to feed him, walk him, act as chief thrower of chaseable objects and general dogsbody – what an apt description! At first it was difficult, but, now that I have learned the wisdom of the Baron's ways, all is well. He's a total exhibitionist. This morning he displayed a full stem for us, the disgusting little beast.'

Coney Island Baby's release in January 1976 brought Reed artistic acclaim and commercial success. Once the album was out Reed was ready to return to the fray with what he considered his 'strongest album, bar none', along with a newborn will to sustain his drive. 'This time I'm gonna do it right,' he said, 'and everybody knows it. *Coney Island Baby* was a statement of renewal, because it was my record. I didn't have much time, and I didn't have much money, but it was mine. Saying "I'm a Coney Island Baby" at the end of that song is like saying I haven't backed off an inch, and don't you forget it.'

The reviews were overwhelmingly positive. 'Evoking Genet decadence ... Warhol chic, European ennui ... [his work] is expressed cinematically by Martin Scorcese and Sam Peckinpah, novelistically by William Burroughs,' wrote James Walcott in the *Village Voice*. He is 'a master narrator, short story writer at heart,' wrote Larry Sloman in *Rolling Stone*. 'I have seen rock's future, and its name is Lou Reed,' wrote Pat Ast, a Warhol superstar, in New York's *SoHo Weekly News*. But to some Lou appeared to be veering away from the hard-core music he had been associated with. Peter Laughner, the lead singer of Pere Ubu, wrote a scathing review of *Coney Island Baby*.

> The damn thing starts out exactly like an Eagles record! And with the exception of 'Charlie's Girl' which is mercifully short and to the point, it's a downhill slide.
>
> Finally there's 'Coney Island Baby', just maudlin, dumb, self-pity: 'Can you believe I wann'd t'play football for th' coach? ...' Sure, Lou, when I was all uptight about being a fag in high school, I did too.

Coney Island Baby came out during the year gay liberation crossed into the mainstream. Once again, Lou's paean to a drag queen, the title song, became the soundtrack of the moment. It caught the gay spirit that was everywhere taking over the parade of New York City, and offered redemption via love. Not since *Transformer* had Lou put out a product that – from the cover to the contents – harboured the opposing sides of his personality so harmoniously. David Bowie's 1976 release *Station to Station* would sell more copies and make him a big star. Twenty years later *Coney Island Baby* would stand out as one of Lou's most memorable self-portraits. Bowie's work would not linger.

Rachel, to whom the title song was dedicated, had proven more than dependable during the siege of the Gramercy Park Hotel. She was increasingly prominent in Lou's public life, appearing in photo spreads in rock magazines and constantly at his side whenever he went anywhere, affording Lou the silent admiration of a dog.

Coney Island Baby marked the end of Reed's commitment to RCA. It was Lou's most commercially successful venture post *Rock 'n' Roll Animal* venture until his *New York* album in 1989, reaching number 41 on *Billboard*'s LP chart. Yet, despite good record sales and Lou's success during the first four years of his solo career, he now reportedly found himself in debt to RCA to the tune of $700,000. Figuring that he would never be able to make money as long as he remained with the label, he decided to shop for another record company.

'Then, I got a call from Clive Davis and he said, "Hey, how ya doing? Haven't seen you for a while,"' Lou remembered. 'He knew how I was doing. He said, "Why don't we have lunch?" I felt like saying, "You mean you want to be seen with me in public?" If Clive could be seen with me, I had turned the corner. I grabbed Rachel and said, "Do you know who just called?"'

Clive Davis had just begun his new Arista label, but he and Reed had known each other for some time. 'Lou and I were friends prior to the business relationship,' Davis recounted.

I remember touting Bruce Springsteen very strongly to Lou and Lou had never seen Springsteen. We went down to the Bottom Line [in 1975 during Springsteen's famous summer run]. At the end of the performance I remember Lou saying, 'Look, he's good.' But he was not turned on, at the time, by what he felt was the rather tame imagery that was being evoked. I'll never forget that Lou took me on a tour of Manhattan the likes of which I've never had. It was an amazing experience. Seeing Lou Reed's world was a very revealing, very eye-opening situation.

Declaring that he was now back in the saddle, Lou signed a contract with Davis.

Having, for all intents and purposes, rid himself of Dennis Katz – although their lawsuits would rage on for two years – Lou acquired a new manager, John Podell, and, in the enthusiasm of the moment, proceeded to talk him up to the press. 'I'm not unmanageable,' he said.

> Not true. It's just that I've never hit on the right people before. John Podell, my new man, is great. He got an MA in business psychology at twenty-one, and he's as good at practice as he is at theory. He doesn't handle my money, I've got all new people to do that, but he gets all the rest together. It's a whole new show now on that front. Anyone who was connected with me on a business level before is out. My accountants, lawyers, record-company manager, his brother quote producer – all out. With Johnny you've got a tiger by the tail. He's ready to go. The product is there. I like that. I'm the product and I call myself the product. Much better than being called an artist – that means they're fucking you, they think you don't know from shit. This time I'm doing it for real, because it seems that's what's supposed to happen.

Eager to follow up the success of *Coney Island Baby*, and recharged by the relationship with Arista, Lou immediately went back into the studio to record his next album. Originally titled *Nomad*, it would be released as *Rock and Roll Heart*. At first, it looked as if all the factors were set up to create a successful record. Lou had a good band, particularly with the increasing input of Fonfara; Davis was fully behind him; his audience was growing; and his relationship with Rachel seemed more stable than any he had had since college. It had turned out to be the longest and best romantic relationship he had ever had. Lou and Rachel were even talking about renting or buying a house in the country.

Clive Davis was well known for taking a hands-on approach with his artists, particularly when it came to picking hit singles. He told Lou he could make him a million dollars if Lou would let him do a little work on the title song for *Rock and Roll Heart*. 'He wanted to sweeten it up,' recalled Lou, 'horns or strings or something. [He argued] that the song had potential to really be radio worthy if we just did that to it.' Though he recognized Davis's talent, Lou turned his suggestion down flat. 'I'm a control person,' he explained. 'I fought so hard to get things to the point of having that control that I wouldn't relinquish it. He said, "You'll be there. Nothing will be done without your approval." "Nah." I'm like a brick wall sometimes.'

Fonfara and the rest of the studio band soon discovered Reed's fresh determination during the recording sessions, where he turned out to be a rigid taskmaster. Lou would present each new song to the group once. Then Fonfara would rehearse the band until they knew the song and had the right arrangement for the vocal.

Lou ended up writing most of the album in the studio. 'I just had the basic progressions, of two or three chords, but no lyrics.' In doing so, he threw himself completely into the songs. To Fonfara, 'it was like method acting'.

Feeling particularly comfortable and connected to the music, Lou picked up his guitar and played lead on the album for the first time since he broke up with the Velvets.

> On other albums I let other people do what they liked; this time I got serious and played what I liked. Every track. There's lots of very dumb rock-and-roll songs on it, but then I like dumb rock and roll. It's very hard to find a dumb guitar player and a dumb piano player, everyone's so much into being technically together. But I fit the bill, because I play very stupid.

According to Reed, this method acting and 'dumb' guitar playing gave him the distance to reflect objectively on his work while remaining a part of it. 'It keeps the more esoteric aspects of my persona, if not exactly anchored down, at least available to anyone who wants to check them out. This may sound perverse, but it helps keep me out of the way so whatever it is that people call creative talent can come through. I don't have anything to do with it, I just have to let it have its own way. I think I've kept out of the way on this album more successfully than ever before. I know what I'm doing. I always look so crazy and disorganized, but I'm not.' In fact, Lou's approach to *Rock and Roll Heart* was, if anything, dictatorial. 'I need things to be done right now and the only person who can do it right is me. I can also accept all the blame if it doesn't work out.'

Beneath the surface buoyancy, all was not well with Lou. Throughout the summer of 1976, during an unexpected drought in the amphetamine market, he was constantly scrambling to find a doctor who would write a prescription for Desoxyn, with only occasional success. The drought became a serious problem when it brought on increasing depression, periods of inactivity and bone-crushers.

After finishing the record, however, Lou managed to muster the energy to begin another project, producing an album by a survivor of one of Lou's Syracuse bands, Nelson Slater. It was called *Wild Angel*. Reed commented, 'RCA released it to about three people, I think. So no one very much noticed it. That was one of the best things I've ever done, I think we sold six copies.' The critics who picked up on it singled out a track called 'We' as a great showcase for Reed's production talents.

Lou was so broke at this time he rarely had $10.00 in his pocket. Part of his problem, he thought, was his incipient honesty. He was going to lectures on Warhol's films by Ondine, and looking for speed connections. 'This is the worst period I've seen,' he told one friend, 'and it's not going to get better.' A short reprieve from his misery came in July when he made a connection with a doctor who wrote him a script for Desoxyn. With batches of drugs boiling on the stove, Lou began rehearsing for the *Rock and Roll Heart* tour with increased energy. But the prescription soon ran out and he had absolutely zero speed again.

In the autumn, Lou and the band were gearing up to go back on the road in what he described as 'that savage jungle called America'. The tour preparations were nearly as chaotic as being on the road. Mick Rock was on his way over to shoot the cover and design the stage and lights. Lister came round on several occasions. Lou's lawyers warned him that his lifestyle could be detrimental to his case against Katz. There was no way he could see it sitting well with the people in the halls of justice.

Rock and Roll Heart, released in October, received fond reviews but lukewarm sales and was a disappointment all around. '*Rock and Roll Heart* is very well produced,' Reed said in his defence.

I produced it. My records are for real. But that song 'I Believe in Love' – coming from Lou Reed is supposed to be a very strange statement. One kid said to me he really liked the lyrics on 'Banging on My Drum'. And I said, 'But there are no lyrics' and he said, 'Frustration'. I thought I'd written a song about fun, fun, fun . . . But apparently not. *Rolling Stone* said that song was about masturbation, so that just goes to show.

Meanwhile, RCA sought to capitalize on the publicity surrounding Lou's move to Arista by issuing *Walk on the Wild Side* – a greatest-hits package notable for its cover Polaroids of Lou and Rachel. It also included 'Nowhere at All', a gritty outtake from the *Coney Island Baby* sessions, which sounded the way the Hunter–Wagner band would have done if they had been let loose in the studio.

Lou was scheduled to tour the US and Europe through December. 'I'll be taking the same bunch of clowns I worked with on the album,' Lou told an interviewer.

I want to make some kind of a show of it. I didn't want the usual horseshit with opening acts and lightshows and all that stuff. None of the dates will be played in very big halls; it's all three or four thousand seaters with hopefully a week of shows in New York City at a small theatre. It'll be for those people who care. Hopefully the more bestial or vitriolic rock fans will be kept out. I'll be picking up from where I left off before I was so rudely interrupted; which spans a good degree of time.

But this time I'll be coming in at a higher level with no dark glasses. It'll be as close to me as you'll ever get. As close to me as I've ever gotten. I want to junk a lot of that old stuff that people seem to get off on.

'The other concerts don't count,' Reed explained. 'This is the first time I had total control.' He was accompanied throughout by

Rachel, who acted as a minder-cum-manager. 'Rachel is very interesting,' Lou said. 'Doesn't react very much, but full of great quotes. The other day it was, "If you're gonna be black be black, but don't give me no shades of grey." Rachel has looked after the money and kept me in shape and watched over the road crew. At last there's someone hustling around for me that I can trust.' She was a good supporter for Lou, loyal, reliable, and protective. What Rachel lacked, however, was the sharp eye that Lou needed to calm his paranoia. He complained to friends, for example, that Rachel was incapable of spotting dangerous people in crowds.

Despite the negative response to the album, Arista supported an extensive, costly tour. Over the previous couple of years, Reed had assembled the most durable band of his career, the Everyman band, led by the keyboard player Michael Fonfara, the lone survivor of the band that had cut *Sally Can't Dance* back in 1974, and saxist Marty Fogel, with Michael Suchorsky on drums. The bass player, Ellard Boles, a.k.a. the Moose, was a mountain of a man who became one of Lou's loyal companions through the end of the decade. Gone was the shambolic rocker of 1975, replaced by the elegant jazz singer of 1976. Lou kicked off the tour in style. Performing in front of a bank of forty-eight TV-sets and accompanied by the surprise addition of Ornette Coleman's trumpet player, Don Cherry, Lou gave one of his most satisfying shows in years.

The Everyman Band was really supportive and worked hard on perfecting dynamics. They would often quieten down to the point where the audience could hardly hear them at all, leaving Lou on his own, knowing that when he was ready, they could explode. Lou loved it.

John Rockwell described the performance in the *New York Times*.

This time around, Mr Reed – who selects his images as carefully as attractive women pick out their dresses for the day – chose the austere look. The hair moderately long, dressed in high-heeled black boots, jeans and a dark, long-sleeved jersey, dragging on the occasional

John Cale, Lou Reed, Patti Smith and David Byrne on stage at the Ocean Club, 1976. *(Bob Gruen)*

Richard Robinson, Lisa Robinson with Lou Reed in New York, 1976. *(Bob Gruen)*

Lou Reed with Diana Ross and Clive Davis, 1976. *(Bob Gruen)*

Andy Warhol holding a Lou Reed cornflakes box by Bobby Grossman *(Bobby Grossman)*

William Burroughs and Lou Reed at Burroughs Bunker in New York, 1979. *(Victor Bockris)*

Left to right: Toby and Sidney Reed, Sylvia Morales, Mr and Mrs Morales and Lou gesturing to and looking directly at his father during his wedding to which Andy Warhol was not invited. New York, 1980. *(Roberta Bayley)*

Right: Bob Quine, the guitar player who would pick Lou up, dust him off and start him all over again in the early 1980s, particularly on *The Blue Mask*. *(Marcia Resnick)*

Below: The cover of *Uptight*, the book about The Velvet Underground that played a role in bringing them back into prominence again, published in England in 1983.

Bottom: Sylvia Reed and Lou outside the church after Andy Warhol's Memorial Service, 1987. *(Bob Gruen)*

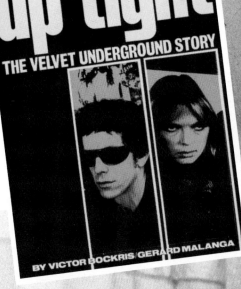

up-tight

THE VELVET UNDERGROUND STORY

BY VICTOR BOCKRIS/GERARD MALANGA

Lou Reed at the time of release of *New York*, 1989. *(Bob Gruen)*

Lou Reed at the photo session for *Between Thought and Expression*, 1991. *(Keith Miller)*

Lou playing at the opening of the Robert Mapplethorpe Room at the Guggenheim Museum in New York, 1993. *(Bob Gruen)*

ou on the Magic and Loss tour in Holland, 1992. *(Marijn Van Rij)*

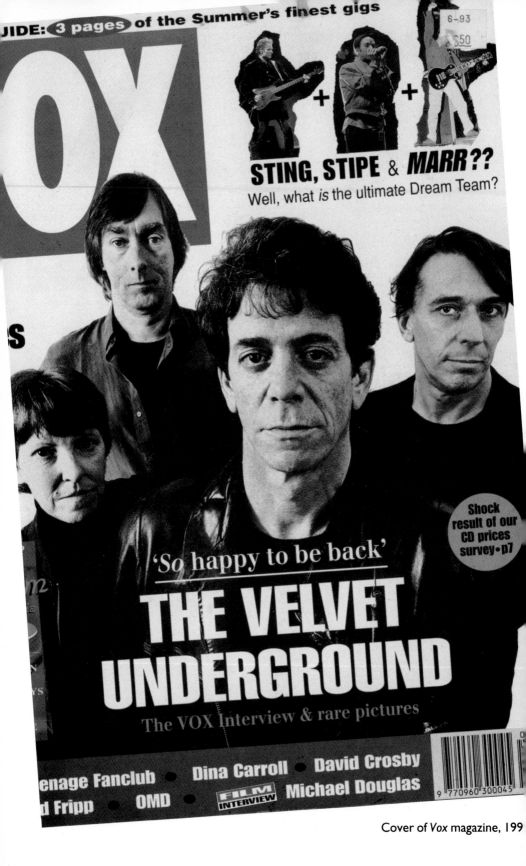

6-93

50

OX

STING, STIPE & MARR??

Well, what *is* the ultimate Dream Team?

s

**Shock
result of our
CD prices
survey• p7**

'So happy to be back'

THE VELVET UNDERGROUND

The VOX Interview & rare pictures

enage Fanclub ● **Dina Carroll** ● **David Crosby**

d Fripp ● **OMD** ● **FILM INTERVIEW** **Michael Douglas**

9 770960 300045

Cover of *Vox* magazine, 199

cigarette and staring out balefully in the direction of the audience without really seeing anybody, he looked compelling indeed.

One realized what was missing only at the very end of the two-hour, fifteen-minute affair, when Mr Reed deigned finally to pick up his guitar. The sound of a twanging electric guitar at long last lent the music – played previously by saxophone, keyboards, bass and drums – a true rock aura.

Unfortunately, the tour ended in personal trauma when Rachel, who was suffering from an infected lung, was mugged in LA. He got kicked in the balls and had some internal bleeding. 'That really had me strung out,' Reed explained. 'This guy jumped him. But Rachel gave him back more than he got.'

As Lou Reed began to recede into the obscurity of *Rock and Roll Heart*, with no clear image or direction, the vehicle which had helped strip him of his mid-seventies Rock 'n' Roll Animal persona, *Metal Machine Music*, surfaced as the inspiration for an entire new movement called punk rock.

As Mark Edwards wrote in the London *Sunday Times*:

Lou Reed's angry reaction to his glitter years serves as the perfect dividing point between the early 1970s and the late part of the decade. Annoyed at the travesty of his original self that he had become, he released *Metal Machine Music*. It's an hour of white noise, feeding endlessly back through a complex studio setup. There is no music on it. Just distortion. He intended it to kill off his glam career; in fact, coming out in 1975, it neatly signalled the end of glam as a whole, while the emphasis of the record on nasty, angry, unmusical noise neatly heralded the punk explosion that was to erupt the following year.

'It was so *boring*,' Reed concluded. 'Then came *Metal Machine Music*. It was like a bomb.'

chapter sixteen

The Godfather of Punk

1975–1978

[In which Lou records and releases *Street Hassle*, records and releases *Take No Prisoners*, and becomes the godfather of punk.]

I couldn't imagine Lou fucking anybody. He was like too hip for sex. Like, 'That's stupid! If you do that, you're an asshole!' I mean that says it all. What's great about that quote is that you can take that out and apply it to everything with Lou and it works. 'If you do that you're stupid and an asshole! If you believe that, you're a stupid kid!' It really sounded like somebody's drunken father.

LEGS MCNEIL,
Punk magazine

When punk rock's New York headquarters, CBGB's on the Bowery, opened its doors at the end of 1973, the NY rock scene was mostly populated by touring superstars. The only remnants of the rock underground were the dying New York Dolls and the *Berlin*-era Lou Reed. Reed's raw reports from the underbelly of the city were an inspiration that helped open the way for punk rock. Fragments of, among others, the Ramones, Blondie,

Television and Talking Heads began to coalesce as early as 1974. By the final months of 1975, while Lou was recording *Coney Island Baby*, two powerful streams of rock were surging forward, threatening to leave him in their wake. In the mainstream, Bob Dylan was going through a resurrection, touring with his Rolling Thunder Review and recording his next album, *Desire*, which would go to number one around the world. David Bowie had, in collaboration with John Lennon, his first number-one American single, *'Fame'*. The new boy, Bruce Springsteen, was simultaneously on the cover of *Time* and *Newsweek*. In left field, all the leading punk bands were poised to make the enormous impact they would soon have. In early 1976, Danny Fields wrote in *Music Gig* that Lou Reed was a fan of the Ramones. That summer Lou released a song from which the line 'Electricity comes from other planets' sparked elements of the London punk movement. At the end of 1976 Lou came second in *Creem* magazine's annual readers' poll in the 'punk of the year' category after Steven Tyler of Aerosmith and before Elton John and Patti Smith.

One of the hallmarks of punk rock was its dismissal of the holdover bands from the sixties. 'We have to fight the entire superband system,' said the Sex Pistols' lead singer Johnny Rotten. 'Groups like the Stones are revolting. They have nothing to offer the kids any more.' And the Clash sang, 'No Elvis, Beatles or Stones in 1977.' 'We're the poison in your human machine,' sang Johnny Rotten. 'We're the future – your future.' To which Lou replied:

> Shakespeare had a phrase for that, 'Sound and fury signifying nothing.' I'm so tired of the theory of the noble savage. I'd like to hear punks who weren't at the mercy of their own rage and who could put together a coherent sentence. I mean, they can get away with 'Anarchy in the UK' and that bullshit, but it hasn't an eighth the heart or intelligence of something like Garland Jeffreys's 'Wild in the Streets'.

With albums like *Coney Island Baby* and particularly *Rock and Roll Heart*, Lou offered little competition to Springsteen's *Born to Run*, Patti Smith's *Horses* or the Ramones' *The Ramones*.

However, as it turned out, no single band and no single performer benefited from punk as much as the Velvet Underground and Lou Reed. According to M. C. Kostek in the *VU Handbook*:

> Brian Eno's quip about how not many people bought the *Velvet Underground and Nico* album but of those who did, everyone went out and formed a band, carries much truth. Many of the most creative people in rock music from the 70s – the Stooges, New York Dolls, Patti Smith, Television, Pere Ubu, Ramones, Richard Hell, Jonathan Richman, Roxy Music, David Bowie, Buzzcocks, Talking Heads, Wire, Cabaret Voltaire and Eno himself strongly reflect and validate the Velvets' massive musical influence.

Lou Reed's career was relaunched in part by punk journalists. This time his life was saved by writers and a cartoonist. It wasn't really until John Holmstrom's *Punk* magazine came along in New York in January 1976, pulling the often disparate music of the punk groups together, showcasing them as if they were major stars, that punk could be looked upon as a movement. It was Holmstrom's view that Reed's independent spirit, enthusiasm and dedication to passion made him the ultimate punk rocker. 'If you were going to do a rock-and-roll time line, Lou's there for every decade,' he pointed out. 'From doo-wop to garage rock to psychedelic to glitter to disco to punk rock and beyond it later to alternative rock and to sober-rock.'

Soon Lou was pouring advice into the ears of Tom Verlaine of Television and David Byrne of Talking Heads – mostly about getting a lawyer. But it was Lou's presence more than anything else that turned everybody on. He went to CBGB's in his uniform shades and black leather jacket with Rachel. They sat at a table and listened to the music like everybody else. Lou didn't grandstand and was obviously enjoying himself. When he saw Patti Smith playing 'Real Good Time Together' at CBGB's, he was genuinely thrilled, clapping with glee and telling everybody at his table that he had written the song. Johnny Ramone remembered how many of them really began to feel something was happening when Lou started coming to the club.

It was during a visit to CBGB's to see the Ramones just before Thanksgiving in November 1975 that Reed had the pivotal encounter which launched him onto the cover of *Punk*. Only some twenty or thirty people were in attendance that night, but the rank, dark little room crackled with the combination of rock in the making. Everyone was happily aware of what was going on and exhilarated. Despite the fact that, as a rule, punks acknowledged no one, Lou *was* the godfather.

'Danny Fields was there and Legs met Danny and everybody went nuts because Lou Reed was there that night,' Holmstrom recalled. To Legs McNeil, the Ramones' performance was the most moving thing he had ever seen in his life: 'The Ramones came out in these black leather jackets. They looked so stunning. They counted off, then each one started playing a different song. Their self-hatred was just amazing, they were so pissed off.'

Sitting at a candlelit table with, of all people, Richard Robinson, Lou was approached by two raw, loony-looking Connecticut teenagers, Holmstrom and the magazine's resident punk, Legs McNeil, who would shortly become the Johnny Carson and Ed McMahon of the punk scene. 'Hey, you!' they accosted him. 'You're going to do an interview with us!' Lou, who was on one of his three-day cruises through the underbelly of the city, watching the parade of geeks and freaks pass before him, fell right into his part, giving one of his best interviews without thinking about it. Lou later claimed no recollection of this incident. Holmstrom commented, 'He wasn't getting too many people to talk to him who liked *Metal Machine*.' After taking in the Ramones fifteen-minute set, Lou spent the next two hours sparring vigorously with the two punk kids and *Punk*'s British correspondent Mary Harron.

Lou apparently enjoyed the show.

PUNK: Do you like the Ramones?
LOU REED: Oh, they're fantastic!
PUNK: Have you seen anyone else that you like?
REED: Television. I like Television. I think Tom Verlaine's really nice.

PUNK: Do you like Patti Smith?

REED: Oh, yeah, yeah.

PUNK: How about Bruce Springsteen?

REED: Oh, I love him.

PUNK: You do?

REED: He's one of us.

PUNK: Thank you.

REED: He's a shit – what are you talking about, what kind of stupid question is that?

PUNK: OK.

REED: I mean, do I ask you what you like? Why does anyone give a fuck what I like?

PUNK: Well, you're a rock star!

REED: Oh . . . I keep forgetting. Why, do you like Springsteen?

PUNK: No, I think he's a piece of shit.

REED: He's great at what he does . . . It's not to my taste, y'know, he's from New Jersey . . . I'm very, y'know, partial to New York groups, y'know . . . Springsteen's already finished, isn't he? I mean, isn't he a has-been?

PUNK: I feel he's a has-been.

REED: Isn't Springsteen already over the hill? I mean – isn't everybody saying that they constructed him because they needed a rock star? . . . I mean . . . Already like groups are coming out and they're saying they're the new Bruce Springsteen, which is really . . . He was only popular for a week.

Holmstrom couldn't believe Lou was talking like this on tape. Legs, however, was not so easily won over. During a long discussion of *Metal Machine Music* and the record business, he started squirming in his seat like an impatient child. 'I thought Lou was boring as hell,' he remarked.

I was an eighteen-year-old guy, I didn't want to talk about art and the record company. I wanted to talk about cheeseburgers, that's all we had in common. I knew he was like so cool, and I was kind of like, we are not worthy, Lou. But, you knew whatever you did this guy was going to think you were an asshole. He was just too cool.

Lou has this vibe of not being anyone. The guy just seems completely threatened by everything. But he's so good you know it's funny because the punk way to appreciate people is to make fun of them. Like Tish and Snooky used to have a song and it was sung to the tune of 'Sweet Jane'. The refrain was 'Lou Reed' instead of 'Sweet Jane'. Lou Reed, then they had all these funny lyrics. So it was paying tribute to him, but I don't think Lou appreciated it.

Halfway through the interview Legs jumped in.

LEGS: Did you ever hear the Dictators' lyrics – what they said about you?
REED: I hope it's nothing bad.
PUNK: Yeah – 'I think Lou Reed is a creep.'
REED: That's funny – because when I ran into one of them he was slobbering all over me saying, 'Hey – I hope you don't mind what we say about you.' And I just pat him on the head – y'know, nice doggie – nice doggie.

Mary Harron, mouth agape, sat through the sparring match with Holmstrom and McNeil. Out in the street after the interview, she recalled, 'John was jumping up and down yelling, "We got our cover! We got our cover!"' But Legs flipped out, screaming, *'Who does fucking Lou Reed think he fucking is?'* Legs felt as if his soul had been taken.

I felt that meeting with Lou, somehow we had been corrupted for ever. You felt it in some emotional stark way. I mean, Lou always seemed like he wanted to go darker than sex, murder, mutilation, further. And you always got the feeling that you were definitely an idiot around him. I didn't want to sit at his feet that night. I didn't like him. He didn't seem like a nice guy. I mean, I wouldn't want to hang out with him.

Holmstrom, on the other hand, was in a trance, totally persuaded that putting Reed on the cover of their first issue was the most exciting choice possible. 'I saw *Metal Machine Music* as the beginning of the punk-rock movement,' he said.

> It was the ultimate punk-rock album. It was the greatest punk
> statement ever made. It was fuck you to the record company and
> everyone who bought it. It was, 'This is what I want to do the way I
> want to do it.' How can you get more punk than that? It was more
> punk than the Sex Pistols, the Ramones, everything that came out
> afterward. I think he meant it that way, and we treated it that way.

Punk #1, containing the interview and a glowing review of
Metal Machine Music, was published in January 1976.
Holmstrom's cover portrait captured Lou's chemical insect
persona as perfectly as the cover of *Coney Island Baby*, released
the same month, put across his chameleon-like MC role. 'Instead
of a photo, the cover was a wickedly accurate cartoon of Reed as
metal man: the feature inside was not typeset but told in fumetti,'
wrote the British rock historian Jon Savage. 'The surrounding
artwork is as important as Reed's insults: when the interviewers
follow Reed down the block, there they are in cartoons. The effect
was both immediate and distanced, a formal innovation on a par
with *Mad* magazine or the Ramones' own manipulations.'

According to John Holmstrom, Lou was impressed. 'He said,
"I barely remember doing the interview and there I am on the
cover of this thing." He thought it had the whole image thing
perfect. I was just knocked out because I was this twenty-year-old
kid. And here was this guy who I'd pay $7.50 to see live gushing
over my magazine when he hated everything in the world. It just
blew me away.' In retrospect, Holmstrom reflected, '*Metal
Machine Music* almost ended his career. He could have become
another forgotten Elton John kind of person if we hadn't put him
on the cover. Instead, he became the godfather of punk and it
resurrected his career.'

Rock stars ranks had swelled by the mid-seventies to such
unmanageable proportions that it was hard to know how to
distinguish one from another. The cover of *Punk* picked Lou Reed
out of the international swamp and placed him squarely in the
vanguard, as a heroic figurehead.

The parallels between Reed's and Cale's careers through the seventies reveal just how important image is in rock. As a body of work, John's solo albums are arguably superior to Lou's. Cale's influence on punk – he produced among other notable works Patti Smith's first and greatest album, *Horses* – was arguably stronger than Reed's. Yet once they went solo Lou's image was always stronger than John's. The competition between them was at once a spur and a thorn, for it was always screamingly obvious, although for many years equally impossible, that they should collaborate again. Cale scoffed at the comparisons between the punk bands and the VU. 'Everybody's talking about this band the Velvet Underground influencing this and that,' he said.

> They're even saying Talking Heads are reminiscent of the Velvet Underground, which has absolutely nothing to do with what we sounded like. And many of these people making these assessments and writing these reviews never saw us live. All they've got to go by are live reissues by Lou Reed, that kind of narcissistic nepotism. He just regenerates the same material over and over again, in different form. Lou has his whole life sorted out now. He's become the Jewish businessman we always knew he was.

But the direct influence of Lou Reed and the Velvet Underground on the punk rock movement was exemplified by their prominent positions in record charts compiled in fanzines in Britain. Though these charts did not reflect the tastes of mainstream rock-and-roll audiences, they established Reed's and the Velvet Underground's popularity with the punk-rock audience. For example, the second issue of *Ripped and Torn* (January 1977), one of the most widely circulated British punk fanzines, gave 'Foggy Notion' by the Velvet Underground the number-five position on its singles chart. The same fanzine's album chart listed six entries (including the number-one position) for Lou Reed and/or the Velvet Underground, and included every Velvet Underground record.

In the autumn of 1977, Lou prepared to record his follow-up to the disappointing *Rock and Roll Heart*. The punk challenge, combined with problems with Rachel which were causing him a lot of pain, led Lou to create one of the great albums of the era, *Street Hassle*.

The most striking thing about Lou's relationship with Rachel was how long it lasted, particularly considering that they spent virtually all their time together. Unlike his relationships with previous girlfriends and his wife, Lou did not immediately try to push Rachel to an edge. Whether this was because he knew how much he needed her, or Rachel's personality was able to absorb Lou's blows without flinching, there's no question that from late 1974 through 1977, Rachel was a mainstay of Reed's life. And her personality permeates the albums from *Coney Island Baby*, a paean to Rachel that put Lou squarely on the map as the poet laureate of the gay world in New York in the seventies, to *Street Hassle*, which documents the sad conclusion to their affair.

The breakdown started somewhere in 1977. A friend visited Lou one afternoon that spring to find him alone and brooding over Rachel's disappearance. Speaking in the tone of a bereaved lover out of a broken-hearts novel, Lou was in despair and blaming himself for the break, crying plaintively that he would do anything to get her back. He was about to go on tour and remarked wistfully that they could have had such a ball together, but now everything was in doubt.

Two days later Lou got a phone call instructing him to go to a downtown bar where a surprise awaited him. Hastening to the specified location, Lou walked in to find Rachel sitting at the bar with open arms and a sweet smile. In such moments, Lou was the most romantic of men. He swept her off her feet again and they did have a ball on the subsequent tour. But in such intense relationships, once a crack like that appears, there is little chance of real recovery.

Although he clearly regretted it, by early 1978 Lou and Rachel were having a trial separation. Again, quite uncharacteristically, when Lou did break up with Rachel, rather than closing her out of his life with a slammed door, Reed admitted that he still had strong feelings about her and missed her. Ultimately, the relationship probably suffered more than anything else from writer's synd-rome. When a writer makes use of his mate for his material, he risks losing the indefinable essence of their connection. Rachel should be remembered in the saga of Lou Reed as the muse who helped give birth to his finest work of the mid-seventies.

Lou, who had in the course of his solo career made an intense study of recording techniques and became something of an authority on the subject, had discovered a binaural recording process created in Germany by one Manfred Schunke. Schunke used computer-designed models of the average human head. The detail was as precise as possible down to the size, shape and bone structure of the ear canal. Microphones fit in each ear so theoretically what they recorded would be exactly what a human being sitting in the position the head was placed in would actually hear.

'I had written these songs on the spot in Germany,' Lou said. 'I tried to teach them to the band really quick. The audience didn't understand a word of English – like most of my audience. They're fucked-up assholes, what difference does it make? Can they count from one to ten?'

Street Hassle was originally recorded at live shows in Munich, Wiesbaden and Ludwigshafen, Germany. Lou brought the live tapes back to New York for overdubbing and mixing. In what looked like an extremely perverse move, he chose Richard Robinson as his producer. Several of the songs were dated. 'Dirt' and 'Leave Me Alone' came from the 1975 *Coney Island Baby* sessions. 'Real Good Time Together' hailed from the Velvets' final years. The title piece, one of the most riveting songs of Lou's solo career, was written in three parts, 'Waltzing Matilda', 'Street Hassle' and 'Slip Away'.

Needless to say, all was not copacetic in the studio. Lou's father–son relationship with Clive Davis came to a head during the *Street Hassle* sessions.

After hearing an early version of the last section of 'Street Hassle', Davis suggested Reed make the two-minute track longer. Although Lou accepted Clive's advice ('I wrote the lyrics for

'Street Hassle' out from beginning to end in about as long as it took to physically write it on paper'), he later complained of

> being betrayed by all the evil people around me! The original producer (Richard Robinson) had walked out, I'd had to change studios because we had a fight there – and then Clive Davis came in and told me I should make a new record and throw this one away. But the record came out, and I wasn't crazy. The head of Arista was stupid.

Making albums allowed Lou to be the Sylvester Stallone of rock. 'Some people make movies of people who interest them,' Reed was quoted in an Arista press release. 'Andy Warhol has been doing it for years . . . Actually, I do it with my songs.'

Displaying what he had learned from Raymond Chandler and Delmore Schwartz, Lou wrote a vivid story with short, neo-Céline-like sentences. The song, which ends the cycle about Rachel that began with 'Coney Island Baby', laments the end of their relationship. As Bob Jones, who was also at the end of his relationship with Lou, said, 'At a certain point the only way to be around Lou was to be secondary to Lou and you either had to become an acolyte – which was a role that I don't think Lou would allow one to continue – or say goodbye. It would very much be part of the attitude of the time that one would say goodbye in a cynical way and be tough and rough about it.'

One of the many nuggets in 'Street Hassle' came from the unexpected contribution of Bruce Springsteen, who sang a few intense lines in the centre of the piece. 'He was in the studio below, and for that little passage I'd written I thought he'd be just perfect, because I tend to screw those things up,' Reed recounted. 'Like "I Found a Reason", it is my best recitation, but I just couldn't resist that "Walking hand in hand with myself" part. I'm too much of a smart ass. But I knew Bruce would do it seriously, because he really is of the street. Springsteen is all right, he gets my seal of approval. I think he's groovy.'

'In a way, the street-rock of Springsteen is the exact polar opposite of the street-rock of Lou Reed,' wrote Robert Christgau.

Reed presents himself as having gone through so much as to have become totally deadened to everything – cocooned so smoothly in his insulating smack bubble that he's an utterly dispassionate observer of everything that passes before his senses, detached to the point where all perspective vanishes and all events are of equal importance (the same trick that Vonnegut pulled in *Breakfast of Champions*, in a way).

The first half of the seventies had been a prolific time for Lou Reed. He produced six studio albums and completed a book of poems, *All the Pretty People*. Several poems were published in literary magazines, ranging from the prestigious *Paris Review* through *Unmuzzled Ox* to underground publications like the *Coldspring Journal*. In late 1977, shortly after he finished work on *Street Hassle*, Lou won a prize as one of the year's five best new poets from the American Literary Council of Little Magazines. He attended the ceremony at the Gotham bookmart in New York and was given the award by Senator Eugene McCarthy. Lou wondered if McCarthy read poems about S&M, noting, 'He was taller than he seemed on TV.'

Street Hassle was released in February 1978 at the commercial height of the new wave, and marketed as a grand statement from the man who invented punk. It received more press than anything he had done before, garnering him reviews across the board from *Time* to *Punk*. It took him to the pinnacle of his career as reviewers around the world praised it to the skies. 'I'm right in step with the market,' he said in *Creem* the week the album came out. 'The album is enormously commercial.'

An article in the *NME* in 1993 looked back at this period:

Signs of his rejuvenation were most vividly apparent on his 1978 tour de force *Street Hassle*, an uncompromising howl of self-lacerating disgust and poisonous venom that against all odds turned out to be one of the major albums of the late seventies. The title track ranks with anything on the more celebrated *New York*, *Songs for Drella*, or *Magic and Loss*. In its final heartbreaking conclusion, Lou sounds exposed and vulnerable and hurt beyond words. 'Street Hassle' takes you to the edge and leaves you there – darkness below, no lights in heaven above.

'I use my moods,' Reed elucidated.

I get into one of these dark, melancholy things and I just milk it for everything I can. I know I'll be out of it soon and I won't be looking at things the same way. For every dark mood, I also have a euphoric opposite. I think they say that manic depressives go as high as they go down, which isn't to say that I'm really depressive.

I keep hedging my bet, instead of saying that's really me, but that is me, as much as you can get on record.

'This album bristles with intensity and Reed pulls no punches,' wrote Mark Kernis in the *Washington Post*. 'His images are direct and frightening, his delivery is blunt and unadorned. *Street Hassle* is haunting and unsettling.'

As usual, Lou gave a series of interviews, including an outstanding one with Allan Jones for a British magazine, *Music Maker*, in which he put himself in perspective:

The Velvet Underground were banned from the radio. I'm still being banned. And for exactly the same reasons. Maybe they don't like Jewish faggots . . . No. It's what they think I stand for they don't like. They don't want their kid sitting around masturbating to some rock and roll record – probably one of mine. They don't want their kid ever to know he can snort coke or get a blow job at school or fuck his sister up the ass. They never have. But how seriously can you take it? So they won't play me on the radio. What's the radio? Who's the radio run by? Who's it played for? With or without the radio I'm still dangerous to parents.

When another interviewer, the kid who had arranged his first solo gig in the US in 1972, Billy Altman, noted, 'One thing that disturbs people about your music is its lack of what might be called a moral stance,' Lou shrugged in disdain.

They're not heterosexual concerns running through that song. I don't make a deal of it, but when I mention a pronoun, its gender is all-important. It's just that my gay people don't lisp. They're not any more affected than the straight world. They just are.

'*Street Hassle* is the best album I've done,' he told another journalist.

Coney Island Baby was a good one, but I was under siege. *Berlin* was *Berlin*, *Rock and Roll Heart* is good compared to the rest of the shit that's going around. As opposed to *Street Hassle* they're all babies. If you wanna make adult rock records you gotta take care of all the people along the way. And it's not child's play. You're talking about managers, accountants, you're talking about the lowest level of human beings. *Street Hassle* is me on the line. And I'm talking to them one to one.

Throughout the 1970s Reed's albums were, for the most part, so individual there was little point in comparing them to their contemporaries except in commercial terms. Who else in rock made albums like *Berlin* and *Metal Machine Music*? However, the release of *Street Hassle* provided an opportunity to measure Reed against Patti Smith (*Radio Ethiopia*), Richard Hell (*Blank Generation*), the Sex Pistols (*Never Mind the Bollocks*), Talking Heads (*More Songs About Buildings and Food*). While Reed's work does not have the energy or freshness of his offspring's, the title track alone possesses the diamond-in-the-rough beauty that is at the core of the purest punk music. And Reed's world was every bit as vital and real as the worlds created in each of the other albums. On that score *Street Hassle* stood up triumphantly to the challenge, without, like the Stones' *Some Girls*, depending on punk influences for its revitalization. Bookends of Reed's punk period, *Metal Machine Music* and *Street Hassle* have the power to change a listener's emotions.

In the second half of March 1978, Reed played a five-night residency at the Bottom Line in New York with his favourite mid-seventies combo, the Everyman Band. Susan Shapiro described the shows in the *Voice*:

On stage he's puckish, like Chaplin, like the cover of *Coney Island Baby*, a live highlight. He moves like a go-go gymnast, awkwardly, authentically, uncorrupted by vanity. He's singing 'I Wanna Be Black', but it's playful, a lie to tell the truth. 'Satellite of Love' and

'Lisa Says' top one another. The force is with him and he's maybe taking 'yes' for an answer. Wallace Stevens has nailed him, 'under every "no" lay a passion for "yes" that had never been broken'. Then he's given them the whammy, 'Dirt'.

'People are always looking for a voice that works,' noted Henry Edwards. 'It took him years to find a very strong performing voice. It was in him and he didn't let it out. Because he was so busy playing the *faux* junky. I was amazed when I went to the Bottom Line in 1978 and he really was a rock and roller.'

Andy Warhol wrote in his diary:

> Lou was late coming out, but then he did and I was proud of him. For once, finally, he's himself, he's not copying anybody. Finally he's got his own style. Now everything he does works. It took years and Lou just kept on working. He's very good now, he's changed a lot.

'Andy always understood where I'm coming from', Reed responded. 'He also said to me that work is the most important thing in a man's life and I believe him. My work is my yoga. It empties me out. Years ago he said I was to be to music what he was to visual arts. The man's amazing. You can't define it, but it's happening just the way he said it would.'

The shows were recorded for a live album to be called *Take No Prisoners*:

> We called it *Take No Prisoners* because we were doing a quite phenomenal booking in a tiny hotel in Québec, where they'd normally have a little dance band. I dunno what we were doing there, but . . . All of a sudden this drunk guy sitting alone at the front shouts, '*Lou, take no pris'ners, Lou!*' and then he took his head and smashed it as hard as he could to the drumbeat. We saw him doing it and we were taking bets that that man would never move again. But he got up and *bam bam* on the table! And that was only halfway through. What was gonna be the encore? He might cut his arm off!

The fastest mouth in rock and roll combined his method-acting stream-of-consciousness spontaneity and Lenny Bruce–style wit to make a record unlike any other in the annals of rock. The songs became mere background to the godfather's monologues –

slapping down members of the audience, reeling off a succession of slick one-liners, throwing darts at Patti Smith or Andy Warhol, playing out every lyric for its full sexual innuendo. Reed saved his most acidic bile for rock critics – notably John Rockwell of the *New York Times* and Robert Christgau of the *Village Voice*. 'Who needs them to tell you what to think?' he railed, before lecturing his audience.

Lou's outbursts on *Take No Prisoners* reveal a Lou who is autonomous because he can talk to himself. 'What are you complaining about, asshole?' he asks himself, answering, 'I just play the guitar.' Later he quips, apropos of literary reference, 'for those who still read,' then turns on himself, snapping, 'What a snotty remark.'

Lou kept in touch with *Punk*'s John Holmstrom, but he was a tough man to have as a fan. 'I would run into him occasionally, but he was very down on the magazine after we did him,' John recalled. 'He'd say, "Oh, you blew it, it's not as good as it used to be." And he was right. He was always drifting away from us, then drifting towards us.'

When *Punk* magazine held its award ceremonies in October 1978, Reed was nominated for the Punk Rock Hall of Fame Award and accepted the invitation to attend the ceremonies. As John recalled that night:

> We thought we were going out of business and we wanted to have a party and go out in style. A day or two before our party, Nancy Spungeon was found dead. So New York went nuts. It was a crazy time and all the insanity focused on our event, because we were the punk event happening at the moment. TV crews came down and wanted to interview all the punk-rock stars about Sid and Nancy and nobody wanted anything to do with this because people were shocked and horrified by what had happened.
>
> The media were always more interested in promoting those aspects of punk. They could have said, for example, that Lou was a great artist who expressed himself differently. But they had to focus on the ridiculous, shaving Iron Crosses in the side of his head. Which to us was not the point. Punk to us was more the attitude: you do what you

want artistically and any other way, lifestyle-related, and screw you. Not that you have a tawdry or decadent lifestyle and get nasty about it. It was more like the ultimate individual against perversion.

What had been intended as a humorous ceremony deteriorated into a horror show owing to the hysterical intervention of the local press. The audience started breaking the furniture and throwing it at the stage and booing.

Legs McNeil remembered 'Lou laughing a lot. We gave him an award. I don't know what for. I'm sure it was really amateurish and stupid. It was the Punk Awards!' But Holmstrom saw a different reaction.

Lou accepted the Hall of Fame award. But he wouldn't come up on stage, he just took it and walked out. That's when I discovered that rock stars are terribly serious when it comes to awards. I always thought it was a big joke, but they take it so seriously. They'll go anywhere to pick up an award. We had a big falling-out over the awards ceremony. It was a disaster, it was horrible. Before the thing he had said, 'If you embarrass me, I'll never speak to you again'. And he was embarrassed. That was the last time he ever talked to me.

chapter seventeen **Mr Reed**

1978–1979

[In which Lou records and
releases *The Bells*, and
embarks on his most
demented tour of America and
Europe. Back in the US, he
decides to see an analyst.]

*I've probably had more of a chance to make an asshole out of
myself than most people, and I realize that. But then not
everybody gets a chance to live out their nightmares for the
vicarious pleasures of the public.*

LOU REED

By November 1978, Lou was ready to go back to work. In a
remarkable confessional interview in *Creem* magazine, he announced a new level of ambition:

> My expectations are very high . . . to be the greatest writer that ever
> lived on God's earth. In other words I'm talking about Shakespeare,
> Dostoevsky. I want to do that rock-and-roll thing that's on a level
> with *The Brothers Karamazov*. I'm starting to build up a body of
> work. I'm on the right track. I think I haven't done badly. But I think
> I really haven't scratched the surface. I think I'm just starting.

November also saw the release of *Take No Prisoners* in the US.
Lou could hardly have announced his next incarnation more
dramatically than with the infamous live album, at least a third of
which was devoted to Lou's Lenny Bruce-inspired running
commentary. Disguising his ravaged singing voice by either

screeching and whining out lyrics, or, more often, talking over the music, Reed filled the two albums with anecdotes, jokes and insults which reflected his state of mind. Meanwhile, the band managed to keep up with Lou, drifting in and out of songs as singing gave way to monologue. 'It presents a portrait of Lou Reed more authentic and vivid than any documentary or any amount of interviews could possibly achieve,' wrote Allan Jones, 'and exploits more fully than on any previous recording the full impact of his often pathologically cruel – but incessantly hilarious – humour.'

Although *Take No Prisoners* was more of a retrospective of Lou Reed than of his music, he was as enthusiastic about the results as his fans. 'I think of it as a contemporary urban-blues album. After all, that's what I write – tales of the city. And if I dropped dead tomorrow, this is the record I'd choose for posterity. It's not only the smartest thing I've ever done, it's also as close to Lou Reed as you're probably ever going to get, for better or worse.'

As the year neared its end, Lou had a feast of work on his plate. He was writing his next studio album, *The Bells*. For the first time since leaving the Velvets Reed wrote songs in collaboration – composing tracks with the guitarist, singer and songwriter Nils Lofgren, Don Cherry and various members of his band. Interestingly, and perhaps uncharacteristically, he also shared credit for those tracks on the album sleeve. In addition to the new record, Lou was planning a spring and summer tour of the US and Europe, where *Street Hassle* was popular and *Take No Prisoners* was soon to be released.

The same month *Take No Prisoners* came out, Lou added another guitarist to the band. Chuck Hammer, a young guitar prodigy from Santa Barbara, felt, by the age of twenty-four, that he had mastered the guitar to the point where he could approach his hero on the grounds of being a 'qualified disciple'. Hammer was a naive, inexperienced version of Robert Quine (who would become Lou's guitar partner in the early eighties). 'As a guitarist coming out of the seventies, you either work with Bowie or Reed,' Hammer declared. 'I also admired John Cale a lot.'

Hammer wrote Lou, telling him that 'I was what he needed', and was astonished when Lou responded with a call. Just as Doug Yule had done when asked to audition for the Velvets, Hammer dropped everything and excitedly rushed to New York. 'I asked, "Does anyone in your band know who you are?" "Not really," he replied. I said, "I do, you're a genius. *Berlin* is a masterpiece, and I know the music." '

Rehearsals were held at the old Star Sound studios where they would work up material through the end of the year. The whole band convened daily for long, regimented practices. It turned out that Hammer was the antithesis of Reed: drug, alcohol and even caffeine-free, he was unprepared for the mind games he would face as a member of the band. The first track Hammer auditioned was 'Sad Song'. He had spent eighteen hours learning Bob Ezrin's string arrangement and as he played it, Lou, with his collar turned up, silently glared at the young musician. Afterwards, Hammer remembered, 'Lou said softly, "You're everything you said you were." '

As a result, Lou began playing more guitar, and, just as Quine would do three years later, Hammer brought out and mirrored his inventive style.

His peers had long since recognized Lou as a guitar legend not only because of his playing, but also because of the number of instruments he had destroyed in the process of customizing them. On one occasion Cale recounted, 'He bought this beautiful guitar, had all the work done to it, and then a week later his guitar roadie gets a call from him. He'd been up all night and found a soldering iron and he plugged it in and his guitar is: goodbye. It's like whhhooom. It's one lump of lead, no more wiring, all of it's melted.'

At the beginning of 1979 he recorded *The Bells* in Germany, working for the last time with the binaural process at Manfred Schunke's Delta Studios on a farm in Wilster, about 60 miles outside Hamburg. Lou had admitted to feeling ambivalent about recording in Germany. 'I wasn't crazy about going to Germany in the first place. And the real reason was that I liked the binaural technique, but I didn't like the board. I don't like any of the sounds they got, across the board. Because they don't have good boards.'

Don Cherry attended the sessions for their first studio collaboration. Though Cherry would play R&B riffs to order, his presence automatically tipped the balance towards avant-garde jazz, allowing Reed to make *The Bells* as much an exploration in sound as an exercise in lyrical composition.

'The Bells' itself is a good example of Lou's method of spontaneous composition. The song was inspired in equal parts by Edgar Allan Poe, whose poem 'The Bells' is among his most famous and lyrical, and one of Reed's musical masters, Ornette Coleman. After listening to Cherry quote a musical line from Coleman's masterpiece 'Lonely Woman', Lou stepped up to the microphone and recited the whole lyric in one take, pouring the words spontaneously into the wash of music around him. To this day he still wonders at their meaning, but the experience was so sublime that 'The Bells' remains one of Lou's favourite tracks.

Unfortunately, there were few fans of the album at Arista. Clive Davis went so far as to write a lengthy critique, concluding that the record was only half finished. Even the loyal Fonfara was never enamoured of the work, agreeing that it needed more time. Naturally, this sort of response only made Lou more determined to release it the way he wanted.

With Lou in control, the record was released in April. No sooner had it come out than he was up on his soapbox proclaiming that it surpassed *Take No Prisoners*, that it was the best record that he had ever made, that if he died tomorrow, etc. One can only imagine the bile he spewed forth on reading in Lisa Robinson's column how disappointed Arista's executives were with the new Lou Reed record. 'I guess that's what happens,' he snapped to the press, 'when you don't respond to the suggestions of the president.'

Though the album stalled at number 130 on the *Billboard* charts, the critics were unusually kind to the flawed work. It was hailed as 'powerfully cogent and authoritative, trenchantly universal' in the *Washington Post*. Christgau 'hadn't found him so likeable since the Velvet Underground'. Rockwell noted 'a new intensity'. Bangs outdid himself, pronouncing it 'the only true jazz-rock fusion anybody's come up with since Miles Davis' *On the Corner* period'.

In the wake of *The Bells*, Lou undertook one last, lengthy, booze-soaked tour that would take him to Britain, the West Coast of the US, back across America and finally to other parts of Europe. The tour would be characterized by the same kind of conflict and violence that had greeted him on the Rock 'n' Roll Animal tour of 1974. The three-month jaunt kicked off in the spring of 1979 with the British and West Coast legs of the tour.

Sterling Morrison, who hung out with Lou between shows in Texas, was saddened by the insularity that characterized Lou's progress.

> The worship surrounding Lou was just awful. I love Lou. That's why it upset me that Lou is making rudeness and obnoxiousness part of his daily life. When he came to Austin, the only person he spoke to in the city was me. I said, 'Lou, what is the fun of going outside of your apartment, if you're not going to talk to anybody? If you never meet a different person?' So we had all kinds of secret rendezvous all over the city, where I wasn't able to bring anybody. It was strange seeing him with a pick-up band. Things were so different – a total sycophantic relationship with the band. Lou is the employer. It's not like an organic unity, it's like these touring mercenaries. People falling over backwards for him.

A reporter from *Rolling Stone* who saw several of the shows found Lou in a remarkably sedate, albeit self-deprecating and reflective mood in his hotel room one night. Watching videos of the previous night's performance of 'Street Hassle', he expressed a kind of identity crisis.

'Look at that guy,' says Lou, pointing at himself on the screen. 'He sure is shameless about occupying his own life. Every time I'm doing that song, when it gets to that awful last line I never know just how it's going to come across. "So the first thing they see that allows them to be, they follow it – You know what it's called?" And here come that line and it should punch like a bullet: "BAD LUCK." The point of view of the guy saying that is so awful. But it's so true.' I only realize sometime afterwards what Lou Reed's talking about. I just try and stay out of the way.

Things moved from bad to worse as the tour progressed into its second leg, returning to Europe in the spring of 1979. A climax came in Germany, where *Take No Prisoners* had just been released and audiences expected a crazed, ranting Lou Reed. One night when the band was playing a concert at a 2,500-seat gymnasium, a particularly rowdy audience of American soldiers and German kids started a riot.

Lou, who played best when he felt in control of his audience, walked off stage three times when he could not get them to calm down. Finally a girl leaped on stage and charged towards him. Acting reflexively, Lou grabbed her and dragged her to the edge of the stage as security men and roadies fought to separate them. In the midst of the melee Lou, whose adrenaline was going full blast, grabbed his large Swedish roadie with one hand and lifted him off the ground. Then, screaming, 'You're full of shit!' at the audience, he ordered the whole band off stage.

Pandemonium erupted in the hall. Meanwhile backstage the police, who had been informed that Reed had bodily attacked a female fan, rushed into the dressing room and arrested him.

They took me to jail alone. How would you like to get into a van with twelve goose-steppers saying they're going to test your blood? They took me me to jail after the show. I slept in the cell overnight. I was tired. Then the next day they came to get me and I thought, oh, they're letting me out. But they came in and said, 'We want your blood.' I couldn't believe it, it was like I said to the guy, 'You must be an American or else all your life you wanted to be an American so you could have a great line like that. And now you said it.' They drove me to Frankfurt to have a blood test and urinology, to see if I had any drugs in my system, as they suspected I had. Of course . . . there was nothing. The guy was sort of nervous because on the way he asked me for a light and his hands were shaking, but, you know, my German's good enough.

No charges were pressed and Lou would later deny responsibility for the violence, claiming, 'The problem was a bunch of American soldiers. They wanted to have a riot, and they had one.'

A young Swedish fan, Stellan Holm, who had seen Lou play every time he had played in Stockholm throughout the seventies, remembered the 1979 show as the most intense and emotional he had ever seen. 'He was crying on "Men of Good Fortune" and saying, "Look at the fortune, the fucking fortune." And he was ranting. And he was really good. Most people hated it because it didn't sound like his songs. But for once he had charisma as a performer.' After the show, Stellan and his best friend Don went to the bar of the Sheraton Hotel and got a table next to Lou, who was drinking with the Moose. There he got a close-up glimpse of the mask behind the mask.

He had big curly hair. He was never a good dresser. He had jeans and maybe a leather vest. He just looked like some guy from Queens. One of us was brave enough to walk over. So he invited us to come and sit with him, which we did. And he bought us drinks. I told him I had met Andy and he suddenly became very defensive. As if he had to live up to the role of Lou Reed. He was very, very obnoxious. He was rude. You'd say something and he'd say something bad back. Then the other guys got up for some reason and we were alone with him. Just me, Don and Lou. And then he looked at us and said, 'I'm crazy, that's my problem.' Sort of like excusing his own behaviour for being an asshole. But it was such a cheap way of trying to be interesting. He knew we really admired him enormously anyway. And he knew by talking to us that we were well informed and we knew the records. He wasn't some old guy and he wasn't crazed on drugs. He was drinking, but he wasn't drunk. He was very together. He was just an extremely uptight and insecure person.

The denouement of what had deteriorated into a two-month international binge came after the last show in London when Lou and his entourage, featuring the oversized, intimidating Moose, dined with David Bowie, whose own career was going through a shaky period.

What began as an ebullient celebration soon disintegrated into an ugly and all too public exposure of the tension that had always existed between the two temperamental stars. Ever since Bowie had produced *Transformer*, he and Lou had flirted with the idea of doing it again. That night, however, when Lou proposed that David produce his next album, Bowie demurred, commenting that Lou needed to do a lot of work on his songs himself. Flying into an hysterical rage like a jilted lover, Lou slapped David hard across the face. Startled but quickly recovering, they made up, embracing across the table. But then, only minutes later Lou exploded again, screaming, 'I told you to never say that to me!' as he slapped Bowie a second time.

Before the two men created pandemonium, they were separated and Lou was led out of the restaurant by Moose who flung one massive arm around his shoulder. Moments later, Bowie made his own dramatic exit, cursing loudly as he smashed the potted plants that lined the stairs from the restaurant to the street. Hastening over to Lou's hotel, where he decided that he should return Lou's slap, David was turned away, informed that Lou could not be disturbed. In fact, he was pretending to be asleep.

'Yes, I hit him,' recalled Reed, 'more than once. It was a private dispute. It had nothing to do with sex, politics or rock and roll. I have a New York code of ethics. Speak unto others as you would have them speak unto you. In other words, watch your mouth.'

The following morning Lou flew back to New York. Angie Bowie, who had dinner with Lou shortly thereafter, witnessed ominous mood swings.

I watched with growing concern as he swung through his changes and then went thataway: from real pleasure to see me, to a venomous but more or less rational attack on David, to a state of bugged-out, all-inclusive paranoia which struck me as truly insane. He was stoned, so his mood was affected by however his pharmaceutical cycles of choice were intersecting during that particular hour or two, but even so . . .

You might get a better sense of Lou if I tell you something he told me during dinner. 'You have to get stoned in the city,' he said in absolute seriousness. 'It's a necessity. The atmosphere is so polluted that you have to put chemicals in your body to counteract it.'

'He had a potbelly after touring,' said Bob Jones.

I think that was because he quit speed. The speed scene ran out. There was no speed. Everyone got busted. Marty got busted. Turtle was sent away for five years. Lister, when I was arrested they wanted Lister, they knew I was dealing with Lister and they wanted me to turn him in and I wouldn't. They wanted the guy behind me.

'I met up with Lou again in 1979,' recalled the DJ Terry Noel, 'when he was blown up. Fat and waddling around the Village. That's when we started going down to Uncle Paul's, right off Christopher and Greenwich. He used to go in there to play the pinball machines. He seemed a lot more sedate and polite and receptive.'

'I believe in all things in moderation – including moderation,' Lou attested. 'I did more than abuse my body in the past. I very often wounded it. I enjoy age. I was miserable when I was younger.'

Several different sides of Lou's personality were revealed during one night in June when he was playing a brief stint at the Bottom Line. Before the first show he was scheduled to have cocktails at the apartment of the writer William Burroughs, a long-time hero, whom he had never met. However, when Lou appeared at the club for a 5 p.m. soundcheck, it transpired that the Moose was nowhere to be found. Conducting a thorough investigation of all members of the band and roadies, Lou became increasingly upset as it emerged that no one had seen the big man since leaving him on a street corner at 2 a.m. the previous night. Soon he was convinced that the Moose had suffered grievous bodily harm and was well into blaming himself. At the same time he worried about his bass player's absence from the upcoming show. Without a bass, there was no way the band could deliver. He decided that if the Moose could not be located by 7 p.m. the shows would have to be cancelled and the money returned.

Meanwhile, the time for Reed's meeting with Burroughs was fast approaching. Just a short while under the gun, the door of the club flew open and the Moose came thundering in, guitar case in one meaty palm, his eyes bugging out of his head as if plugged into a electric socket. He had overslept. Reed went ballistic. Ordering everybody but the band out of the room, he attacked the trembling giant in a tirade that could be heard out on the street. Then, storming out of the club with a final threat that if anything like this ever happened again the Moose would instantly be fired, Lou, a bottle of Scotch in hand, accompanied by two band members, leaped into a limousine and motored over to Burroughs's apartment on the nearby Bowery.

He arrived a full one and a half hour late at the home of the great writer, a punctilious gentleman of the old school who had cocktails at six and dinner at eight. Rather than apologizing for his tardy arrival, Lou cast a withering glance around the room, rudely asking if there was a chair or whether he was expected to sit on the floor. Then he proceeded to take apart each of Burroughs's cocktail guests with deft one-liners that perfectly pinned their weakest points. Turning to Burroughs, he opened the conversation by asking him if it was true he had had to sleep with publishers in order to get his books published. A few seconds later he asked the writer whether it was true that he had cut off his toe to get out of the draft. A lesser man than Burroughs might have got his back up against the wall at such an obviously inebriated onslaught. However, as it turned out, the author of *The Naked Lunch* was charmed by what turned into a hilarious exchange about, among other things, how to shoot heroin with a safety pin, should the need arise.

After a whirlwind visit in which Reed left everybody in the room, except Burroughs, feeling as if they had been mentally raped, Lou gathered up his entourage and swept back to the club where he was shortly due to go on. In the dressing room before the show he appeared to be so drunk that he was returning to a state of infantilism. However, as soon as the time came for him to go on stage, despite dripping with sweat and looking like an updated version of the late sixties bellicose Jack Kerouac, he proceeded to deliver a masterful set.

Reed raged around the stage in a temper, smashing microphones against each other. Beginning the revamped 'Heroin', he greeted the audience's applause by calling out, 'How do you think it feels, when I hear you calling for a pop song called "Heroin"? The evil of that drug – you don't know. When I say it's my wife and it's my life, do you think I'm kidding?' Reed's anger and frustration about his career was reaching a climax. When he spotted Clive Davis in the audience, Lou paused to give him the finger. 'Here, this is for you, Clive,' he said through the microphone. 'Where's the money, Clive? How come I don't hear my album on the radio?' As the show came to an end, Reed kept his fans waiting over twenty minutes for an encore. When he did emerge again, he received a standing ovation.

Lou issued a press release later that week through Arista to explain himself and straighten things out. 'I've always loved Clive,' he said, 'and he happens to be one of my best friends. I just felt like having a business discussion from the stage. Sometimes, out of frustration, you yell at those you love the most. I have a mouth that never sleeps, and I suppose that's why I make rock and roll records. Trying to read anything deeper into all this is pointless.'

In the autumn Lou took stock of his situation and scurried back once more to memories of Syracuse. In times of great distress, it was Lou's custom to call upon those figures from his past that had been pillars of support. Lou's college years, which represented Lou at his strongest, frequently provided the answers to conflict in later life.

Returning to his first mentor, Lou drew upon his memory of a conversation he had with Delmore Schwartz in his senior year at Syracuse when the drunken poet had given him an astute piece of advice. 'He told me,' Lou remembered, 'that I should see an analyst, and it should be a female analyst, because I wouldn't listen to anybody else.' Lou had always been adept at finding the right person at the right time. Now, his powers of survival still intact, one of the great misogynists of the era went through a series of intense sessions with a woman to whom he had been introduced by a mutual friend. As a result, he emerged claiming that he had never before been in such good shape mentally, spiritually and physically.

'It's like I'm really healthy these days,' he told John Holmstrom,

physically and mentally. Physically because mentally. I went to a doctor, a lady psychiatrist, which I'm sure will turn every Lou Reed fan off and say, 'Oh, what a fag.' But, you know, in case there are people out there who might want to go see someone . . . I met this woman who is really fantastic . . . I talked to her and she stayed with me practically like for hours every day during what was going on. And I was really in trouble. I mean, it's all the things that were going on but I wasn't coping with it. I was not handling it because of some things that were going on. It's like I had a problem, you know, so she solved the problem. Isn't that amazing? And ever since that day, literally, a couple of months ago, my whole life has changed. And I'm totally different. You can probably tell. And I'm saying to you, isn't it amazing that if you try hard enough and if you have some friends who are OK and that, you know, I believe there's a God or something. I really do. Because there are things that go beyond coincidence. And I think a lot of it has to do with if you're a good person. I mean, if you've been honest on a certain level, and I think you get paid back for that in the oddest way, in ways you don't think of and it's my honesty that let me meet her, for instance.

I'm delighted [he concluded triumphantly], because I think I've become an adult. I think I have a 24-hour-a-day job I like, and I think I do it really good and everything. It's like I love being in a rock band. I mean, that's all I ever really wanted. And I got it.

chapter eighteen

The Second Mrs Reed

1978–1983

[In which Lou meets Sylvia
Morales, records and releases
Growing Up in Public, tours
Europe, gets married and
joins A.A.]

*I think I've found my flower, so it makes me feel more like a
knight.*

LOU REED

The end of the seventies signalled a surprising rebirth for Lou. No
sooner had he finally got his head straight about being in a rock-
and-roll band than he met the woman who was to become his
second wife and most influential companion through the 1980s.
Lou's new 'best friend' was a sexy, dark-skinned, black-haired,
half-Mexican who bore a startling resemblance to Rachel. He met
Sylvia Morales in New York in early 1978 at a meeting of an S & M
group called the Eulenspiegel Society. Sylvia, twenty-two, was a
regular at CBGB's, and known on the punk scene primarily as the
sidekick of her striking roommate, the punk star Anya Phillips. A
Chinese-American photographer, stripper, underground movie
star and spirit, Phillips was the most erotic, threatening woman at
CBGB's. Under Anya's thumb, Sylvia joined her as a stripper and
part-time dominatrix. According to a mutal friend, Terrence
Sellers:

> Sylvia was always the butt of jokes and was always being teased and
> criticized by Anya – 'I hate your shoes' and 'do this' and 'dress up'. So

she lived in Anya's shadow. But I liked her. She was nice and very serious-minded but very flat compared to Anya's constant theatricals. Sylvia was kind of a coarser version of Anya. She was pretty but she had a larger nose, darker skin – she looked more ethnic.

Basically, the sultry Sylvia – who could resemble in photographs the classic image of the GI's oriental pin-up – was lady-in-waiting to the regal Anya. Underneath her patina of punk glamour, Sylvia was also a much straighter, steadier character than her flamboyant roommate. Lou could not have been more titillated.

Morales came from a military family. Her father was an old-world Hispanic, a lifetime military man. Army brats are often lost souls, but Sylvia was grounded by the goals of the 1950s. Her aim in life was to get behind a good man and devote herself to his success. Sylvia had a strong ambitious streak. In between stripping and socializing at CBGB's, where she made several friends, she went to college to study writing. At 2 a.m. while everybody else was raving it up in the club, Sylvia could be found slumped at the bar, her nose buried in a big, fat college textbook as she waited patiently for Anya to choose whom she was going to take home. Glenn O'Brien 'always thought she was a cool and sexy girl. And I think the fact that Anya went out with Sylvia as a duo makes Sylvia a major person. She was a great presence at CBGB's. Sylvia and Anya were awesome together. But I also thought she really had a brain. Sylvia is really talented at writing.'

John Holmstrom 'was shocked that Sylvia was going out with Lou, because Sylvia seemed like such a quiet person. Anya was the boss and dominant person and Sylvia was just her roommate and friend. And the fact the Sylvia and Lou met and fell in love was so funny. It was hilarious, it was nice.'

What made her the perfect candidate for the vacant position of Mrs Reed was her duality. Lou liked his women to have a suggestion of trash about them, but that had to be balanced by their domestic, supportive, subservient sides. Wasting no time with pleasantries, Lou whisked away Sylvia right from under Anya's nose to take a closer look.

Terrence Sellers recalled Anya's rage that night when the friend she considered to be her dowdy little slave went home with a prize as grand as Lou:

Lou just spirited her off, leaving Anya standing on the street corner ranting and raving and screaming. Sylvia did not come home for about a week and a half. When she and Lou got back, Anya was in such a rage she went completely crazy and Sylvia moved out. And that was really the last we heard of Sylvia. She never came back to the scene. She never came back to the clubs and hung out. She just went off with him and that was it.

Once he got hold of a woman, Lou's would demand her total attention, amputating her from her friends and family, just as he had done to Shelley.

Sylvia moved to a building on East 12 Street that housed, among others, Allen Ginsberg and Richard Hell. One of Allen's friends, Rosebud, recalled seeing Lou uncharacteristically carrying Sylvia's garbage downstairs on more than one occasion.

One small fact that Sylvia neglected to mention to Lou up front when she met him was that she was also seeing John Cale. It wasn't such a coincidence, considering how small the downtown music scene was. It just indicated how similar their tastes in women were, plus what a good catch Sylvia was. But it was another ironic chapter in their history of competition for women, particularly the still simmering case of Nico. It is not clear exactly when Lou found out about Sylvia's relationship with John, but it ended shortly after Lou met her.

Lou started going to Times Square to watch Sylvia strip at the Melody or the Madame Burlesque. Sylvia and the others were required to perform six times a day for twenty-five minutes at a stretch. A higher class of strip joint, more like theatres than bars, they didn't serve alcohol, and the dancers would go on in costume – though most of their clothes would come off very quickly. The dancers performed on stage while the audiences sat and watched, but the onlookers could also approach the stage and stick money in their garter belts or panties. That year, Sylvia also starred in an underground film by Beth and Scot B. Wearing a skimpy bustier which exposed her breasts, and brandishing a whip, she played a dominatrix torturing a nerdy customer.

Her blunt, impassive face, partially obscured by a hank of black hair, gave her the right look for the part. Lou must have been assured that he had chosen the real thing, that Sylvia wasn't a fake. However, a cooler head might have realized that in both stripping and acting, Sylvia was just playing a part.

At the same time Lou was falling in love with Sylvia, he was struggling through the aftermath of his relationship with Rachel. After Lou moved to Christopher Street, they had taken separate apartments. Lou's four years with Rachel had been emotionally charged on the deepest levels. Her loss left him despondent and cynical. Continuing to use quantities of amphetamine and alcohol, he often found himself alone and desperate. During the remainder of 1978 Lou kept in touch with Rachel while he privately nurtured his relationship with Sylvia.

The few Syracuse friends he was still in touch with looked down on Sylvia as a second-rate choice for a man of Lou's calibre. Shelley, however, understood that the relationship could work because Sylvia had two for Lou essential characteristics: experience in New York's trashy underground world, and a down-to-earth and old-fashioned attitude to romantic relationships. And that it was the straight side of her that really attracted Lou most. 'She's a very fifties-type girl,' Shelley remarked. 'Lou's a very fifties-type guy. He's ultimately straight, I want my woman to do what I want her to do, and I want her to take care of me, cook that pound of bacon when I want it and dress up in a suit. One of the things I noticed on the cover of *Growing Up in Public* is that he looks like his father.'

While continuing to be a multiple drug user through the end of the decade, by 1978 Lou was finding it harder to get speed. The Lister group had broken up. He tried to stop taking drugs by drinking, which led to such harrowing songs as 'Underneath the Bottle' and 'Waves of Fear'. Alcohol began to take a noticeable toll on his thirty-six-year-old frame. It also began to erode the glamour of his relationship with Sylvia. One visitor to Christopher Street found Lou lying on the couch, and just as he had carped at Shelley about Seymour, he was whining at Sylvia: 'You gotta take the dogs out so they can shit!'

Apart from walking the dogs, Sylvia also attempted to bring Lou back to his family. She arranged, for example, for them to visit Freeport at Hanukkah. A friend pointed out that Lou would have loved it,

> as long as he could say he didn't like it. As long as he could announce, 'I don't like being here, this was not my idea, I don't do this stuff, I'm much too hip, where's my present?' And, 'Why didn't you make what I like?' I bet his mother made his favourite meal. You bet he liked it. He's got to be clever enough to pick someone who's going to do that. It's perfectly safe.

It was the consensus of opinion among Lou's friends that Lou's obsessive misery came from his family. 'His parents are totally dismissive of his achievements, and it's very irritating,' observed one. 'His parents are very insulated,' explained another friend. 'They're really, really straight. For example, they never travelled. On one occasion they had planned a trip to Hawaii. But they disliked it so much on their first day they just went back to Long Island the next day. They could not relate to what he was doing at all. They couldn't accept anything about the reality of his life. They thought Sylvia was a nice girl.'

For his part, in the mirror of his family Lou appeared to have changed little since he was a child. He was not afraid of his mother. She was accessible and she did not threaten him, he knew she would always love him. The problem was she was never going to choose him over his father. Lou could not get his head around this idea. It seemed as if he wanted to be afraid of his father as a way of finding conflict. He didn't want to attack his father, but everything he did was a way of repudiating everything Reed *père* stood for. He had, for example, illustrated his refusal to take money seriously by losing it in the sixties and again in the early seventies (even after Sidney had gone to Lou's manager's office to sort the paperwork out). When Lou did have money he spent it in a fashion that suggested he couldn't get rid of it fast enough. Living with Rachel had been another way of saying to his father, 'See, I repudiate everything!' By introducing Sylvia to his parents he raised the prospect of supplying them with grandchildren and a continuation of the Reed line. It was an effective trap that would soon give Lou another way to disappoint them. The Reeds clearly understood Lou in 1979 better than they had twenty years earlier when they had dispatched him to Creedmore. Still, Lou's friends felt that he really loved his father, and hoped the old man would live long enough to get some gratification, if Lou could ever open up to him. Lou did love his little sister, as he would make clear in a song with that title, but even she had incurred the Reedian wrath when she got married to a man whom Lou celebrated in another song for being big, fat and without a brain. Sylvia discovered that there was actually no basis for an active relationship between Lou and his family, who were too close-minded to really accept him.

In a move that signalled another kind of return to his roots, Lou bought a sizeable property in rural Blairstown, New Jersey. There he could fish on a man-made lake, shoot hoops in his back yard, and follow his latest diet of fresh fruit and nuts. The move led so-called friends to smirk that Lou was safely 'back in suburbia now'.

The Blairstown property, some eighteen wooded acres approximately one and a half hours from New York by car, was beautifully situated, but the house itself was nothing more than a simple cabin dating back to the 1930s. Over the years Lou and Sylvia would add several haphazard extensions. Not ready to go completely back to nature, Lou installed a satellite dish and hooked up TVs and other electronic equipment, ranging from a jukebox and computer games to a pinball machine. Video equipment, amplifiers and guitars were stashed everywhere. The master bedroom was cozy, and they had some big comfortable couches in the living room. In the garage, Lou had a collection of vehicles ranging from motorcycles to snowmobiles.

For the most part, Lou entertained himself with inanimate objects, over which he had some control. When not composing songs, he spent his time tinkering with his bike, shooting hoops, working out, and trying biofeedback therapy. Sylvia studied writing at Sarah Lawrence College. Together they worked on video projects and took kung fu classes.

Sylvia's brother was also a help, introducing Lou to Wu-style Tai Chi Chuan, or Chinese boxing. According to Master C. K. Chu:

> Tai Chi enables students to cultivate 'chi' (or 'qi') – the intrinsic energy or life force of the body. The circulation of the chi revitalizes the internal organs and all the biological systems. As an active meditation, Tai Chi promotes the integration of body, mind and emotions. As a result, the student will find he or she is better able to deal with the internal contradictions and external stress.

Lou found it to be 'a sport where the ritual of combat is as important as the outcome. It's an aesthetic and physical discipline that I find exquisite. The discipline is in the ability to relax. It's very beautiful to watch.'

Spending long weekends out of the city with Sylvia and his two dachshunds, Duke and Baron, for the first time since he had been at Syracuse, Reed had plenty of time to think. 'I really love it,' he beamed. 'It smells great. Even if you wanted to do something, there's nothing there. It's appalling how much sleep I get.'

In early February 1980 Lou was back in New York making arrangements for his wedding to Sylvia. The event would signal the beginning of a new life for Lou. Just before the day, the Sex Pistols' Sid Vicious, awaiting trial for murdering his girlfriend, died of a heroin overdose. Asked by a British journalist if Sid died for Lou Reed's sins, the band's singer Johnny Rotten replied, 'Yes. There was that horrible movement from New York to London, and they brought their dirty culture with them. Sid was so impressed by the decadence of it all. God! So dreary. Too many Lou Reed albums I blame it on.'

'If you meet the perfect woman,' Lou said, 'you should pick her up in your arms and dash off with her.' On Valentine's Day, 14

February, Lou Reed and Sylvia Morales, whom he described, invoking Poe, as his 'child bride', got married in Reed's Christopher Street apartment. The vows, written by Lou, were taken from two poems by Delmore Schwartz: 'I used, "Would you perhaps consent to be my many branched little tree?" in my wedding ceremony,' he said. 'I just really adored him and his writing – that you could call up so much in so few words, in very simple language. It serves you well if you're trying to put a lyric in a song, where they go by so quick. A lot of my ideas come from him.'

The formalities were overseen by New York Supreme Court Justice Ernest Rosenberger and witnessed by the families of Sylvia and Lou, Lou's band members, his old Syracuse friend Garland Jefferys, a member of the punk band the Erasers, Susan Springfield, his new manager-lawyer Eric Kronfeld, and the RCA president Bob Summer and his wife.

The wedding marked a break from their pasts for both Lou and Sylvia. Anya wasn't invited. 'They had been best friends since they were like eleven – they were military brats together,' observed one friend. 'One can see Sylvia's point of view because Anya would probably have caused a big scene or done something to really get the attention of everything on her. Sylvia really did have this traditional, calm, sedate sort of wedding. But Anya was really bummed out.'

Another friend of Sylvia's wasn't allowed to attend because he was homosexual. Much to his chagrin, Andy Warhol was not invited either. 'I don't understand why I wasn't invited to the wedding,' he complained in his diary. 'They had a big reception and everything.' According to Glenn O'Brien, 'Andy was totally sentimental about weddings. If Andy wasn't invited it was real deliberate on Lou's part because that's the only person that he wanted there. Lou was trying to punish Andy. Maybe he felt he had to get revenge because Andy had forced him to fall in love with a transvestite. Lou had to break away in order to achieve that hetero bond.'

Lou appeared in wedding photos by Sylvia's friend Roberta

Bayley with Sylvia and his and her parents wearing a suit and tie, looking like a younger version of his father. Lou, thirty-eight but looking, according to those present, nineteen, appeared happy. Sylvia, twenty-four, wore her mother's satin and tulle wedding dress with gardenias in her hair. After the ceremony, everyone toasted the couple, then went off to a nearby restaurant on Barrow Street for wedding cake and champagne. Afterwards Lou and Sylvia changed into casual attire and joined their friends. Piling into limos, they sped off to Times Square where they played pinball at the Broadway Arcade, whose proprietor, Steve Epstein, was a friend. 'You know you won't be stabbed in Steve's place,' commented Lou, who was an avid pinball player. 'I got the highest score I've heard of on the Rolling Stones game,' he boasted. '29,180,880. It's actually a pretty easy game, but I was there two hours getting my 29 million.'

The only ripple in an otherwise perfect wedding was the failure of Mick Rock, who was unable to attend, to take pictures. Lou, who knew how to hold a grudge, was so furious he did not speak to Mick for the next ten years.

To Reed, the wedding marked another attempt to take full control of his life. 'I know now that certain things will get taken care of and looked out for on the home front, where you can get hurt a lot,' he said soberly. 'It's nice to have a trustworthy situation at home, a security situation. It's good to know that you're covered, and beyond just friendship. I'm a great one for commitment. I like to look at centuries past, when knighthood was in flower – I'm still a great one for that.'

In April 1980 in the US and May elsewhere, *Growing Up in Public* was released. The new album once again dealt with Reed's most personal problems. 'Everything on that album is about one particular character, why he's that way, and what causes that kind of viewpoint,' commented Reed. 'I think it's a fairly prevalent attitude and viewpoint that a lot of people grow up with, that I've seen in a lot of people around me. Not necassarily myself – although that's always possible.' Certainly the specifics chronicled in 'Standing on Ceremony' or 'My Old Man' were not strictly autobiographical, but, as Lou suggested, the general tone and sentiment of the songs on the album were inspired by Lou Reed. 'My mother's not dead, and my father never beat my mother – you've got to take it like I'm a writer. I'm not restricted to me. Whether my mother's dead or not really doesn't matter, it's the attitude I'm interested in. I want to express a view, so I manipulate the events to justify the view.'

Despite Arista's aggrandizing trailer for the album, 'There are seven million stories in the city, *Growing Up in Public* is all of them,' the album was not well received, and there was little company support for it. 'Lou Reed is the smartest person regularly recording rock and roll,' wrote Jeff Nesin in *Creem*.

> But one of the great rock singers of the late sixties simply cannot sing any more. Though he uses sharp rhythmic phrasing and some expressive dynamics to disguise the problem, he has no tonal pitch or control any more and a drastically reduced overall range.
>
> I have witnessed Lou Reed in many strange incarnations over the years, but I never could have imagined him as a prattling, self-absorbed Central Park West analysand. No song is utterly without redeeming virtue, but all of them could stand considerable work. As a follow up to the *The Bells*, Reed's best recorded work since *Coney Island Baby*, *Growing Up in Public* is truly depressing, and I wish Lou would get off the couch and back into the streets.

Praise for the Velvets was increasing. In the *New York Times*, Robert Palmer compared Reed and the Velvets to the beat writers of the fifties and sixties. Turning to Reed's latest work, Palmer was more guarded. 'Lou Reed's latest album, *Growing Up in Public*, is reminiscent of some of Jack Kerouac's later books . . . and he runs the risk of veering too close to sentimentality.'

'For the last few years,' Reed said in defence of his music,

> I was working with musicians who were into jazz and funk. I wasn't playing guitar on my records because I really couldn't play with those

guys, being a simple rock-and-roll player. I thought it would be interesting to explore that direction, but there was a gap between me and them. You can hear it on the records. So I said, 'You've carried this experiment far enough. It's not working. The ideas are there and then they disappear, the music isn't consistent, you seem isolated, there's a certain confidence that's not there because you're not really in control.

Now, Lou's long-term strategy of slowly building a large European following paid off when he played 60,000-seat stadiums instead of medium-sized venues. For the first time, Lou made a lot of money touring Europe. June 1980 saw the kick-off of a brief European tour.

Relations between Lou and the band seemed to decline in direct proportion to the growth of his bond with Sylvia. Drugs were off limits on the tour and, though Lou continued to drink, he was toning it down. Not only did Lou maintain tyrannical leadership and control of the band, continually criticizing their performance, but he refused to share the high profits. When they got back to the US, they played some shows in California, but Lou was getting increasingly annoyed with the band.

Lou repeatedly expressed the desire to produce records by other people, perhaps to demonstrate that he was better at it than Cale, but something always went wrong. He had been negotiating with Jim Carroll to produce his second album, after the success of Carroll's *Catholic Boy*. That fell through when Lou started rewriting all Carroll's lyrics, telling him that he didn't know what he was doing, attempted to persuade Carroll's manager to make a record with him and forget Jim Carroll, and then insisted that the whole thing be recorded in Berlin. As one man who attempted to do business with him observed, 'Lou is a lovely person, and one of the most charming people in the world – as long as you don't have to do business with him. As soon as you start working with him he changes into an impossible monster and everything has to be his way, or else.'

One had the feeling that whatever was suggested, Lou would find a way to make it impossible. The next unfortunate candidate for the Lou Reed treatment was his acolyte Chuck Hammer. At first everything seemed fine. Arista was happy for Lou to produce a record by Chuck. Lou and Chuck began meeting daily at Lou's apartment after Sylvia had gone to school. Every morning as they walked his two dogs, Lou would cheerfully begin the day's work by tearing apart each member of the Everyman Band he had been working with for the previous two years. Then Lou's *shpilkes* came to the fore. One by one he fired every musician Hammer wanted to play with. When Hammer remonstrated that these were people who had been with him for years, Lou sneered that he had no choice now but to tell the record company that Chuck was too difficult to work with. The project was abandoned, but there was a cute denouement. When they bumped into each other in the street several months later and shared a cab uptown, Lou made Chuck admit that he had made a mistake and should have done everything Lou told him. (One of Lou's more powerful abilities was to make everybody see things his way.)

According to a close friend, 'Head games were his true life's passion. He had an ability to manipulate other people that is unmatched, at least in my experience. He could not take the responsibility for his life and his mistakes so he spent a lot of time making them the responsibility of other people. He needed a psychiatrist, but there isn't one in this world that's a match for him.'

The year end brought the release by RCA of *Rock and Roll Diary*, a retrospective album which traced Reed's development from the Velvet Underground to the present. 'The full span of impact of a seminal career,' commented *Time* magazine, listing Reed with the Clash, the Ramones, Smokey Robinson and Bruce Springsteen among the best rock of 1980. 'Ultimately, what *Rock and Roll Diary* makes one realize,' wrote John Rockwell in the *New York Times*, 'is the delicate balance between reportage, self-destruction, scorn and compassion in Mr Reed's work.'

Since it was on his old label, who had the rights to the songs, and its cover was a series of Polaroids of himself with Rachel, a relationship he was now denying, Lou had little to do with the album's creation and chose to ignore its appearance on the scene. After a Christmas 1980 show at the Bottom Line in New York, he temporarily stopped performing.

For years, along with Keith Richards, Lou Reed had been on everybody's list as 'rock star most likely to die'. It may be that on some level Reed blamed drugs for his lack of commercial impact in the marketplace. *Growing Up in Public* turned in disappointing sales figures. Certainly the drugs and alcohol were now having a deleterious effect on Reed's appearance. Furthermore, in addition to erratic behaviour on and off stage, he was experiencing problems with his writing and in retaining his ideas. 'It's very difficult to retain things, to learn things and keep track of everything if it starts to get out of control, which it was,' he said. 'Then it got very out of control. So it was just obvious it had to stop. To really get a grip on my career and be true to the talent and everything I like to have control.'

At the beginning of 1981, Lou joined both Alcoholics and Narcotics Anonymous.

The last thing in the world I would be interested in is blowing it, on a personal health level. I think drugs are the single most terrible thing, and if I thought there was anything I could do which I thought might be effective in stopping people dealing in drugs and taking them, I would do it. I just think it's the worst conceivable thing in the world. Before, I didn't care.

To accomplish his radical transformation, Lou needed a period of retreat. For this, his Blairstown estate was ideal. The home – replete with basketball hoop, electronic devices and other toys that gave Lou boyish delight – was the perfect substitute for his parents' house, just as Sylvia was an ideal replacement for Toby Reed.

For a while, struggling to remain sober and married was all he could concentrate on. 'The Last Shot' and 'Bottoming Out', two songs composed during his Blairstown retreat, described a Lou Reed desperate for a drink and reeling from emotional instability.

The AA recruit's desire for alcohol represented the classic conflict between what Lou knew was good for him, and what he craved for release and catharsis. And his resolve was undermined by the reckless, drug-dependent image his audience demanded. In the light of this, he now revealed a remarkable ability to open himself up in front of a different kind of audience: hundreds of other alcoholics and drug addicts. In each AA meeting, one person tells the story of how they became an alcoholic, and what led them to stop drinking. Lou's speech was honest and unadorned. He admitted that while recently riding his motorbike he had spotted a bag of white powder on the side of the road and pulled over in the wild hope that it might be speed. On closer inspection he discovered that it was talcum powder, but ruefully admitted that had it been amphetamine he would have been hard-pressed to leave it there. The anecdote received appreciative laughter and applause for its candid honesty. 'Basically he said being sober was beyond his wildest dreams,' recalled one member who witnessed his AA speech. 'And to hear Lou Reed say that, a guy who achieved a lot, who was cool in everybody's eyes . . . He was very grateful, he was just very regular. He talked about how alcohol and drugs had affected his life and how it still made him stop.' Another friend commented, 'When I went to Narcotics Anonymous Lou was there, I would see him and talk to him at the meetings and he seemed perfectly normal. But he wouldn't hang out afterwards.'

Outside of his contact with people at AA and NA meetings, Lou suspended or ended most of his personal relationships. 'I ran into Lou one night at a movie theatre and we had a very friendly fifteen-minute talk and vowed to get together and I haven't seen him since,' recalled his old Syracuse friend and Eldorados manager, Donald Schupak.

I guess he was sober, clean, straight, hetero, married, lifting weights, looking great. I think one of the rules laid down was no contact with your prior life – like an AA thing. Rather than differentiating between the good contacts and the bad contacts. It was like a cult, you've got to cut off everyone from your past life. It says something that he'd go along with that.

Discipline and control were the central themes in Lou's life, and he was characteristically unapologetic about his new lifestyle. 'I'm not interested in any morality plays,' he said of his attempts to clean up. 'I'm not proselytizing, but as far as my early demise goes, I've made a lot of efforts in the other direction. Such things you might consider dull – working out, playing basketball, keeping my head together and all that. I find destructive people very, very boring, and I'd like to think that I'm not one of them.'

Even though Lou had quit drinking and was attending AA, Sylvia continued to indulge. She didn't see herself as having a problem, claiming that she often went without a drink for days or even weeks without missing it. According to one friend, however, when she did get drunk she could get crazy and out of control. In most respects, though, Sylvia was the epitome of the devoted wife, often submitting to Lou's wishes despite her own. Now, living far from New York and strictly limiting all visitors, Lou could successfully isolate Sylvia. She had transformed from a downtown diva into a 1950s-style housewife. Where once she had said that if he ever broke up with her she would sue him for palimony, the now domesticated Sylvia was happy to be with Lou and was flattered by the songs he wrote about her. 'Sylvia is 100 per cent for Lou,' noted Eric Kronfeld. 'She's supportive. He relies on her a lot. He's certainly happy.'

Sylvia was evidently just what Lou needed; he changed in ways that surprised his old friends. 'Since he got married he's been really happy,' said Mo Tucker, 'which makes me happy. Recently I dropped him a line to say we had a new baby. I didn't expect a reply – I mean, what does he care? – but I got a very sweet letter back.' According to Lou:

> Sylvia's very, very smart, so I have a realistic person I can ask about things: 'Hey, what do you think of this song?' She heped me so much in bringing things together and getting rid of certain things that were bad for me, certain people. I've got help, for the first time in my life

[he had said the same thing about Bettye and Rachel]. I'm surrounded by good, caring, honest business people. In my life, that's a real change. I don't know what I would have done without her.

Sylvia also had a positive influence on his writing. 'There's this real myth, as if by getting married you suddenly become old and senile and move to the suburbs and never do a meaningful piece of work again,' Lou said. 'I envision marriage as the romantic thing it is. How can you write about love when you don't believe in it?'

Lou defended himself against the charge that he had retired to the suburban married life and was no longer a relevant artistic force.

I've run up against resentment in the press about this. Getting married, if you're in rock and roll, seems to strike these people as if you'd been put out to pasture somewhere in the suburbs and stripped bare of your vital organs. Whereas another point of view might be that marriage could revitalize you. It could help you, make you stronger, more insightful, more perceptive, have even more ability to go about doing what you want to do in writing and all that. And make you a better person for it. I have a place in Jersey so I read these things now: 'He's a suburbanite.' It's as though I donated my brain to science and I was now making rock and roll totally on a shallow field: 'Memories of the dark underbelly of New York from before.'

The few friends Lou still saw were characterized by extreme loyalty. Being one of those people who always express astonishment and disbelief that everybody is not following their example, Lou now preferred to socialize with couples. He couldn't understand people who were no longer married. Married was the thing to be, and friends who messed up their marriages found themselves persona non grata at the Reeds'. Even Reed's oldest friends and collaborators remarked on the change. 'We don't keep in touch,' said John Cale. 'He's turned into a regular home bird, settled down on a nice farm out in Jersey. I don't see him. I don't even listen much to what he does.' Andy Warhol, writing in his diary, commented that all Lou was interested in was his rural retreat. Ronnie Cutrone, who visited Lou in the country, told

Warhol that Lou had 'always just bought another motorcycle and another piece of land'.

Blairstown was great for Lou's writing, but

the great breakthrough was the computer. My main thing is rewriting. I can edit in my head pretty well but because of the handwriting and because I don't have the ability to contain one thought for very long, if I'm interrupted, that's it.

I used to seek out extreme situations and live through them. Now I try to avoid them. I've discovered I'm a person who works best when there's no tension. I like to watch other people in extreme situations. I would have made that change all along if I could have.

The change in the lyrical content of his songs was not the only by-product of his new life. Reed also toned down his image in an 'Average Guy' motif.

Some people like to think I'm just this black-leather-clad person in sunglasses. And there's certainly that side of me; I wouldn't want to deny my heritage. But I'm not saying I'm a primitive. I work really hard to make my songs sound like the way people really talk. My concerns are somewhat similar to what Sam Shepard and Martin Scorsese are doing, talking about things that people growing up in the city go through. I'm trying for a kind of urban elegance, set to a beat.

In his Blairstown retreat Lou found himself trying once again to reinvent the setup he'd had at Syracuse – going so far this time as to summon up the ghost of Delmore Schwartz. One night at the cabin Schwartz put in an appearance via a Ouija board. 'Something very strange happened,' recalled Reed. 'After a while we just had to stop, it was becoming too much for me to handle.' The incident did inspire a song, 'My House', in which Lou claimed Delmore Schwarz occupied a guest bedroom.

For a while, the Lou–Sylvia axis worked close to perfectly. She gave him the complete loyalty he needed. He rewarded her by writing songs which really flattered her. And Sylvia got caught up in the myth of Lou and herself as the new John and Yoko.

She could not have understood the price attached to saving Lou's life. Once she got him out of his alcoholic funk, Lou transferred to Sylvia those qualities he would have associated with his mother. Unfortunately, the moment he gave that power to Sylvia, he had to hate her for having it, just as he, for example, hated Cale for having brought his music to fruition in 1965. As soon as Sylvia saved Lou, she set him on the path to separating from her, although in this case, since Sylvia was a tougher customer than he had reckoned, the process would take considerably longer than in the past.

chapter nineteen

The Lou Reed Quartet

1981–1984

[In which Lou joins forces with Robert Quine, records and releases the *The Blue Mask*, records and releases *Legendary Hearts*, and returns to the road where he records *Live in Italy*. Lou then records and releases *New Sensations*, embarks on a lucrative world tour and breaks up with Quine.]

I think he loves his lives and I think he hates them.

ROBERT QUINE

Once Lou was married to Sylvia and had the ghost of Delmore living in his house, all he needed was a third person to complete the triangular collaboration he had favoured since his life with Shelley and Lincoln. In 1981, he found that person in the guitar player Robert Quine. Quine was from Akron, Ohio, where Alan Freed got his start. Though he had gone to law school and become a member of the Missouri Bar, Quine had never practised. Instead, he moved to New York to pursue his love affair with the guitar. A staunch Velvets fan who had seen the band perform numerous times in 1969, Quine had developed a slashing, tension-filled style. 'Lou Reed became such a big influence on my playing,' he recounted. 'He was a true innovator on the guitar who was never appreciated at the time. I completely absorbed his style. I've always liked those basic, simple rock-and-roll changes.' In the space of a few years he hooked up with Richard Hell, formed the Voidoids, and recorded the groundbreaking punk album *Blank Generation*. His spare, impeccably timed sonic assaults were in the vanguard of 1970s punk music. As Robert Palmer wrote in the *New York Times*, 'Robert Quine's solos were like explosions of shredding metal and were over in 30 seconds or so.' His playing was so inspired that he developed a cult following. In one of her best contributions to Reed's career, Sylvia recognized Quine's talents and talked Lou into hiring him.

Quine knew Sylvia through Anya. They were both big Voidoids fans and attended all their shows. 'Around October 1977 we were playing at CBGB's,' he recalled,

> and I didn't know Lou was there, but he was at the front table. We had done a pretty good set and I was walking by the table and he grabbed me and said, 'Man, you're a fucking great guitar player.' Then in early 1981 Sylvia called me, and then he called me, and we got together and had a hamburger at one of those Sheridan Square places. It happened on the day Reagan got shot.

They went to the apartment on Christopher Street. Lou showed Bob a few of his guitars and laid out his plans for a new band, adding that he wanted to play more guitar himself. 'That's absolutely great!' Quine exclaimed spontaneously. Reed quickly discovered that he had found 'a guitarist who could play my way'.

Playing was about the only thing Quine did Lou's way. During the thirty years Reed has fronted bands, after Cale and Nico, Bob Quine was the only person who ever upstaged him. Bob, who dressed conservatively and adopted a laconic stance on stage and off, unlike any other guitar superstar, could have passed for a retiring shoe salesman or pious cleric. His head was mostly bald. His small, tight facial features were shielded by the trademark black sunglasses he wore clamped over his sensitive eyes like a visor and the perennial cigarette that dangled from his lip. The purest of musicians with the highest of standards, Quine let his music speak for him. Whereas he could have passed for Mr

Anonymous in a crowded room, as soon as he played a single, inimitable note on his guitar there was no question that Mr Quine was in control. If an artist's work can be judged by how quickly it is recognized, then Bob Quine was one of the all-time greats. Passionate, generous, vulnerable, Bob was the perfect and much needed musical foil for Lou. On top of that, he was as opinionated and articulate as Reed. For someone who was constantly bored, as Lou was, this provided a big relief. They had endless discussions. A shared love for EC Comics probably bonded them as much as their love for the guitar playing of James Burton.

When Quine showed Reed his collection of vintage horror and science-fiction comic books, in particular a patently gory and offensive series put out by EC Comics,

> Lou really lit up. A typical comic would be a guy jealous of another team player on the baseball team would put poison on his spikes and spike the guy and he dies. So the other guys on the team find out about it and invite the guy to a midnight game and the last few shots are these players playing baseball with this guy's body parts. His intestines are the baselines, his limbs are the bat, head the ball.

In October 1981, they started work on Lou's next solo album, *The Blue Mask*. As Lou saw it:

> Everything shifted around the time of *The Blue Mask*. I was playing guitar with a sympathetic guitar player. A monumental bass player, Fernando Saunders. And Fred Maher on drums. Plus a good engineer. And I'd made some strides in the improvement of the production. I do the writing, that's separate. But when you're working out with the guys, doing the songs, playing, trying to bring it to life, it's a mysterious process – recording. I'll tell you: all really good musicians – forget about the notes they play – it's their tone that's important. They have a certain tone and you're trying to capture it. They work quite hard on it.

Quine recalled:

> Lou gave everyone a demo of him on acoustic guitar. He was playing a lot of open chords in D, which was very nice, but to try and get a second guitar part to complement that was difficult. So I dropped my

tuning a whole step. When he was playing an open D chord I was playing an open E chord. That's partly the reason why that album sounds the way it does.

Quine knew that he was working with a major talent.

There are people like David Bowie or Prince, people who have had millions of books written about them and are regarded widely as geniuses. I would admit that they are creative, intelligent people who have done some worthwhile things, but they are completely second-rate next to some of the things Lou's done. I don't even mention Bruce Springsteen, how could any intelligent person ever like him? But the other two at least could be regarded – still they're not even close to being in the same league as Lou Reed.

Robert Palmer would later write enthusiastically about the band:

The four musicians, especially Mr Reed and Robert Quine on guitars, interact with a sort of empathy and lucidity one expects from a seasoned jazz combo and the music always reaches out to invite the listener in, even at its most intensely personal level. There are no ego contests, no power plays. When he was asked why *The Blue Mask* succeeded so brilliantly where his other albums had been uneven, Mr Reed laughed and said, 'You mean, has there been a tremendous personal change in me that made possible this clarity of vision? No, it's mostly working with the right musicians.'

The way in which Reed worked with and used Quine's abilities to temper his own provides an example of Lou Reed at his best and worst. Reed was an enormously seductive character, not just in a sexual sense but socially. To really *be* with him, to play with him, was a joy for musicians of the calibre of Cale, Chuck Hammer and Bob Quine. And Quine, perhaps more than the others, was such a perfect match for Lou because he knew how to listen to both music and words.

Though he had built his own personal style, Quine also worked from an encyclopedic knowledge of Reed's guitar playing. Within a short time he became the key musician in the creation of the new Lou Reed band. Most importantly, he bolstered Lou's faith in his own guitar playing. As a result, on *The Blue Mask*, for the first time since *WhiteLight/White Heat*, Reed came in with some great guitar solos. Just as David Bowie had given a part of Lou back to himself ten years earlier, Quine urged Reed to take his guitar playing back to his subtle, insightful style. With Quine's help, Reed interpreted most of *The Blue Mask* as guitar songs, relearning much of what he had left behind with the break-up of the Velvets. Rob Bowman speculated in the *Between Thought and Expression* booklet, 'One imagines that major chunks of his being had to be rebuilt and that, to some degree, at least, he had to relearn how to write songs.'

Lou needed receivers – people he could talk to endlessly through the day and night in person or on the phone – just as much as he needed musical collaborators. And Quine, who was, if anything, more articulate and opinionated than Lou, fit the mould almost too well for his own good. Lou loved to talk to Bob. 'Sometimes we talk about the traditions our music comes from. The other day I told Quine, 'There are just these few basic chords in rock and roll, and I've spent all these years just trying to strum these chords right, in a really good traditional way, but souped up a bit.'

Backed by Quine and the excellent new band, Reed was once again on his own rock-and-roll turf. Gone were the experiments with funk and jazz, and the musicians with whom he couldn't play. 'I was alarmed by the last album he had done, *Growing Up in Public*, which was my least favourite of his,' said Quine. 'But he said he didn't want to do anything like that again. He wanted a whole new band, he wanted to play guitar, he wanted a new record company.'

To accentuate the aura of a fresh start, Reed elected to drop Arista in favour of RCA, the company he had left in 1976 in the wake of the infamous *Metal Machine Music*. His superstar success was enough to persuade them that, once again, Reed was a good investment.

To underscore the music's spontaneity, Reed insisted on keeping the studio effects to a minimum. For years his records had been recorded virtually dry with little or no studio enhancement. 'There was a reason for that,' Reed explained.

> I couldn't stand working with these engineers and they were always trying to fuck around with me. At least you essentially got to hear what went down before this guy fucks around with it and takes the fucking guts out of it. I'd rather you heard it with the guts in than with a fucking pop sheen to it. Going back to Andy Warhol, that was the worst of anything that could happen as far as Andy was concerned, that it gets slicked up. I believe that, too. If you want to hear slick shit, my God, you could just buy everybody else.

On *The Blue Mask* – originally called *Heaven and Hell* – Lou would go back to his seminal experience with Andy Warhol and try to make a record that was alive in the studio. He fought for the control of his work that Warhol had handed him on a plate. He chose an engineer who would specifically 'not fuck around with the shit'.

Reed's comfortable relationship with his musicians made for spontaneity and a raw vitality missing from some of his previous albums. 'About a week before going into the studio,' Reed said, 'I got together with the guitar player, and we ran down the songs together. Everyone knew the songs up to a point, but nothing was too structured.' Bob Quine remembered how liberating this approach was. 'We did *The Blue Mask* under very unusual circumstances. Lou gave everyone in the band a cassette of him just strumming these songs on an acoustic guitar, and I was free to come up with whatever I came up with. Total freedom. We went in with no rehearsals. I'd never done a record like this before or since. We went in and ran the songs down and started doing them.'

In October 1981, the band recorded the basic tracks for *The Blue Mask* in less than ten days. For the first time since 1978 and *Street Hassle*, Reed didn't share songwriting credits, and he controlled the mix. Nonetheless, he did share the feeling of success with his new collaborator and friend. 'I remember the first track we did was "My House",' said Quine. 'There was such a sense of elation and relief when he and Sylvia and I went out to dinner. We knew we had it. I wish it had gone on longer on that kind of level.'

Quine was happy with the results. 'None of us had ever played together before, but it just clicked immediately,' he said.

What you hear on the record is totally live. Like 'Waves of Fear', it was one of the best things I ever did. I just let it go. The spontaneity was there. I said to Lou at the end of the song, 'I have an idea for a solo,' and he said, 'Just do it.' There are no overdubs, except one track . . . any mistakes that happened are on that record. If I take a solo, I stop playing rhythm. There's no rhythm-guitar fill going underneath. It's the way they used to do things in the fifties.

This method paid off especially well for Lou, who let go with his strongest guitar solos in years. 'It was a turning point,' continued Quine,

you can hear it on *The Blue Mask* when Lou starts his guitar solo. He did it, and there it was as good as anything he had done ten years earlier. It was like a vindication.

When he approached the end of *The Blue Mask* I saw his confidence increasing day by day and it was a great thing, even when it resulted in things like 'The Heroine' which he did by himself. But he got so exasperated with the band. He said, 'Screw it, I'm doing this myself.' The last few songs he took complete charge of. There was still spontaneity, but even then he saw what was possible. A song like 'Average Guy', which was one of the last songs, he changed the whole chord structure and said, 'Do it this way, this way.'

Working so closely in the studio, Lou and Bob struck up a close relationship, though Quine tried to discourage Lou from calling him fifteen times a day – an invasive habit Lou maintained with all his friends and collaborators. 'We hung out for about six months and we got to be pretty good friends,' recalled Quine, adding,

which may have been a mistake in the long run. Who knows if you should become close friends with the people you work with. But we would go to see horror movies all the time; 3-D was making a comeback and we'd go see all the trashy 3-D horror movies. And he'd drag me to see the crappy kung fu movies in Chinatown. He'd want to watch ten in a row, but I couldn't absorb any more after three or four.

'I remember at the beginning of it I ran into them a couple of times just hanging out together, going out to eat Chinese food, stuff like that,' said Robert Palmer. 'Which is very unusual – I've never run into Lou sort of hanging around the Village way the way you would run into Quine or somebody.'

Quine would often join Lou and Sylvia out in Blairstown.

> As a general rule we just hung around. He had his motorcycle and in the winter he had his snowmobile. I was fairly terrified of the motorcycle. I took one ride with him and decided never again. His eyes aren't that good. We'd sit around and listen to records. I don't think we jammed too much, but he had some nice old ancient Fender amps and stuff out there. They must have been from when he was a kid. And he had a jukebox in his house with a lot of nice oldies on there. He had boxes of 45s in the closet. Pinball. Pool. And he had those dogs. It was sort of like a cabin, but a gigantic cabin with a second floor. Very rustic. It was very nice. But personally I like being close to the ocean, and being in the woods surrounded by ponds, it makes me claustrophobic.

As they spent more and more time together, the friendship spilled over into other areas. Lou had suffered from insomnia for many years. Quine, who also found it hard to go to sleep, had discovered an across-the-counter pill called Unisom, which he turned Reed on to with positive results. Lou was gratified, but when Lou was gratified, resentment was sure to follow.

The Blue Mask was released in February 1982. Lou felt *The Blue Mask* fulfilled his higher literary ambitions, and dedicated it to Delmore Schwartz. 'I spent a lot of time on the song order,' Reed said.

> These things are important. If you can get a feeling of continuity from the album, a feeling of somebody trying to speak to you, that's the difference between a good album and something that's much finer. I'm not above appreciating my own work. And I don't think *The Blue Mask* is just a good album. It's way better than that.

The songs on *The Blue Mask* fall into several categories. 'My House' – about summoning up the spirit of Delmore Schwartz to

Blairstown – and 'The Day John Kennedy Died' take us back to Syracuse and the beginning of Lou's quest. 'Underneath the Bottle' and 'Waves of Fear' chronicle Lou's frightening passage through withdrawal from drugs and alcohol. 'The Blue Mask', 'The Gun' and 'Average Guy' present a series of new definitions of Lou – a man who can stretch from being average to being a complete masochist. The final group, 'Women', 'The Heroine' and 'Heavenly Arms' offer the great misogynist's new view of women through whom he hopes to find redemption. The work holds up well and deserves the rich praise it received both for its reinvigorated music and high standard of lyric content.

Robert Palmer interviewed Lou when the album came out.

I said something very early on like, 'Well, this is really a good one, it is really a high-water mark.' And he said, 'I know that.'

I suspect, and Lou sort of admitted as much, he has a certain inferiority complex about his guitar playing. Because it is, from one point of view, very basic. But from another point of view it's very cool because conceptually he's got the ability to go over the top and then beyond that. The fact that he plays so hard and so intensely and sort of transcends his instrumental limitations.

He was actually still taken enough with his own work to be quoting lines and lyrics. I remember talking about the lyrics to 'Waves of Fear', the one really concrete example, and him pointing out phrases or little parts of it that really gave you a lot of information in very compact series of images.

The thing about *The Blue Mask* that's so impressive in that respect is that he really escaped his own clichés. I think he was in danger there before *The Blue Mask* of just becoming just a total parody of himself. I think he was very well aware of it. I think to a certain extent he was playing the rock-and-roll animal as a role and then the role kind of swallowed him up. Which, as we know, frequently happens. I think there was a definite sense of liberation there – of having escaped from that. It's a very impressive thing to do – especially at that stage in such a long career.

There's one other aspect of vocal influence on Lou that I remember him bringing up, which was his real and intense love of doo-wop. He pointed out during the interview one or two songs on *The Blue Mask* that were very influenced by fifties doo-wop records. You would never hear it just listening to the records because it's set in the middle of this raging guitar noise and stuff. But when he pointed it out to me – 'Heavenly Arms'. That's been a really important source for him all the way through.

Although they failed to compare Lou to Shakespeare, several important critics heaped him with praise. *Trouser Press* compared *The Blue Mask* to John Lennon's *Double Fantasy* and commented, 'Precious few people in rock deserve the accolade of genius, but Lou Reed is surely one of them.' And Robert Palmer in the *New York Times* called *The Blue Mask* Lou's best in years, and the first rock masterpiece of 1982. Later he said:

The thing about Lou's guitar playing is he's able to use all of these nonmusical elements, really screeching feedback, and integrate them into something musical. But, he does tend to ramble. Certainly even on some of the Velvets stuff, to me, the guitar solos – I love what he plays, but sometimes it doesn't seem to have a beginning, middle and an end, it doesn't build. On *The Blue Mask*, Lou's playing is as concise as Quine's. There's a certain kind of real raging thing going on within it yet it's all very directed towards the song.

Between the release of *The Blue Mask* in February and the commencement of work on the next album, *Legendary Hearts*, in the summer, the relationship between Bob Quine and Lou Reed was put to the test. The first cracks appeared when Lou noted that Quine was receiving as much attention as he was in the reviews. Ever since Lou had so unwisely fired Cale from the VU, it had been clear that he could not stand sharing credit. Quine, who was not restricted by the desire to be a star and more singularly focused on the music, was not at first aware of the problem, but even he could not fail to notice Lou's negative reaction when a fan came up to their table in a restaurant and asked Bob for an autograph, ignoring Lou as if he did not know who he was. Lou retaliated like a ten-year-old, grabbing the opportunity to put Quine down to mutual friends. Finding it hard to light upon an intelligent criticism of his playing, Lou was reduced to spitting out really nasty, spiteful, personal, stupid insults about Bob being bald, or something equally puerile.

By the early summer of 1982, Lou began working up material for the next album. However, with his confidence soaring, Lou depended less on his collaborators, and often got angry when they didn't perform as he wished. 'There started to be a slight strain in our friendship,' said Quine. 'He's a strong and intimidating personality, but this didn't keep me from being outspoken at various times. I have a couple of theories about *Legendary Hearts*. It's more of a subdued record.'

On one occasion, said Quine,

when we were doing *Legendary Hearts*, he was doing the vocals for 'Pow Pow' in the vocal booth. He wasn't sure what approach to take so he started going through his catalogue of voices. He said, 'I think I'll do my *Transformer* voice on this one.' It was amazing. He did his voice from *Transformer*, and then he said, 'Nah, I think I'll do my — voice,' and he did three or four. He certainly has a handle on it, but it's a conflict.

Before the album was completed, Lou resorted to an old tried and true trick. Going back into the studio without informing anyone on the record, he remixed the entire album so that his voice and his playing stood out. Some of Quine's best playing was either mixed down so as to be barely distinguishable, or was cut out altogether.

This time around, however, Quine, who smashed the cassette to smithereens with a hammer, was not elated with the results. 'I got very upset when I heard the mix of that album,' he said. 'I ended up working with him for two more years, but things were never the same after that.'

When *Legendary Hearts* was released in March 1983, Lou got a mixed reaction to his latest product. At best, the press embraced the virtues of a new Lou Reed. 'Much of the tension that has made his records and songs compelling, and often unsettling, derived from the apparent dichotomy between his more or less conventional roots and the succession of bizarre roles he has chosen to play,' wrote Robert Palmer in the *New York Times*. 'But recently the two Lou Reeds, one a literate craftsman, the other a self-styled "monster", have been coming together.'

'I was always dissatisfied with the mix on *Legendary Hearts*,' Palmer explained.

> Both on the album and live it seemed like Quine was not quite loud enough. And I think the songs are stronger on *The Blue Mask*. It's more focused and it's got a sharper sense of cutting. Having made that breakthrough with Quine on *The Blue Mask*, it seems like Lou then started being a little self-conscious. And I guess what happens to him when he gets self-conscious is that he starts exercising control. It seemed like there was more and more of him exercising control and less of the music itself controlling it, which you got the impression happened on *The Blue Mask*.

At their worst, the reviews accused Reed of being exactly what he was: over forty, married, countrified, sober – all unacceptable states by rock-and-roll standards. 'Lou ended up doing album after album of reissues of the same song,' said John Cale. And Chris Bohn, writing in the *NME*, saw a more subtle desperation in Reed's latest attempts, 'You can always tell a bad Lou Reed song by the level of urgency he imparts it with.' *Melody Maker* dismissed Reed's work altogether for being 'so out of touch and unreal that it's shocking . . . the most insultingly appalling release in years by any major artist.' *Legendary Heart*'s sales were predictably pallid.

The year 1983 brought new albums from the Police, David Bowie, Talking Heads, and a $28-million contract to the Rolling Stones. In the spring, Mickey Ruskin died, only a few short months after the closing of his most famous club and restaurant, Max's Kansas City.

In February, Lou returned to the road. The tour started at the Bottom Line in New York. There were no drugs or alcohol allowed in the dressing rooms. The first show was filmed for video release as *A Night with Lou Reed*. (Another Quine-era video, entitled *Coney Island Baby*, recorded at the Capitol Theater in New Jersey, was issued in 1987.) What was surprising, however, was the fact that much of the show's material was reworked Velvets and Lou Reed hits. The set included sixties favourites like 'Sunday Morning', 'New Age' and a closing medley of 'Sister Ray' and 'Rock & Roll'. There were also a few improvements, and perhaps an attempt to disguise his commercial turn. Andy Warhol, in the audience the first night, wrote, 'Lou's lyrics you can understand now, and the music was really loud. He did a lot of familiar songs, but you didn't recognize them, they sounded different.'

The shows sold out, and got an overwhelmingly positive response from critics and audience alike. The *New York Times* review gushed: 'The new Lou Reed quartet is one of the most distinctive and powerful bands in all of rock.' Once again, Lou was upset by reviews that singled Quine out for the same amount of praise that he got. In collaborating, Lou was good at sharing the work, but never the praise.

'The music was just ferocious,' Palmer later recalled. 'And you'd look and Quine was sitting there with a bemused expression on his face ripping the stuff out of the guitar and Lou too. There was definitely a sense of Quine pushing Lou as a guitar player and they were really digging that, I felt. I didn't really feel anything competitive between them.'

Lou had not had a musical collaboration on the level he had with Quine since working with John Cale. Interestingly, Quine shared a number of characteristics with Cale. Both men were agoraphobic. Both men were high-strung, emotional people who had a wonderful ability to share their own light with others. These qualities made them both particularly vulnerable to Lou Reed. Lou's reptilian mind loved nothing more than to disassemble such creatures, who were not adept at protecting themselves from his brutal, piercing attacks.

After the resounding success at the Bottom Line, and coaxed by an RCA record offer, Lou decided to take the show to a few cities in Europe where he could fill stadiums. In September 1983, Reed,

Quine, Saunders and Maher made the trip to Italy, where the local RCA Records branch was to tape the shows for a double album – *Live in Italy* – to be released in Europe in early 1984. The album material was taken from dates at the Verona arena and Rome Circo Massimo, where Reed played in front of thousands of screaming fans.

Live in Italy wasn't the finest achievement of the Reed–Quine partnership, though it was still a powerful, if slightly anonymous, double live album. Reed fired up 'Kill Your Sons' as if the scars of the past would never disappear, while Quine helped create a storm of guitar noise on a memorable fifteen-minute medley of 'Some Kinda Love' and 'Sister Ray'. In effect, Reed was presenting a greatest-hits show – half Velvets, half solo – but performed with enough grace to give the concerts a craftsmanlike air.

The British critic Matt Snow wrote:

Lou's going on 42, and *Live in Italy* documents how he regards his history as of September, 1983, just as *Take No Prisoners* did in '79, *Rock 'n' Roll Animal* and *Lou Reed Live* five years before that. And when I say history I mean that seven out of fifteen tracks are the Velvet Underground's greatest hits, and two others are 'Walk on the Wild Side' and 'Satellite of Love'. Of the rest, only two each come from his latest pair of LPs, *The Blue Mask* and *Legendary Hearts*, the latter providing the line-up of musicians who play here. Lou and Quine mesh in an empathetic steel-and-glass grid, an aluminium sound which spirals into jaggedly lyrical solos, even psychedelic as on a stunning 'Kill Your Sons'; Verlaine and Lloyd spring to mind. And, like Television, rhythms are crisp and slightly jazzy.

By now, the tension Reed created between himself and Quine became detrimental to the results. 'Unfortunately they didn't present that band at the best,' recalled Quine.

We were very tense at the first concert, we did not play as well as we could. Only the encore. We had a guitar roadie who would consistently put our guitars out of tune. And the result was almost none of the ballads could be used. We had great arrangements to 'Sunday Morning', 'I'll Be Your Mirror', 'Femme Fatale'.

Another highlight was 'Heroin' at the Rome concert. We were

teargassed at that one and we were playing Circus Maximus – an outdoor place. Apparently a crowd had gathered outside the fence before the concert and the police dispersed them using teargas the moment before we came out. When we came on stage the wind blew the teargas directly on us. So during the first forty-five minutes of the show I could not see a thing. I could not even see the little dots on the neck of my guitar. And there was snot running down my face and they were throwing wine bottles full of piss on the stage. People said we were really brave to stay on stage, but we had to. There would have been a riot. There were God knows how many of them. And it was a pretty emotional performance.

For his next album, *New Sensations*, Reed recorded from December 1983 through February 1984. Robert Quine, who by now had suffered through a major falling-out with Lou, was not involved. It was the same way Lou had behaved towards all of his worthwhile collaborators – rather than being grateful, he resented them. At the last minute, he told Quine that he didn't need his help with the project. 'It's very complicated,' said Quine, 'but maybe he just wanted to try doing the guitar himself.'

Lou's inability to continue the fruitful collaboration with Quine had negative results comparable to his firing Cale. In dumping Quine, Lou came across to friends as a cutthroat Machiavelli. 'With Quine it was a little too even for Lou,' said one friend. 'Bob is a really smart guy, a little bit too equal. So that had to go.' Another friend recalled, 'Bob gave Lou a lot of musical credibility and really good musical direction and then Lou just fucked up the friendship. Lou really couldn't handle having a friend. Lou doesn't have any friends, he just wants a guy to sit around and listen to him discussing equipment, guitars, recording and just go, "Really, really, really . . ."' Officially, Reed told the press Quine wasn't available for the sessions because he was recording his own solo album, *Basic*.

'Quine hated every minute of playing with Lou after *Legendary Hearts*,' recounted one close friend.

He thought that Lou was losing it. Their falling out had to do with Lou's megalomania, with stealing credit. Lou would enjoy hurting Quine, humiliating him. There were real problems in the music. Although he adored Quine and was using Quine, he was jealous of him. It was obvious. He was jealous of him as a guitar player. If Quine would come up with something great, Lou was jealous. I mean, he was a jealous person. The impression I got was that he was a really fucked-up, vindictive, sick . . .

'Miserable' was his favourite word for Lou. Not just once, not just twice, many, many times. Lou Reed was the incarnation of misery. For many people misery is an attractive, seductive subject. Teenagers identify with suffering, basically. The thing that's intriguing about a lot of Lou's music is that it makes suffering happy. He celebrates it. And the music itself is catchy, it's dancey, and so it's embracing the suffering, making it lovable. But in embracing it, you're not trying to change it, you're just dressing it up, you're recognizing it and you're wallowing in it. Lou wallows in it, and he makes sure everybody else is wallowing in it. Maybe he got stuck in it because it became his subject matter. It's a self-fulfilling prophecy. That's what misery's about, it's about obsessiveness. The nature of being a miserable person requires that you obsess about it. And you do this over and over and over, and you absorb things and turn them in on yourself.

New Sensations was released in 1984. The album's single, 'I Love You, Suzanne', was released with 'Vicious' as a B-side. 'I Love You, Suzanne' captured significant radio airtime and MTV video play. A second video, 'My Red Joystick', boosted sales of Lou Reed albums present and past. Where sales of *The Blue Mask* and *Legendary Hearts* were disappointing, the two reaching only 169 and 159 on *Billboard's* LP chart respectively, *New Sensations* peaked at 56, his best showing since *Coney Island Baby. New Sensations* was also number nine in the *Village Voice* albums-of-the-year poll.

Hand in hand with the Reeds' move towards a more commercial career came a physical move from downtown Christopher Street to a high-rise on the Upper West Side, at 81st Street and West End Avenue. The new home was not, however, to provide them with the harmony they had experienced on Christopher Street.

Robert Quine was brought back for the *New Sensations* world tour of 1984, restoring the band to the five-man line-up that had given the 1979 tours their high pitch. 'He called me to go out on tour in early '84,' recalled Quine, who signed on more for the money than anything else. 'I thought it was fairly curious to be asked to go out and support this record. And his manager Eric Kronfeld was shocked and amused that I accepted.' The keyboard player Peter Wood signed on for the tour along with Fernando Saunders, though Fred Maher was replaced on drums by Lenny Ferrari.

Ferrari gave an amusing account of his first meeting with Lou. 'I go to the session and I walk in and there's Robert Quine, Fernando Saunders, Lou and myself,' he recalled.

The first thing Lou says to me is, 'The last thing I want to do is audition a drummer.'

And I looked at him and said, 'But you called me!'

We didn't know each other yet. I could see he was annoyed he had to audition somebody. So after I get to meet everybody he says, 'OK – I usually like to start out with "Sweet Jane".'

I said, 'Excuse my ignorance here, but "Sweet Jane", what's that?' Robert Quine's sort of holding his hand over his mouth, and Fernando Saunders sort of knew what I was saying because he's an R&B player too. Lou looked startled that I had said this – like it was the bible or something, and I later found out it was. So I said, 'Hey, Lou, never mind, just hum a few bars and I'll fake it.'

Robert Quine falls over laughing and Fernando said, 'I can't believe you just said this to Lou.'

So Lou counted it off and I sort of figured it out that this was my first song with him and they're gonna try and mess me up and see if I'm gonna hold the beat, which, as a drummer, is your main job. So I just locked into the beat and they tried to pull the rhythm against me and I felt it but I just held strong. After he does this Lou stopped and said, 'Gee, we were trying to mess you up and you didn't move, so I was wondering if you'd like to do a world tour with us starting in two weeks?' It was sort of serious and hilarious at the same time. We did eight days of rehearsal.

'I saw Quine shortly before he went on the tour,' recounted a close friend.

He was anxietized. He agreed to go on the tour, but had made a lot of demands on Lou. Quine was a passionate person, deeply and profoundly emotional. He loved Lou's music. He gave him back himself. He was very bitter about the fact that Lou did not give him credit for that, and in fact went in the other direction to put him down. The only good thing about the trip was the playing part. The before and after he hated. Lou was a sick person. A mean person. I had a sense that he derived great pleasure out of hurting people. Not just any old people, though, people who threatened something in his own sense of self. For example, if Quine had too much integrity, he would make Lou face his own lack of it. Quine would be a reminder to him of certain things about himself that he couldn't face, so he would lash out at Quine and try to hurt him. And because Quine was such a lovely person, such a polite person, he was an easy target.

'We did America in the first two months,' recalled Lenny Ferrari.

Lou was moody and it was a crucial point in his life. At the beginning of the tour he pissed Quine off by saying, 'No sunglasses on this tour.' Every day he was a different person. He was being Mr Clean. We weren't allowed to do anything, we couldn't have a drink, actually we couldn't have any fun so we renamed it the No Sensation tour. The whole band was not having a good time together. Quine also called it the No Sensation tour. Lou didn't want the temptation back in his life. Nobody was drinking. Except the manager was sneaking it, and the bodyguards. And the crew members were having fun. We had about sixty dates around the world. There were sixty parties scheduled but he cancelled fifty-eight of them so we only had a party in New York and LA. We were not allowed to have any fun so it was a business thing, which was OK with me.

'It would be a drag sometimes because we would be so isolated there would be nowhere to go and nothing to do,' said Quine. 'We'd be in the airport Hilton in Rome with no car. I'd be looking out the window at Rome – I hadn't seen it in thirty years.'

'We'd get back to the hotel and talk about the show,' recalled

Ferrari. 'It was business. There wasn't any passion. Lou's a square. A week before I got the call from Lou I had decided to quit smoking grass, which was about the extent of my drug taking, and maybe a glass of wine. But after four months, five months, man, we were crying – you're crying for some fun.'

Aside from being forbidden drugs, alcohol and after-concert partying, the band members felt Lou's nervousness in other ways. To prepare for a show Lou would hang out with Sylvia in the dressing room, smoke a few cigarettes and do some Tai Chi to calm down. But on stage, he would often lash out at various band members, leaving them humiliated and angry. For the first part of the tour he took out his frustrations on the new kid, Ferrari. Then he switched to Wood and Saunders and, finally, Quine.

But these incidents were more than offset by the good pay and per diem expenses for his band members. Moreover, the group was housed in the finest hotels, fed in the finest restaurants and transported by limousines.

Still, Lou's mania for maintaining complete control over his environment got on their nerves. 'Everything was Lou's way,' said Ferrari.

I knew Sylvia from the TV party days before she met Lou. And she liked the way I dressed, and would be saying, 'Lou, look at that suit he's got on.' And Lou would start getting a little uptight, 'cause he was like in a leather jacket and it looked like I was in a different band, and I didn't want that to be the case. So I was trying to dress down. I would wear just a cravat instead of a tie. But I just didn't want to wear blue jeans. I wore blue jeans in Vietnam, I didn't want to wear blue jeans in civilian life.

There were many funny moments on stage when Lou was very honest with the audience. We were playing some college, a music school somewhere, and Lou said, 'You probably figured it out, I'm playing the same song over and over and changing the lyrics.' Another funny thing was, Lou would say to me, 'I couldn't believe it, I'm singing an older song and I'm making up the lyrics 'cause I can't remember them and then the audience is singing the right lyrics and I'm reading their lips.'

When we played the Beacon Theater in New York on what was Lou's biggest tour of the time, the Beacon was sold out three or four days. We were given two names each per night on the guest list. So the first night I had Andy [Warhol] and Jean-Michel Basquiat and when I put the names down Eric Kronfeld made sure Lou didn't see Andy's name down there or I would have been on the shit list.

He gave me *ageda*. That's an Italian term for an upset stomach. I have to say Lou was a strange bird. He would never pump up the band members. Eric Kronfeld told me, we were in LA and *Entertainment Tonight* were interviewing him after a show and they said, 'Who's your tremendous drummer?' and he told them to scratch that from the tape.

He acted like a dick so many times on stage. He felt he was under pressure and he released it on me, the new kid.

Despite the friction within the band and Lou's new bid for sobriety, the tour managed to reach its Olympian moments. ' "Am I glad to see you," said a lean and clean Lou Reed to last week's crowd at the Beacon Theater in New York before launching into "Waiting for the Man",' wrote one reviewer.

The feeling was mutual. But the show's real centrepiece was Reed's brilliant orange guitar. He couldn't keep his hands off the instrument, only shifting it to his back to hitch-hike his way through 'Walk on the Wild Side', soloing seraphically in 'Legendary Hearts' and 'New Sensations', and goading Saunders and especially Quine to increasingly dazzling flights. Indeed, Quine's playing was practically an illegal stimulant, sending the band rushing back into a song after every solo.

But other critics felt Lou had lost a lot of his former edge. A reviewer for the *Washington Post*, noting that 'Lou Reed has no stage moves and not much of a voice', commented that Lou managed to transfix the crowd anyway. Ferrari had also noticed Reed's awkward stage presence, and joked that when he tried to clap his hands Lou looked like the comedian Jerry Lewis.

'I don't think I'm a pop star,' Lou told the British journalist Jessica Berens in London, where he was playing two nights at the 4,500-capacity Brixton Academy. 'Domestic bliss is a little difficult to associate with the over made-up *minceur* and high priest of oblivion who symbolizes the decadence of the Warhol Factory,' she wrote. 'However, marital stability has helped to free him from drugs and Reed is straight (in every sense of the word) at last.'

'Now I combine a love for rock and roll with a love of writing,' he told her. 'It's a very rare art and I'm not kidding one word I've ever written.' To the question 'How does it feel to be more famous than rich?' he replied, 'Commercial success would mean that people were enjoying the records, and I don't make them for myself. If only fame could pay the rent.'

Ferrari, who went from resenting Lou to feeling that he wanted to give him a hug when he saw him, realized Lou was extremely ambivalent in his feelings about other people, swinging from hot to cold and from kindness to cruelty in a matter of seconds. 'It's interesting that he wrote the bible on hip but personally he was not hip,' the drummer remembered.

> He was just intelligent enough to know what was hip. I think that's what led to his longevity in the music industry.
>
> Lou tried not to get close to anyone. He said to me, 'I already have enough friends, I don't need any more.' It was stressful, because the only thing he'd say to me is he'd turn around and say, 'Play harder', and I was playing harder than you can imagine. I was breaking everything and I broke two snare drum stands, which I'd never done before in my life. One time in Germany my roadie comes out and was saving the day by holding the snare drum. His ears are in there without earplugs, and the band is playing loud and the snare drum is ear-piercing, so I'm worried about his ears, and Lou knows this, yet Lou turned around and said, 'Play harder.' If I wasn't such a professional I would have put my sticks down and walked offstage because that was just inhumane. He didn't respect that roadie who was saving the show that night in Düsseldorf.

But Ferrari also remembered times when Lou could relax and enjoy his company.

> Then we went to Australia. We were in Perth, Perth is lovely, it was warm. And Lou just looked at me one day while we were at the beach

and said, 'They really have it down, here.' There was always moments like that – when he was really with you.

Lou and I went out and had a bite to eat a few times. It was very amicable – Sylvia was there. And as usual, Lou [just like his father] would divide the check up, he would never pick the check up. I used to say, 'Give me the check, I'll take it.' Lou wanted to hang out with us, but we didn't want to hang out with him. Peter Wood had his wife, so now it's the honeymoon tour, Peter and his wife and Lou and Sylvia. They were always doing things together to the point that we were a little ill about it. And they wanted us to go to the zoo with them, to a petting farm, as a band, to pet the koala bears or something. I just couldn't bring myself to suffer that much. We passed it up. But when they came back they were sure to tell us about it.

It was a passionate, intellectual group of people. The music was simple, but the personalities were complex. Nobody was mean to each other, but it was the underlying thing with Robert Quine and Lou, we knew that was there. They were headed for a big break-up and it was that tour that did it. Quine and Reed were like the odd couple. It was a love–hate relationship. Mostly the love was coming from Lou. And Quine hated to go on tour. He's a funny guy, he's a sleeper and he acts like he's not on top of things completely. The only thing that held Lou and Bob together was Quine's infatuation with Jim Burton. He was Quine's favourite guitarist and ended up becoming Lou's favourite guitarist and whenever we would have a tour bus to take us to the hotel from the airport or something, it was all that was played on the bus. I felt like Lou was into it to brown-nose Quine. Lou really wanted to get tight with Quine, but Quine wasn't letting it happen. No matter what. Still to this day I'll run into Quine and he'll have something not nice to say about Reed. I don't even want to tell you what Quine was saying.

Lou was starting to get off on playing the guitar solos a bit more. Quine was a master of the obscure notes, and Lou was catching the groove and at times it was very good. When it was good I would let him know. And then Lou would tell Quine, 'I'm gonna take this solo in this song again.' And then he was torturing Quine to the point where Quine said, 'Well, what do you want from an ex-junkie homo?' [Quine denies saying this.] The way Quine delivers a line, he's so cold-faced and so intellectually witty that you start to pee your pants because he's so funny.

A big fight in Australia [in December 1984] ended it. That's when Quine was coming off the stage getting really upset because Lou was stepping on Quine's turf. Lou was taking all the solos. And then Lou cancelled Japan.

'There was a definitive break right at the end of the tour,' Quine confirmed.

He has his version and I had mine, but it was a major falling-out. Allegedly over musical problems. It's nothing that didn't happen with other members of the band, but I wouldn't stand for it. I will not take shit from anyone. Whether he had his reasons for being annoyed with me – I'm hardly a saint, but I did deliver the goods. By the second concert in Australia I called my wife and said I'm certainly never playing with him again, ever. I like to think I stoically endured it, but he was not a moron, he probably saw my attitude. Some stupid little incidents happened. The last thing we did was a concert in New Zealand. We were doing 'Sunday Morning'. It was pretty much just the two of us – the bass and drums and keyboards were just so subdued. And I was looking out into the crowd thinking, This is a total drag. I'm never going to play this song with him ever again. And that's the end of the story.

chapter twenty

The Legendary Lou Reed

1984–1987

[In which Lou appears in a
series of advertisements,
writes film music, plays
benefit concerts for altruistic
causes such as Amnesty
International, and records
and releases *Mistrial*.]

Who else could make a scooter hip?

LOU REED

Ever since making *New Sensations*, Lou had become increasingly
visible. Besides the interviews he gave for the album, Lou began
attending private and public functions which, intended or not,
served to keep his name in the press. In February 1984, for example,
he attended a banquet with seventy-five other guests at the Limelight
club in New York to honour William Burroughs's seventieth
birthday, where he sat at Burroughs's table with Kurt Vonnegut and
Edie Kerouac (the beat writer's first wife), looking uptight.

Throughout the summer of 1984, videos for 'I Love You,
Suzanne' and 'My Red Joystick' appeared repeatedly on MTV,
and Lou was the subject of an hour-long Rock Influences show
where he invited the Chantelles to perform their girl-group classic
'Maybe', performed himself and was interviewed by the series
host Carla DeVito. In August, he joined James Brown, George
Clinton, Peter Wolf (who had left the J. Geils Band the previous

year to go solo) and Madonna on the artists' panel of the New Music Seminar in New York. They discussed industry issues like the impact of new technology on rock and the $30 ticket ceiling on that year's Jacksons tour.

In September, Lou acted as MC for part of the Manhattan Poetry Video Contest at Joseph Papp's Public Theater where Allen Ginsberg, among others, performed his works. A week later, on Friday 14, he was spotted at the MTV music awards by Andy Warhol, who noted in his diary, 'I don't understand Lou, why he doesn't talk to me now.'

At the end of 1984 Lou also did interviews on the CBS Morning News, Cable News Network's Sandy Freeman show, and on another cable channel, USA, which did a profile of Reed with his *New Sensations* videos and a brief interview.

In early 1985, after returning from the *New Sensations* world tour, Lou signed an advertising contract with Honda Motor Scooters. With 'Walk on the Wild Side' playing in the background, the quick-cut heavy TV ad, directed by Steve Horn, showed a leather-clad Lou wearing shades perched on a scooter in a variety of Manhattan locations. The official line, 'Take a walk on the wild side,' came from Mr Neil Leventhal, Honda's motor-scooter manager, who proclaimed, 'Reed is an innovator – one of the pioneers of new music. His music is unique and experimental – much like scooters.'

When they appeared in June, the Honda commercials were widely reviewed. 'Rock singer Lou Reed flings off his sunglasses, unbuttons his jacket and with a cool stare declares, "Don't Settle For Walking!"' read one. 'Posed astride a red, two-passenger scooter in front of New York City music club the Bottom Line, Reed is the latest in a string of unusual celebrities [like Miles Davis and Devo] Honda has chosen to advertise its scooters.' The commercial became one of the most acclaimed ads filmed in New York. In addition to the TV spots, Honda ran a full-page colour ad of Lou astride the bike by Manhattan's Hudson River docks in several prominent magazines. Honda reported the commercials helped sell as many as 60,000 scooters. This kind of exposure was a surer sign of commercial success than anything Reed had ever done.

Although some members of the rock press found the spot ironic, snapping, 'Do they have any idea what kind of song they're using to sell scooters?', it was clear that Reed and his signature song had become integrated into the mainstream. Not only had Reed's lyrics lost their bite, but Lou, too, was approaching the same fate.

That spring, another step in Lou's climb up the ladder towards mass recognition and acceptance took place at L'Expo, a French computer exposition which featured the latest in technological advances and the brochures marketing them. Among them was a brochure from IBM featuring the first official software recognizing Lou Reed, the Velvets, the Clash and the Sex Pistols, among others, on what *PC* magazine called the first 'punk computer'.

In May 1985, Lou signed a contract with American Express to advertise their credit cards. Lou, appearing beneath the tag line 'How to buy a jacket' in print ads aimed at college students, posed casually in his trademark leather jacket and shades. The ads directly addressed the audience he had been cultivating with his MTV appearances. He appeared to have few qualms about selling out in return for the money and exposure. 'Look who's recording you – the same companies who manufacture missiles,' he argued in his defence. 'You could really start tearing it apart.' Besides, he said, 'the thing that I would like to do at this time in my life is the thing that would sell out.'

Reed's drive for media exposure and increasing revenue was aided by Sylvia, who ran a campaign to further her husband's career. Apart from commercials, Sylvia had Lou doing a rash of interviews, TV spots, films, public appearances, celebrity concert tours and assorted publicity outings, culminating in hundreds of mentions of Lou and his work in virtually every media venue available. Their efforts helped sell Lou Reed's latest product, and renewed interest in his large back catalogue.

Lou accepted assignments to write songs for other projects which appeared to have little in common with his own work. In the early 1980s, he had accepted a commission to write songs for an album called *Music from the Elder* by the glitter-metal group Kiss.

'Lou was so into the project that when we called him and explained it over the phone to him, he said, "I'll get back to you in an hour,"' recounted Paul Stanley, Kiss's lead guitarist. 'And he called back an hour later with good basic lyrics to "Mr Blackwell", "World Without Heroes" and a lot of other stuff that hasn't been used yet.'

'It's fascinating and flattering,' Reed expounded, 'to be given a set of characters or whatever and be asked to write songs around them.' His enthusiasm for the project, however, was not shared by the media. It was Kiss's worst-selling album since 1974. The negativity was due, in part, to the declining reputation of glam bands, who were seen as passé. 'Yes, a Kiss album, can you believe it?' commented a reviewer in *What Goes On*. 'I assume Lou did this for the bucks, not a very good excuse for such a piece of trash. It's a long way down from "European Son" to this.'

In the mid-1980s, Lou attempted to develop this vein by contributing songs to, and in some cases appearances in, four films. In 1984, he contributed 'Little Sister' to the film *Get Crazy*, and made a playful comment about aging rock stars by appearing in his first scene in the famous Dylan pose on the cover of *Bringing It All Back Home* – though in his version, Reed was covered with cobwebs. The song was well received despite the film's failure. In 1985 Lou contributed another song, 'Something Happened', to the film *Permanent Record*. In 1986 he wrote a zany, three-chord dance track reminiscent of his 1964 Pickwick compositions, 'Hot Hips', for the film *Perfect*, starring John Travolta and Jamie Lee Curtis. The same year he came up with a disco number, 'My Love Is Chemical', for the film *White Nights*, starring Mikhail Baryshnikov. The director Taylor Hackford felt Reed's song gave depth to Baryshnikov's character. 'When they're alone in the dance studio, you expect him to put on Mozart and instead he puts on Lou Reed.' Late in the year, Lou contributed a song to a rock cartoon, *Rock and Rule*. The soundtrack also included songs from Debbie Harry, Iggy Pop and other punk performers.

Despite the commercial and critical failure of all but *White Nights*, Lou enjoyed the work, declaring, 'I really love it if someone wants me to contribute a performance or a song and they give me a subject.' Taking a line from a book that had particularly influenced him, *The Philosophy of Andy Warhol*, he continued, 'And it's even better if they tell me what kind of attitude they want. I can divorce myself from it completely.' Reviewers, however, saw Reed's film flirtation as a bald-faced bid for exposure. '*White Nights*' sound track,' sniffed the *Los Angeles Times*, 'is a perfectly acceptable, standard-issue film sound-track album, which means it's got a big hit ballad (Phil Collins and Marilyn Martin's 'Separate Lives') and songs from quality performers working below their potential (John Hiatt, Lou Reed, Nile Rodgers).'

Reed found greater success in branching out when he stuck to the medium he excelled in. Joining another star-studded project in the early summer of 1985, including Sting, Tom Waits and Marianne Faithfull, he recorded Kurt Weill's 'September Song' for a tribute to the German composer most famously associated with Bertolt Brecht. It was a project he felt particularly close to. 'I want to be a rock-and-roll Kurt Weill,' said Lou, who seemed unaware that Weill was not a lyricist.

> My interest – all the way back with the Velvets – has been one really simple guiding light idea: take rock and roll, the pop format, and make it for adults. With subject matter written for adults so adults, like myself, could listen to it. There is the theory that really good rock and roll is all below the waist. The theory continues – if I understand it right – that as you introduce any other kind of thought to it it starts to stutter and become less rock and roll, less danceable, less everything. Until it's no fun at all. There is that point of view. Then there's my point of view that says if you do it right you should be able to have everything you had before and – if you want it – you should be able to have these other levels. I'm trying to resolve that problem of how to keep it a rock and roll record. That's my primary interest.

By the mid 1980s Lou had come full circle. The release of his recording of the Weill song on the album *Lost in the Stars* coincided with another strong resurgence of interest in the VU, largely perhaps because culturally in New York, the first half of the eighties was a re-run of the first half of the sixties.

In the 1980s, the international scene saw the emergence of a new wave of rock and roll heavily influenced by such groups as the Velvet Underground. Many new, post-punk and experimental bands, previously relegated to college and alternative (indie, or independent) charts, began to break into the mainstream. As happens so often in rock, truly inventive and progressive bands become popular only after years of existence in the marketplace, and after their songs have been rerecorded and their sound widely imitated. By 1985, British bands ranging from the Smiths, Echo and the Bunnymen, Lloyd Cole and the Commotions and Simple Minds to a host of other chart-toppers paid tribute to Reed and the Velvets. Morrissey, then lead singer of the Smiths, for example, was called a 'reasonable post-liberation version of the early Lou Reed'. The Scotsman Lloyd Cole owed a large debt to Lou Reed, as his singing voice evoked Reed and his material was redolent of what the *LA Times* called the 'sparse, beat-era expressionism of the Velvet Underground'. Responding to comparisons drawn between him and Lou Reed, though, Cole told the *LA Times*, 'I don't think we've got a lot in common other than we don't sing properly and we've both got small vocal ranges.' Jim Kerr, Simple Minds' lead singer, claimed Reed as one of his greatest influences. Simple Minds performed a bunch of cover songs, doing a poorly received version of 'Street Hassle' on their 1984 hit album *Sparkle in the Rain*.

Similarly, there were quite a few American bands who, by the mid-eighties, had brought the Velvets' work a degree of fame. Ric Ocasek of the Cars was often compared to Reed in voice and delivery, and the singer also claimed many of the same beat-generation roots as Reed. His first solo work, *Beatitude*, was to be taken as meaning 'beat attitude'. Georgia's REM with Michael Stipe also drew Velvet comparisons, and often performed such Velvets material as 'Femme Fatale' and 'Pale Blue Eyes'. The

Violent Femmes' Lou Reed–derived vocal style put them on top of the college charts in 1986. More cutting-edge eighties rockers were bands like Sonic Youth and Scotland's Jesus and Mary Chain, who developed the Velvets' love of feedback and drone. Contemporary groups like Nirvana, Jane's Addiction, and the Cowboy Junkies, embryonic in the mid-eighties, would bring the Velvet influence into the 1990s. 'The Velvet Underground were so far ahead of their time,' wrote Lynden Barber in *Melody Maker* in 1984, 'that hearing them now it seems scarcely believable that they're not a contemporary group.'

In fact, there were so many VU-influenced bands on the scene that Sterling Morrison commented, 'I didn't really think about my years with the Velvets much until recently, when the climate seemed the same again. With New Wave, the music went back to the people who were kind of screwing around on records, who knew they couldn't possibly achieve mass appeal, and didn't care. I was looking at all these little punk bands and thinking, "Well, there goes us again."' Even Moe Tucker felt the effect of this proliferation. 'Stuck out here [Tucson, Arizona] in the middle of nowhere, the only friends we have are my husband's, from work. But quite a few of them have heard of the Velvets, and they're impressed.'

The Velvets and Lou Reed influence had also crossed the boundaries into other art forms. The US playwright Sam Shepard was a drummer in a band called Lothar and the Hand People, who had apparently opened for the Velvets one night in an experience that would shape his later work in the theatre. Reed wrote a song about Shepard in the mid-eighties: 'Doin' the Things That We Want To'. The fashion designer Rifat Ozbek, 'who dressed like a rock-and-roll animal at school' and who would be the rising star on the fashion scene in 1987, attributed many of his designs to the Lou Reed influence.

In the wake of the July 1985 Live Aid concert, the Reeds saw the opportunity to join in with what was fast becoming the greatest rock media blitzes of all time – the mega-charity concerts of the mid-eighties. Lou's most famous quote about rock and politics had been made from the stage at the Bottom Line in 1977 when he'd snapped, 'Give me an issue, I'll give you a tissue, wipe my ass with it.' He certainly hadn't been recruited into any political party in the 1970s, being, if anything, a political liability. He made a tentative entry into politics in 1984, singing backup vocals on Carly Simon's theme song for the disastrous Democratic Convention that summer, 'Turn the Tide', alongside Shirley MacLaine, Mia Farrow, Dick Cavett, Mary Travers and Phoebe Snow. But when Bob Dylan invited Lou to play the Farm Aid benefit on 22 September 1985, he jumped, delivering a blistering set.

On the country-musician-heavy bill next to Johnny Cash and Willie Nelson, and lined up for performance between George Jones and Loretta Lynn, Lou's presence sparked humorous speculation on whether he and John Denver might team up for a duet on 'Rocky Mountain High'. Reed gave plenty of interviews without saying much. 'What's it like playing with all these country artists?' asked one interviewer. 'I'll tell ya, two guitars, bass and drums,' replied Lou blankly. Addressing the issue in more detail, he told David Fricke of *Rolling Stone* that he had overcome his city-dweller attitude and could appreciate the problems the farmers were having. 'I'd show up out there in Blairstown and go, "What the fuck is going on? It's raining here. What is this, another weekend with rain?" Finally they sat me down to tell me the facts of life, such as there are farmers out there and they're getting killed by the drought. I became aware of what weather means, besides New Yorkers going away for the weekend.' However, there were more than a few cynics who questioned Reed's use of a charity event to gain publicity. 'How do people in New York perceive Farm Aid?' asked one journalist who appeared to be surprised to see Lou in Champaign, Illinois. 'I don't know how the people in New York perceive anything,' Lou riposted. 'We're like snowflakes, we're all different.' Farm Aid eventually generated $50 million to help save 2.3 million American farmers from over $212 billion of debts.

Once Lou got going in a new direction, he couldn't be stopped. No sooner had he done Farm Aid than he volunteered to take part in the Artists United Against Apartheid Sun City project. He sang one line on the record 'Ain't Gonna Play Sun City', a multiracial effort headed by 'Little' Steven Van Zandt, who had left Springsteen's E Street Band the previous year. The Sun City gang comprised artists from a variety of musical disciplines, and included Dylan, Springsteen, Jackson Browne, Bono of U2, Jimmy Cliff, Kurtis Blow, Run DMC and Afrika Bambaataa. Besides the record, the Sun City project released a video, a book and eventually a concert campaign to force the release of the South African nationalist leader Nelson Mandela. An acquaintance of Reed's, the Panamanian superstar Rubén Blades, whose lyrics were on a par with Reed's, had suggested that Lou take part in the effort. 'I couldn't not be vocal about apartheid,' Lou explained. The organization got more than they bargained for when Lou came to the studio and started advising them on how to produce the record. The *LA Times* called the album 'a refreshing attack on the practice of isolating musicians by category'. Lou appeared in the video of the song and was also in several scenes of the documentary *The Making of Sun City*.

On 13 November, the reclusive Bob Dylan attended an exclusive party honouring his achievements at New York's Whitney Museum. His guest list featured dozens of rock-and-rollers, including Lou Reed, Pete Townshend, Billy Joel, Little Steven, Dave Stewart, Ian Hunter, David Bowie, Roy Orbison, Yoko Ono, Judy Collins and members of the E Street Band, as well as the writer Kurt Vonnegut Jr, the artists Andy Warhol and Keith Haring, the filmmakers Robert DeNiro, Brian DePalma and Martin Scorsese, and the actors Mary Beth Hurt and Griffin Dunne. 'There's no way you can be a pop artist today or do anything in contemporary music without being influenced by Bob Dylan,' said Billy Joel. Dylan was photographed with an uncomfortable-looking Reed on the steps of the museum.

During the sixties and seventies, Lou had been an outspoken critic of Bob Dylan. However, since cleaning up his act he had made a point of aligning himself with the man whose mantle he sometimes felt was his to such an extent that he had made his friend Jim Carroll remove negative remarks he had made about Dylan from Carroll's *Downtown Diaries*. Dylan, whose camp had been at war with Warhol's in the sixties, had been mending his own fences in the 1980s and singled out both Andy and Lou for thanks and praise in interviews. Lou was one of the few living songwriters, he said, whose work always moved him.

At the beginning of 1986, Lou recorded *Mistrial*. After doing four albums with RCA he once again became dissatisfied with their handling of his work and determined to find another label. It was also the last record he would make with Fernando Saunders – although they would play the Grammies together in 1988. *Mistrial* marked the end of another period in Reed's career.

The album, released in April 1986, was designed to follow up on the pop vein originally tapped into by *New Sensations*. RCA released a promo tape called *He's Got a Rock and Roll Heart* based on an MTV interview and a number of remixes and special editions of his songs. In addition to Reed's customary print interviews, on 19 May he was on the *David Letterman Late Night* talk show, along with the basketball player Michael Jordan and the actor Alan Alda, promoting *Mistrial* and its single, 'Video Violence'.

Mistrial, the lowest rung of Lou's mid-eighties trilogy commencing with *Legendary Hearts*, received bored reviews and ran into problems. The video for its second single, 'No Money Down', was cut from the MTV play list for being too violent. It contained a segment where a Lou Reed look-alike robot has its face torn apart, which Lou thought was hysterically funny. 'My wife didn't,' he reported gleefully. 'My mother felt the same way. She looked at it and said, "What can I say, Lou? I'm sure it's very clever, but I don't like seeing that happen."'

That summer Lou partially redeemed himself by making his strongest altruistic commitment when he joined a tour celebrating the twenty-fifth anniversary of Amnesty International, the human-rights organization that seeks the release of prisoners of conscience throughout the world.

Although the Reeds' commitment to Amnesty International fit neatly into their commercialization campaign – AI offered participation in a highly visible series of stadium concerts across the US, Europe and Asia with some of the biggest stars around – Lou's continuing work with the programme grew not only in involvement, but also in intensity. Perhaps because he often saw himself as a persecuted artist, he could sympathize with others who suffered for their convictions. 'I had never been a member of a group besides a rock band,' he said. 'But I've joined Amnesty International.'

By the time the Conspiracy of Hope tour kicked off on 4 June at the Cow Palace in San Francisco in front of 13,000 fans, the permanent line-up included Lou Reed, U2, Sting, Bryan Adams, Peter Gabriel, Joan Baez and the Neville Brothers. Guests who popped up along the way included Bob Dylan, Tom Petty, Jackson Browne, Bob Geldof, Dave Stewart and the comedian Robin Williams. During the course of the tour, Lou would be called a great guitar player by some of the greatest guitar players ever. At the Amnesty concerts, he was introduced as 'the legendary Lou Reed'.

Reed managed to slip some of the new material, such as 'Video Violence', into his Amnesty set, but remained dependent on the old stand-by 'Walk on the Wild Side'. According to the *New York Times*, 'With Baez, the obligatory "do-gooder", out of the way, the crowd was happy to move on to some rock and roll ably provided by Lou Reed. One of rock's genuine originals, Reed and his band performed 'I Love You, Suzanne', 'Turn to Me' and 'Walk on the Wild Side' to the crowd's appreciative cries of "Loooooooo."' At the end of each show he joined the ensemble in performances of freedom-oriented songs such as 'Biko' and 'I Shall Be Released'. Along the way, barnstorming across the country in the tour's Boeing 707, he composed a song called 'Voices of Freedom' for the Amnesty cause – again sparked by his friend Rubén Blades – which he premiered at the European shows.

Ironically, despite Lou's heartfelt involvement, several members of the press were more cynical about this venture than they had been about Farm Aid or Sun City, openly questioning his motives for enlisting. 'Lou Reed is a washed-up ex-rocker who couldn't fill my garage with paying fans,' commented a particularly riled journalist. 'Somehow he managed to cash in on a Honda Scooter commercial, and now he's turned up on television and the Amnesty tour with his latest product, *Mistrial*, in tow.' And another scowled, 'The Amnesty line-up consisted of such superstars as Sting, U2, Peter Gabriel, the Neville Brothers, and other has-beens such as Lou Reed, Jackson Browne and Joan Baez also attempting to rekindle their flagging careers.' Even positive reviews were tinged with similar sentiments, as in the *New York Times*, 'These concerts also helped seasoned, consistently creative artists like Mr Gabriel and Mr Reed reach the wider audience their work has long merited.'

On the road Lou cemented his friendship with Bono, whom he had met on the Sun City project, urging him to read 'a really great short story', Delmore Schwartz's 'In Dreams Begin Responsibilities'. According to U2's biographer Eamon Dunphy, 'There was a part of Bono that could have lived where Reed had lived, in the drug-induced twilight of New York City. Reed understood what U2's music was trying to say, the difference between freedom and responsibility.'

Bonded by the cause, mutual respect, as well as 'fun' (a word he used to counteract criticism of his intentions), a strong sense of camaraderie developed between the musicians. When the Amnesty tour arrived in Atlanta, Georgia, they celebrated at the Ramada Renaissance Bar. When the house band finished their set, a number of the Amnesty musicians jumped on stage. 'Bono, high on the absurdity of the night, got up to sing. He started Lou Reed's "Sweet Jane" and sang it to a raunchy young lady posing at the bar,' wrote Dunphy.

They jammed the night away, Baez, Gabriel, Adams, the Neville Brothers, Larry, Adam and Bono. When they heard about it the next day Lou Reed and Edge were sorry to have missed it. 'If you ever do that again, be sure to wake me,' Reed chastised Bono. 'Okay, we'll do it again tonight,' Bono replied. Only this time it was contrived. The magic was missing on Tuesday night. But not the pleasure. Reed was one of Bono's heroes. Bono had been no great record collector when he was young, but one of the few good records he had was of the Velvet Underground . . . Bono called on Lou to play the next night at the Ramada. Reed, after much persuasion, shyly consented, offering rare renditions of 'Sweet Jane' and 'Vicious'.

Amnesty International's annual report the following year said that although governments were responding to increasing pressure to respect human rights, there 'is a gulf between commitments and reality'. At a news conference attended by Paul Simon, Lou Reed and Little Steven, the human-rights group also introduced former prisoners of conscience, including Yuri F. Orlov, a Soviet dissident, who described their experiences. Lou gave his support to the Amnesty programme called Freedom Writers under which people were asked to write letters to heads of government appealing for the release of specific political prisoners. Between shows on the 1986 tour, Reed also found time to join Sting in a protest over the US execution for murder of Jerome Bowden, a man who was mentally retarded.

The subtlety of the new Lou and the Amnesty gigs may have been lost on the fans. When asked what Amnesty International was all about, one of them replied, 'Doesn't it help people who have lost their memories?' Reed made a stab at explaining. 'In a country where Reagan is president, it is very easy to be cynical,' he said. 'But I'm really fascinated about why people are arrested and what happens to them in jail. I mean, for the rock-and-roll records I've made, I'd be dead ten times over if I was over there.'

On 15 June, after two weeks of sold-out touring across the country, the concert's core perfomers mustered their combined efforts and enthusiasm for a grand finale. From noon until midnight MTV presented, live from Giants' Stadium in East Rutherford, New Jersey, the last show in the Conspiracy of Hope tour. Lou, who had done his set earlier, returned to the stage during U2's set to join Bono and the rest of the band in the antiapartheid song 'Sun City'.

At the end of the month, Reed was back on the road, touring behind the *Mistrial* effort. 'The most surprising thing about Lou Reed's Monday night 19 August concert at the Universal Amphitheater was that the hall was only half-filled,' commented one reviewer. 'Those who attended, however, saw what amounts to Lou Reed's Rock and Roll Survivor Travelling Roadshow – nearly two hours' worth of two-chord rockers, third-person story-songs and seven tunes off his latest album, *Mistrial*.'

In October, Lou teamed up with Sam Moore of Sam and Dave to record the duo's 1960s smash 'Soul Man' for a film of the same title. 'What I like about this new version is that Lou didn't come in to copy Dave,' said Sam. 'He does it his way – that kind of talk singing. This is better than the original!' A video made from film clips to publicize the soundtrack album was relased that month. The song eventually gave Lou his first hit record in Britain since 1973.

In the autumn of 1986, Lou was recruited into RAD, a series of MTV Rock Against Drugs public-service announcements, joining the ranks of ex-drug-addict rock stars behind slogans such as 'Drugs suck'. Although eager to participate, Reed was concerned about being hypocritical:

I had a lot of problems with that spot. When all these rock people make these announcements – 'I did it, you shouldn't' – my attitude when I was out on the street was now he's had his fucking fun, and he's going to turn around and say, 'Don't have any fun because I tell you it's not worth it.' Who the fuck are you to tell me anything? I was prefacing it, saying, 'I don't want to tell you what to do, but speaking for myself, da, da, da . . .' And the director said, 'Lou, no offence, but this is aimed at eight-year-olds. You do that and they'll go to sleep.' So I thought about it, and that's when I came up with what I said: 'I did drugs . . . Don't you.'

UPI reported in November 1986:

Lou Reed's wife was a bit on the riled side when a group of college students dropped by the rock singer's house – apparently unannounced – in Hardwick Township, NJ. Seven students from Somerset County College went to the rock singer's home to ask if he would perform at Home Aid, a benefit for the county's first shelter for the homeless. 'His wife answered the door,' said Clair Wargaski, one of the students. 'We left as soon as she showed her displeasure with our being there. We didn't have a chance to explain anything.' State police were called in to shoo the students away and the firm that provides security at Reed's home has since called the students demanding an apology. 'Lou is a very private person,' said RCA Records publicist Pat Baird. The incident left student Regina Black disaffected. 'I'm going to give away all my Lou Reed albums,' she said.

As 1986 drew to a close, the sporadic *Mistrial* publicity was on hiatus, as were the Amnesty tours. To keep his schedule full, Lou concentrated on more collaborations. Tipping his hat to an early influence, he joined his friend the bass player Bob Wasserman on a version of Frank Sinatra's 'One for My Baby', which wound up on Wasserman's *Duets* album. Lou also worked through early 1987 with Rubén Blades on the latter's first English-language record, *Nothing but the Truth*. 'Lou and I finished a draft for a song about a son coming back to a painful reunion with his parents,' Blades recounted. While Blades sat in the library of Reed's New Jersey home, Lou played the melody to the song on his guitar in the music room above him. The tune prompted Blades to write some lyrics, and from this partnership came 'The Calm Before the Storm'. 'We were both emotionally exhausted,' he recalled. 'I almost had an anxiety attack that night.'

On 22 December, Lou joined rockers from the Soviet Union, the US, Europe, Africa and Japan at the Japanese Jingu Baseball Stadium before some 32,000 listeners in a benefit concert the performers called Hurricane Irene after the name of a Greek peace goddess, at the close of a two-day UN International Year of Peace Conference. Hurricane Irene's aim was to raise public awareness as well as money to establish a computer-based information network at the University for Peace in Costa Rica.

At the beginning of 1987 Reed flew to London to play the yearly

Amnesty International benefit, the Secret Policeman's Third Ball, with Peter Gabriel, Duran Duran, Mark Knopfler, Jackson Browne and many others at the London Palladium. Reed performed 'Voices of Freedom', accompanied by Rick Bell on sax with Peter Gabriel and Youssou N'Dour contributing background vocals. Lou was not without his own following at the show, and his set was continually beset with a barrage of calls for 'Heroin' and 'Sweet Jane'. Lou played a mix of new and old material which included 'Rock & Roll', 'I Love You, Suzanne', 'No Money Down', 'Walk on the Wild Side' and 'Video Violence'. Lou also contributed background vocals to Gabriel's 'Biko' on the *Secret Policeman's Third Ball* album released later that year, as was the Amnesty concert film of the same name.

By May Lou was back on the road in the US, promoting *Mistrial* again. That summer his tour met up with U2 in Europe. This was the first time Lou had ever worked as a support act at a commercial concert. Interestingly, in a dramatic departure from his days with Clive Davis and Arista, the usually reticent Reed eagerly accepted the U2 singer Bono's suggestion on how to commercialize his work while performing to U2's fans. 'The audience come in completely fresh – "Gee, what's this?" ' he said.

It's interesting that I connect with them. Sometimes, with an audience like that, I try to cut down the songs that have a lot of words, or maybe ease them into it. I'll give you an example. We're doing 'Street Hassle'. Bono loves 'Street Hassle'. And after we did it one night, he told me, 'You know, if you sang "sha-la-la-la" more, the audience would sing along with it. That's the fun part of the song; I love it when you do that. Stay with it – they'll love it.' Next time out, I did that – changed the words around and did the 'sha-la-la-la' more. Sure enough, they really liked it. Funnily enough, I liked it, too.

In October, as a mark of his final acceptance, *Rolling Stone* magazine's twentieth-anniversary issue came out carrying long interviews with Mick Jagger, Paul McCartney and Lou Reed, among others, and the Syracuse local paper published an interview with a Scottish punk rocker who had demanded to know whether there was a 'monument to Lou Reed at Syracuse University'. Around the same time, one of Lou's instructors, the poet Phillip Booth, recalled discovering such a monument in the English Department men's room where somebody had scrawled LOU REED SHAT HERE above the toilet.

In December, Reed played a benefit concert for homeless children in New York. His concern for the city's problems would increase during the coming years, and he would devote his next album, *New York*, to the subject. The event, held at Madison Square Garden, was organized by Paul Simon. The first of a number of celebrity surprises came when Debbie Harry and Grace Jones introduced Lou Reed, and sang backup on 'Tell It to Your Heart', 'New Sensations' and 'Walk on the Wild Side'. Reed, in turn, introduced Dion, who sang 'The Wanderer' and 'Run-around Sue'. Then Dion was joined onstage by Reed, Paul Simon, Rubén Blades, James Taylor, Billy Joel and Bruce Springsteen, who called themselves – after Dion's legendary group – the Belmonts. As they sang Dion's 'Lonely Teenager', the crowd leaped to its feet and went bananas. 'These guys all loved being Belmonts,' Dion marvelled, adding, 'Lou Reed, it was like, he knew the part.'

Sylvia had been remarkably successful, where so many before her had failed, at turning Lou into a moneymaking machine. Lou had at last acquired the funds to make him secure for the rest of his life. He had also gained the widespread acclaim and recognition he had always wanted – in short, he could believe that he controlled everything and everyone he saw. The problem was that the more commercially successful, the less artistically successful he became. The guitarist and composer Glenn Branca ranted:

> Lou Reed is a wasted, mediocre, half-assed nothing who came along and ripped off somebody else's idea and turned it into something that somehow clicked with a few of the idiot critics and has made a career for someone who never should have had a fucking career in the first place and to me his music has proven that to be true.

'I think his records are less than they could be, and also that we'd do it better,' said Moe Tucker.

I just don't really like many of his songs since he left the group. Not that I loved every song that we ever did, but I truly enjoyed, and still do, and like our songs as interpreted by the four of us. I just don't like his music that much. I like what could be done with them, the lyrics, some of them. But I do think that we, just because of who we were, the four of us, interpreted his music the best way. I wish he'd play more feedback guitar. I wish he'd play his guitar the way he can. I wish he wouldn't be quite so slick in a lot of his stuff.

chapter twenty-one   # The Crowning Achievement

1987–1992

[In which Andy Warhol dies, and Lou records and releases *New York*, and *Magic and Loss*.]

How long do you try to do it [make that grand comeback]? At some point you have to actually start doing it. He hasn't been trying to start doing anything as far as I can see. I think he would do a situation comedy at this point if they paid him enough money. Doesn't Lou Reed think he's Delmore Schwartz? Absolutely!

GLENN BRANCA

During the 1980s, Lou's relationship with Warhol had fallen off at the same rate as the quality of his work. Yet, when Warhol surprised the world for the last time by suddenly dying at the age of fifty-nine, in February 1987, Lou was stunned into silence. He released no albums in 1987 and 1988, after having put out one a year for twenty years. Eventually, Lou responded to Warhol's death with the trilogy *New York*, *Songs for Drella* and *Magic and Loss*. It was a moral and creative task which he carried out with élan.

Second in significance only to the final end of Lou's protracted love for Shelley in 1978 was the curtain coming down on his relationship with his father figure Andy Warhol. Still hurting from Reed's refusal to hand over the money due him from their early collaboration, and envious of Reed's commercial success, Warhol had stepped up his critical remarks and cold-shouldering of his former protégé. People in Warhol's entourage recalled Warhol treating Lou 'very, very badly' on several occasions when Reed had visited the Factory in the 1970s, which, considering how mean Andy could be when he put his mind to it, is a pretty chilling description. According to another Factory acolyte,

> Lou totally idolized Andy and Andy rejected Lou very deliberately so that Lou was aware of it. And so Lou always had to be the kind of prodigal son, who was trying to prove himself to Andy. See, if Andy liked you he rejected you in that way. He did it to everyone who worked for him. And then he would go and put everybody down to everybody else, so he would say, 'What's wrong with Lou, he's so talented, it's such a waste.' I don't think Lou ever outgrew Andy.

According to Lou, the final break came late in 1981 when he and Sylvia were riding in a car with Warhol.

> It was snowing out and the driver was speeding. I asked him to slow down. Andy turned to me and in a fey, arch, whiny voice said, 'You wouldn't have said that a few years ago.' He was being so evil I never spoke to him again. He stirred me up and he did it on purpose. He got me very mad that he did it. You see, Andy had to be the leader.
> The Factory was a really strange place. People came and went, got used up, then moved on. One particular person became dominant there for a while and I just didn't like what was happening there and stopped going. Andy would moan at me but I really couldn't face it. Things build up between people, but basically – and this is going to sound strange – he just wanted me to call him. On the phone. I'd see him around, but I wouldn't call him.
> We had a very major falling-out. I was in touch, but not close. I didn't want the things I said regurgitated into the diaries I knew he was going to put together. I wanted to have a normal personal conversation with Andy and that wasn't possible. He used to tape record everything, every conversation he ever had, and I didn't want our talk to end up in some publication, which is what would have

happened. He would only talk to me on his terms. Everything always had to be on Andy's terms.

Indeed, Warhol had been recording entries in his diaries for years. In several of them Lou figured. For example, 'I hate Lou Reed more and more, I really do, because he's not giving us any video work.' And he couldn't understand why Lou had turned his back on him. Andy had thought of Lou as a friend and was very hurt. He suspected it had something to do with Lou's marriage, he noted, suggesting that maybe Lou 'didn't want to see peculiar people'.

On 22 February 1987, Andy Warhol died in New York Hospital following a routine gall-bladder operation. Andy's exit forced Lou to confront not only his sense of grief, but the sense of himself he had gained through his association with the pop artist and his entourage at the Factory.

As memories of Warhol and the Factory came flooding back, a shape began to coalesce out of the jumble of images. Retreating to Blairstown, Lou threw himself into a protracted writing binge. He worked like a man freed from a long sleep of vagueness, waking to hunch over his word processor day after day at 5 a.m.

> I suffer from insomnia, I only sleep about three hours a night. So that's when I write. I get up, no one else is around, it's relatively quiet. That's when you can tag in. I'm not getting it from out there, I'm getting it from in here. Everything else doesn't exist.

The album taking shape was, appropriately, a musical sketch of his life in New York.

Writing about the landscape of New York, Lou looked back to the Halloween Parade, and friends who had died of AIDS. Yet he ferreted out the beauty among the decay, and humour and compassion amid the despair.

When the writer Jonathan Cott, one of America's most literate critics, commented to Lou that the New York album was nihilistic and contained not one love song, Reed pointed out the redemption written into 'Dime Store Mystery', which he saw as a love song, 'dedicated to Andy Warhol, whom I really miss and had the privilege to have known.'

'Supposedly when you get older, you get something from all of it before, or you drop dead and that's the end of it,' Reed mused. 'I think I know about certain things better than other people. And I'll fight for it. And I don't think that's being difficult. I mean, it sounds tacky, but it's like being true to your vision.' He told Jonathan Cott:

> I spent almost three months writing those words, and I tried to find a way to surround them properly to get the rhythm of the words working in the right way against the beat, and get the nuances in the vocals so that the listeners could hear the words – that was the *raison d'être* of this record. This is my vision of what a rock-and-roll album can be. Put it this way: I'm writing for an educated or self-educated person who has reached a certain level. I'm not aiming *New York* at fourteen-year-olds.

To emphasize another new beginning, Lou chose this moment to leave RCA and sign with Sire Records, an arm of Warner Brothers that had played a major role in the punk-rock explosion ten years earlier, putting out records by, among others, the Ramones and Talking Heads. Sire was run by Seymour Stein, generally considered to have the most sensitive and intelligent ears in the industry, and certainly someone who knew and understood Lou Reed. A younger version of Clive Davis, Stein was more on Lou's wavelength than any other record-company president he had ever worked with. Their relationship would usher in the most creative and commercially successful period of Lou's entire career.

Lou recorded *New York* in the second half of 1988 working with a new guitar partner, Mike Rathke, who was married to Sylvia's sister, on custom Pensa-Suhr guitars. Rob Wasserman was on bass; Fred Maher and Moe Tucker alternated in the drummer's seat. Lou worked hard getting the words, the music and the sound right, taking longer with this record than anything else he had ever recorded.

New York was released in January 1989, and pitched Lou back into the centre of the rock scene, near the top of the mountain, bringing him legions of new fans and returning to him some who hadn't bought a Lou Reed record for more than a decade. The *New York Times* suggested that it was finally time to 'think about taking him seriously'.

It was also his best-selling album since *Sally Can't Dance*, reaching number one on *Rolling Stone* magazine's college chart and getting into *Billboard*'s top fifty. The reviews were, for the most part, excellent. Jonathan Cott wrote:

> This record provides the perfect musical medium for Reed's highly charged depiction of and verbal onslaught against an AIDS-stricken New York in which friends are continually 'disappearing' – a city of abused children and battered wives; of child police-killers, teenage bigots, and racist preachers; and of thousands of homeless people panhandling, rummaging for food in trash baskets, and sleeping in streets, alleys and doorways. It is a world of hypocrisy, greed, ugliness, selfishness and degradation – in comparison Bob Dylan's *Desolation Row* is like a weekend outing to the Hamptons.

While most of the reviews were positive, a few cutting ones slipped into the press. 'Unfortunately, the product (as record companies call their output) at hand displays just how unsubtle and fuzzy the new Lou Reed's social awareness is,' commented the *Nation*'s music critic. 'There's "Common Ground", a muddled anti-anti-Semite attack on Kurt Waldheim, the Pope and Jesse Jackson. Vet homilies of "Xmas in February"; and the jejune pseudo-myth called "Last Great American Whale".' The *Rolling Stone* and *Daily News* video critic Jim Farber said, 'The 9 million printed raves try to excuse his indefensibly clunky lyrics with some of the most ornate rationalizations in rock-critic history. Apparently, critics feel the need to take this record as seriously as it takes itself.'

'The Velvet Underground sucked from beginning to end, and then they still sucked,' snapped the innovative guitarist Glenn Branca. 'Bon Jovi did New Jersey and Lou Reed does New York. Gimme a break! Lou Reed has been dead for at least ten years. This is a simulacrum; this is not a real person!'

'In *New York*, the Lou Reed image doesn't exist as far as I am concerned,' Reed told Cott. 'This is me speaking as directly as I can to whoever wants to listen to it.'

In the *New Musical Express*, Sean O'Hagen wrote the best review in the British press, describing the album as

one of the hardest, strongest, most cohesive and perfectly realized rock statements of 1989. '*New York* is like this huge person that's shaped me as much as genetics,' Lou Reed tells me in that same deadpan drawl that is his consistent signature. 'This album is a result of a convergence if you like, of everything that went before,' Lou Reed says of his ongoing work in progress. That means all the learning, all the mistakes, all the twisted fuck-ups from a legendary life. Like his friend, Keith Richards, Lou Reed is an individual for whom the term survivor is an understatement. Personal survival is measured against impending social and global collapse with AIDS, pollution and the death of the American dream at the top of the agenda. In this doom-laden context, you keep asking yourself why *New York* is such an, at times, hilarious record? 'Good, good, I'm glad you got to that. People who say, "Oh, Lou is just bitching on and depressin' everybody," they're missin' the point. I mean, it ain't about moral admonishment. Shit, I walk away fast from all that stuff. It's funny and urgent.'

'People don't talk enough about Lou's wit,' said Penn Jillette of the entertainers Penn and Teller. 'Like the tension in a horror movie, there's tremendous proper use of wit.'

So effective was the new Lou Reed that *Rolling Stone* put him on their cover of the 4 May issue. To cap his success, on 10 May the *New York Times* published the lyrics to 'Hold On' from *New York* on the op-ed page.

Lou's euphoria over the album's success was interrupted in February when his friend from Syracuse, Lincoln Swados, was found dead in his East Fourth Street storefront slum apartment. This caused a small sensation and a good deal of local press coverage because of the suggestion that his death was hastened by a greedy landlord who was in the process of forcing Lincoln to abandon the premises so he could renovate. Lou, who had turned his back on Lincoln in the mid-sixties, incurring the wrath of

Swados's sister Elizabeth, made no comment at the time, but would later react in the way he knew best, by writing a moving song about him on *Magic and Loss*.

In the spring of 1990, Lou was invited to sing at Wembley Stadium in London in front of 72,000 people at a benefit for the South African political leader Nelson Mandela, recently released from prison after twenty-seven years. Returning to the folk roots of his college days, Lou performed two songs from the *New York* album, playing an acoustic guitar. Unlike every other act performing that day, Lou made no attempts to meet Mandela or make any statements of his views about the momentous occasion. Instead, he watched Mandela's speech on a backstage TV monitor.

From London he travelled to Prague to interview Czechoslovakia's new president, the writer and former dissident Václav Havel, for *Rolling Stone*. Havel was a big fan of his and in the interview he commented on what an important influence Lou had been on the Czechoslovakian 'velvet' revolution that eventually threw off Soviet domination.

Reed spent half the interview time talking about himself – explaining that he didn't want to play in Prague because he was a very private person who didn't like to have his photo taken, why he didn't like to be interviewed and didn't like to perform in public, and how he insisted on having total control of any situation he was involved in.

'I myself was one of the first three spokesmen of the Charter 77,' Havel explained. 'By this I mean to say that music, underground music, in particular one record by a band called the Velvet Underground, played a rather significant role in the development [of democracy] in our country, and I don't think that many people in the United States have noticed this.'

'He was amazing – the whole thing was amazing! – and I found out how much the Velvet Underground meant to those people in Eastern Europe all these years ago,' boasted Reed. 'They were listening to us, only we just didn't know it.' Not since Delmore

Schwartz or Andy Warhol had he met and been recognized by such a heavyweight character.

Reed later said he was 'dumbstruck' when Havel presented him with one of the 200 hand-printed editions of his lyrics ('From the Velvet Underground straight through'), which had circulated among Czech dissidents in pre-*glasnost* Prague.

After the interview, Lou was invited to play with a local band in a small club in front of Havel and his friends and associates.

> I did a few songs from my *New York* album. I started to leave and Kocar [his guide] asked me if the band could join me. They did and we blazed through some old VU numbers. Any song I called they knew. It was as if Moe, John and Sterl were right there behind me and it was a glorious feeling.

In between *New York* and his next solo album, *Magic and Loss*, Lou, in collaboration with John Cale, made an album called *Songs for Drella*, released in 1990 – which is dealt with in the following chapter.

Reed's *Magic and Loss* focused on the value of lost friendship, a subject which has always been at the core of his writing. The album commemorated the deaths of two close friends in the early 1990s. One was the songwriter Jerome 'Doc' Pomus, whom Reed had befriended in 1988. Pomus had penned hits in the 1950s and 1960s for, among others, Dion and the Belmonts, Elvis Presley and the Drifters. The other friend, Rotten Rita, was the Callas-loving diva in the speed world whom Lou had known since 1966.

> These were people who were inspiring me right through to the last minute [said Lou]. These were people I was lucky to have known all the way through. Within a short period, two of the most important people in my life died from cancer, so the piece is about friendship and how does it transform things.
>
> Though I only got to know him in the last couple of years, I really loved Doc. He was an amazing creature. A mutual friend said we should meet and I only lived two blocks away from him so I started traipsing round. I went to his Writers' Workshop and it was a real

thrill for these people to have their songs edited by him. I went over to talk, but not as much as I wished. It's really sad not being able to call Doc Pomus up right to this day, because he was like the sun. He was just one of those people that you feel good when you're around them. You could be feeling bad, and you go visit them and they say two words and you feel good. But it would have been even worse not to have known him at all. That's part of the whole *Magic and Loss* deal.

It's inspiring to see how a real man and a real woman face death. I could visit Doc while he was going through these extreme medical processes, and I still felt great when I was around him. Both of them made jokes straight through. Unbelievable. I had said there's this great wide-screen colour TV I could get for you, and I'll hook up all the wiring for you, you don't have to worry about any of that. And he said, 'Lou, this is not the time for long-term investments.'

Recording *Magic and Loss*, Reed and Rathke spent 'incalculable hours' in research and refinement. 'I practically studied with some technical people who really helped me out. Because there's millions of choices out there and even if you had a zillion dollars and bought all these to try them, it'd take forever. So you really need someone knowledgeable and talented to guide you. Even down to the kind of tape you record on. I find the sound on this album awe-inspiring.'

Lou finished writing and recording *Magic and Loss* between January and April 1991, and then waited until January 1992 for its release.

'If a song cycle about a friend's death from cancer seems to be the stuff hits are made of, well . . . it's not,' commented one reviewer.

But what *Magic and Loss* lacks in pop appeal is more than made up by emotional impact. With arrangements so skeletal they're barely noticeable, the album stakes everything on its songs. Reed makes them work with sly melodic twists and a well-framed narrative, assuring that we not only understand his emotional turmoil, but share in it. Which, in the end, makes this a perfect modern blues: heartbreaking, thought-provoking, involving as life.

Newsweek called it 'the most grown-up rock record ever made'.

The album received some of the best reviews he had ever had around the world, but there were, as always, some dissenting voices. Adam Sweeting commented:

> Reed has suggested a link between *Magic and Loss* and 1973's *Berlin*, but the telling difference is that the latter mediated its harrowing subject matter through powerful, vivid music. Though *Magic and Loss* touches upon a range of styles, Reed is so immersed in the minutiae of suffering that his musical ideas remain undeveloped, while the subject matter has squeezed out the sardonic wit and throwaway cynicism of his best writing. What's left is a slim volume of morbid verse, set to half-finished music.

While finishing *Magic and Loss*, Reed also completed his selected lyrics and poems, published in the summer of 1991 as *Between Thought and Expression* by Disney's Hyperion Press. 'I took those songs that satisfied two criteria,' said Lou. 'One, that, as most of the lyrics are supposed to do, they did not need the music. They could survive on the printed page. Two, they helped rhythmically advance a narrative, following someone through New York over three decades – the sixties, the seventies and the eighties.' There were also two poems first published in 1976 ('The Slide', 'Since Half the World is H_2O'), and interviews with Václav Havel and the novelist Hubert Selby Jr.

'The collection vividly traces how he swam up and out of his original bookish gloom so cherished by a vanished dropout demimonde,' wrote Milo Miles in the *Voice*.

To publicize the book's release, Lou gave two readings in New York, one at Central Park's Summer Stage in July, the second at the NY Center for Ethnic Studies in November. They were both as successful as his 1971 reading at St Mark's Church had been and harkened back to it also in marking another new beginning of sorts. At the Summer Stage Lou held a crowd of several thousand spellbound on a hot night as his acrid voice recited some of his most famous lyrics devoid of music. He ended both performances with an impassioned reading of material from the as yet unreleased *Magic and Loss*, none of which appeared in the book.

These shocking lyrics tangled the feelings of loss and guilt, gallows humour and dark despair [reported Bobby Surf in the *NME*]. The standing ovation that greeted this unnerving finale was more genuine and heartfelt than anyone connected to this bald promotional stunt could have dared wish for. Here was an audience who recognized an artist at the height of his powers nearly twenty-five years after they were first saluted.

Reed's audience had grown over the years. Many of the early bohemian fans of the Velvets and the gay fans of *Transformer* had stayed with him. They were joined later by supporters of punk rock in the 1970s and of political and vintage rock in the 1980s and 1990s – particularly on college campuses.

In November 1991, Lou made a triumphant visit to London where he was presented with the *Q* magazine Award of Merit for his outstanding contribution to rock music. Reed was introduced to the audience as a man who

> still says, on occasion, that there's nothing to beat two guitars, bass and drums – but his work has broadened our vision of rock's possibilities, forming it into something more real, more literate and more grown-up than we'd probably have settled for otherwise. Scores of musicians will readily admit their debt to this man's influence, and any that won't are probably lying.

In December, RCA released Reed's solo boxed set, also titled *Between Thought and Expression*.

> Bruce Springsteen may be more user-friendly, and Neil Young may own the territory west of the Mississippi, but Lou Reed's loud works of art speak with the same extra-large authority, and burn with the same enduring dedication to authentic feeling and hard answers [wrote a reviewer in the *New Yorker*]. His new greatest-hits boxed set, *Between Thought and Expression*, is an utterly convincing document made up of equal parts of nastiness, tenderness, and sorrow, and it is astonishingly mature from start to finish. When he's playing those songs live, this man is the King of New York.

In 1992, Reed was informed that the French government had decided to make him a knight of the order of arts and letters. On 18

February, he flew to Paris for the investiture ceremony conducted by the French minister of culture, Jack Lang. 'Some have seen you as a star of malaise, perhaps even of evil,' Lang pronounced. 'I prefer to see in you a great poet of our anguish and, perhaps, of our hopes.'

'I'm deeply touched and moved,' Reed responded.

In a world of many negative capabilities, it is wonderful to live long enough to experience something so directly opposite and pristine, something so unilateral which looked at from my age remains thrilling and challenging. I'll tell you what it really is. I think the most important thing in life is art. It's art that I turn to for sustenance. It's the art that elevates things to the finest level where you can go for examples of greatness and that's what I want to try and impart.

Before him lay a world tour on which he would share the emotional transformation of *Magic and Loss*. 'Death is one of the great themes,' he began to tell interviewers.

There's a lot of what you might call violent or vicious songs in my work but I feel compassion for the characters in them. Because I know what it's like to be outside. I know what it's like to have an unhappy childhood. And I delineate these people because either I identify with them or I think they deserve their moment in the sun.

Still, for all its promise of transformation and redemption, *Magic and Loss* was a doleful album that dredged up feelings a lot of people might rather forget. It was the kind of album that people owned but rarely played. And the album's promotional concert tour, though impressive in its dignity and detail, left Lou's fans and critics feeling uncomfortable. According to Lou's dictates, audiences were instructed to listen in stony silence. No one was to smoke, eat, drink, take photographs, talk or react in any way that would break Lou's concentration. If the ticket-holders obeyed, Lou rewarded them with an uptight, highly controlled act which lacked both passion and spontaneity, except in performing 'The Dream' from *Songs for Drella*.

*

Much as Lou had transformed himself professionally, he remained stuck in the same groove personally. Just like everyone else who had taken on the onerous task of being his manager, Sylvia, despite all her hard work and success, fell foul of Lou's temper, often drawing his resentment and wrath. Sylvia, in turn, harboured her own resentment which, as she exercised the power of her position, she was increasingly willing to show. In the midst of all the rock and roll, Lou and Sylvia started reeling from the blows their psyches had been delivering to each other. The competition between them reached an impasse over the question of having children. As Sylvia approached thirty, she told Lou the time had come for them to have children, characterizing it as a great adventure. Lou, however, saw the question of children through realistic eyes. Admitting that it might be fun to have a small version of himself to kick around, he rejected the proposition on the grounds that he had neither the time nor the patience for children. This created a chasm between Lou and Sylvia. She was not prepared to give up the idea of having children. Consequently Lou, perhaps, fearing an accidental pregnancy, stopped sleeping with her. During their final years on the Upper West Side they had separate bedrooms. Sylvia professed to be stunned by the development, telling friends that Lou used to like her and she couldn't understand why he did not seem attracted to her any more. They started to live separate lives, going out with friends rather than each other. Despite the deep fracture, Sylvia continued to play, if anything, a stronger role in Lou's business affairs.

Worse than the lack of sexual intimacy was Lou's growing tendency to use Sylvia as a psychic punching bag. A comparison of photographs of her in 1978, the year they met, and 1992, the year Lou reached his great climax, are starkly revealing. The sultry, sexy girl he had picked up at his S&M society had turned into a rumpled, overweight hausfrau, who looked as if she had for years been beaten mentally and spiritually to a pulp. And when he couldn't take out his frustrations on Sylvia, he found sexual and aggressive release elsewhere. Rumours abounded that Lou was visiting S&M houses, and even there he was considered a bad risk, coming across as too mean and reluctant to tip.

Now that Lou had Sylvia more trapped than he had ever had a woman before, he could torture her all the more for it. After ten years of being Mrs Reed, with all the glamour, power and wealth that went with the title, she had nowhere to turn. Not allowed to make any friends during their marriage, she had also alienated most of the people she dealt with in business matters by becoming rude and aggressive. It was a tendency that would grow worse over the coming years.

Lou, meanwhile, continued to manifest the arrested emotional development that is often the bane of rock stars. Though he could be a most charming person at social functions so long as he was the centre of attention, he became a petulant eight-year-old when the spotlight faded, often insisting on leaving precipitately when the conversation turned away from him.

With his cleaned-up image so celebrated – and remunerated – Lou underwent a period of denial about his past. Many friends reported that, as far as Lou was concerned, he had never been a drug addict or a homosexual. He was straight, he said, and always had been. He didn't take drugs or drink and never had. And anybody who brought up the subject in his presence was thrown out of the room. Since she couldn't bring herself to leave Lou, Sylvia had no choice but to go along with his make-believe. In Lou's world one lived by Lou's rules or perished. Sylvia never seemed to accept, for example, that Lou had ever been gay, referring to Rachel, if at all, as simply another girlfriend. During this period of denial their friends found it increasingly difficult to be around either one of them. As the decade drew to an end, Lou cut off his long-term friendships with the poet Jim Carroll and the painter Ronnie Cutrone, ostensibly because he objected to the fact that the two men had left their wives. Lou chose instead to surround himself with yes-men like Sylvia's brother-in-law Mike Rathke, who massaged his ego with attentiveness and praise.

Ironically, the impending collapse of Lou's marriage did not do him any harm on the professional front. In fact, the worse things got for the Reeds, the more Lou appeared to bask in the across-the-board success he had always craved.

By the time Lou had completed work on *Magic and Loss*, his relationship with Sylvia had reached an impasse. They began to talk about getting a divorce and consulted their respective lawyers. At the beginning of 1993, Lou moved back downtown – to the same block of Christopher Street he had lived on between 1978 and 1983. Shortly thereafter, Sylvia rented an apartment on nearby 10th Street. At her housewarming party in August, Lou made it obvious he was pissed off. Accompanied by Mike Rathke, who was in the process of divorcing Sylvia's sister, Lou turned up a couple of hours late. He entered the flat without a word or glance to anybody, and sequestered himself in the kitchen, feeding on the assorted food and glaring ferociously at anybody who dared enter the room. A short while later he departed without saying a word.

Sylvia had been turned into a mother figure whom Lou could order around. Indeed, it now fell to her to take primary care of the dog, Champion Mr Sox. Any time Lou felt the need for the mutt's company, usually somewhere around three or four in the morning, all he had to do was pick up the phone and Sylvia would come scurrying over with the hapless hound in tow.

'He's got an image to keep up,' said a friend.

Beyond the fact that he's thinking, God, I'm alone, I've got to find somebody else. I'm sure in the middle of the night, that's the reason he calls Sylvia, because that's when it hits him – 'Oh, my God, I'm by myself.' That picture of him on the cover of *Vox* [in May 1993] was so awful. He looks like a ghoul. You heard this thing about his liver. I'm surprised he's still alive.

Whether out of fear of loneliness or his fear of losing a lot of money, Lou suddenly pulled an about-face with Sylvia, deciding he didn't want to proceed with the divorce. Caught once again in a delicate transition between image and album, Lou, aged fifty, could not operate unprotected. As a tough and dedicated manager, an intelligent sounding board, a submissive wife and somebody to bounce anything off, Sylvia had remained remarkably resilient. Even the self-destructive side of Reed must have realized that at this stage of the game he would have been insane to have cut himself loose from her. But there was certainly no plan to resume living or even spending time together.

Still, isolated and in control, Lou had himself to contend with – and his self wasn't good enough. That one thought made up for any torture that could have been inflicted by anyone in the outside world. In *Magic and Loss*, he had said it all. He was stuck with himself and a rage that could hurt him.

chapter twenty-two **I Hate Lou Reed**

1987–1990

[In which Lou joins forces with John Cale, and they record and release *Songs for Drella*.]

Even today he looks unhappy, like a walking disaster. What's wrong with him? He married a man, he married a woman . . .

PAUL MORRISSEY

Throughout Lou's solo career, he had been haunted by the Velvet Underground and had repeatedly toyed with the idea of reforming the band. But his attitude towards John Cale made it impossible. During the first half of the eighties, as Lou's star rose and John's fell, their relationship languished. As Mary Harron pointed out, 'John Cale, who was as brilliant as Lou Reed, has been more consistent [than Lou], but throughout his solo career he has not simply avoided success, but tried to throttle it with both hands.' After Lou married Sylvia, the door that slammed shut on Lou's past closed Cale definitively out of his life.

But by the second half of the 1980s, the two men were drawn back together by circumstances beyond their control. The Velvet Underground seemed to spring to life through the sheer willpower of its fans. In 1978 a young VU enthusiast, Phillip Milstein, started publishing *What Goes On, the Velvet Underground Appreciation Society Magazine*. In 1983, Britain's leading music publisher, Omnibus Press, published the illustrated history of the group, titled *Uptight: The Velvet Underground Story*, which went on to gain an impressive readership, being published in Japan, Germany, Spain, Czechoslovakia and the US. Meanwhile, on college campuses a new generation of rock-and-roll fans discovered the old Velvets albums, venerating the vintage vinyl and newly released discs. In *The 1983 Rolling Stone Guide*, Billy Altman wrote, 'The Velvets' influence hovers over all current music seeking to do more than entertain. Reed's songwriting rang with an honesty and compassion that few songwriters ever reach.' By 1985, there were so many bands that were proud to be indebted to the VU, and so many Lou Reed clones, that a radio station in Los Angeles ran a popular programme called the Battle of the Lou Reeds, and a radio station in Austin, Texas, had a 'Sweet Jane' contest.

The Velvet Underground's famous lost album of 1968, titled *VU*, was discovered in Polydor's vaults, and was remixed and released by that company's new owner, Polygram Records, in February 1985. The favourable critical response to the album must have been confusing to Lou. Just as he was moving into the mainstream at last, after twenty years of hard work, his past was pulling him back into the underground. Juxtaposed to *Mistrial*, *VU*, with Lou's scrappy guitar playing and razor-edged hysterical voice, reminded listeners of what had been lost in the intervening years. The renewed attention to the Velvets was a success for Lou and Sylvia. Still, Lou so wanted to succeed on his solo career that he kept his back turned on the Velvet Underground.

That summer, the BBC was busy making a documentary about the Velvet Underground. Reed, Cale, Morrison, Nico and Tucker also agreed to be filmed for the English television *South Bank Show* which was doing a special on the band's history (aired in 1986). Cale and Nico even indulged in some nostalgic performances for the cameras, but Reed, the only member of the band not to go to the London studios, kept his distance, being interviewed in front of a graffiti-covered building on the street in New York, wearing leather and sunglasses.

One place you could see the band, albeit briefly, was on MTV.

Their 1985 Video Music Awards show featured a segment of Lou outside CBGB's. As Lou told how it was for the VU – 'hadda play small clubs' – and how it is for today's bands, they showed a clip from the black-and-white film *The Velvet Underground and Nico – A Symphony of Sound*. The fifteen-second clip showed the band informally rehearsing, 'children frolicking about,' as Lou described it. 'The Velvet Underground 1966 Courtesy of Andy Warhol' was superimposed on the screen.

'These guys were a great rock-and-roll band,' commented *Stereo Review* in 1985, 'and it's good to hear from them again, even fifteen years after the fact.'

In September 1986, a second compilation of Velvets tracks, *Another View*, was released, feeding off the renewed interest in the now legendary band. 'Yet another surprisingly upbeat, energetic brace of previously unreleased material from this seminal New York band, circa 1969,' wrote *Playboy*. 'And believe it or not, Lou Reed actually sounds as if he's enjoying himself here.'

Along with the resurgence of interest came several crucial business decisions for Lou. *VU* and *Another View* created a flurry of interest and rumours of a reunion. Lou flatly refused to take part, snapping, 'It'll never happen.'

By the mid-eighties, there were so many Velvet lookalikes that Lou could not escape his past. He was increasingly cast as the leader of the Velvet Underground rather than an 'adult' solo artist. His bid to become commercially viable was undercut to some extent by his roots in the anticommercial punk scene, just as his new, clean persona was subverted by the Velvets' legend. This new attention to Reed's early work, however, also paid him homage, helped sell his back catalogue, and placed him in the company of the greatest rock legends. In an article about artists as visionaries, Robert Palmer wrote in the *New York Times*, 'The best artists – such as John Lennon of the Beatles, Lou Reed of the Velvet Underground and Bob Dylan – broke down the barriers, creatively reimagined present-day conditions and future possibilities, and redefined themselves with almost every record release.'

Lou's business entanglements with his former partners multiplied as sales of the VU catalogue increased internationally. While the publishing royalties poured into Lou's coffer, the other band members threatened a lawsuit. None of them was making much money, and Moe, a single mother, was skirting poverty as she brought up her five children in a Georgia small town.

Cale's New York–based British lawyer Christopher Whent, who brought to his profession a sharp legal mind wedded to a love of music, made it his goal to straighten out the VU's tangled legal affairs. He took on representing Maureen and Sterling as well as John. Lou was involved in the matter inasmuch as he admitted that the distribution of VU royalties had been unfairly biased in his favour and he was willing to share some of what was legally his with the others. This gesture opened channels of communication with Morrison that had been closed for years. By 1986, Whent was able to deliver renegotiated contracts to his clients, and they started to receive royalty payments, which, though not enough to live on, considerably improved the lots of Morrison and Tucker. 'The band went into the black with the record company in about '83,' said Whent. 'That's when they started spitting out royalty cheques. It's not a bad chunk of change. Not enough to live on. But a comfortable settlement.'

Still, Lou continued to display an ambivalent attitude to the subject of the VU, cutting off every interviewer who asked him the obvious question, 'Will there be a VU reunion?' with curt answers like, 'I don't believe in high-school reunions.' John thought Lou would never come around. 'I don't really know what that sixties period means to Lou,' he said. 'He's spent so much time saying it was a time of sophomoric activity.'

Then, in February 1987, the death of Andy Warhol caused Lou to admit the Warhol influence. 'Andy had a great effect on my formative years. His way of looking at things I miss. I owe him that. His whole aesthetic. I still wonder, if I look at something new and interesting, oh, I wonder how Andy'd think about that.'

By the time Lou went to Warhol's memorial service at St Patrick's Cathedral in New York on 1 April 1987, he realized how much he missed Andy's vision and humour. Later, at the post-service luncheon, as his recorded voice sung VU tunes over the chattering mob, Lou expected Andy to materialize and say that it all had been a joke. Then he found himself standing on one side of Billy Name, and John Cale was standing on the other. Not knowing that they had hardly spoken in years, Billy drew them both into the orbit of his conversation. Lou and John talked and John felt that the tension between them had eased.

At the same lunch the painter Julian Schnabel told Cale that he should write a memorial for Warhol. Cale spent several months working on an instrumental piece, but discovered that writing about Warhol was not easy. For those who appreciated him, Warhol was such a dominant figure that they feared their work would not measure up to his level. He was also such a mercurial figure that it was hard to capture him in conventional ways.

In May 1988, when he had finished a first run-through, John asked Lou if he would listen to the piece and tell him what he thought. They got together and talked about Andy, filling in gaps in each other's knowledge. Cale, for example, was astonished to discover twenty years later that Lou had fired Andy back in 1967.

I was stunned that Lou fired Andy, I thought Andy left. For Lou to have fired Andy was a real tragedy, a real mistake. Andy gave us the environment to do whatever we wanted and we took full advantage. The next step was to have commercial success. So Andy said, 'I've done this, now you've gotta make up your mind,' you know, shit or get off the pot. Have a hit. And we were very close, y'know, 'Sunday Morning' . . . But there was a lot of pressure on us, and Lou couldn't handle Andy telling him that.

'John Cale and I got together in a little rehearsal place to see how it felt to play and to have some fun,' Reed recalled.

John had already written an instrumental piece for Andy, a mass of sorts, but then the opportunity arose to do the bigger thing. We were both keen because, after talking at length about Andy, there seemed to be a great need for us to put the record straight. The things I was disturbed about with Drella was these evil books presenting Andy Warhol as just a piece of fluff. I wanted to show the Andy I knew. I wouldn't call it working through emotions. There's a craft to all this – it's not just spewing out emotions. It's very ordered and very specific work.

They quickly discovered that the musical chemistry was still there. In the next ten days they composed fourteen chronologically biographical songs. Lou handled the majority of the lyrics while John focused more on the music.

'John and I just rented a small rehearsal studio for three weeks and locked ourselves in,' Reed said. 'I was really excited by the amount of power just two people could get without needing drums,' said Cale, 'because what we have there is such a strong core idea that the simpler the better. I wanted to see if the power was still there between us, and I found out that it was, very quickly. Working with Lou again is enthralling. We're still tiptoeing around, but in all the sessions that we've worked together, the results have been very exciting.'

'I very much like playing with John,' said Reed. 'He's a very exciting musician. It's fun playing with him. We play very well together.'

'It was done by osmosis,' Cale explained.

When we first sat down and started playing, there was this amazing energy – it was aggressive. We sat down and talked about all these memories we had, and then Reed shut himself in with a tape recorder running and showed up later with a kind of summation of what had happened. We sat there and bandied them around. It's difficult for him to collaborate on that level – it's difficult for him to collaborate, period. And he admits it.

They called the collection *Songs for Drella*.

Although the collaboration was eventually successful, it was fraught with problems from the onset. Cale and Reed worked in noncomplementary manners. When Lou went into the studio he worked from a series of lists composed by Sylvia and had to have everything sheduled to the second. Cale, on the other hand, was accustomed to coming into the studio, reading through six newspapers, making a number of international phone calls, then launching himself at the work with ferocity.

'In order for things like that to happen again between Lou and me, we had to go through the same sort of process; we had to play these things over and over just like we had in the past,' said Cale. 'And we did that. But this time we kind of knew what the landscape would look like and we were prepared for those things that we needed to be aware of – the distractions and stuff.'

'Things would be 1,000 times better without that tension,' Lou said. *Drella* was 'an excruciating son-of-a-bitch to write. I did it on my word-processor – what a tool! – and had to do rewrite after rewrite. And all the time I was finding out more about what I really felt about Andy and trying to put that into the right words.'

As he had with Delmore Schwartz, Reed identified strongly with Warhol and focused on the similarities between them so that what was a Warhol biography also became a Reed biography. In public statements, however, he tried to play down the similarities, declaring that *Drella* was 'entirely fictitious', and the words 'A Fiction' were added for its appearance on vinyl.

Eerily, just as Lou and John were working on the collection they received the sad news that on 18 July 1988 Nico had died as unexpectedly as Andy in a bicycle accident on the Spanish island of Ibiza. She was forty-nine.

'Recording *Drella* with Lou was very difficult,' Cale admitted after the event.

> There was a lot of banging heads. It was exhilarating, and working with Lou is never dull, but I wouldn't want to go through it again. I'm much more interested in the spontaneity of playing live.
>
> Lou felt that I didn't appreciate how much effort he had put into the words. He never actually said this to me ... personally. The comment was made to a lot of other people. That was a shocker; it's very difficult to fight with, or argue. If someone thinks that you don't really appreciate what they're doing, well, then what can you say? It's

just a very sad and disappointing turn of events. I mean – and whether you actually base it on anything substantial or not – it's just the clincher.

In the liner notes to the album, however, Cale appeared very appreciative when he wrote, '*Songs for Drella* is a collaboration, the second Lou and I have completed since 1965, and I must say that although I think he did most of the work, he has allowed me to keep a position of dignity in the process.'

In January 1989, Reed and Cale staged two workshop performances of their Warhol suite at St Ann's Church in Brooklyn under the auspices of the church and the Brooklyn Academy of Music. '*Songs for Drella* is a brief musical look at the life of Andy Warhol,' ran the programme notes for the initial performances, 'and is entirely fictitious.' In the small church they created the most enlightened of memorial services for Andy Warhol. They played the fourteen songs in chronological order, gradually building up a prayer-service atmosphere that was perfect for the moment and the setting. Backstage after the show, Billy Name held court once again, finally introducing Lou to his other guru, LaMonte Young.

In the spring, just as John and Lou were putting the finishing touches on *Songs for Drella*, Warhol's *Diaries* were published. Despite the caution he had taken in not talking to Andy, Lou was mentioned some fifteen times in caustically negative entries from the 1980s. The last reference to Lou Reed was, 'I hate Lou more and more.' Asked if it bothered him, Reed replied, 'Not at all. I know Andy; he's like a child. He would have said that in the way a child says, "I really hate you!" It's not meant like real hate.'

Although both Lou and John thought the diaries were an unfitting epitaph to Warhol, they realized how much they captured the artist's quirky personality, and decided to use them in an added song. What they came up with was an imagined diary entry, 'A Dream', in which Cale employs the same tone he used in 'The Gift', but this time using Andy's words about his day, his friends and, ultimately, his death. 'It was John's idea,' said Reed.

He had said, 'Why don't we do a short story like "The Gift"?' But then he went away to Europe saying, 'Hey, Lou, go write a short story.' But I thought, no, not a short story, let's make it a dream. That way we can have Andy do anything we want. Let me tell you, man, it was really hard to do. But once I got into Andy's tone of voice, I was able to write for a long time that way. I got to the point where I was able to, you know, just zip-zip-zip away – just because I really liked that tone so much. It's certainly not my tone of voice at all. I really don't talk that way. I had to make myself get into that way of talking.

Strangely, Lou seems not to have realized that 'A Dream' was not his writing, but mostly a cut-up of quotes from the diaries.

Twenty-three years after getting together to create the sound of the VU, Reed and Cale had pulled off another successful collaboration. What had changed and what hadn't? Cale was still intimidated by Lou and there was a tension between them based on creation and control. Lou wrote the 'Dream' sequence but gave it to Cale to read. It was not coincidental that the only two prose pieces Lou recorded were 'The Gift' (a letter to Shelley Albin) and the 'Dream' letter to Andy Warhol. Cale rose to the occasion, sensitively understanding the nuances of the work for Lou. Writing *Drella* was a healing process for Lou and a difficult challenge because it had to be written in the right tone or else they would be accused of cashing in on the artist's death.

In November 1989, Lou and John performed the completed *Songs for Drella* to a much larger audience at the Brooklyn Academy of Music. The BAM shows got great reviews and set people thinking about a VU reunion again. However, Moe thought Lou still wasn't interested because 'he's worked so hard to get his own career going, and especially with the success of his latest album [*New York*], I really don't think he'd want to plunge in and have everybody talking about the Velvets again'. But Cale saw it differently.

For the time being I'm really happy with the results, now that we've accomplished that and shown that we can do it, we can move ahead to something more challenging. Collaboratively, I think Lou and I could come up with something very imaginative that would be more in the form of a dramatic situation. We're really efficient, and I think we could do anything. I don't think there's a limit.

Songs for Drella was released in April 1990. Reed and Cale shared songwriting credits and split the money fifty-fifty. Some of the tunes, such as 'Nobody Like You', were catchy pop songs, others were dirgelike. 'A Dream' was the outstanding track on the record and in performance. Although after completing *Songs for Drella* Lou swore that he would never, ever work with John again, the album would eventually lead to the reformation of the Velvet Underground.

chapter twenty-three

The Reformation of the Velvet Underground

1993

[In which the Velvet Underground reform, tour Europe, and are, once again, destroyed by Lou.]

You can just say that John Cale was the easygoing one and Lou Reed was the prick.

LOU REED

In the aftermath of Warhol's death, the artist's stock had risen tremendously. Between 1989 and 1990, a retrospective of his work travelled to museums around the world. The original members of the Velvet Underground, along with Billy Name, the Warhol superstar Ultra Violet and the art historian David Bourdon, were invited by the Cartier Foundation to Paris for the inauguration of the Andy Warhol Exposition in June 1990, at which Lou and John performed *Songs for Drella*.

The band's first reformation, which took place at the opening, was largely unexpected. Nick Kent wrote:

Everyone ate separately on their first day together, while Lou Reed announced flatly at a press conference during the same afternoon,

'You'll never get the four of us together on one stage again . . . *ever*. The Velvet Underground is a story.' At the same event, however, John Cale showed himself more open to such a possibility. 'So many ideas were left unfinished in the Velvet Underground. If it's possible to do it again, I think we should really take the bull by the horns . . . I think we have a lot left to give.'

Sterling Morrison found himself in an awkward position. The French journalist Christian Fevret, who met him the evening before the opening in his Paris hotel, recounted:

He was tired, anxious and suddenly became very agitated. He wanted to know what Reed and Cale were playing the next day. 'What a blow for me! What am I supposed to do? Stand at the back of the stage and watch them play – paralysed by bitterness and rage? And what are people going to think? That I can't play guitar any more?' It's another stab in the back, the most cruel yet, for somebody who thinks that his role in the band has been horribly underestimated by history. On the most important day, he is put to one side and humiliated.

'Still, he wanted it on record that "he held nothing against Lou Reed",' added Nick Kent.

He just wanted to play with the Velvet Underground once again. He even brought his guitar over. Only Lou Reed didn't want to play with them.

Lou Reed quite rightly has his own slew of bitterness regarding the Velvet Underground; only he more than anyone else was openly nursing them pretty much up to the last minute. Whatever, he was clearly overtaken by something approximating the spirit of *glasnost* at midday on Friday; for, as some two to three hundred guests were arriving, Reed broke a ten-year silence with Morrison, inviting him, Cale and Tucker all to have lunch together.

Fevret set the scene:

11.30. On the balcony of a private house, isolated at the back of the park, three silhouettes were chatting. The vision of Cale, Morrison and Tucker together was already a bit of an event for those who managed to see it. Three minutes later a pair of dark glasses, curly hair and a leather jacket came forward timidly. He shook Sterling Morrison's hand nervously, even a little reluctantly. The four of them sat down at a balcony table and didn't leave until lunch was over.

3.30. Lou and his wife Sylvia drove a few hundred metres across to an open-air stage. Cale and Reed were supposed to be playing in ten minutes. 'I think it would be nice to ask Sterling and Moe to come up on stage for a while,' said Lou. There was an astonished silence in the car. Even Sylvia Reed was choking. 'And what about doing "Pale Blue Eyes"?' he reckoned, before someone discreetly mentioned that John Cale hadn't been around when they recorded that one. It would be 'Heroin' then.

'The occasion was the grand opening of the Andy Warhol Exposition, a majestic celebration of the artist's art and times', noted another observer. The organizers had not only assembled an unrepeatable collection of Warhol's work, including films like the *Symphony of Sound* portrait of the Velvets in rehearsal which had remained unseen for almost twenty-five years; they had also succeeded, through their devotion to the cause, in persuading the remnants of the Factory empire to attend. When they arrived at the festival site, the Velvets were overwhelmed by what they saw; though they insisted to the last minute that a reunion was impossible, they realized that it would be churlish not to respond in kind to the efforts of the organizers. And so it was that Reed, Cale, Morrison and Tucker occupied the same stage for the first time since the late summer of 1968.

'In the late afternoon of 15 June 1990, two musicians strolled onto an open-air stage in Jouey-en-Josas, twenty miles from Paris. One clutched an electric guitar; the other took up position behind a simple display of electronic keyboards. Lou Reed, clad in his uniform shades, leather jacket and blue jeans, nodded curtly to his companion; and John Cale, hair shaved severely above his ears, fringe flopping decadently over his eyebrows, began to play their canny evocation of Andy Warhol.' After a few songs from *Drella*, Reed announced, 'We have a little surprise for you. I'd like to introduce Sterling Morrison and Maureen Tucker.' There was a moment of stunned silence, before the Warhol audience knew that they were about to see something that, according to Lou Reed, could never happen: a reunion of the original Velvet Underground.

Afterwards, everyone – audience and performers alike – seemed giddy from the experience. While Cale softly bemoaned the lack of rehearsal, everyone else was jubilant, particularly Lou Reed, that sullen old smile of his creased into one big irrepressible smile.

'That was one of the most amazing experiences I've ever had in my few years on Earth!' Lou exclaimed to Maureen. 'That was extraordinary! To have those drums behind me, that viola on one side, and that guitar on the other again, you have no idea how powerful that felt. I moved up into the pocket between you, John and Sterl, and . . . holy shit!' Even John was overwhelmed. 'Three hours ago this was not possible,' he admitted. 'Now I'm overcome by emotion.' Lou Reed was reportedly moved to tears.

That night the band and Billy Name had dinner together – and the night after that, and the night after that. They even visited the Louvre Museum together. John and Lou were considering playing some *Drella* concerts in the US and Europe. The band talked of getting together to play in a club in Paris, although nothing came of it.

In August 1990, Lou toured Japan with Maureen Tucker's band as his support group. During the tour Lou and John played what may have been the last *Drella* show in Tokyo. By this time, both *Songs for Drella* and *New York* had come to represent a reborn Lou Reed – a Lou Reed finally unafraid of recognizing the vast influences of Warhol and the Velvet Underground.

The spring of 1992 brought Lou together again with Moe and Sterling. Lou was touring Europe with *Magic and Loss* at the same time Moe was touring behind her album with Sterling on guitar. The three of them ran into each other in Paris, where Lou appeared at one of their gigs. Sylvia hung out with Sterling and Moe and threatened to move in with them if Lou screamed at her one more time. Sterling got the feeling that Lou might be open to the possibility of a reunion. He saw clearly that Lou wasn't enjoying himself on stage any more because he had become such a control freak. When Lou admitted that he had fun playing with Moe and Sterling in Paris, Sterling replied, 'Well, see, Lou, if you'd only consider . . . '

In 1992, Polygram started work on a boxed set of VU music. This led to a couple of band meetings in New York in December. 'It was really great meeting, because we were all friends again,' Tucker recalled. 'We were fooling around, when Lou suggested that we get back together to play Madison Square Garden for a million dollars. It was just a joke, but it was the first time any of us had said anything like that in front of the other three. After a lot of thought, we all decided, 'Yeah, a Velvets reunion is a really cool idea.'

On 5 December Cale played a concert at New York University accompanied by Sterling. Lou joined them on stage for two songs.

> The evening's biggest treat came when Lou Reed strode on stage in suburban casuals, guitar strapped to his chest [wrote Ann Powers in the *New York Times*]. Mr Cale, Mr Reed and Mr Morrison launched into 'Style It Takes', from *Songs for Drella*. Only the crucial absence of drummer Maureen Tucker kept this from being a Velvet Underground reunion. Mr Reed's aggressive playing dominated the proceedings, but the three men did listen to one another, building a fractured reflection of the foundational Velvet sound.

After that, Lou started talking eagerly about a reunion. Sylvia began investigating the possibility of the Velvet Underground doing some shows in Europe in 1993. Shortly thereafter, Cale went on the *Tonight Show* and told Jay Leno that they were planning to reform ('for the money!').

In February 1993, 'we all got back together in New York for rehearsal,' Tucker recounted. 'We played music together for five or six hours. Everybody was feeling a bit nervous at first. We really didn't know what was going to happen. None of us had any idea how the others would react. But, in the end, we were all extremely happy with the result.' So they agreed to do a short tour of Europe that summer. In retrospect, though Lou insisted that it was just a whimsical notion based upon having fun, this would turn out to be a brilliant career move for him.

As soon as word of the agreement was out, the business people – spearheaded by Sylvia, who would also become the VU's road manager – set up the dates and worked out the contracts for a three-week tour, followed by a live album and video to be recorded in Paris. It was left to the band to carry out a series of rigorous rehearsals not unlike the rehearsals of 1965 that had bolted the musicians to their sound. They were conducted, fittingly, in a former factory on West 26th Street in Manhattan.

Although glad to get back together, they were not without apprehension. It was not possible simply to erase the years of bitterness between the rest of the band and Reed. Even now, he held the whip hand over them because he owned the publishing rights to the vast majority of the VU's material. According to the proprietor of the Mudd Club, Steve Mass, who had many conversations with Cale in the early 1980s:

John would say to me – he would crow – that he wanted to extract the Velvet Underground, the history, the culture, from Lou Reed. Reed wanted to kill the Velvet Underground and Cale was the carrier of the virus. The way Cale would express it to me was in terms of the financial elements, the lawyers and the accountants, and Lou Reed just controlled it. He had the legal power and had it all tied up.

At first Cale emerged as their spokesman, telling Richard Williams, in a piece for the *Independent on Sunday* magazine:

Nothing would have gotten done without Lou thinking it was a good idea. There was nothing happening for him this year, so he decided to try it. We had two days of playing to see if it was fun, and it turned out to be fantastic. All the original enthusiasm was there.

It's good that Lou has about 20,000 guitars, or he'd be spending hours retuning between every number. That's what we used to do, and it drove people crazy. But Lou is being Lou Reed again – he's turning up his guitar and wailing. Which is how most of those songs work anyway: turn it up and crank it out.

In another interview with Allan Jones for *Melody Maker* earlier that year in Paris, Cale had reflected upon their motives for performing.

As far as I'm concerned, this is an opportunity to take care of some unfinished business. The business we started when we first put the VU together. We never saw it through.

He seemed hopeful about the possibilities of doing new work.

I've got three pieces I've almost finished that I've already talked to Lou about and he wants to do them. I don't really think he's interested in doing something that'll come out as just another Lou Reed solo album. From what he's said, he sees this very definitely as a group thing.

When Jones remarked 'that sounds uncommonly democratic of him', Cale snapped, 'Lou, democratic? Let's not go too far. Let's put it this way, if he thinks I'm going to turn up to play "Walk on the Wild Side", he's going to be very disappointed.'

Once they had found their groove and felt as comfortable with each other as they ever would, the band agreed to receive a series of European journalists whose publications were willing to treat their reformation as a major story. Sylvia made it a condition that all interviews be guaranteed cover status. Matt Snow from *Q* came away with a sharply etched image of the four veterans.

The first is small, late forties, dressed in black with a paradoxically mumsy face. The second wears jeans, T-shirt and a pair of hexagonal glasses, giving him the aspect of an intimidatingly intelligent monkey. The third sports a Gothic profile, grey-edged chestnut Eton crop. The fourth, like the previous two an alarmingly well-preserved fiftyish, has the ranginess, acne-scarred complexion and greying, slightly receding Prince Valiant haircut of a perpetual student. They are Maureen 'Mo' Tucker, Lou Reed, John Cale and Sterling Morrison, the names as hallowed to the alternative rock fan as John, Paul, George and Ringo are to everyone else.

Every journalist who interviewed the band emerged with some colourful images. Despite his repeated insistence that they were there primarily to have 'fun', Lou Reed's uncomfortable presence dominated the sessions. Max Bell, writing in *Vox*, described Lou as alternately staring at Sterling 'like one of the Gorgons' and speaking 'in a voice that creaks like the cellar door at Frankenstein's castle'. He thought that the band and everyone involved in the project were living in 'Lou's world'.

Reed was undoubtedly calling the shots. It was he, for example, who made their much-debated decision to open for U2 on several dates in Europe after their own tour. And it was he, not Cale, who conducted the rehearsals. Despite his often dour mien, Lou attempted to present their position in as light a vein as possible. He repeated over and over again like a mantra:

> The only *raison d'être* for this is fun. Fun. To play for fun. This is not about money. I like playing with them; we had fun in France; we had fun sitting in with one another. And so long as money doesn't get in the way of anything and you can afford to do it just for fun and not lose any money and it doesn't become a career – that is, it's in essence pure, driven only by the instinct to make something nice – that's a nice, pure thing to do.

Ever since they had started meeting in late 1992, Sterling and Lou had appeared to old friends to have fallen in love, giving each other messages of appreciation as strong as Valentines. Consequently, Sterling was shocked and hurt when Lou started screaming at him one Friday during rehearsals. Morrison told friends that if he had had a day like that at the beginning of the rehearsals, he could have saved everyone the trouble of going through with them. But then, much to everyone's surprise, at the end of the day Lou actually called up Sterling and apologized. Lou's handlers put the tantrum down to his nervousness about the fast-approaching shows, pointing out that he was as nervous now about performing as he had been when he was fifteen.

Reed, Cale and Morrison all suffered from paranoia, taking a conspiratorial view of the world. The difference between 1968 and

1993 was that Sterling and John were able to regard Lou with enough detachment to feel sorry for him. With a little help from their handlers, they could see that Lou was trapped inside this paranoia like a mastodon in an Arctic icecap, that he was not to be condemned for his brattish mouth, but rather pitied for the pain his every waking minute contained.

By then, though, they were all suffering from some of the anxiety that goes hand in hand with any international rock tour in the 1990s. The sheer financial logistics were terrifying, as was their vulnerability before the rock press. Veteran rock writers were warning that the Velvets had more to lose than any other band in rock history if they blew even one gig on the three-week tour. Many fans voiced the opinion that they should never have threatened the VU myth by reforming in the first place. It was seen as short-sighted and mercenary, and the band was criticized for the outrageously high ticket prices – as much as $75 in London and Amsterdam.

For the most part, the positive chemistry of the foursome overcame their collective fear, and Sterling and Moe worked as a buffer between Lou and John. In fact, the reunion might have been a great success, and perhaps even a long-lasting one, if it hadn't been for the added pressure of Sylvia, whose ego had ballooned out of proportion to her job. According to several people involved with the shows, Sylvia made no secret of her contempt for the other members of the outfit, particularly John, whom she called stupid and untalented. John was convinced that she had learned everything she knew in this department from Lou, but others were not so sure. After lasting through twelve hard, embattled years with Lou, Sylvia had developed a tough shell and an instinct for self-preservation that led her to lash out at others. Despite the rumours floating around New York that Lou was now sharing his Christopher Street apartment with a man, Sylvia seemed more intent than ever on shoring up Lou's image and, by extension, her own.

With the people she dealt with in the rock business, Sylvia appeared incapable of beginning a conversation without a string of expletives. She virtually showered contempt on Cale, whom she had left for Lou in 1978, going so far at one point as to make the curious remark that John had become exceedingly ugly while Lou had grown more and more handsome as he had grown older. Sterling and Moe were also subjected to foul-mouthed put-downs. Sylvia seemed to think that the 'lesser' band members should feel grateful to Lou for stooping to their level to help them.

Being tough and highly self-confident themselves, the band members could have shrugged off Sylvia's cutting remarks, had she not been their road manager. Worse still was the fact that Lou put Sylvia between himself and the band. Despite living with Lou for over a decade, Sylvia did not understand the value of collaboration in creative rock-music chemistry. Because of this, she had no conception of how important Cale was to Reed. In the long run, it was Sylvia's separating of Lou from the band that would do the most damage.

In the opinion of one observer, Lou was simply reverting to the adolescent pattern he had never grown out of. 'Mother is going to take care of this for Lou,' she said.

> I mean, there are people who don't grow up. I think as an adolescent Lou probably went through the same thing that all kids do, which would tell you something about his intelligence. He isn't smart. Sometimes very simple propositions take an incredible amount of time to explain to him. I mean, he doesn't understand simple things about dealmaking, like if you want to get a higher royalty rate, you'd better have something to trade off for it. A simple rule of life. If you give me something, I'm going to have to give you something. Most people have a sense of this. Lou doesn't. Lou thinks the way you're going to get a higher royalty rate is just go and ask for it. Which I suppose is like an eight-year-old.

Even though Lou managed to place a certain amount of distance between himself and the band, it wasn't long before the rivalry surfaced between Lou and John, just as it had twenty-five years earlier. The dispute that emerged centred on who was going to produce the live recordings of their reunion tour. Each man thought he was the only one capable of pulling it off. Soon, they were both preparing for a pitched battle. Lou told everybody when the tour started, 'Catch it while you can, it's probably not going to last that long.'

'Somebody said Lou Reed wouldn't have existed if it hadn't been for John Cale,' commented one friend.

> Lou recognized that and that was one of his biggest problems. The sad thing about it was that John didn't recognize this. John represented everything that Lou wanted to be, in terms of the musical reputation and the other intellectual things. John is probably the most highly trained musician ever to play rock and roll. Cale was very insecure about what he wrote, but he was not stuck in the sense that Reed was – stuck in adolescence.

With Lou predicting its early demise, the tour kicked off in Edinburgh on 1 June. The first show did not live up to the expectations of an audience geared up for an exciting set composed largely of the VU's new material. After waiting for the five-minute standing ovation to quieten down, Lou yelled 'One-two-three-and . . . ' and the band launched into 'We're Gonna Have a Real Good Time Together'. Much of the ensuing material, however, failed to make good on the band's promise to premiere new songs and improvise on the classics, leading one attention-seeking Caledonian to shout, 'This is the most boring load of shite I've ever seen.' Chris Whent heard other things being shouted that night that were highly positive. 'I thought it was like a lovefest. I have never felt such a warmth of emotion. And the sound was different than anything I'd ever heard before. The entire evening sounded utterly and remarkably like the Velvet Underground.'

By other accounts the band was tense on the first night. 'The first thing you notice as the Velvet Underground stutter and stumble through their first few numbers is the inappropriate rude health of Lou Reed,' wrote Pat Kane in the *Guardian*. 'He bulges out of his black T-shirt and blue denims like a cross between Bryan Adams and Nosferatu; the pebble glasses make him look more like a pop professor than real pop professors do.'

'"I Can't Stand It" ends the set,' wrote one critic.

But everyone knows they'll be back, and the cheers are just turning to impatient boos when Lou leads them back out for two encores: a tense, neurotic and inevitable 'Waiting for My Man', and a spellbinding trip through 'Heroin'. At the end they line up like chorus girls or the cast of *The Mousetrap*. Cale puts his arm around Lou. Lou jumps. You get the feeling that the last time Cale touched him, his fists were probably clenched. There's still a lot of history between these two. Lou smiles, puts his arm around Maureen. Sterling taps her on the head.

The following night's show was far superior.

The revelation on Thursday, though, was the diminutive Ms Tucker's drumming [wrote John Rockwell in the *New York Times*]. Standing at her kit and whacking away, she makes a tom-toms of doom sound that inspired straight-ahead punk drumming for a generation. The effect is not quirky or amateurish; it is rocklike in the granitic sense of that word, the foundation on which the band could build a creative future to match its potently nostalgic past.

From Edinburgh they travelled down to London for two shows on 5 and 6 June. The first was at a 1,200-capacity club, the Forum. David Fricke wrote in *Rolling Stone*:

You could definitely feel the invisible lightning flashing between Reed and Cale as they faced off during the extended guitar-viola jousting in 'Mr Rain', Reed lancing Cale's agitated Arabic droning with paint-peeling feedback.

From Britain they went to the Netherlands for shows in Amsterdam and Rotterdam. Back in 1988 a poll of Dutch journalists had voted the first VU album the best record of all time. Since then Lou had received the Dutch equivalent of a Grammy – the Edison Award – for the *New York* album. The tour was turning into a triumphal procession.

The Paris shows at the Olympia Theatre were recorded on 15–17 June. Asked by a member of the audience if he could repeat the name of the new composition 'Coyote', Lou replied, 'Of course. We're the Velvet Underground. We can do anything.'

'I slowly made my way out of the Olympia thinking about Reed,' wrote an American critic, Ira Kaplan, in *Spin*.

Why had he, with a thriving solo career, made this dive into his past? Now 51, he's used his two most recent records, *Songs for Drella* and *Magic and Loss*, to consider mortality. The flipside of the bitterness that Morrison expressed (though he denied the term 'bitter', preferring 'cold') is a past yet unreconciled. And while you obviously can't change the past, by reuniting the band gets a chance to change the ending. The Velvet Underground reunion provides an opportunity – not just for Reed, of course – for closure, for vindication. I hope that when his fists rose at the end of their show, it meant he's found it.

From Paris they travelled to Berlin for two final shows. As soon as the tour was over the Velvets joined U2 in Italy for four stadium concerts in front of audiences of up to 60,000. After these concerts they returned to the UK to play a short set at the Glastonbury festival.

Though press reaction to the tour was soberly positive, criticism came from purists who objected to the fact that Lou allowed 'Venus in Furs' to be used for a Dunlop tyre commercial in the UK. Others viewed the VU's opening for U2 as a further sellout.

According to tour insiders, the group got along reasonably well until the U2 dates in Italy, when friendly relations soured. The band members had grown tired of Lou's screaming at them on stage with a live mike in front of him. 'I've never seen him be so uptight on stage,' Cale later commented, 'And giving the fascist salute during "Heroin" in Italy . . .' 'I'm always nervous,' Lou responded. 'I'm nervous about life. I'm calmer on stage, I have my guitar. Offstage, that's something else.' Morrison, too, was upset by Lou's nasty jibes. By the time they left Britain he was already wishing he had never agreed to tour in the first place. Lou's behaviour was not his only beef. He was also put off by Lou's primadonna posturing for the press and record executives. Sterling complained later, for instance, that during the tour nobody from Sire Records ever said a single word to anybody in the band except Lou.

Making matters worse for Morrison, Cale and Tucker was the overbearing presence of Lou's surrogate, Sylvia. One observer drew the conclusion that Lou and Sylvia had lasted so long together because she was not a nice person, that she mirrored his nastiness and encouraged that side of him, that she recharged his unpleasantness and gave it back to him. In other words, they deserved each other. Or, as one friend put it, 'They were fucking each other's brains.'

By the time the Velvet Underground returned to the US, their camaraderie had dissipated. Once home, they scattered in their separate directions – Moe to Georgia, Sterling to his tugboat on the Gulf of Mexico, Lou and John to their separate camps in Manhattan. On the positive side, they had received a massive amount of good publicity and both Sterling and Moe, who would each end up with something like $75,000–100,000 when the smoke cleared, had been rescued from penurious conditions.

No sooner had Lou safely retreated from face-to-face contact with the band members than he initiated an all-out fax war. Previously a phone-aholic, Lou had now become a fax maniac, spending hours composing messages and then keening over the machine in anticipation of a snappy reply. It was the perfect mode of communication for the hermitic Reed, who now had written into his contracts that people who worked for him were forbidden to make eye contact with him. He began with a four-page fax to John, explaining in formidable detail that though John was a very good friend of his, Lou never wanted to play on the same stage with him again. He then proceeded to delineate all the things that John had done wrong throughout the brief tour.

Cale, who had maintained his reserve and dignity through-out the entire episode, replied, 'I can understand what you're saying, but we just got back, we're too close to it all happening, we're exhausted, and we shouldn't be dealing with this now.' There was too much at stake for him to take Lou's fax seriously. Not only was the band anticipating the release of its upcoming live album and a video of the Paris shows, but Polygram was working on the VU box set. Moreover, MTV had invited them to record an 'unplugged' acoustic concert. Most importantly, an autumn tour of the US would reap considerable profits for all involved. Warner Brothers, whose Sire label was due to release the live album in October, was urging the band to seize the moment.

Even though reports were circulating in the media that the band was definitely scheduled to tour in October and November, the fax battle heated up through the end of September. Lou demanded that he be given complete control of producing any records the reunited band released, with particular emphasis on the MTV unplugged album. Sterling was sequestered on his faxless tugboat, leaving John and Moe to take the brunt of the attack.

It wasn't long before Lou took the game one step too far and sent Moe a hurtful note, charging her with being ungrateful for all he had done for her. As a result, the scales finally fell from Moe's eyes and she decided to stand up for the band. On listening to the live album, mixed adequately by Lou's man Rathke, and studying the video they had made together, she realized where the weakness lay in the group and why Lou was so insistent on controlling the production. Lou's failing ability to sing and his less than inspirational guitar playing had not been completely covered up in the live record and video. She figured that Lou's need to produce any VU product came in part from a desire to protect himself from the discovery of his musical shortcomings. Realizing that she would rather get the music right than cover it up, Moe sided with John in issuing a definitive negative to Lou's demand. As Cale pointed out in one of the many reply faxes he sent to Reed, their communication had from the outset revolved around a series of ultimatums from Reed to the band. They had to draw the line somewhere, otherwise they simply dissolved into Reed's backing band and a third-rate rock group.

In the midst of all this, as a sure sign of his schizophrenia, Lou spent a weekend at Cale's Long Island place as if nothing out of the ordinary was going on and their friendship was unaffected. Later, in the first week in October, Lou attempted a reconciliation, sending John a fax saying how much the group meant to him and that that was a reason why he had been so insistent about producing the MTV unplugged album. John replied, 'Lou, I didn't realize how much it meant to you, let's cut the crap and start playing.' The next day a fax came back from Sylvia saying, 'It's a good thing you've seen sense, and, of course, Lou will have to get the producer's fee.' When Cale simply refused to go along, he received a cold-blooded fax saying, 'Good luck in your future career,' signed, Sylvia and Lou.

While Lou had been manning the fax machine, Sylvia had been working behind the scenes booking and unbooking the tour, designing a cover for the live album, and worrying about her financial settlement with Lou. However, in light of the conflict with John, Sterling and Moe, the three people to whom he had been referring back in June as among his few real friends, there were those in the VU camp who seriously worried that Lou was finally going over the edge. He seemed, they mused, to have little sense of how much harm he had done to himself with his record company by blocking the potentially lucrative VU tour. They also wondered how his US fans would respond to the return of the solo Lou, and indeed how he could possibly follow up *Magic and Loss* with anything that could stand up to what he might have done with the Velvets.

With the release of the live album, *MCMXCIII*, in late October, the searchlights of the press were once more turned upon him. 'Following a quarter-century's hiatus, the reunited Velvets are less concerned with re-creating what was than with exploring what could have been and what might still be,' wrote a reviewer in *Rolling Stone*.

With the exception of Neil Young, there isn't a rocker who understands as well as Reed does that stylistic extremes have more in common than either edge shares with a safer middle ground. Reed's streetwise eye for detail and ear for everyday poetry find common spirit – and frequent challenge – in Cale's conservatory-trained experiments with dissonance, decibels and repetition, while the jittery precision of Maureen Tucker's garage-band drumming is as crucial to the Velvets as Charlie Watts' is to the Rolling Stones. After the professorial tone of Reed's recent tours and the elegiac turn of his nineties albums, the physical rush of this music has him sounding like a man possessed.

Reviews for the video were not so favourable.

Four chronologically advanced musicians performing basic, broody adolescent rock songs with about as much passion as a quartet of railway announcers [wrote Roger Morton in the *NME*] makes for a strange spectacle. Sawing away at his violin, the curate-like Cale deports himself with bizarre solemnity. Morrison just stands there and follows the notes. Maureen Tucker whacks out the mono-beat with at least some commitment. And Reed croaks on, seemingly viewing it all with detached amusement. The whole thing has the deadening atmosphere of an angst-pop masterclass.

On 11 November, Lisa Robinson reported in her *New York Post* column that the VU would once again disband. 'We won't continue because John Cale and I and other members of the band can't agree on certain things,' Reed told her. Phoning Lisa from Buenos Aires, where he was on a brief tour, Cale countered, 'He's a control freak. I wanted to try and create new music – more songs like 'Venus in Furs', 'All Tomorrow's Parties'. I don't want to just go in and become some third-rate rock-and-roll band. We didn't contribute anything to ourselves on this tour; we didn't step outside ourselves again and reach for that extra bit.'

Reed's reply: 'I didn't want to get involved in writing any more songs unless I knew that I would be involved in the production of anything that came out of it. I am a control freak, I'm a perfectionist when it comes to music and writing, and I want it to exist on the level I know I can deliver, and I won't settle for anything less.'

chapter twenty-four   *Queen of Scars*

1993–1994

[In which Lou fires Sylvia,
and finds himself alone.]

*It always worries me that people actually think there's
something wrong with me and what I'm doing. What is this
thing that they want me to correct?*

LOU REED

Lou maintained a high profile at the end of 1993 and into early
1994. He had started having an affair with the coolest
performance artist in the world, Laurie Anderson, who bore a
passing resemblance to the young Shelley Albin. They were
spotted smooching in the back of limousines and in restaurants.
At first, Sylvia welcomed the affair since it helped quell rumours
that Lou had dumped her for an older black guy, a guard at the
Natural History Museum, with whom he regularly had breakfast
at a local café. In November, Lou and Laurie went to the
premiere of *The Black Rider*, an opera by Robert Wilson,
William Burroughs and Tom Waits, and smiled for the cameras
at the dinner party after it.

He was rehearsing at the Guggenheim Museum for a benefit
performance for the opening of the Robert Mapplethorpe
Gallery. On the night of the show, 8 November, playing
acoustic guitar with electronic pickup, accompanied by a single
guitarist and a stand-up bass, he complained acidly about the
acoustics, but seemed otherwise to enjoy himself with the band.
Wearing tight blue jeans and a skin-tight black leather T-shirt

zipped up the side, he played folk versions of 'Satellite of Love', 'Walk on the Wild Side', and 'Sweet Jane'. The audience, though enthusiastic, was not entirely attentive. Many people maintained conversations during the show, a practice outlawed by Lou in most clubs and concert halls. His craggy face suggested a cross between his father and Delmore Schwartz.

In December, the German director Wim Wenders's film *Faraway, So Close*, starring Willem Dafoe, Nastassia Kinski and Peter Falk, with a cameo by Lou singing a new composition, 'Why Can't I Be Good?', opened in New York. Lou performed the song at a party after the premiere, telling the press, 'It's always a privilege and an honour to be involved with Wim Wenders.'

On 2 February 1994 Lou was not so complimentary to Kris Kristofferson when they performed at a songwriters' night at the Bottom Line. According to a reporter for the *New York Observer*'s Transom column:

Kris Kristofferson seemed eager to jam with Lou Reed at a concert that also featured Suzanne Vega and Victoria Williams. When Mr Reed began a solo version of his classic 'Sweet Jane', Mr Kristofferson tried to accompany the former Velvet Underground member on harmonica. But Mr Reed did not seem to want his spare song cluttered. 'No harmonica, Kris,' said Mr Reed, interrupting his singing. Mr Kristofferson stopped, but later tried to pick his acoustic guitar along to Mr Reed's electric one. Again, Mr Reed broke off his singing. 'Shhh,' he said. Mr Kristofferson, looking a bit like a reprimanded child, obeyed.

Later in the month Lou flew to Los Angeles and appeared at an Artists' Rights Foundation benefit with Los Lobos and Chris Isaak. Lou had become interested in interpreting other people's material. According to Tom Chao in the *Los Angeles Reader*:

His crack four-piece touring unit really locked into its huge, monolithic sound with a fiery reading of Bob Dylan's 'Foot of Pride' and Reed also interpreted works by Pete Townshend, Victoria

Williams and Elvis(!). His recasting of the Kurt Weill–Maxwell Anderson classic 'September Song' as a slow soul number was hypnotic; and who would have guessed that Reed could make 'Tracks of My Tears' indisputably his own.

According to Erik Jasen in *LA Village View*, 'He proceeded to perform a hauntingly stark version of Elvis Presley's "Mystery Train". Considering Lou Reed's appearance was much awaited by the crowd, it was strange to see hordes of people exit during his set.'

On 21 February to promote the Velvet Underground live album Lou was on *The Tonight Show*. He glared into the camera. His 'Waiting for the Man' was less exciting than Cale's on the album. After the performance Lou looked distinctly vulnerable.

From Los Angeles, Lou jetted back to New York, where he appeared at a tribute to Pete Townshend at Carnegie Hall. Singing 'Now and Then' from Townshend's recent album *Psychoderelict*, he made the song his own with the same phrasing as 'Sweet Jane'. On 26 March Lou played at a group concert at the Beacon Theatre in New York to mark the release of Rob Wasserman's album *Trio*. 'A sardonic Lou Reed growling iconoclastic versions of "The Tracks of My Tears" and "One for My Baby" was the high point of the nearly three-hour benefit concert,' wrote Stephen Holden in the *New York Times*. 'Intoning these classic songs in an impassioned monotone, Mr Reed demolished and reconstituted them in his own image. Lovelorn ballads became minimalist rock anthems whose tearful emotions were transmitted into a more generalized, barely suppressed rage.'

At the same time that he was fighting with John, Moe and Sterl, Lou was brawling with Sylvia over getting divorced or not getting divorced. Having decided not to get divorced, he started considering the financial settlement.

On Lou's fifty-second birthday, 2 March, the *New York Post* ran his photograph above a horoscope which read, 'Although no one can really question your motives or undermine your confidence, a marvellous aspect between Venus and Neptune on your anniversary signifies that it might be wise to make an adjustment, especially when dealing with projects which involve a large number of people.'

Many people who knew Lou were sure that Sylvia could not last much longer. Sylvia, however, seemed to have lost contact with reality just as Lou's previous wife, Bettye, had. Not only did Sylvia take it for granted that she would continue to manage Lou, she started thinking about managing other stars too. When Kurt Cobain of Nirvana overdosed in his Rome hotel suite during the first week of March 1994, Sylvia rang Lou suggesting they send flowers and a note. No, Lou replied, he wanted to talk about their financial settlement. She should come over.

When Sylvia got there she was met by a barrage of figures. Lou would pay her a salary of $150,000 a year, but no percentages. Since Lou earned approximately $1 million a year and a standard managerial contract gave the manager 20 per cent, and since Sylvia had been instrumental in bringing Lou to this level of income, she reacted negatively. She threatened to send appraisers to his apartment to assess how much of their money he had spent on having his new place fixed up. It was more than $100,000 and she knew Lou had recently taken Laurie Anderson to Antigua for a week's vacation, on which he spent $25,000.

On the following day Lou fired Sylvia as his manager, cancelling her credit cards, car service and other accounts. Now she had no choice but to sue him for divorce. However, one friend noted:

I wouldn't be surprised if he and Sylvia went back and forth like this for years. Now Sylvia has left him for whatever reason, but whether he said 'Get out', whether he stomps on her, kicks her out, throws her out, beats her up, she's not supposed to get out. She's supposed to say, 'No, I'm coming back.'

Meanwhile, Reed's lawyer, the venerable Allen Stein, dismissed him as a client. 'Don't underestimate the fact that Lou was fired by his attorney,' one observer pointed out.

Allen Stein is in his seventies and he has been one of the top entertainment lawyers for years. He began to represent Lou because one of his close friends is Lou's accountant, David Gottehrer from Mason and Co., whom Lou has used for many years and who seems to be one of the few people he trusts. Allen is a class act. Allen represents Seymour Stein and has done for many years. So this was a heavy rejection.

'When you hit fifty there are a lot of frightening changes,' noted an acquaintance. 'A lot of doors close, new possibilities no longer open up. You suddenly realize that that's it.' Lou knew, for example, that closing the door on Sylvia was dangerous. Laurie Anderson was not going to become his mommy, manager and protector. She had as healthy a career as he did and as strong and ambitious a personality. 'He may fantasize that he's going to replace Sylvia with Laurie Anderson,' his friend continued, 'but he's going to make a horrible discovery. You may be a fucking rock star but if you're fifty-two years old you're an old fart.' Changing his life by rejecting whole groups of people had been his recurring tactic but it was the consensus of opinion among Lou's acquaintances that he was scared of spending the rest of his life alone.

Lou Reed had upset all the fans in the US who had looked forward to seeing the Velvet Underground. His last trilogy of solo albums had left off with the depressing *Magic and Loss*. Where could he go from there? He claimed to be working on a novel. Allegedly, he approached Warner Brothers with the desire to make a covers album. Warner Brothers had been fully informed of Lou's behaviour during the collapse of the VU reunion and cannot have been particularly pleased with how he had undermined the commercial potential of the live album by refusing to tour with the band.

Some observers thought Lou might escape by blaming everything on Sylvia. During the VU negotiations she had drawn hostility even from the kind-hearted Moe. 'At the very least Lou must have seen she made him vulnerable,' one go-between commented, 'that she had been incompetent. And frankly I don't think he need do very much more than highlight her incompetence, which has been gross.' Sylvia responded to complaints by saying, 'You don't understand how hard it is to deal with Lou. If it hadn't been for me this whole Velvet Underground reunion would never have happened which, according to Lou, was true.'

'Lou may be particularly mean now because I would believe that he is twice as scared,' stated one long-term friend.

Lou can stand in front of the world and say I'm rich and famous and pearls of wisdom drop from my teeth. Yet I think what he really is still is the boy who wants all his mother's attention. If I wake up at four in the morning and I want you to cook me a pound of bacon and two hot dogs, of course you're going to do that, or I'm going to smack you, or I'm going to be real cold and withdrawn – that's the way an artist does it. To punish her. And he watches himself as all writers do, he stands back and restructures the scene a little and edits.

I would think he must be pretty crazy right now. Lou's pretty crazy about Sylvia as I understand, so for him not to be happy is the most dismaying thing because more than anybody else he's such a romantic. And I think in some ways that Lou is bewildered, lost in a way that a young kid in love might be. Here he is rejected, and how can you reject someone who's so smart and good? That's what really makes him tick.

Lou Reed has said that he hoped his music would lift children out of their confusion.

If you play my albums all in a row, one of the things that I think is fun about me is that if you follow me, in each and every way from day one up till now, you're following a person. A real person I've tried to make really exist for you – Lou Reed.

If you line the songs up and play them, you should be able to relate and not feel alone – I think it's important that people don't feel alone.

In 1994, Lou Reed often sat alone in his Christopher Street penthouse playing his guitar with an array of machines he controlled with his foot.

Source Notes

I really like people.

LOU REED,

The primary source for *Lou Reed: The Biography* is information that the author gathered from interviews with: Penny Arcade, Cathleen Aiken, Gretchen Berg, Philip Booth, Jessica Berens, Chris Charlesworth, Jim Condon, Tony Conrad, David Dalton, Henry Edwards, Mick Farren, Lenny Ferrari, Mark Francis, Bernie Gelb, Larry Goldstein, Mary Harron, Clinton Hevlin, Barbara Hodes, John Holmstrom, Allen Hyman, Andy Hyman, Jim Jacobs, Alan Jones, Bert van der Kamp, Gary Luke, Earl McGrath, Legs McNeil, Gerard Malanga, Steve Mass, Miles, Phil Millstein, Richard Mishkin, Glenn O'Brien, Robert Palmer, Bob Quine, Matt Snow, Chris Stein, Andy Warhol, Michael Watts, John Wilcock, Barbara Wilkinson, Carol Wood, Mary Woronov, Doug Yule and Tony Zanetta.

Other interviews and articles drawn on in this book come from work by Al Aronowitz, Bobby Abrams, Billy Altman, Katrine Ames, Thomas Anderson, Dan Aquilante, Lester Bangs, Bill Barol, Steve Beard, David Belcher, Max Bell, Peter Blauner, Michael Bonner, Glenn Branka, Allen Brown, Peter Buck, Keith Cameron, Cath Carroll, Paul Carroll, Tom Carson, Chris Carter, David Cavanagh, Robert Christgau, Jay Cocks, Scott Cohen, Mark Coleman, Jim Condon, J. D. Considine, Mark Cooper, Jonathan Cott, Richard Cromelin, Giovanni Dadomo, Stephen Dalton, Jim DeRogatis, Dave DiMartino, Peter Doggett, Dan Durchholz, Ben Edmonds, Richard Fantina, Christian Fevret, Bill Flannagan, Emma Forrest, David Fricke, Stephen Gaines, Mikal Gilmore, Tony Glover, Danny Goldberg, Robert Greenfield, Paul Grein, Richard Guilliatt, John Harris, Richard Hattington, Martin Hayman, Gary Hill, Geoffrey Himes, David Hinkley, Brian Hogg, Stephen Holden, Scott Isler, Waldemar Januszczak, Betsey Johnson, Allan Jones, Cliff Jones, Nick Jones, Pat Kane, Lenny Kaye, Mark Kemp, Nick Kent, Jim Koch, Marek Kohn, M. C. Kostek, Wayne Kramer, Kurt Loder, Andrew Lycett, Jim Macnie, Jessie Mangaliman, Greil Marcus, Dave Marsh, Kenny Mathieson, Annalena McAfee, Ed McCormak, Adam McGovern, Wayne McGuire, Helen Mead, Lisa Mehlman, Milo Miles, Jim Miller, Phillip Milstein, Mike Nicholls, Jeff Nisin, Richard Nusser, Sean O'Hagan, Robert Palmer, Anastasia Pantsios, John Pareles, Sandy Pearlman, John Peel, John Piccarella, Steve Pond, Edwin Pouncey, Ann Powers, Lou Reed, Simon Reynolds, Allan Richards, Jonathan Richman, Lisa Robinson, Mick Rock, John Rockwell, Alex Ross,

Robert Sandall, Ed Sanders, Mark Satlof, Jon Savage, Karen Schoemer, Robin Smith, Matt Snow, Jean Stein, Zan Stewart, John Strausbaugh, Caroline Sullivan, Barry Taylor, Ben Thompson, Nigel Trevena, Richard Walls, Peter Watrous, Michael Watts, Chris Welch, Kevin Westenberg, David Wild, Jane Wilkes, Richard Williams, Simon Williams, Ellen Willis, Emma Willis, Tom Wilson and Carlo Wolff.

They were published in *Advertising Age, Aquarian, Arena, Aspen, The Bob, Chicago Sun-Times, Circus, Cover, Crawdaddy, Creem, Details, Entertainment Weekly, Esquire, Evening Standard, Evergreen Review, The Forced Exposures, Freeport Leader, Fusion, GQ, The Guardian, Guitar, Guitar World, High Times, Hit Parader, Independent, Interview, Jazz and Pop, Life, Little Caesar, The Lonely Woman Quarterly, Los Angeles Free Press, Los Angeles Times, Ludd's Mill, Melody Maker, Musician, The New Musical Express, Newsweek, New York Magazine, New York Newsday, New York Post, New York Rocker, The New York Times, The New York Times Magazine, New Yorker, The Observer, Option, Partisan Review, People, Phonograph Record, Playboy, Pulse, Punch, Q, Rapid Eye, Record, Record Collector, Record Mirror, Reuters, Riverfront Times, Rock, Rolling Stone, The Scene, Select, Smart, Sounds, Spin, The Sunday Correspondent, The Sunday Times, Tatler, Time, Time Out, The Times, Trouser Press, USA Today, Utne Reader, Vanity Fair, Vibrations, The Village Voice, VOX, Washington Post, Weekend Guardian, What Goes On: The Velvet Underground Appreciation Society Newsletter,* and *Wire.*

Bibliography

Indispensable were the numerous books about Lou Reed, particularly, *Between Thought And Expression: Selected Lyrics of Lou Reed*, by Lou Reed (New York, Hyperion, 1991), *Beyond The Velvet Underground*, by Dave Thompson (London, Omnibus Press, 1989), *Up-Tight: The Velvet Underground Story*, by Victor Bockris and Gerard Malanga (London, Omnibus Press, 1983), *The Velvet Underground Handbook* by M. C. Kostek (London, Black Spring, 1992), *Lou Reed & The Velvet Underground*, by Diana Clapton (London, Bobcat Books, 1987), and *Growing Up In Public*, by Peter Doggett (London Omnibus, 1991)

Other books include:

Abate, Anna, *Lou Reed: The Life, The Poems, and The Music of a Hero of American Rock*, Milan, Savelli Editori, 1980.

Albertoli, Carlo, *The Velvet Underground*, Rome, Redazione, 1993.

Alexander, Franz G. M. D. and Sheldon T. Selesnick, *The History of Psychiatry*, New York, Harper & Row, 1966.

Algren, Nelson, *A Walk on the Wild Side*, New York, Fawcett World Library, 1957.

Aquila Richard, *That Old Time Rock and Roll: 1954–1963*, New York, Schirmer Books, 1989.

Artaud, Antonin, *The Theater and its Double*, New York, Grove Press, 1958.

Atlas, James, *Delmore Schwartz: The Life of an American Poet*, New York, HBJ, 1977.

Bangs, Lester, *Psychotic Reactions and Carburator Dung*, New York, Vintage Books, 1988.

Barkentin, Marjorie, *James Joyce's Ulysses in Nighttown*, New York, Modern Library, 1958.

Bellow, Saul, *Humbolt's Gift*, New York, Viking, 1973.

Bergerot, Frank, and Arnaud Merlin, *The Story of Jazz: Bop and Beyond*, New York, Harry N. Abrams, 1991.

Bockris, Victor, *The Life and Death of Andy Warhol*, London, Hutchinson, 1989.

Bockris, Victor, and William Burroughs, *With William Burroughs: A Report From the Bunker*, New York, Seaver Books, 1981.

Botts, Linda, *Loose Talk: The Book of Quotes From the Pages of Rolling Stone Magazine*, New York, Quick Fox Press, 1980.

Bourdon, David, *Andy Warhol*, New York, Harry Abrams, 1989.

Bowie, Angela, with Patrick Carr, *Backstage Passes: Life on the Wild Side with David Bowie*, New York, Putnam, 1993.

Broadman, Evan, *Social Guide to New York Bars*, New York, Collier, 1973.

Bruce, Lenny, *How to Talk Dirty and Influence People*, Chicago, Playboy Press, 1963.

Bowman, Rob, and Jim Campbell, *Between Thought and Expression* (Booklet to the Lou Reed Anthology Box Set), New York, BMG/RCA, 1993.

Christgau, Robert, *Rock Albums of the Seventies*, New York, Da Capo, 1981.

Carducci, Joe, *Rock and the Pop Narcotic*, Chicago, Redoubt, 1990.

Carroll, Jim, *Forces Entries: the Downtown Diaries, 1971–1973*, New York, Penguin Books, 1987.

Chandler, Raymond, *The Lady In The Lake*, New York, Vintage, 1976.

Chandler, Raymond, *The Simple Art of Murder*, New York, Ballantine, 1972.

Chaplin, J. P. *Rumor, Fear and the Madness of Crowds*, New York, Ballantine Books, 1959.

Chapple, Steve, and Reebee Garofalo, *Rock 'n' Roll is Here to Stay: The History and Politics of the Music Industry*, Chicago, Nelson Hall, 1977.

Charters, Ann, *The Portable Beat Reader*, New York, Viking, 1992.

Cohen, Harvey, *The Amphetamine Manifesto*, New York, Olympia Press, 1972.

Cohen, Stanley, *Dodgers! The First 100 Years*, New York, Carol Publishing, 1990.

Colacello, Bob, *Holy Terror: Andy Warhol Close Up*, New York, Harper Collins, 1990.

Coleridge, Samuel Taylor, *The Rime of the Ancient Mariner*, Van Goor Zonen Den Haag, 1965.

Crane, Paul, *Gays and the Law*, London, Pluto Press, 1982.

Davis, Clive, with James Willwerth, *Clive: Inside the Music Business*, New York, William Morrow, 1975.

Davis, Stephen, *Hammer of the Gods: The Led Zeppelin Saga*, New York, Ballantine, 1985.

de Grazia, Edward, *Girls Lean Back Everywhere: The Law of Obscenity and the Assault on Genius*, New York, Random House, 1992.

Denselow, Robert, *When the Music's Over: The Story of Political Pop*, London, Faber & Faber, 1989.

Diamant, Anita, and Howard Cooper, *Living a Jewish Life*, New York, Harper Perrenial, 1991.

Dickson, Morris, *Gates of Eden: American Culture in the Sixties*, New York, Basic Books, 1967.

DiMucci, Dion, with Davin Seay, *The Wanderer: Dion's Story*, New York, William Morrow, 1988.

Duberman, Martin Bauml, *About Time: Exploring the Gay Past*, New York, Sea Horse, 1986.

Dunphy, Eamon, *Unforgettable Fire: The Story of U2*, London, Penguin, 1987.

Edelstein, Andrew J., and Kevin McDonough, *The Seventies: From Hot Pants to Hot Tubs*, New York, Dutton, 1990.

Edmiston, Susan, and Linda D. Cirino, *Literary New York: A History and Guide*, New York, Gibbs/Smith, 1991.

Ehret, Arnold, *Arnold Ehret's Rational Fasting*, New York, Benedict Lust Publications, 1971.

Ferlinghetti, Lawrence, *A Coney Island of the Mind*, New York, New Directions, 1958.

Finkelstein, Nat, *Andy Warhol: The Factory Years, 1964–1967*, New York, St. Martin's Press, 1989.

Flanaggan, Bill, *Written in My Soul: Conversations with Rock's Great Songwriters*, Chicago, Contemporary Books, 1987.

Freeman, Gillian, *The Undergrowth of Literature*, London, Panther Books, 1968.

Frommer, Arthur, *New York: A Practical Guide to . . .*, New York, Frommer/Pasmantier, 1964.

Goldman, Albert, *Ladies and Gentlemen, Lenny Bruce!*, New York, 1974.

Goldman, Albert, *Sound Bites*, New York, Turtle Bay, 1992.

Goldman, Eric F., *The Crucial Decade and After: America, 1945–1960*, New York, Vintage, 1956.

Goldstein, Richard, *Goldstein's Greatest Hits: A Book Mostly about Rock and Roll*, New York, Tower Books, 1966.

Goldstein, Richard, *The Poetry of Rock*, New York, Bantam Books, 1969.

Gooch, Brad, *City Poet: The Life and Times of Frank O'Hara*, New York, Knopf, 1993.

Hadleigh, Boze, and Leonard Bernstein, *The Vinyl Closet: Gays in the Music World*, San Diego, Los Hombres Press, 1991.

Hardin, Evamaria, *Syracuse Landmarks*, Syracuse, Syracuse University Press, 1993.

Hemphill, Paul, *The Nashville Sound: Bright Lights and Country Music*, New York, Pocket Books, 1971.

Henry, Tricia, *Break All Rules! Punk Rock and the Making of a Style*, Ann Arbor, UMI Research Press, 1989.

Herman, Gary, *Rock and Roll Babylon*, London, Plexus, 1982.

Hester, John, *Soho is my Parish*, London, Lutterworth Press, 1970.

Hewison, Robert, *Too Much: Art and Society in the Sixties, 1960–1975*, New York, Oxford University Press, 1987.

Heylin, Clinton, *From The Velvets to The Voidoids: A Pre-Punk History for a Post-Punk World*, London, Penguin, 1992.

Heylin, Clinton (Ed.), *The Penguin Book of Rock and Roll Writing*, New York, Viking, 1992.

Hopkins, Jerry, *Bowie*, New York, Macmillan, 1985.

Hutchinson, Larry, *Rock and Roll Songwriter's Handbook*, New York, Scholastic, 1972.

Joyce, James, *Ulysses*, New York, Random House, 1990.

Kavan, Anna, *Asylum Piece*, New York, Michael Kesend Publishing, 1981.

Kavan, Anna, *Julia and the Bazooka*, London, P. Owen, 1970.

Kelly, Kitty, *His Way: The Unauthorized Biography of Frank Sinatra*, New York, Bantam Books, 1986.

Kesey, Ken, *One Flew Over the Cuckoo's Nest*, New York, New American Library, 1962.

Knight, G. Wilson, *The Wheel of Fire: Interpretations of Shakespearean Tragedy*, Oxford, Oxford University Press, 1930.

Koch, Stephen, *Stargazer: The Life, World and Films of Andy Warhol*, New York, Marion Boyars, 1973.

Koestenbaum, Wayne, *Double Talk: The Erotics of Male Literary Collaboration*, New York, Routledge, 1989.

Kostelanetz, Richard, *The Theatre of Mixed Means*, New York, Dial Press, 1968.

Krassner, Paul, *Confessions of A Raving Unconfined Nut and Misadventures in the Counter-Culture*, New York, Simon & Schuster, 1993.

Lait, Jack, and Lee Mortimer, *New York: Confidential*, New York, Dell, 1951.

Lazell, Barry, *Rock Movers and Shakers*, New York, Billboard Publications, 1989.

Lehmann, John, *Three Literary Friendships*, New York, Quartet Books, 1983.

Leigh, Michael, *The Velvet Underground*, New York, McFadden, 1963.

Lindesmith, Alfred R., *The Addict and The Law*, New York, Vintage Books, 1965.

Litweiler, John, *Ornette Coleman: A Harmolodic Life*, New York, William Morrow, 1992.

Loder, Kurt, *Bat Chain Puller: Rock and Roll in the Age of Celebrity*, New York, St. Martin's Press, 1990.

MacInnes, Colin, *Loving Them Both: A Study of Bisexuality and Bisexuals*, London, Martin Brian & Okeeffe, 1973.

Malina, Judith, *The Diaries of Judith Malina: 1947–1957*, New York, Grove Press, 1984.

Murray, Charles Shaar, *Shots from the Hip*, London, Penguin Books, 1991.

McShine, Kynaston, *Andy Warhol: A Retrospective*, New York, The Museum of Modern Art, 1989.

Margolis, Dr Isadr, and Rabbi Sidney L. Markowitz, *Jewish Holidays and Festivals*, New York, Citadel, 1990.

Marsh, Dave, *Rock & Roll Confidential*, New York, Pantheon, 1985.

Matlock, Glen, with Pete Silverton, *I Was A Teenage Sex Pistol*, London, Faber & Faber, 1990.

McLuhan, Marshal, and Quentin Fiore, *The Medium is The Massage: An Inventory of Effects*, New York, Bantam Books, 1967.

Meltzer, Richard, *Gulcher: Post-Rock Cultural Pluralism in America 1964–1993*, New York, Citadel Press, 1993.

Miles, Barry, *Words & Music – Lou Reed*, London, Wise Publications, 1980.

Miles, *David Bowie: Black Book*, London, Omnibus Press, 1980.

Miller, Alice, *The Drama of the Gifted Child*, New York, Basic Books, 1981.

Mottram, Eric, *Blood on The Nash Ambassador*, London, Hutchinson Radius, 1983.

Nietzsche, Friedrich, *Twilight of the Idols/The Anti-Christ*, New York, Penguin, 1978.

Peelaert, Guy, and Nik Cohn, *Rock Dreams: Rock and Roll for Your Eyes*, New York, R&B, 1982.

Perelman, S. J., *The Last Laugh*, New York, Simon & Schuster, 1981.

Platt, John, Chris Dreja and Jim McCarthy, *Yardbirds*, London, Sidgwick &Jackson, 1983.

Poe, Edgar Allan, *Selected Stories and Poems*, New York, Airmont, 1962.

Pynchon, Thomas, *The Crying of Lot 49*, London, Picador, 1966.

Ragni, Gerome, and James Rado, *Hair*, New York, Pocket Books, 1969.

Reed, Lou, *Velvet Underground: Lyrics*, Milan, Arcana Editrice, 1982.

Reed, Lou, *Lou Reed: Words and Music*, New York, Warner Publications, 1991.

Research Inc, *Incredibly Strange Music*, San Francisco, Research Publications, 1993.

Ribowsky, Mark, *He's a Rebel: The Truth About Phil Spector – Rock And Roll's Legendary Madman*, New York, Dutton, 1989.

Rinzler, Alan, *The New York Spy*, New York, David White, 1967.

Rivelli, Pauline, and Robert Levin, *Giants of Rock Music*, New York, Da Capo, 1981.

Rock, Mick, *Ziggy Stardust: Bowie 1972/1973*, New York, St. Martin's Press, 1984.

Rolling Stone, *The Rolling Stone Rock Almanac*, New York, Collier Books, 1983.

Rolling Stone, *The Rolling Stone Illustrated History of Rock and Roll*, New York, Rolling Stone Press, 1976.

Roszak, Theodore, *The Making of a Counter Culture*, New York, Anchor Books, 1969.

Santoli, Al, *Everything We Had: An Oral History of the Viet Nam War . . .*, New York, Ballantine, 1981.

Savage, Jon, *England's Dreaming*, New York, St. Martin's Press, 1992.

Schwartz, Delmore, *In Dreams Begin Responsibilities and Other Stories*, New York, New Directions, 1978.

Schwartz, Delmore, *Summer Knowledge: Selected Poems (1938–1958)*, New York, New Directions, 1967.

Selby Jr., Hubert, *Last Exit To Brooklyn*, New York, Grove Press, 1957.

Shakespeare, William, *Hamlet*, New York, Washington Square Press, 1957.

Smith, Joe, *Off The Record: An Oral History of Popular Music*, New York, Warner, 1988.

Smith, Patrick S., *Andy Warhol's Art and Films*, Ann Arbor, UMI, 1986.

Smith, Patrick S., *Warhol: Conversations About the Artist*, Ann Arbor, UMI, 1988.

Smith, Patrick S., '*Art in Extremis*: Andy Warhol and his art' (3 vols, unpublished PhD dissertation, Northwestern University, Evanston, Illinois, 1982. A shortened version was published 1986 by UMI Research Press, Illinois, as *Andy Warhol's Art and Films*.)

Somma, Robert, *No One Waved Goodbye: A Casualty Report on Rock and Roll*, London, Charisma Books, 1973.

Spoto, Donald, *Lenya: A Life*, Boston, Little Brown, 1989.

Stallings, Penny, *Rock and Roll Confidential*, Boston, Little Brown, 1984.

Stein, Jean, edited with George Plimpton, *Edie, An American Biography*, New York, Alfred A. Knopf, 1982.

Stevenson, Ray, *The Sex Pistols File*, London, Omnibus, 1978.

Swados, Elizabeth, *The Four of Us*, New York, Plume, 1993.

Symons, Julian, *The Tell-Tale Heart: The Life And Works of Edgar Allan Poe*, London, Faber & Faber, 1978.

Szatmary, David P., *Rockin' In Time: A Social History of Rock and Roll*, New York, Prentice Hall, 1991.

Thomas, Donald, *The Marquis De Sade: A New Biography*, New York, Citadel, 1993.

Thompson, Hunter S., *Fear And Loathing In Las Vegas*, New York, Popular Library, 1971.

Time, Inc., *Time Capsule/1968*, New York, Time Life Books, 1968.

Tosches, Nick, *Hellfire: The Jerry Lee Lewis Story*, New York, Dellecourt, 1982.

Tosches, Nick, *Unsung Heroes of Rock and Roll*, New York, Scribners, 1984.

Tracy, Jack, with Jim Berkey, *Subcutaneously, My Dear Watson*, Bloomington, James A. Rock, 1978.

Tynan, Kenneth, *Oh! Calcutta!* New York, Grove Press, 1969.

Violet, Ultra, *Famous For Fifteen Minutes – My Years With Andy Warhol*, New York, HBJ, 1988.

Viva, *Superstar*, New York, Putnam, 1970.

Warhol, Andy, *A.* New York, Grove Press, 1968.

Warhol, Andy, edited by Pat Hackett, *The Andy Warhol Diaries*, New York, Warner Books, 1989.

Warhol, Andy, *Andy Warhol's Index Book*, New York, Random House, 1967.

Warhol, Andy, *The Philosophy of Andy Warhol*, New York, HBJ, 1975.

Warhol, Andy, and Pat Hackett, *Popism: The Warhol 60s*, New York, HBJ, 1980.

White, E. B., *Here Is New York*, New York, Harper & Brothers, 1949.

White, Theodore H., *The Making of the President: 1964*, New York, Signet, 1965.

Wilcock, John, with a Cast of Thousands, *The Autobiography & Sex Life of Andy Warhol*, New York, Other Scenes, Inc., 1971.

Wilson, Colin, *The Occult: A History*, New York, Random House, 1971.

Witts, Richard, *Nico: The Life and Lies of an Icon*, London, Virgin Publications, 1993.

Woodlawn, Holly, with Jeff Copeland, *A Low Life In High Heels*; *The Holly Woodlawn Story*, New York, St. Martin's Press, 1991.

Wrenn, Mike, *Andy Warhol in His Own Words*, London, Omnibus Press, 1991.

Young, James, *Songs They Never Play on the Radio: Nico, The Last Bohemian*, London, Bloomsbury, 1993.

Zappa, Frank, with Peter Occhiogrosso, *The Real Frank Zappa Book*, New York, Poseidon Press, 1989.

Every attempt has been made to track down the original sources of this book. If anybody whose work is quoted herein is not mentioned above, the author apologizes and would be glad to rectify the mistake.

Index

394; 'Underneath the Bottle', 346, 369; 'Venus in Furs', 89, 94, 97, 101, 102, 104, 121, 169, 445; 'Vicious', 225, 233, 289, 299, 376, 396; 'Video Violence', 393, 394, 399; 'Voices of Freedom', 399; 'Walk on the Wild Side', 204, 233–4, 235–6, 237, 242, 243, 284, 299, 374, 380, 385, 386, 394, 399, 400, 434, 444; 'Waves of Fear', 346, 367, 368; 'We're Gonna Have a Good Time Together', 438; 'White Light/White Heat', 48, 117, 160, 174, 181, 230; 'Why Can't I Be Good', 447; 'Women', 369; 'Wrap Your Troubles in Dreams', 101; 'Xmas in February', 406

Reed, Sidney George (father), 2, 3, 5, 7, 8, 9, 10–11, 12, 13, 14, 15–16, 35–6, 37–8, 46, 48–9, 60, 75, 134, 137, 190, 204, 206, 226, 347–8, 350, 351, 352, 382, 444

Reed, Sylvia (née Morales; 2nd wife), 343–4, 345–6, 347, 348, 349- 51, 353, 354, 355, 357, 358, 359–60, 361, 362, 366, 368, 379, 382, 386, 393, 397, 398, 400, 403, 414, 415–16, 418, 419, 430, 432, 433, 434, 436–7, 441, 443, 447, 449, 450, 451, 452

Reed, Toby Futterman (mother), 2, 3, 5, 6–7, 8, 10–11, 12, 35, 36, 37–8, 46, 48–9, 60, 64, 83, 89, 90, 137, 190, 206, 235, 347, 348, 350, 351, 352, 355, 360, 393

REM, 389

Reserve Officers' Training Corps (ROTC), 20, 90

Rice, Ron, 100

Richards, Keith, 26, 115, 192, 284, 355, 407

Richman, Jonathan, 316

Riddle, Nelson, 270

Rimbaud, 25, 290

Ring, Bob, 211

Ripped and Torn fanzine, 321

Robbins, Tim, 173, 178

Robins, Wayne, 268–9

Robinson, Lisa, 209, 210, 211, 212, 215, 223, 227, 236, 334, 445

Robinson, Richard, 209, 210, 211, 212, 213, 215, 217, 218, 219, 223, 226, 227, 236, 282, 317, 323, 324

Robinson, Smokey, 354

Rock, Mick, 229–30, 234, 235, 249, 278, 283, 304, 310, 351

Rock 'n' Roll Animal (persona), 283, 286, 313

Rock 'n' Roll Animal tour, 252–9, 260, 264–6, 267, 274–5, 335

Rock and Rule (cartoon), 387

Rock Against Drugs (RAD), 397

Rockwell, John, 250–1, 298, 312–13, 329, 335, 354

Rodgers, Nile, 388

Rolling Stone magazine, 159, 186, 218, 249, 250, 251, 268, 298, 306, 311, 335, 391, 399, 406, 407, 408, 439, 444

Rolling Stones, The, 26, 97, 102, 141, 143, 205–6, 215, 242, 284, 289, 315, 327, 372, 444

Ronson, Mick, 211, 229, 232, 233, 236

Rosebud, 345

Rosenberger, Justice Ernest, 350

Rothschild, Charlie, 131

Rotten, Rita, 290, 409

Rotten, Johny, 111, 315, 349

Roughnecks (band), 76

Roxy Music, 316

Rubin, Barbara, 100, 101, 105, 106, 114, 149

Ruff, Hope, 143, 155

Run DMC, 392

Ruskin, Mickey, 140, 141, 372

Russell, Leon, 102

Ryder, Mitch, 245

Saint-Laurent, Yves, 225

Sam and Dave, 397

San Francisco Chronicle, 136

Sanders, Ed, 119

Sarah Lawrence College, 349

Sartre, Jean Paul, 22

Saunders, Fernando, 364, 374, 377, 379, 380, 393

Saunders, George, 223

Savage, Jon, 320

Schnabel, Julian, 422

Schunke, Manfred, 323, 333

Schupak, David, 42–3, 44, 74, 76, 77, 82, 91, 356–7

Schwartz, Delmore, 2, 8, 9, 51, 53–8, 59, 64, 65–6, 67, 68, 69, 75, 87, 92, 111, 138–9, 207, 244, 324, 342, 350, 359, 361, 368–9, 395, 402, 408–9, 424, 447

Scorsese, Martin, 306, 359, 392

Scott, Sir Walter, 42

Second Fret club, 160, 186

Secret Policeman's Third Ball, 398

Sedgwick, Edie, 106, 112, 114, 116, 121

Selby, Hubert, 68, 156

Selby Jr., Hubert, 411

Selesnick, Sheldon T., 2

Sellers, Terrence, 343, 344, 345

Sesnick, Steve, 150, 152, 153, 154, 157–8, 160, 161–2, 165, 167, 168, 170, 171, 172, 175, 176, 177, 182, 183, 187, 188–9, 190, 191, 199–200, 204, 205, 282, 283

Sex Pistols, 315, 320, 327, 349, 386

Seymour (dog), 59–61, 85, 91, 305, 347

Shakespeare, William, 54, 315, 331, 370

Shapiro, Susan, 327–8

Shebar, John, 195

Shepard, Sam, 210, 359, 390

Shepp, Archie, 21

Sigal, Richard, 237–8

Simon & Garfunkel, 134

Simon, Carly, 391

Simon, Paul, 12, 396, 400

Simple Minds, 389

Sims, Jimmie, 77, 78, 80

Sinatra, Frank, 1, 27, 28, 102, 209, 220, 270, 271, 398